In Memoriam Paul Kahle

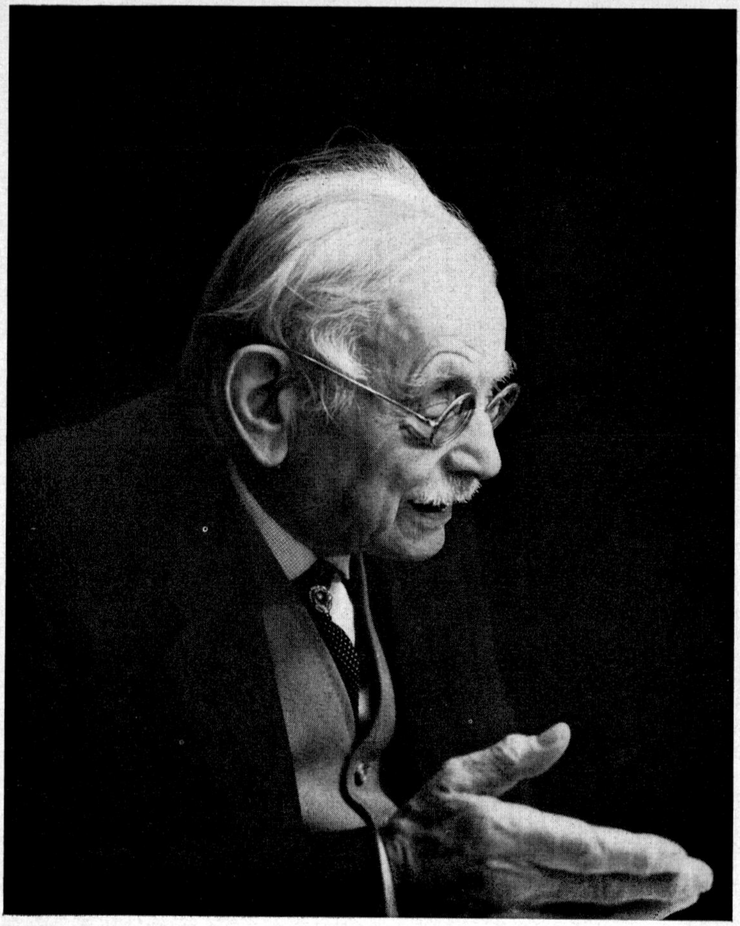

In Memoriam Paul Kahle

Herausgegeben von

Matthew Black und Georg Fohrer

Verlag Alfred Töpelmann

Berlin 1968

Beiheft zur Zeitschrift für die alttestamentliche Wissenschaft
Herausgegeben von Georg Fohrer

103

Printed in Germany
Satz und Druck: J. J. Augustin, Glückstadt
Archiv-Nr. 38 22 682

Preface

The idea of a commemorative volume to form a tribute to the life and labours, as Old Testament scholar and Orientalist, of the late Professor Paul E. Kahle was one which occurred independently to several of his many friends shortly after his lamented death in 1965; and it at once commended itself to the still wider circle of colleagues, former pupils, and pupils of his pupils. The first proposal was to collect a volume of personal reminiscences from close friends and acquaintances of long standing, but this suggestion was subsequently abandoned in favour of a collection of scholarly essays in Kahle's own main fields of learned activity, namely, the Old Testament and Judaica, the volume to be prefaced by a brief personal tribute from one who had known him for many years as fellow-Semitist and friend, Professor Nyberg of Uppsala.

It was felt that any such volume, while it should reflect by representative contributions Kahle's own wide range of interests in the Oriental field, in particular in Islamica, ought nevertheless to concentrate mainly on the field of Old Testament studies and Judaica where Dr. Kahle's most notable contributions to learning had been made.

When Professor Fohrer, Editor of the *Zeitschrift für die Alttestamentliche Wissenschaft,* was asked if such a volume could be accepted for the series of *Beihefte,* he readily agreed and later accepted my invitation to act together with me as joint editor of the volume. While the volume appears under the joint editorship of Professor Fohrer and myself, it is only right to put on record that the main burden of actual editorial labour has fallen to the Editor of the *ZAW.*

As I have written elsewhere[1], Kahle was, for nearly a generation before his death, the doyen of European Orientalists; and that eminence was attained and maintained by an achievement in the field of Oriental study which is in many respects without parallel in this century. The secret of his great distinction is not far to seek: he was

[1] Obituary, Paul E. Kahle, *British Academy Proceedings,* 1965, p. 494.

filled with an unbounded zeal for his subject and in his total dedication to his chosen life work he never spared himself. Zeal for his subject, however, and painstaking industry were only part of Kahle's greatness as a scholar. His achievement lay not only in his ability to uncover historical data but, in the light of them, to open up new and important points of view and above all to stimulate others to follow in the paths he had opened up. He introduced his pupils to fresh vistas of historical understanding and showed us new solutions for problems old and new.

To all his many pupils throughout the world Kahle's scholarly generosity was unbounded: *meum et tuum* did not matter in scholarship — what really counted was the advancement of the subject. The following words were written by a pupil and protégé in a review of the second edition of *The Cairo Geniza*: 'Throughout its pages, it is apparent that the author is not only an indefatigable pursuer of new ideas, but also a generator of new scholars, in that his unselfish love of learning has led him to share with them not only his opinions and knowledge, but even the unpublished manuscripts in his possession. His example is particularly bright and conspicuous in these gloomy times, when dissatisfied students, their work brought to a halt, fret after fragments inaccessible and languish after Scrolls still unseen'[2]. Kahle's scholarly generosity was matched by the great hospitality of his home: his home in Oxford became like his Seminar in Bonn, a centre of learning which attracted students from all over the world.

This volume is not only a tribute to his memory; it is also a token of the immense gratitude his friends and pupils feel for one who himself gave so freely and so unstintingly throughout his long and active life of his scholarly labours and discoveries.

St. Mary's College, St. Andrews. January 1967.

MATTHEW BLACK

[2] G. Vermes, in NSt 6 p. 325.

Inhaltsverzeichnis

Paul Kahle

Von H. S. Nyberg

(St. Johannesgatan 9, Uppsala)

In den protestantischen Ländern führte in früheren Zeiten der Weg zur Orientalistik fast immer über die Theologie, über das Studium des Alten Testaments und des Bibelhebräischen. Prof. Paul Kahle gehörte in diese alte Tradition hinein, denn er begann seine Laufbahn als protestantischer Theologe und ist über das Hebräische zum Studium der anderen semitischen Sprachen hinübergelangt. Dem Hebräischen blieb er auch sein Leben lang treu, und auf diesem Gebiete liegt sein Hauptwerk in der Forschung. Aber er gehörte andererseits zu den ersten Generationen moderner deutscher Orientalisten, die in den Orient gingen und orientalische Sprachen und orientalisches Leben aus eigener Anschauung kennenlernten. Der Orientalist der älteren Generationen war ein Stubengelehrter, dem z.B. das Arabische eine tote Sprache war und der seine arabischen Autoren so las, wie er in der Schule seine lateinischen und griechischen Autoren zu explizieren gelernt hatte. Diese Arbeit soll gewiß nicht unterschätzt werden, die Orientalisten des 18. und 19. Jh. haben mit unzulänglichen Hilfsmitteln Großartiges und Grundlegendes geleistet, aber vom Orient hatten sie oft ganz weltfremde Vorstellungen, was seinerseits nicht selten in ihren wissenschaftlichen Arbeiten nur allzu deutliche Spuren hinterließ.

P. Kahle kam als junger Pfarrer nach Kairo, um der dortigen deutschen Gemeinde zu dienen, und während eines fünfjährigen Aufenthalts dort (1903–1908) lernte er das damalige modernisierte, aber doch noch ziemlich mittelalterliche Ägypten, seine Volkssprache und sein völkisches Leben gründlich kennen. Das war damals nicht ganz gewöhnlich. Heutzutage gehört ein Aufenthalt in einem orientalischen Land zum Bildungsgang eines Orientalisten.

Den Jahren in Kairo, denen ein längerer Aufenthalt in Palästina folgte, verdankte er seine Vertrautheit mit gesprochenem lebendigem Arabisch, das nun einmal für einen Orientalisten die hohe Schule zur Einführung in orientalisches Denken ist. Wer einmal gezwungen worden ist, sich auf Arabisch auszudrücken, in Arabisch zu denken, dem eröffnen sich ganz von selbst unerwartete Blicke ins orientalische Wesen. Er verdankte aber diesem Aufenthalt in Kairo auch das

Interesse für die Schattenspiele und das Puppentheater, die beide in der orientalischen Welt weit verbreitet sind und eine lange Geschichte, ein sehr interessantes Stück Kulturgeschichte, hinter sich haben. Er erwarb Material und Texte, und es gelang ihm, mit Hilfe einheimischer Kenner mit den ungemein schwierigen Texten zurechtzukommen. Diese Spiele waren ja schon früher in der Literatur erwähnt worden, aber ihre wissenschaftliche Bearbeitung hat erst P. Kahle unternommen. Er war auf diesem Gebiet eine unbestrittene Autorität und regte zu weiterer Arbeit an.

Ende des vorigen Jahrhunderts wurde die Geniza, die Rumpelkammer für verbrauchte Bücher der karaitischen Synagoge in Kairo zum ersten Male seit dem Mittelalter durchgestöbert. Es quoll hervor ein ganzer Strom von alten jüdischen Handschriften, Werke umfassend, die teils ganz unbekannt waren, teils als seit langem verschollen galten. Diese Funde kamen zu rechter Zeit, um den richtigen Mann zu finden. Für P. Kahle wurden sie zum Ausgangspunkt für sein großes Lebenswerk, die Aufhellung der Geschichte der Arbeit, die die Masoreten verschiedener Schulen an den hebräischen Texten des Alten Testamentes Jahrhunderte hindurch geleistet hatten, ehe die jetzige Textform endgültig fixiert wurde. Die Forschungen P. Kahles auf diesem Gebiete zogen immer weitere Kreise. Keiner hat wie er das Handschriftenmaterial für das hebräische Alte Testament so umfassend und eingehend gekannt und studiert. Keiner hat die diesbezüglichen Probleme mit solcher Kraft angefaßt, so tief durchgedacht und so abschließend geklärt wie er. In seinen Theorien gibt es natürlich Verschiedenes, das weiter diskutiert und vielleicht anders aufgefaßt werden muß; ich nenne z.B. seine Auffassung von der Abhängigkeit der Masoreten von den arabischen Grammatikern. Aber die Grundlagen liegen fest, und auf ihnen hat jede weitere Forschung zu bauen.

Die Größe P. Kahles lag in seiner wissenschaftlichen Leidenschaft. Er hat wie kein Zweiter für seine Forschung gelebt, unbeirrt von der grimmigen Wut der Zeit, über die Schicksalsschläge erhaben, die über ihn einbrachen, in gefährlichen und kritischen Lagen unerschrocken, ein gerader und aufrechter Mann, ein *integer vitae* in einer Zeit, wo allzu viele ihre Integrität nicht zu wahren vermochten. Seine wissenschaftlichen Ideen gab er verschwenderisch freigebig an seine Schüler und Mitarbeiter weiter, und sie wurden immer zwanglos und vorbehaltlos, in Bonn wie in England, in seinem Haus als Gäste empfangen und bewirtet. Sein Haus war ebenso international wie heutzutage ein internationales Studentenhaus, und der geistige Austausch war immer frei und rege. Er bildete Schulen, nicht zumindest dadurch, daß er sich seiner Schüler so persönlich annahm.

Maṣḥafa falāsfā ṭabībān

Von Franz Altheim und Ruth Stiehl

(Nienberge, Krs. Münster, Gieselbertweg 8)

I.

Von Demokrit heißt es bei Clemens Alexandrinus, strom. 1,15,69 (vgl. Euseb., praep. evangel. 10,4): λέγεται ... τὴν Ἀκικάρου στήλην ἑρμηνευθεῖσαν τοῖς ἰδίοις συντάξαι συγγράμμασιν. An späterer Stelle wird überdies berichtet, Demokrit sei in Babylonien gewesen. H. Diels hat diese Angabe für ungeschichtlich erklärt, und W. Kranz ist, trotz einiger Abstriche an der Beweisführung seines Vorgängers, ihm darin gefolgt[1]. Demgegenüber konnten wir den Nachweis liefern[2], daß keiner der angeführten Gründe stichhaltig ist. Indem auf unsere Darlegung verwiesen sei, mag hinzugefügt werden, daß in späterer Zeit eine ähnliche Stele, diesmal in Ninive aufgestellt, begegnet. Amyntas, der Bematist Alexanders d. Gr., wußte von einer steinernen Stele, die Χαλδαικοῖς γράμμασιν die Lebensmaximen Sardanapals enthielt und von Choirilos metrisch übersetzt worden war (FGrHist 122 F 2). Es war eine Fortsetzung dieser Praxis, wenn Aśoka in der aramäischen Inschrift von Pul-i Darunta Zeile 7f. mit *šymll mktb b'm[wd'* „der gesprochen hat, indem er schreiben läßt, auf der Säule" auf sein Edikt verweist[3].

Weisheitsprüche Aḥīḳars sind innerhalb der literarischen Überlieferung Bestandteile des gleichnamigen Romans. Ein Bruchstück des Aḥīḳar-Romans begegnet erstmals auf einem aramäischen Papyrus aus Elephantine, der im späten 5. Jh. n.Chr. geschrieben worden ist. Er war sozusagen ein Zeitgenosse von Demokrits Schriften, was um so bedeutsamer ist, als der Roman selbst wenige Zeit zuvor, unter dem fünften Achaimeniden, auf Aramäisch verfaßt worden ist[4]. Die originale Fassung, die zweifellos in dem Elephantine-Papyrus vorliegt, ist in der Folge mannigfach übersetzt und erweitert worden. Unter den bei Stobaios erhaltenen ethischen Bruchstücken Demokrits

[1] In der sechsten Auflage der Vorsokratiker, 1952, steht die Nachricht unter Nr. 299 als unechtes Bruchstück.

[2] Altheim-Stiehl, Die aramäische Sprache unter den Achaimeniden I (2. Lfg. 1960), S. 185–187.

[3] C. Brockelmann bei F. Altheim, Weltgeschichte Asiens, I 1947, S. 29.

[4] Altheim-Stiehl, a.a.O., S. 184f.

findet sich keines, das mit irgendeinem der unter Aḥīḳars Namen laufenden Weisheitssprüche gleichgesetzt werden könnte[5]. Doch Th. Nöldeke[6] hat bereits gesehen, daß unter den bei Šahrastānī überlieferten Sprüchen des *dīmoḳrāṭīs* sich zwei, zwei weitere in der syrischen Fassung des Aḥīḳar-Romans, ein fünfter in der armenischen und slawischen finden.

Diese Sprüche gehören zweifellos Demokrit. Sie ordnen sich dem wertvollen Gut ein, das Šahrastānīs *kitāb al-milal wa-n-niḥal* auch sonst erhalten hat. An bestimmten Kennzeichen vermag man zu erkennen, daß die originalen Sprüche mit Sicherheit auf Thrasyllos' Ausgabe zurückgehen, wo sie in den ὑπομνημάτων ἠθικῶν (mit fehlender Buchzahl) unter der ersten Schriftengruppe, den ἠθικά, gestanden haben müssen (Diog. Laert. 9,46 = A 33 Diels[7].) Die mannigfachen Übereinstimmungen mit den in griechischer Sprache erhaltenen Bruchstücken Demokrits wurde von uns bemerkt[8], die systematische Einordnung in Demokrits Gedankenwelt von D. Kövendi vollzogen[9].

Von Bedeutung war eine weitere Beobachtung, die Nöldeke entgangen war. Die Übereinstimmungen der bei Šahrastānī erhaltenen Sprüche Demokrits beschränkte sich bisher auf die späteren Fassungen und Übersetzungen des Aḥīḳar-Romans. Darüber hinaus gelang uns der Nachweis[10], daß Šahrastānī 305,20 Cureton *lā takun ḥulwan ǧiddan, li'allā tublaʿ, wa-lā murran ǧiddan, li'allā tulfaẓ* »Sei nicht allzu süß, damit du nicht verschlungen wirst, und nicht allzu bitter, damit du nicht ausgespieen wirst« im ursprünglichen Aḥīḳar vorliegt. In der aramäischen Fassung aus Elephantine (Z. 148) lautet er: *'l tḥly w'l [yblʿ]wk 'ltmr [w'l yrḳwk* »Sei nicht süß, auf daß man dich nicht verschlinge, nicht bitter, auf daß man dich nicht ausspeie«. Damit ist die Benutzung der ältesten Fassung durch Demokrit erwiesen: er muß in der Tat Aḥīḳars Sprüche im Laufe des späten 5. Jh. kennen gelernt haben.

In den äthiopischen Bereich führt das unter Chusrō I. Anōšarvān entstandene Florilegium, das ursprünglich mittelpersisch verfaßt, dann ins Arabische übersetzt wurde und heute allein in der äthiopischen Fassung als *maṣḥafa falāsfā ṭabībān* erhalten ist[11]. Dort entspricht der 25. Spruch, nach der Zählung der Frankfurter Handschrift, wiederum einem der bei Šahrastānī überlieferten demokritischen Sprüche. Er lautet: *taḳārānī mā'ĕmĕr yĕḥĕyĕs ĕmĕna abd radā'ī,* nach

[5] Ebd., S. 186.

[6] In: Abh. Gött. Gesellsch. Wiss. N.F. 14, 4 (1913), S. 22.

[7] Altheim-Stiehl, a.a.O., S. 191.

[8] Ebd., S. 191f.

[9] Bei Altheim-Stiehl, Geschichte der Hunnen, V 1962, S. 72–94.

[10] Altheim-Stiehl, Die aramäische Sprache I, S. 188.

[11] Geschichte der Hunnen, V 1962, S. 215–224.

unserer Übersetzung: »Ein kluger Gegner ist besser als ein törichter Helfer«, und entspricht damit genau Šahrastānī 305,15f. Cureton: *ʿālimun muʿānidun ḫairun min ǧāhilin manṣaf*[12]. Allerdings ist der im *maṣḥaf* angeführte Spruch ohne den Namen Demokrits gegeben.

Anders steht es mit einem zweiten Spruch Demokrits bei Šahrastānī, der nach unserer Übersetzung[13] lautet: »Der Schwanz des Hundes erwirbt ihm das Fressen, und sein Maul erwirbt (ihm) die Schläge«. Im *maṣḥaf* entspricht eine Mahnung, die unter Nr. 215 steht, auf fol. 115b Zeile 11ff. der Frankfurter Handschrift. Der äthiopische Text lautet: *waldĕya ašanī ḳālaka wagĕʿĕzaka, ĕsma ansāḥsĕḥāt zanabū lakalb yĕhūbō ḫabzĕta wamankasūhī zebṭata baʾaʾĕbān.* Übersetzt: »Mein Sohn, mache schön deine Rede und dein Benehmen, denn das Schweifwedeln des Hundes gibt ihm Brot, aber seine Kinnlade Steinwürfe«[14]. Da stimmt der zweite Teil fast genau zur Fassung Šahrastānīs. Nur daß im *maṣḥaf* nicht Demokrit als Gewährsmann entgegentritt, sondern *ḥēḳār ṭabīb*. Obwohl bisher nicht bemerkt[15], wird damit niemand anderes als der »weise Aḥīḳar« gemeint sein. Wieder beobachtet man die Übereinstimmung zwischen ihm und Demokrit.

II.

Ein weiterer Spruch aus dem *maṣḥafa falāsfā ṭabībān* soll uns noch beschäftigen. Fol. 151a der Frankfurter Handschrift findet sich als Nr. 251 auf den Zeilen 11–17:

yĕbē ērāḳlīs fĕlsōf	»Es sagt *ērāḳlīs* der Philosoph,
ĕsma faṭārisa lōtū sĕb-	daß der Schöpfer — ihm (sei)
ḥat lalīhū ḫēr waḫayāl	Preis — selbst ist der (oder: das) Gute und der Starke,
zayāwḥĕz ĕmbĕrhāna lĕ-	der fließen läßt aus dem Glanz seines λόγος
būnāhū lĕbūnā wayĕswĕ-	den λόγος. Und er ergießt
ṭ manfasa aʾĕmrō bāʿĕla	den Geist der Weisheit über die
nafs.	Seele«.

Die erste Frage, die sich stellt, ist die nach dem Autor des Spruches. C. H. Cornill[16] spricht von »Heraklius«, und da er den Namen von anderen, die für ihn unbestimmbar sind, scheidet, kann er wohl nur den Kaiser gemeint haben. Wenn dem so sein sollte, wäre dieser neben Alexander d. Gr., Salomon, David genannt worden. Jedoch

[12] Ebd., S. 218.

[13] Altheim-Stiehl, Die aramäische Sprache I, S. 190.

[14] C. H. Cornill, Das Buch der Weisen Philosophen, Diss. Leipzig 1875, S. 20, 40.

[15] C. H. Cornill, a.a.O., S. 19. Erstmals gesehen bei Altheim-Stiehl, Geschichte der Hunnen V, S. 220 Anm. 13.

[16] A.a.O., S. 15.

kennt man sonst keine Einordnung des Kaisers unter die Weisen. Auch seine Kennzeichnung als eines Philosophen bliebe ungewöhnlich, während in einem anderen ein ungenannter *negūša rūm* ausdrücklich als solcher entgegentritt (Nr. 43) und David mit *dāwīt nabīy* bezeichnet ist (Nr. 181). Nicht einmal Herakleios' Gegenspieler Chusrō I. Anōšarvān erhält die Bezeichnung »Philosoph«, die er sicherlich nicht verschmäht hätte. Denn daß *kĕrsīs, krĕsīs, kasrī* Nr. 38 kein anderer als der Sasanide gewesen ist, hoffen wir gezeigt zu haben[17].

Man muß an anderem Ort suchen. Angesichts der Tatsache, daß Šahrastānī Heraklit als *herakil* (*hrkl*) bezeichnen kann (296,16 Cureton), liegt allein vom Namen aus gesehen nahe, den Epheser im *ērāklīs* des *maṣḥaf* zu erkennen. Die Kennzeichnung als Philosoph würde gewiß auf ihn passen. Aber Heraklit in äthiopischer Fassung? Und wie sollte der angeführte Spruch die geringste Aussicht haben, als solcher heraklitischen Ursprungs anerkannt zu werden? Er ist in der Tat kein solcher, doch eine Beziehung zu dem Mann, unter dessen Namen er steht, ist gleichwohl vorhanden. Wer unseren früheren Erörterungen[18] über das neue Heraklit-Bruchstück und über die Herkunft des gesamten, über Heraklit handelnden Abschnittes in Šahrastānīs *kitāb al-milal wa-n-niḥal* 296,11–297,9 Cureton gefolgt ist, wird sich erinnern, daß dort, im Gegensatz zu dem sonst vorliegenden Auszug aus Porphyrios' Φιλόσοφος ἱστορία, ein vollständiger Abschnitt erhalten ist. Man ist in der seltenen Lage, die über Heraklit innerhalb des Auszuges erhaltenen Sätze 277,4–8 mit der Übersetzung des vollständigen Wortlautes im vorliegenden Fall zu vergleichen. Am Schluß des gesamten Abschnittes stehen die neuplatonisch gefärbten Worte, die an den äthiopischen Spruch erinnern. »Er (Heraklit) hat gesagt, daß der Schöpfer in jedem Zeitalter jene Seelen berühre, um sich ihnen zu offenbaren, bis sie sein reines Licht, das von seiner wahren Substanz ausgehe, schauten«. Diese wörtliche Übersetzung bildet die Voraussetzung des äthiopischen Wortlautes, der von einem »fließen lassen« und »ergießen« spricht. Denn erst die Berührung mit der Hand schafft die Möglichkeit, daß der λόγος und »der Geist der Weisheit« über die Seele herabströmen. Auch sonst zeigt sich die Zusammengehörigkeit, vor allem wenn der arabische Text vom »reinen Licht«, der äthiopische vom »Glanz des λόγος« spricht. Denn daß bei Šahrastānī *an-nūr* die Übersetzung des heraklitischen λόγος ist, konnte in eingehender Erörterung gezeigt werden.

Daß dem Verfasser des Florilegium ein Werk Porphyrios' vorlag, sagt er selbst (fol. 16b–17a)[19]. Es war bisher auffällig, daß trotz

[17] Altheim-Stiehl, Geschichte der Hunnen V, S. 222f.

[18] Altheim-Stiehl, Die Araber in der Alten Welt, IV 1966, S. 76-91.

[19] Altheim-Stiehl, Geschichte der Hunnen V, S. 220.

dieser Versicherung unter den Autoren der Sprüche niemals Porphyrios begegnet. Jetzt erklärt sich diese Besonderheit. Denn zweifellos hat der Verfasser aus Porphyrios' Φιλόσοφος ἱστορία, und zwar aus dem Abschnitt über Heraklit, einen Satz genommen, den er nach der Art, wie er eingeführt wird (»er hat gesagt«), für ein Bruchstück des Ephesers selbst halten durfte. Daß er sich vergriff und Porphyrios' neuplatonische Ausdeutung zu fassen bekam, wird man ihm kaum verargen. Dafür wird uns durch sein Verhalten ermöglicht, ein geschichtliches Ergebnis auf unerwartete Weise zu bestätigen.

Es wurde gezeigt, daß das Florilegium, das heute allein in äthiopischer Übersetzung vorliegt, aus einer arabischen Vorlage geflossen ist[20]. Deren Vorhandensein zeigt sich an unserem Spruch, indem der Schöpfer sein: *lōtū sĕbḥat* erhält. Die arabische Fassung geht nun ihrerseits auf eine mittelpersische Fassung zurück, die im Kreise des an griechischer Philosophie interessierten Chusrō I. Anōšarvān verfaßt wurde. Die Nennung Chusrōs selbst als *kĕrsīs, krĕsīs, kasrī* und seines Arztes Burzoë, des Übersetzers des Buches *Kalīla wa-Dimna* ins Mittelpersische, unter dem unverkürzten Namen *barzamĕhār* (*brzmhr* = mittelpers. *burzmihr*) lassen sich nur unter dieser Voraussetzung verstehen[21].

Auf der anderen Seite war Porphyrios' Φιλόσοφος ἱστορία dem spätantiken Osten in einer syrischen Übersetzung bekannt[22]. Die ausdrückliche Nachricht des Fihrist (260,7f. Flügel) bestätigt sich gerade an dem uns angehenden Heraklit-Abschnitt, insofern dort das syrische *esṭuḵsā* für »Element«, gebraucht wird[23]. Auch von dieser syrischen Übersetzung haben wir nachzuweisen gesucht, daß sie in der Zeit Chusrōs I. Anōšarvān und in seiner Umgebung angefertigt wurde[24]. Nunmehr bestätigt sich dieses Ergebnis. Denn in das mittelpersische Florilegium konnte jener Satz aus Porphyrios' neuplatonischer Ausdeutung, der als vermeintlich heraklitisches Originalbruchstück übernommen und gekennzeichnet wurde, nur eingehen, wenn Porphyrios' Werk zugänglich war, will sagen: wenn es in syrischer Übersetzung bereits vorlag. Jene seltsame Episode der ost-westlichen Berührung, die sich in Chusrōs Bemühungen um griechische Philosophie, in den gleichartigen Bestrebungen seiner Umwelt und nicht zuletzt in der (freilich erfolglosen) Heranziehung der letzten Neuplatoniker verkörperte[25], hat sich nunmehr nach neuer Richtung hin verfolgen lassen.

[20] Altheim-Stiehl, a.a.O. V, S. 216f., 223, 224 Nachtrag.

[21] Altheim-Stiehl, a.a.O. V, S. 221–224.

[22] Altheim-Stiehl, Porphyrios und Empedokles, 1954, S. 18.

[23] Altheim-Stiehl, Die Araber in der Alten Welt, IV 1966, S. 91.

[24] Altheim-Stiehl, Porphyrios und Empedokles, S. 22–26.

[25] Altheim-Stiehl, a.a.O., S. 23.

Eine weitere Bestätigung des zuvor Ermittelten ergibt sich dadurch, daß Porphyrios und seine Schriften auch sonst innerhalb des *maṣḥafa falāsfā ṭabībān* benutzt worden sind. Freilich an einer Stelle und unter einer Form, die man schwerlich erwartet hat.

III.

Unter den Philosophen, deren Name im *maṣḥaf* angeführt wird, begegnet auch Cicero. Sein Name steht über den Sprüchen 247 und 248: er lautet in seiner äthiopischen Form *ḳōḳōrōs*. So steht es zumindest in C. F. A. Dillmanns Lexic. linguae Aethiop. (Neudr. 1955), 1414 Zeile 2, und die Folgezeit hat diese Angabe übernommen. Niemand hat bisher daran gezweifelt, daß *ḳōḳōrōs* als Cicero zu verstehen sei, und die Verfasser schließen sich ausdrücklich ein. Sie haben ihn in die Reihe der im *maṣḥaf* angeführten Autoren aufgenommen[26] und aus diesem Umstand Folgerungen chronologischer Art gezogen[27]. Sie müssen sich jetzt berichtigen.

Zunächst die Übersetzung der beiden Sprüche:

247. »Es sagen Cicero (*ḳōḳōrōs*) und Aristoteles, die Weisen, daß die Seele
seiend ist und sich nicht verändert«.

248. »Und wiederum sagt Cicero der
Tyrier (*ḳōḳōrōs ṭīrōsāwī*), daß die Seele gezüchtigt
und erhoben wird, wann immer einer
lernt. Und alles, was berührt wird (zu lesen: *zayĕtgasas*)[28],
ist (von) dicht(er Substanz), und die Seele
ist (von) fein(er)«.

Es wird schwer fallen, diese angeblichen Anführungen aus Cicero in seinem erhaltenen Werk nachzuweisen. Auch die Zusammenstellung Ciceros mit Aristoteles ist merkwürdig, und gar nicht läßt sich erklären, warum der Arpinate ein Mann aus dem phönizischen Tyros (*ṭīrōsāwī*: C. F. A. Dillmann, a.a.O., 1423 Zeile 44) gewesen sein sollte. Aus dieser Stadt jedoch stammte als ihr berühmtester Philosoph Porphyrios, und ihm zusammen mit Aristoteles zu begegnen, darf nicht wundernehmen. Allerdings wird Porphyrios, wie gesagt, im *maṣḥaf* an anderer Stelle genannt: in der Aufzählung der philosophischen Werke (fol. 16b–17a), die der dort redende »Weise« als die Umgebung, in der er lebt, bezeichnet[29]. Hier heißt Porphyrios *farfōryōs*,

[26] Geschichte der Hunnen, V 1962, S. 215.

[27] Ebd., S. 223f.

[28] C. F. A. Dillmann, a.a.O., S. 1159 Zeile 17.

[29] Ebd., S. 220.

was genau der arabischen Namensform (*frfwryws*) entspricht. Daß dem äthiopischen Übersetzer des *maṣḥaf* eine vorangehende arabische vorlag, ist anerkannt. Es fällt freilich auf, daß Porphyrios, obwohl in dieser einleitenden Äußerung ausdrücklich genannt, hernach mit keinem Zitat begegnet. Denn auch der zuvor behandelte Spruch Heraklits aus Porphyrios' Φιλόσοφος ἱστορία nennt den Namen des Tyriers nicht. Aber auch die in jener Aufzählung genannten *aḳlandīnōs* (Apollonios von Tyana[30]) und *pawlōs* bleiben in der Spruchsammlung ohne Vertretung, und so könnte es bei Porphyrios gleichfalls geschehen sein.

Woher stammt Dillmanns Gleichsetzung von *ḳōḳōrōs* mit Cicero? Zweifellos ist sie sein Werk; zumindest in H. Ludolfs Lexicon von 1699 begegnet nichts dergleichen. Gab es außer unserer Stelle noch eine andere, innerhalb der äthiopischen Literatur, die *ḳōḳōrōs*-Cicero anführte? Schwerlich, hingegen weiß man, daß Dillmann unseren *maṣḥaf* kannte. Das zeigt nicht nur *ṭīrōsāwī*, das wie *ḳōḳōrōs* der zuvor übersetzten Stelle entstammt, sondern auch die Tatsache, daß in der 1865 erschienenen »Chrestomathia Aethiopica« als drittes Stück erstmals ein Teil des *maṣḥaf*, nach einer Tübinger Handschrift, veröffentlicht wurde. Dementsprechend nennt Dillmann in dem Verzeichnis der Abkürzungen, das er seinem Lexicon vorausgeschickt hat, auch den *maṣḥaf* (XXVIII Zeile 28) und führt später (6 Zeile 31f.) den Spruch 247 an: »Aristoteles docet: *nafs halāwīt yĕʾĕtī waʾītĕtwĕlaṭ* anima substantia immutabilis est Fal. f. 82«.

Auffällig bleibt indessen, daß Dillmann nur Aristoteles, nicht auch Cicero an dieser Stelle anführt. Er verändert pluralisches *yĕbĕlū* in »docet«, und wie er sich mit dem Tyrier Cicero abgefunden hat, wird nicht gesagt. Man hat den Eindruck, als sei es Dillmann bei seiner Gleichsetzung nicht ganz geheuer gewesen. In der Tat dürfte eine andere Lösung auf der Hand liegen, wenn sie auch bisher niemandem eingefallen ist. Denn *ḳōḳōrōs* ist nichts anderes als verlesenes arab. *frfwryws*. Falsche Punktation hat aus arab. *f* ein *ḳ* gemacht, *w* und *r* sind, wie so häufig, verwechselt, und daß der Haken des *y* vor dem letzten *w* unberücksichtigt blieb, wird kaum ins Gewicht fallen. Des äthiopischen Cicero sind wir damit ledig.

[30] Ebd., S. 220, 224 Nachtrag.

The Arabic and Turkish Scrolls of Mount Sinai

By Aziz S. Atiya

(Middle East Center, University of Utah, Salt Lake City, Utah)

The Mount Sinai Expedition (1950) for microfilming[1] the priceless manuscripts accumulated over the centuries in the Library of the Monastery of St. Catherine was an event of capital importance in the field of Biblical scholarship. Apart from bringing home to scholars in the form of microfilms one of the most comprehensive collections of Biblical manuscripts of all ages in varied languages[2], pre-eminently in Greek and Arabic, partly in Syriac and Georgian, the Expedition revealed to the world numerous new items of particular value which can hardly be fully appraised in one paper. The »Codex Arabicus«[3] — a ninth century quintuple palimpsest with its five layers of texts in Syriac, Greek and Arabic, — the oldest Arabic versions of Job and the Pauline Epistles[4] together with other Old and New Testament dated or undated books, the »Codex Georgianus«[5] which comprises the oldest known Georgian Psalter on Egyptian papyrus, and a whole

[1] Participants in the Expedition were the Library of Congress in Washington, the American Foundation for the Study of Man in New York City, and the University of Alexandria.

[2] Manuscripts in twelve languages were found in the collection. The Greek MSS numbered 2289 and 1073 were microfilmed. The Arabic 602 and 306 were microfilmed. Of the 257 Syriac MSS, only 159 were microfilmed. The rest were completely microfilmed. These were 90 Georgian, 40 Slavonic, 6 Ethiopic, and one of each of the following languages: Coptic, Armenian, Polish, Latin and Persian. For the Arabic and Turkish Firmāns, see text and further notes below.

[3] Cf. A. S. Atiya, The Arabic Manuscripts of Mount Sinai, 1955, p. xxviff., 9 (MS no 514). See also short notices on the »Codex Arabicus«, Bulletin of the Egyptian Historical Studies 2 (1952), p. 22–24; and The Indian Archives 7, No. 1 (January –June 1953), p. 1–4.

[4] The *Book of Job* is included in the 'Codex Arabicus' (MS 514) and the *Epistles* in MS 151 dated 867 A.D. Cf. Atiya, Arabic Manuscripts of Mount Sinai, p. 6f. for other ancient versions of the *Epistles and Acts*.

[5] I found that Georgian Codex wrapped in old newspapers and afterwards mounted what remained of its folios under glass. This was executed after the Expedition had completed its course and thus it remained unmicrofilmed. On that occasion, too, I did the same towards a number of New Testament Greek papyri used as stuffing in some old book bindings.

host of other materials were brought to light and made available for use by specialists. Of no less importance was the discovery of the vast collection of scrolls, hitherto unknown or at best very little known. These comprised a unique series of official documents, largely in Arabic from Fatimid times, and partly in Turkish covering the whole of the Ottoman period. Since this unusual hoard of original archival materials has been increasingly captivating the attention of some historians[6], it may be appropriate here to recapitulate the romance of the discovery and assemblage of that documentary harvest as necessary and legitimate background for future studies.

Up to the time of the 1950 expedition, little had been said about the Scrolls or *Firmāns*, as they were later called after Turkish times, of Mount Sinai. However, it must be recorded that the first glimpse of those scrolls occurred just before the outbreak of the First World War. In 1914 the Prussian Academy of Sciences[7] in Berlin had commissioned two great German scholars, namely C. Schmidt and B. Moritz, to go to the Monastery of St. Catherine and photograph a selection of Biblical treasures. In the course of the operation, they appear to have accidentally stumbled over a limited number of those scrolls, approximately one hundred, which they readily identified to be Mamlūk. After photographing them, they were set aside in a special chest of drawers. Then on their return with the negatives from Sinai in the spring of 1914 after the outbreak of the War, the two scholars were intercepted by the British Military authorities in the Suez Canal Zone and all their goods and chattels were confiscated, including of course the negative plates which were destroyed as espionage material. Thus came to pass the unhappy ending of the first chapter in the story of the Scrolls of Mount Sinai.

The second chapter was resumed in 1940[8], when I visited the Monastery and found the aforementioned scrolls set aside in the special chest of drawers. Most of them were dated on the verso side in modern ink, evidently by the two German scholars, and we must

[6] See, for example, J. N. Youssef, A Study of Documents from the Fatimid and Ayyubid Periods Preserved in the Library of the Monastery of St. Catherine in Sinai (in Arabic), Bulletin of the Faculty of Letters (University of Alexandria) 18 (1964), p. 179ff.

[7] C. Schmidt–B. Moritz, Die Sinai-Expedition in Frühjahr 1914, Sitzungsberichte der Preußischen Akademie der Wissenschaften, Gesamtsitzung vom 4. März 1929, VIII. Moritz published separately Beiträge zur Geschichte des Sinai-Klosters im Mittelalter nach arabischen Quellen, Abhandlungen der Königl. Akademie der Wissenschaften, 1918, Phil.-Hist. Klasse Nr. 4, Berlin 1918.

[8] This occurred during a trip to the Monastery undertaken by the staff of the Cairo Faculty of Arts under the leadership of the late Shafīk Ghorbāl, then Professor of Modern History and Dean of Faculty.

assume that this is the set they knew and photographed. On further enquiry into the matter, the friendly monks revealed to me the existence of two other greater chests stacked with other scrolls where Arabic documents were mingled with Turkish Firmāns in heaps. My estimate of the Collection then rose to 500 scrolls, and I hastened to bring the matter to the knowledge of the official authorities at Cairo in the hope that something might be done towards photographing this valuable material or transcribing it for publication[9]. Though quite sympathetic with the project, none could do much in the circumstances of the Second Great World War; and so the project had to be postponed until better times. Finally, better times came with the Mount Sinai Expedition which opened up the third and last chapter in the episode of the Firmāns[10]. I realized at once that this was my unique chance. The Expedition was at first launched with an eye on the Greek Collection in the service of Biblical studies. Nevertheless, in the course of preliminary negotiations, I made a drive for the inclusion of this new field in the project and put the matter before the Library of Congress authorities in Washington; and, thanks indeed to their foresight and appreciation, the Arabic Collection was admitted at par with the Greek, and it was further stipulated that the Firmāns should be microfilmed wholly as a set.

While at work in the Monastery, however, the number of scrolls kept mounting by leaps and bounds. Apart from the material already handled by Schmidt and Moritz, the late Father Joachim then Librarian brought me the two new chests which I had already seen in 1940. But this was not the end. Two other huge cases emerged from another secluded corner in the Library annex where I again hit upon a great big medley of Turkish and Arabic scrolls of which many were of singular beauty and importance. It became clear to me that there were more documents than I had visualized, and I therefore began a systematic scroll hunt in the whole place. My efforts yielded good results. Fresh lots unknown to and unseen by scholars in untold and untrodden corners of the Monastery Library furnished new additions to the Collection. For instance, I found a whole heap wrapped up in

[9] I submitted an official memorandum dated July 1940 on this question to the late Maḥmoud Fahmy el-Noḳrāshy Pasha, then Minister of Education.

[10] The idea of the Mt. Sinai Expedition started as early as 1947 when members of the University of California African Expedition visited the Monastery during their wanderings in the Sinai Peninsula. They included eminent scholars such as W. F. Albright the great Orientalist and H. Field the well-known anthropologist. The Expedition was lead by Wendell Philips the young President of the American Foundation for the Study of Man. They were struck by the magnitude of the manuscript collections in the Library and started negotiating the Microfilm Expedition on their return home.

old newspaper unknown even to the Librarian. Further, I found a large bunch concealed behind a row of books on one of the upper shelves including an early Fatimid scroll of considerable dimensions. And so the story dragged on even after the classification of the bulk of our first large finds, so that newly discovered material had to be treated separately in a special Addendum to the main Collection. In the end, the total rose to the staggering figure of 1072 Arabic and 671 Turkish scrolls. Some of them were of unusual length. One deed or indenture written on both sides of a scroll of oiled paper reached approximately twenty-five metres or eighty feet[11]. This is really what is left of it, since its inception was worn out and fell off. Most of the decrees and firmāns emanating from the royal courts bear the signs and signatures of the Caliphs and Sultans of Islam.

It would be hard to over-exaggerate the value of this treasure-trove which is a real paradise for the bibliophile and the historian. All I can do now in the course of an introductory paper is to try to tabulate some of the main bearings of these scrolls on the various fields of study.

I. Palæography and the Evolution of Arabic Calligraphy

The scrolls of Mount Sinai are of inestimable value for this department of knowledge, and no other collection in existence is comparable to this tremendous accumulation of documents. This is mainly due to the following characteristics:

1. Provenance of these documents from official sources, more particularly from the Courts of the Sultans and the Courts of Justice.
2. Continuity and sequence. The scrolls form an almost unbroken chain from century to century, in some sections of the collection from year to year. Starting with the Fatimid Dynasty, they keep increasing in numbers until they reach the Age of the Khedives in modern or contemporary history.
3. Of paramount importance is the fact that, on the whole, these documents are dated and in many cases signed and sealed.

II. Diplomatics of the Islamic Dynasties

Hitherto, scholars have depended in this field on literary sources or secondary material, notably al-Qalqashandi's encyclopedic work

[11] This is Scroll No. 353 dated 20 Dhul-Qui'dah 927 A.H.–21 November 1521 A.D. Its exact dimensions are 2426 × 28 cm. Another example is Scroll No. 49, a decree dated 20 Dhul-Ḥijja 815 A.H.–23 March 1413 A.D., and its dimensions are 1400 × 14 cm.

»Ṣubḥ al Aʿshā«[12]. In recent years, I have been able to add to this a small number of official documents in the form of eight scrolls which I discovered in 1932 in the Archivio de la Corona de Aragon at Barcelona[13]. These are the original epistles which the Mamlūk Sultan al-Nāṣir Muḥammad b. Qalā'ūn sent to King Jaime II of Aragon between 1300 and 1330 A.D. The Mount Sinai Scrolls offer the researcher in this field endless possibilities with a multitude of documents from the royal *Dīwāns*, in many cases signed by the Muslim monarchs themselves.

III. Constitutional History of the Islamic Polity in the Middle Ages

This is an obscure subject on some aspects of which the Scrolls of Mount Sinai will shed much light for our illumination.

IV. Legal History

Here we have two capital sets of documents of immense value: the *Fatwās* or legal opinions, and the marvellous array of deeds covering the period from the Fatimids in the eleventh century to the present day. The *Fatwās* generally bear the signatures of the *Imāms* of the four Muslim sects, and the deeds are mostly marked by the seals of judges and official witnesses in courts of justice.

Further, the deeds supply us with some useful knowledge in two subsidiary spheres: first, they give some idea of the fluctuations in the Monastery property through the ages; secondly, in delineating the limits of property in the city, they record some particulars about the topography of Cairo.

V. Economic History

Ledgers, Accounts, Bills, Receipt-Books, and Taxation notes from various periods will necessarily be of some service to the economic historian.

VI. Social History

The Scrolls will undoubtedly add to our stock of knowledge on Egyptian society in various periods.

[12] H. Lammens, Correspondances diplomatiques entre les sultans Mamlouks d'Égypte et les puissances chrétiennes, Revue de l'Orient Chrétien 9 (1904).

[13] A. S. Atiya, Egypt and Aragon–embassies and diplomatic correspondence between 1300 and 1330 A.D., Abhandlungen für die Kunde des Morgenlandes 23, 7 (1938). Ibid., The Crusade in the Later Middle Ages, 1938, 1965², p. 510–16.

VII. Historical Geography

Odd data of great interest on Sinai and its adjacent territories are to be found scattered in many documents.

VIII. International Relations

Relations between the Muslim potentates and the non-Muslim minorities under their rule will be elucidated from the Decrees and the *Firmāns* to a degree hitherto unattained from other sources. These are supposed to begin with the Covenant of the Prophet whereby he ordered the safeguarding of Monastery property and the lives of the monks of Mount Sinai.

IX. Signs and Signatures of Mediæval Sultans

To my knowledge, the present collection is unique in this respect. I have never seen so many royal signs and signatures representing the Islamic Dynasties from the Fatimids onwards grouped together in one and the same place. As a rule, the regular stout signature of the Sultan appears in the Mamlūk period. In earlier periods, a sign of a phrase is recorded by the Caliph or Sultan surrounded by other signs or phrases representing the heads of the royal *Dīwāns* to indicate approval and knowledge of the contents thereof. In the Middle Ages, these were inserted at the head of each document in much the same way as the Papal Bulls.

I have classified this *Firmān* Collection into the following categories[14]: Covenants of the Prophet, Royal Decrees and *Firmāns*, Treaties, *Fatwās* or Legal Opinions, Procès-Verbaux, Proclamations, Current Affairs, Letters, Inventories, Accounts, Bills, Receipts, and Miscellaneous. The last category includes, amongst other things, a statement on the foundation of the Monastery, an elegy, and an important account of the Jebeliya clans. The Jebeliya were originally a company of legionaries sent from Dacia Felix or modern Roumania by Emperor Justinian in the sixth century to serve and guard the monks of Mount Sinai. At the Turkish Conquest of Egypt in 1517, they sent a delegation to Sultan Selim I to express their wish to adopt the Muslim faith and to ask him to transfer them to the Nile Valley. The Sultan accepted their Islam and enjoined them to remain in Sinai in the service of the monks of St. Catherine. Though they still retain some of their original features, they necessarily have changed a great deal through inter-marriage with the nomadic tribes of Sinai. They speak a special dialect of Arabic, and some of them can speak Greek.

[14] A. S. Atiya, Arabic MSS. of Mt. Sinai, p. 26ff.

Juxtaposed to the Arabic Scrolls are the Turkish *Firmāns*[15] from the Ottoman period. Without dwelling too long on this Collection, some of its data are worthy of note. The royal *Firmāns* issued by the Sublime Porte to the Monastery since 1517 total 210 scrolls from twenty-four Sultans in succession. They include three *Firmāns* from Selim I, eighteen from Suleiman the Magnificant, and they soar to thirty-one from Sultan ʿAbdul-Ḥamīd. Some of these *Firmāns* reach the highest degree of accomplishment in the field of Ottoman artistic workmanship and calligraphy with their beautiful *Ṭu͟ghras* surrounded by floral and architectural frames in gold and attractive colours.

On the whole it would seem that if the Mount Sinai Expedition had done nothing else in the department of Arabic besides the establishment, arrangement, and microfilming of this unique collection of scrolls, its labours would have been more than compensated. Nevertheless it would be a mistake to assume that this was the end of the archival material in the Monastery. Few other documents in Greek, Latin and even French are known still to exist in the Library including a charter from Emperor Charles V and another of Napoleonic origin issued during the French Expedition of 1798–1801. Amidst the Greek documents are to be found some curious pieces in the Turkish language but transcribed in Greek characters. All these were deemed to be outside our jurisdiction which was confined to the Arabic and Ottoman materials and were thus left for another future endaevour.

[15] Ibid., p. 80 (Appendix).

Aramaic Studies and the Language of Jesus

by Matthew Black

(St. Mary's College, St. Andrews)

The remarkable thing about Paul Kahle was that, in every branch of scholarship he entered, he soon became, not only a leading authority in that subject, but himself a pioneer, opening up new avenues into unknown and untrodden fields. There was no subject in the field of Oriental learning in which he was content simply to take over, at second hand or on another's authority, the conclusions of the past, unless he had himself thoroughly proved and approved them. This was most notably true in the areas of Biblical or Oriental study where his major contributions were made, such as his identification of the Ben Asher text, his studies in Hebrew punctuation or his Islamic studies: it was no less true, however, of his Aramaic studies, and in particular of his contributions to the elucidation of the history of the Aramaic Targums, and to the understanding of their language and its relevance to the problem of the language of Jesus. The impetus he gave to such studies led to the rise of a 'Kahle' school of Targumic or Aramaic studies, in which pupils of Kahle (or pupils of his pupils) carried forward his pioneering work[1].

The purpose of this tribute to Kahle's memory is to provide a brief review of the main work (some of it still unpublished) of this Kahle school of Targumic and Aramaic studies, based on an account and estimate of Kahle's own work in this branch of learning.

Kahle's first interest in the history of the Aramaic Targums and the problems of their language goes back to his Semitic studies as a pupil of F. Praetorius in Halle: they certainly were one of his chief interests in the Semitic field long before the appearance in 1913 of his »Masoreten des Ostens«[2] followed in 1930 by his »Masoreten des Westens, Band II«, in which for the first time Aramaic Targum fragments from the Cairo Geniza were published by him. It was in these studies, however, that Kahle began his pioneering work in the field of Targumica et Aramaica.

The Geniza Targum fragments, according to their first editor, represented a Palestinian tradition of free paraphrasing of the Hebrew

[1] Cf. Kahle's own remarks in this connection in ZNW 51 (1960), p. 55.

[2] BWAT 15 (1913).

Old Testament which ante-dated the introduction of the official and authoritative 'Onkelos'[3]; the latter was written in an artificial Aramaic which had to be such as could be understood by both Babylonian and Palestinian Jews; it was fundamentally a Babylonian composition. Kahle's views on the history and relationship of the Targums finally crystallized in his Schweich lectures[4]. He held that Onkelos had been without importance in Palestine, and, indeed, that it had not even existed there till it was introduced from Babylonia, and then scarcely before 1000 A.D. It was entirely a product of Babylonian Judaism: the native Palestinian Targums were preserved in his own Geniza fragments and the related 'Jerusalem' Targums.

This was a view in marked contrast to that hitherto held and first propounded by A. Geiger[5] and A. Berliner[6], viz., that the Onkelos Targum was a native product of Palestinian Judaism dating to the second century A.D. whence it had been transplanted to Babylon (like so much else, e.g., Calendar, Mishnah, etc.) and where it had undergone a certain local influence[7]. Berliner's views had been substantially accepted by Dalman who, also following the Geiger-Berliner tradition, tended to dismiss the so-called Fragment or Jerusalem Targums as late Palestinian compositions of no great value linguistically for the recovery of the spoken language of the time of Christ, and without any authority from the synagogue; they were private Jewish Aramaic paraphrases of the Middle Ages. With the exception of Pseudo-Jonathan, Kahle classed the Fragment Targum with the Geniza Targum as pre-Onkelos Palestinian tradition; Pseudo-Jonathan also belonged to this tradition at a later stage of development, only it included Targum Onkelos, or rather, those haggadic expansions, of which Pseudo-Jonathan mainly consisted, had been packed, as it were, into the framework of Onkelos. What held for Onkelos was also true of the so-called Targum of Jonathan to the Prophets or the Targum to the Hagiographa.

Kahle's theory of the Babylonian origin and linguistic character of the Onkelos Targum had important consequences for the question of the language of Jesus. Following the assumptions of Geiger-Berliner about the Palestinian provenance and language of the Onkelos Targum, G. Dalman had argued that its language was our nearest

[3] Masoreten des Ostens, p. 204ff.; Masoreten des Westens, p. 11ff.

[4] The Cairo Geniza[2], p. 191ff.

[5] Urschrift und Übersetzungen der Bibel, 1857, p. 162ff.

[6] Targum Onkelos, 1884, p. 107ff. Berliner was inclined to the view that the first authoritative written Targums were introduced under the influence of the work of R. Akiba.

[7] See especially Berliner, Targum Onkelos, p. 107ff. Cf. also F. Rosenthal, Die Aramaistische Forschung, 1939, p. 127ff.

representative, next to the old *Reichsaramäisch*, of the type of Aramaic language spoken in Palestine in the time of Christ[8]. Kahle now argued that the language of the Palestinian Pentateuch Targum of his 'pre-Onkelos' tradition was much more representative of first century Palestinian Aramaic[9].

Since the publication of Kahle's views in »Masoreten des Westens II«, and subsequently in his Schweich lectures, a new edition of the Onkelos Targum has appeared[10], and other important work has been done. Sperber's magnificent work has resulted in an edition of Onkelos which must remain a model of its kind: Sperber did not, however, concern himself with questions of the history and development of the Targum tradition. The same is true of other scholars, like Diez Macho, who edited fragments of the Targum to the Prophets[11], and in 1956 announced the discovery of an entirely new Targum to the Pentateuch, Codex Neofiti[12]. The question of the *Überlieferungsgeschichte* of the Aramaic Targums has been raised recently by E. Y. Kutscher and Kahle's view challenged[13]. Kutscher's arguments, however, which will be considered later in this essay, were anticipated by the work of a younger scholar, G. J. Kuiper, now Associate Professor of New Testament at the Theological Seminary, Johnson C. Smith University, Charlotte, North Carolina. Kuiper undertook, under my supervision, an investigation into the relationship between the different strands of the Targum tradition, and in particular the question of the relationship of the Pseudo-Jonathan Targum and Targum Onkelos[14]. The results, which it is hoped will be published soon, have proved surprisingly interesting: Onkelos, while admittedly showing traces of Babylonian influence, appears nevertheless to have been an authoritative redaction *of the same kind of Palestinian Targum tradition which is preserved, still in its fluid state, in the Fragment Targum, the Geniza Fragments, Pseudo-Jonathan and Targum Neofiti I.*

We need not, therefore, be so sceptical about the value of Dalman's »Aramaic Grammar« as Kahle was: at the same time, it must be admitted with Kahle that the more idiomatic and freer Aramaic of

[8] Aramäische Grammatik², p. 12ff.

[9] The Cairo Geniza², p. 200ff.

[10] A. Sperber, The Bible in Aramaic I, The Pentateuch according to Targum Onkelos, 1959.

[11] See infra, p. 22.

[12] See Estudios Biblicos 15 (1956), p. 446ff. Cf. also M. Black, The Recovery of the Language of Jesus, NSt 3 (1957), p. 306. See further, infra.

[13] See infra, p. 22.

[14] G. J. Kuiper, The Pseudo-Jonathan Targum and its Relationship to Targum Onkelos, Ph. D. thesis, St. Andrews, 1962. Kuiper spent some time in Oxford, where he had the privilege of consulting Kahle.

the pre-Onkelos Palestinian Targum tradition, uninfluenced by the Babylonian dialect or the need to translate the Hebrew word by word, is a much better source of knowledge for the Aramaic of the New Testament period.

Work on the problems of the connections and interrelations of the different strands in the Palestinian Targum tradition is still in progress, and must inevitably be delayed until the (long-awaited) publication of the *editio princeps* of Neofiti I, promised by Diez Macho of Barcelona as part of the great modern Spanish Polyglot project[15]. Nothing so far, however, has led anyone to cast serious doubts on Kahle's view that what we have in the extant Palestinian Targum is a free, developing tradition with very substantial differences between the different manuscripts: indeed, this has, if anything, been confirmed by the text of the Neofiti manuscript, which seems to represent an entirely different and independent translation from anything we know of in the Geniza fragments or the Fragment Targum. The importance of this work cannot be overemphasized, since it forms an essential preparation for an edition (or editions) of the Palestinian Targum (or Targums), without which the study of their vocabulary, grammar, syntax, etc., is premature. Kahle himself was convinced of the need for a new edition of his Geniza fragments, and entrusted this task several years ago to his pupil Pater G. Schelbert[16]. My own pupil, M. C. Doubles of Laurinburg, N. Carolina, worked, under the joint supervision of myself and Kahle, on the problem of the Ginsburger edition of the Fragment Targum: that edition did much less than justice to the Vatican manuscript of these fragments, and the full text of this is now available in Doubles's work[17]. There is still an enormous amount of preparatory work to be done, but some rough pattern of relationships appears to be emerging. As Kuiper's work seems to point to Onkelos as an official redaction of one Palestinian tradition, so the close connection of the Paris, Nürnberg, Leipzig and Vatican manuscripts of the Fragment Targum seem to point to a likewise official rabbinical redaction undertaken in the Middle Ages, with the purpose of preserving something (in addition to the official Onkelos) from the previous Palestinian Pentateuch Targumic tradition. Neofiti I is still a vast open question, and its marginalia, some of which can be traced in the Fragment Targum,

[15] Cf. Kahle, The Cairo Geniza[2], p. 201ff. The Bibliotheca Vaticana is also proposing to bring out a facsimile edition (Kahle, ibid.).

[16] See The Cairo Geniza[2], p. 201.

[17] The Fragment Targum: A Critical Examination of the Editio Princeps, Das Fragmententhargum, by M. Ginsburger, in the Light of Recent Discoveries, St. Andrews, Ph. D. thesis, 1962.

may further enrich our knowledge of the Palestinian Pentateuch Targum[18].

So far as the language of the Targums was concerned, Kahle was firmly convinced that Dalman was wrong in taking Onkelos and the related Targum to the Prophets as his main authorities for first century Palestinian Aramaic, the so-called 'Jerusalem' Targums having been relegated to a secondary position[19]: the latter, together with such close relatives as Samaritan Aramaic and Christian Palestinian Syriac, seemed to Kahle to be much closer to the original language of Jesus and the best post-Christian sources for the reconstruction of the Aramaic of the *verba Christi*. This he sought to demonstrate by his now well-known discovery that *ribboni* (my Lord) in Onkelos was pronounced *rabbouni* in the Geniza fragment targum, exactly as at Jn 20 16 (cf. Mk 10 51)[20]. In view of this, Kahle held that a study of the grammar, syntax and vocabulary of his Geniza fragments, and indeed of the whole of the Palestinian Targum tradition, so far as it was extant, was the next urgent task in Aramaic studies. This view was shared — and to a large extent reached independently through the study of »Masoreten des Westens II« — by the late A. J. Wensinck, who carried his work to the point of preparing, on the basis of existing editions of the Palestinian Pentateuch Targum, a lexicon of these texts to supplement Levy's »Chaldäisches Lexicon« (or the smaller lexica of Jastrow and Dalman)[21].

No one will deny the urgency or the need for grammatical and lexicographical studies in those particular areas if we are to extend our knowledge of the Aramaic language, and particularly of the language as it was spoken and written in the New Testament period. The situation, however, has changed in some important respects since the publication of »Masoreten des Westens« (or »The Cairo Geniza«). There are the new Qumran Aramaic texts to study, for the most part exhibiting a language closer to the old *Reichsaramäisch*, but also in their literary form and character, no less than in language, exhibiting a literature which serves as a much closer prototype of the Aramaic portions and especially the original Aramaic poetry of the Gospels[22].

[18] One of my pupils, Miss S. Lund of Boston, is at present engaged on a study of the Neofiti text of Deuteronomy. A short study of the *marginalia* of Neofiti appears in this volume (p. 167 ff.).

[19] Aramäische Grammatik, 1905² (reprinted, 1964), p. 30ff.

[20] See The Cairo Geniza², p. 204, and my Aramaic Approach to the Gospels and Acts², p. 21.

[21] This material was very kindly lent by Mrs. Wensinck to Kahle and myself for a period (see my Aramaic Approach to the Gospels and Acts², p. 231 n. 2). It is now in the care of Professor Jansma of Leiden.

[22] See my article on The Recovery of the Language of Jesus, NSt 3 (1957), p. 313.

There is also the inestimably valuable text (450 folios) of Neofiti, which will also have to be scrutinized by the philologist, once an edition is available. In fact, it is this last difficulty, applying to all the Palestinian Pentateuch Targums, which makes grammatical investigation or lexicographical studies at present difficult, if not impossible. *Our first and most urgent needs are for editions of the Palestinian Pentateuch Targum (or Targums) similar to Sperber's splendid edition of Onkelos*, which must also, however, not be overlooked in any full study of early Palestinian Aramaic.

It was characteristic of Kahle that he lost no opportunity of presenting positions with which he had once identified himself in the light of the latest developments in his field; and he could be a doughty opponent in controversy. Thus, just shortly before the second edition of his Cairo Geniza was published he wrote a long article in ZNW entitled »Das palästinische Pentateuchtargum und das zur Zeit Jesu gesprochene Aramäisch«[23] in which he took cognisance of the new Qumran discoveries, in particular of the so-called Genesis Apocryphon (or Genesis Midrash, as he himself preferred to describe it). The article (which forms most of Chapter III of »The Cairo Geniza«[23]) brought inter alia an up-to-date report on work on the Targums and the scrolls by W. H. Brownlee[24], N. Wieder[25], Diez Macho[26], etc. In the course of the article Kahle had occasion to criticize some of the methods of E. Y. Kutscher of Jerusalem in his dating and localizing of the Genesis Midrash, and this criticism drew a lively rejoinder from Kutscher in which he not only replied to the points of Kahle's criticism but called in question Kahle's general position on the relation of the Palestinian Pentateuch Targum to Targum Onkelos, and on its value linguistically as a primary source for the language of Jesus[27]. Kutscher's reply called forth in turn an equally lively riposte from Kahle[28].

The controversy centred mainly on the exception Kahle had taken to Kutscher's methods of determining the date of the Genesis midrash: he accepted Kutscher's conclusions that this text, composed in a literary Aramaic (of the type we find in Daniel, Ezra, etc.), was Palestinian, belonging to the first century B.C. or earlier. Kutscher's attempt to show that the language of the Palestinian Pentateuch Targum was not one of our best representatives of the spoken language

[23] ZNW 49 (1958), p. 100–116.

[24] The Dead Sea Habakkuk Midrash and the Targum of Jonathan, Duke University, 1953. Cf. JJS 8, p. 169–186.

[25] The Habakkuk Scroll and the Targum, JJS 4 (1953), p. 14–18.

[26] Un nuevo Targum a los Profitas, Estudios Biblicos, 15 (1956); Cf. also Sefarad, 16 (1956).

[27] Das zur Zeit Jesu gesprochene Aramäisch, ZNW 51 (1960), p. 46–54.

[28] Op. cit., p. 55.

of the time of Christ was unconvincing. It is true, the view that Onkelos is a purely Babylonian composition is doubtful[29], but the fact that it may have had its origin in Palestine does not mean that its language is, therefore, a pure spoken Aramaic of the time of Jesus: it is, in fact, as Kahle held, an artificially literal translation of the Hebrew, composed in its present and final redaction in a form of 'literary' Aramaic which is neither pure Palestinian nor pure Babylonian dialect.

In one point Kutscher challenged Kahle's claim that the Palestinian Pentateuch Targum alone knew the New Testament word *rabbo(u)ni* (ῥαββουνί, Mk 10 51 Jn 20 16)[30]. Kutscher is, of course, right in maintaining that the *word* does appear in rabbinical texts, and this Kahle never sought to deny: it was the pronunciation of the word in the Palestinian Pentateuch Targum as *rabbo(u)ni* in contrast to the rabbinical *ribboni* which was unique and adduced as proof by Kahle that it was this Palestinian Targum tradition which correctly preserved the accents of the living speech and dialect of Palestinian Aramaic. To prove that this was not so, Kutscher adduced one instance from one Mishnah codex where the pronunciation *rabbouni* is preserved, evidently as a 'Verbesserung': but all that this, in fact, proves is that at least one scribe knew of this particular pronunciation and objected to the probably artificial (Babylonian?) pronunciation *ribboni*. The instance from the Mishnah confirms rather than refutes Kahle's argument: it is a reminiscence of how the word was actually pronounced in Palestinian spoken Aramaic.

In comparison with the extensive Hebrew discoveries, only a small number of Aramaic texts have so far come to light at Qumrân. They consist, for the most part, of small fragments, miscellaneous ›bits and pieces‹, sometimes containing no more than one word or even just a single letter[31], and only occasionally extending to several lines of text, as, for instance, in the fragments from ›apocryphal works‹ (from the Book of Enoch, or the Testaments of the Twelve Patriarchs)[32]. Where, in one case, a longer text has existed, it has been preserved in so dilapidated a condition as to be at times barely legible[33]. In view of this situation, the discovery at Qumrân of an entire scroll of twenty-two columns, with approximately thirty-five lines to each

29 Cf. above, p. 19, and see especially Kutscher, op. cit., p. 48 n. 11.

30 Kutscher, op. cit., p. 53.

31 See Barthélemy, Milik, and others, Discoveries in the Judaean Desert I, Qumrân Cave I, 1955, p. 97, 147.

32 Ibid., p. 84, 87.

33 Cf. M. Baillet, Fragments araméens de Qumran 2. Description de la Jérusalem nouvelle, RB 62 (1955), p. 222ff.

column[34], makes a welcome and significant addition to the Qumrân library, and, in particular, to its sadly decimated Aramaic contents.

Most recently the remains of an ancient Targum of Job have been discovered: they consist (a) of twenty-seven small fragments, all that is left of a scroll with twenty-eight columns, containing portions of the text of Job xxvii. 14–xxxvi. 33; (b) in addition, a scroll of some ten columns with connected text of Job xxxvii. 10–xlii. 11. J. van der Ploeg who has edited the text[35] thinks the manuscript comes from the first century of the Christian era, and would place the language nearer to Daniel than to the Genesis Apocryphon; he estimates the second half of the second century B.C. as the period of composition of the translation. The translation is literal, not free or paraphrastic, and without haggadic expansions. (It seems to be based on a Hebrew text closer to the Massoretic Text than the LXX.) The editor has been widely followed in his identification of this ancient Targum with the banned Job Targum of the Talmud[36]: it is quite different from the familiar Job Targum of the Polyglot Bibles[37]. Here we have a literary monument of the written Targum of inestimable importance, posing a whole new set of problems for the Targum's history. The question of the existence of written Targums in the time of Jesus is now relegated *ad acta*.

The now so-called Genesis Apocryphon is a kind of *midrash* on Genesis xii and xiv[38]. The date is not absolutely certain, but, if we accept the general conclusions of the archaeologists, the scroll itself must have been written before A.D. 70. Affinities with the apocrypha and the pseudepigrapha (especially the Book of Jubilees) support this early dating. Before a sufficient number of characteristic Aramaic idioms of a particular period can be adduced to identify the period of the scroll by linguistic criteria, we shall have to await publication of the whole text[39]. The published folios, however, already yield one important philological fact: the scroll makes use of the Aramaic

[34] A Genesis Apocryphon. A Scroll from the Wilderness of Judaea, Description and Contents of the Scroll, Facsimiles, Transcription and Translation of Columns II, xix–xxii, by N. Avigad and Y. Yadin, 1956.

[35] J. van der Ploeg, Le Targum de Job de la grotte 11 de Qumran (11 QtgJob). Première Communication, 1962, p. 15.

[36] B.T. Shabbat 115a.

[37] See W. Bacher, MGWJ 21 (1871), p. 208–223.

[38] Earlier I was inclined to regard the so-called ›Apocryphon‹ as a ›Targum‹ (Recovery of the Language of Jesus, p. 309ff.: The Scrolls and Christian Origins, p. 193ff.): in fact, it is much more of the character of a *midrash* than a targum.

[39] The ›apocryphon‹ has been made the subject of an extensive linguistic study by E. Y. Kutscher of Jerusalem: The Language of the Genesis Apocryphon, Scripta Hierosolomitana 4 (1957), p. 1–35.

temporal conjunction אדין, באדין (e.g., col. xxii, lines 2, 18, 20), found no less than twenty-six times in Daniel alone, but *never* in Targumic Aramaic. Mr. Peter Coxon has drawn my attention to the employment of *'ashkah*, literally, ›to find‹, in the sense of ›to be able‹ at IQ Gen. Ap. xxi. 13[40]. The use of εὑρίσκειν in this sense is a well-known Gospel Aramaism[41], but hitherto the meaning ›to be able‹ for *'ashkah* has been attested in Syriac only. Further close affinity with East Aramaic is attested by the form אבי at 1 Q Gen. Ap. 2, 19, 24, where Neofiti and all Jewish Targums have the familiar אבא, attested for the Gospel period by its transcription in the New Testament. The presence of the form with final Yodh in West Aramaic is not only an indication of the great antiquity of the Genesis Apocryphon, but, in view of the firmly attested *Abba* for first century Aramaic, clear evidence that the split between West and East was pre-Christian.

The discovery of fragments of an Aramaic Enoch in Cave 4 at Qumrân was first made known in a communication of Père J. T. Milik to the Revue Biblique in January 1956[42], though the first fragments had been identified by Pères de Vaux and Milik as early as September 1952. Milik's communication mentioned eight different manuscripts of I Enoch, all in Aramaic and containing portions of four out of the five books of Enoch. Three manuscripts contained Book III only, the astronomical section, in a much larger, more detailed and more intelligible redaction than that of the Ethiopic version, in which alone this section is otherwise extant; two of these manuscripts seem to have practically identical texts. So too in the earlier Books, where the fragments happen to contain the same portions of the text, different manuscripts offer an almost identical text. One fragment purporting to be a letter of Enoch which Milik conjectured was addressed to a certain Shamazya and his companions, is not found in any of the versions. Book V was contained in a small scroll which Milik suggested was possibly the original of the *Epistle of Enoch* of the Chester Beatty-Michigan Papyrus (Enoch 97_6–107_3).

In this preliminary announcement Milik drew attention to the complete absence of any fragment from Book II, the *Book of the Parables* (containing the famous Son of Man passages which have been the subject of so much controversy). This omission, Milik ventured to add, could scarcely be accidental.

So far two only of these fragments have been published, in an article by Milik in the Revue Biblique entitled »Hénoch au Pays des

[40] See now also J. A. Fitzmyer, Genesis Apocryphon, 1966, p. 134.

[41] An Aramaic Approach, third ed., p. 133.

[42] Tome 63.

Aromates«[43]. They are fragments containing some eight to ten verses from Book I, chapters 30, 31, 32. They are typical of the extent and character of the larger fragments which have been preserved. There are several fragments which do have a larger portion of text than these; and these are mostly in the astronomical section of the Book. Unfortunately some of these longer fragments are preserved in the Ethiopic version only. The script varies from manuscript to manuscript, but is very close in form to that of the *Hymn Scroll* or the *Genesis Apocryphon*. There seems little doubt that they come from the same period, usually put before A.D. 70.

It cannot be sufficiently emphasized that we are dealing with ›classical‹ Aramaic literature of the Daniel-Ezra type, of very considerable, indeed at times remarkable literary merit, both in the Enoch poems and in the Genesis Midrash which (like the later targums and Midrashim) contains poetic passages. An example is the description of Sarah's beauty at col. xx and the Parable of the Palm and the Cedar at col. xix. The second (in Avigad and Yadin's English version) reads:

›And I, Abram, dreamed a dream . . .
and lo! I saw in my dream one cedar tree and one palm
. . . And men came and sought to cut down and uproot
the cedar and to leave the palm by itself.
And the palm cried out and said, ›Cut not down the cedar . . .‹
And for the sake of the palm the cedar was saved.

(The cedar is Abraham, the palm Sarah, through whose offer of herself Abraham was saved in Egypt.) These are probably the closest literary parallels we possess in Aramaic to the original (poetic) parables and poems of Jesus.

It is abundantly clear that linguistically these newly discovered Aramaic scrolls belong to the period of the Daniel-type or *Reichsaramäisch* (or classical Aramaic). Both from a linguistic and a literary point of view they are invaluable witnesses to the Aramaic language and literature of the time of Christ.

The problem of the original language (or languages) of Jesus has been reopened more than once in recent years. A. W. Argyle and others have sponsored the claims of the *Koine* as a 'second language' of Jesus[44]. The Qumrân discoveries have also shed fresh light on the problem: M. Wilcox writes:

'With regard to the matter of language, we ought to note that the discovery of the Dead Sea Scrolls has now placed at our disposal information of a highly interesting and relevant nature . . . The non-Biblical texts show us a *free, living language*, and attest the fact that in New Testament times, and for

[43] Tome 65 (1958), p. 70ff.

[44] See ET 67, p. 92, 246, 317, 383.

some considerable time previously, Hebrew was not confined to Rabbinical circles by any means, but appeared *as a normal vehicle of expression*'[45].

It would seem from this description of Hebrew in the time of Christ as a 'free, living language' and 'a normal vehicle of expression' that Wilcox intends us to understand that Hebrew was in fact a spoken Palestinian language in the time of Christ, and not merely a medium of literary expression only or a learned language confined to rabbinical circles (as well, of course, as being the sacred tongue of the Hebrew Scriptures). If this is a correct estimate of the Qumrân evidence, where Hebrew certainly vastly predominates over Aramaic, then it may be held to confirm the view identified with the name of Segal that Hebrew was actually a spoken vernacular in the time of Christ[46].

This view — or a closely similar one — has been argued in recent years by H. Birkeland of Oslo, who set out, in a learned article[47], to challenge the usual view that Aramaic was the regular spoken language of first century Palestine, and, therefore, the spoken language of Jesus: according to Birkeland, Hebrew not Aramaic was the regular and normal language of the Jews in first-century Palestine, and certainly so, so far as the masses of the Jewish people were concerned; it was only the educated upper classes who spoke (or used) Aramaic and only the learned who were familiar with both languages[48]. The Aramaic Targums were intended for the benefit, not of the masses of the people who could understand the Hebrew Scriptures without an Aramaic paraphrase, but for the upper classes who understood Aramaic only[49]. This extreme position has found little if any support among competent authorities: the evidence of the Aramaic *ipsissima verba* of Jesus in the Gospels is impossible to explain if Aramaic was not his normal spoken language[50]. Moreover, it is absurd to suggest that the Hebrew Scriptures were paraphrased for the benefit of the 'upper classes'; these Scriptures were provided with a Targum for the benefit of the Aramaic-speaking masses who could no longer understand Hebrew. The use of the term 'Hebrew' to refer to Aramaic is readily explicable, since it described the peculiar *dialect of Aramaic* which had grown up in Palestine since the days of Nehemiah and *which was distinctively Jewish* (with a no doubt distinctive Hebrew script associated with it, and a large proportion of borrowings from classical Hebrew).

[45] The Semitisms of Acts, 1964, p. 14. Italics mine.

[46] Mishnaic Hebrew Grammar, p. 17.

[47] The Language of Jesus, in: Avhandlinger utgitt av Det Norske Videnskaps-Akademi i Oslo II, Hist. Filos. Klasse, 1952, No. 1.

[48] Op. cit., p. 39.

[49] Ibid., loc. cit.

[50] For *effatha*, T. Neof. Gen 3_7 marg.

It is these differences to which the letter of Aristeas is referring and not to two different languages, Hebrew and Aramaic (Syriac)[51].

While this extreme position must be rejected, there is nevertheless a case, certainly for a wider *literary* use of Hebrew in New Testament times. This much is certain from the Qumrân discoveries. It is also possible, however, as Segal argues, that Hebrew did continue as a spoken tongue; it seems unlikely, however, that this was outside the circles of the learned or the educated, i.e., learned Pharisaic, priestly or Essene circles. We must nevertheless allow possibly more than has been done before for the use of Hebrew in addition to (or instead of) Aramaic by Jesus Himself, especially on solemn festive occasions. There is a high degree of probability that Jesus began his career as a Galilaean rabbi who would be well versed in the Scriptures, and able to compose (or converse) as freely in Hebrew as in Aramaic.

[51] Cf. Birkeland, op. cit., p. 14. See also R. H. Charles, Apocrypha and Pseudepigrapha of the Old Testament II, p. 95. The passage in the Letter of Aristeas reads: »'They (the Hebrew Scriptures) need to be translated', answered Demetrius, 'for in the country of the Jews they use a peculiar alphabet, and speak a peculiar dialect. They are supposed to use the Syriac tongue, but this is not the case; their language is quite different'«. The reference is to the peculiar dialect of Aramaic spoken by the Jews, a dialect of West Aramaic, quite different from Syriac, the dialect of East Aramaic which was in regular use as the standard Aramaic language.

Some Difficulties in the Reconstruction of »Proto-Hebrew« and »Proto-Canaanite«

By Joshua Blau

(Department of Arabic Language and Literature, The Hebrew University, Jerusalem)

New finds, not in the least owing to the insight of the late Kahle, have considerably enlarged our knowledge of Hebrew and Canaanite in comparison with the 19th century[1]. Nevertheless, this widening of our horizons with regard to particulars, despite their importance, has not solved the main problems of »Proto-Hebrew« and »Proto-Canaanite«. On the contrary, in some respects it has brought out into relief some of the difficulties which thwart the possibility of establishing this reconstruction on firm ground. In this paper we shall try to treat of some of these difficulties.

1. Defective Knowledge of the Canaanite Dialects

Even our knowledge of Biblical Hebrew, no doubt the best known Canaanite dialect, is rather restricted. The main problem is not the quite limited corpus of texts with their restricted vocabulary, but rather the lack of vowel signs, the vocalization belonging to a much later period[2]. It goes without saying that we possess no indica-

[1] Cf. W. L. Moran, The Bible and the Ancient Near East, Essays in Honor of W. F. Albright, 1961, p. 54ff.

[2] We are in a better position with regard to the vowel system of Syriac. Nevertheless, even it raises problems, cf. the important paper of H. Birkeland, The Syriac Phonematic Vowel Systems, in: Festkrift til Professor O. Broch..., 1947, p. 13ff., dealing, inter alia, with the correspondance of Nestorian *ê* with Jacobite *e* and *i* and assuming that in Nestorian *ê* two sounds, *ệ* and *ê̜*, coalesced. (One may add that one has the impression that originally in Proto-Syriac stressed *áj* > *ệ*, but weakly stressed *aj* (as in st. c., prepositions) > *ê̜*; this was, however, obscured by many analogical formations. But this problem is already beyond the scope of this paper). — Even Arabic grammatical tradition is deficient in some points. Suffice it to mention the well known fact that we have no knowledge whatever of the role of stress in Arabic. Moreover there is the problem of the so-called *alif maqṣûra bi-ṣûrat al-yâ* (as بَكَى »he wept«), whether or not it represents *-aj* (as claimed for pausal pronunciation by Ch. Sarauw, ZA 21 (1908), p. 38–40; H. Birkeland, Altarabische Pausalformen, 1940, p. 74ff., and even for context forms Ch.

tion of the speech rhythms[3]. As to the Canaanite inscriptions and Ugaritic, we, as well known, do not possess any tradition as to their vowels and depend entirely on *scriptio plena* (in Canaanite) and the diverse *alif*-signs (in Ugaritic).

2. Pitfalls of Transcriptions in Other Languages

For lack of other sources, we are often forced to depend upon transcriptions of Canaanite names and phrases (e.g. in Greek and Latin). It is always, however, rather difficult to derive clear inferences from them, since one has to take into account also the intricacies of both the transcribed and the transcribing languages. We shall illustrate our contention by some examples.

One of the vexing questions of the Hebrew vowel system is the problem of the quantity of originally short vowels in pretonic open syllables (as **maΘal > mAʃâl, *ʿinab > ʿEnâḇ*). Whereas e.g. H.

Rabin, Ancient West Arabian, 1951, p. 115ff. 160; cf. against them H. Fleisch, Traité de Philologie Arabe, I 1961, p. 318). One will not, however, propound a markedly different pronunciation of *alif maqṣûra bi-ṣûrat al-yâ* (as *aj*) as against ـَا, since after *yâ* it is spelled *alif*, only in order to avoid two successive *yâ*. Rabin, op. cit., p. 117, it is true, claimed that in this case phonetically *jaj > jâ*. This explanation, however, is contradicted by يا frequently rhyming with ـَى in the Qurân (e.g.—I am quoting according to the »royal« Qurân—20, 71–74 ابقى —
يحيى] موسَى — لاوَلَى — ابقى — الدنيَا — فصلَى — تزكى — يحيَى 87, 13ff. يحيَى — ابقى — الدنيَا
is always spelled in the Qurân in this way, even as a verbal form; Rabin's assumption, op. cit., p. 124 n. 32, that this is due to purely graphic confusion with the proper noun, is only possible, if their pronunciation was quite similar!]). Accordingly, for the Qurân one will postulate the pronunciation *ê* for *alif maqṣûra bi-ṣûrat al-yâ*. On the other hand, we do not believe that Arabic orthography was as much influenced by Aramaic (Nabataean) spelling as hinted by A. Spitaler, WZKM 56 (1960), p. 220 n. 25. Had this been the case, one would have expected *tâ ṭawîla* as the spelling of the nominal feminine ending *-at* in *status constructus* (in accordance with Nabataean usage) rather than *tâ marbûṭā*. So the simplest explanation of Arabic orthography remains that every word was spelled as if standing in *pausa*.

[3] C. Brockelmann, Grundriß der vergleichenden Grammatik der semitischen Sprachen, I 1908, p. 103, 375f., assumes that *mâʿôz, mâḡên* (and add also *mâsâḵ*) preserve their *â* in the first syllable because they were pronounced slowly (lento forms). This is well possible. On the other hand (v. § 5), these forms may be borrowed from a dialect that preserved *ă* even when remote from the stress. In this case the original *pataḥ* changed to *qameṣ*, because in Biblical Hebrew the *pataḥ* could not occur in open syllable. For other interpretations v.e.g. Th. Nöldeke, Mandäische Grammatik, 1875, p. 130 n. 4, who considers *mâ* as a very old form of the prefix *ma*, further J. Barth, Die Nominalbildung in den semitischen Sprachen, 1894², p. 234, who considers *mâ* as prolongation of *ma*.

Grimme[4] and P. Joüon[5] regarded them as short[6], now, since C. Brockelmann's paper[7], it is commonplace that these pretonic vowels are long[8]: Brockelmann relies upon Syriac (Nestorian) and Arabic loans of Hebrew proper nouns, which exhibit these pretonic vowels as long. Accordingly, he concludes, these vowels must have been long in Hebrew as well. This inference, however, overlooks the phonetic conditions of Aramaic (Syriac): in Aramaic short vowels in pretonic open syllables cannot subsist. Aramaeans, when borrowing a word like *dawîḏ* »David« (let us, for the argument's sake, assume that the *a* was short), could pronounce it only in one of the following ways: by reduction of the short pretonic vowel (i.e. *dəwîḏ*) — but this form was, it seems, too different from the original; by reduplication of the consonant following the short vowel (i.e. *dawwîḏ*)[9], or by lengthening the short vowel: *dâwîḏ*[10]. Accordingly, the long *â* of Aramaic *dâwîḏ* does not necessarily reflect a long *â* in Hebrew[11]. The same applies to the Arabic loans, as well as to the Arabic place names of Palestine, which continue Hebrew ones, since they were not borrowed directly from Hebrew, but via Aramaic[12].

Nevertheless, we do not claim that these pretonic vowels were not long. All we wanted to demonstrate was how difficult it is to determine the phonetic values of the sounds of a language from transcriptions in another language. As a matter of fact, we even prefer to regard pretonic vowels in open syllables as long[13]. There

[4] Grundzüge der hebräischen Akzent- und Vokallehre, 1896, p. 34.

[5] Grammaire de l'Hébreu biblique, 1923, p. 23.

[6] I.e. the first vowels in *mAʃâl* and *ʿEnâb* have changed their quality only (from *a* and *i* respectively) rather than their quantity. Joüon, it is true, regards *qameṣ* etc. as longer than *pataḥ* etc. (»voyelles moyennes«).

[7] ZA 14 (1899), p. 343.

[8] I.e. *mâʃâl*, *ʿênâḇ*. V. also e.g. Brockelmann, Grundriß ... I, p. 101, G. Bergsträsser, Hebräische Grammatik, I 1918, p. 117.

[9] Cf. e.g. Syriac *ʾattûnâ* < Accadian *atûn*.

[10] Cf. e.g. Syriac *Tâmûz*, representing, it seems, Accadian **Tamûz*; Syriac *kânônâ*, »stove«, corresponding to Middle-Assyrian *kanûnu*.

[11] This oversight on the part of two such great scholars as Brockelmann and Bergsträsser is the more striking, since both of them explain the lengthening of pretonic vowels (v. loc. cit.) by the assumption that Aramaic speaking Jews prolonged these vowels in order not to reduce them in accordance with Aramaic phonetic pattern! We may justly assume the same for Hebrew loans in Aramaic.

[12] V. for them e.g. H. Bauer-P. Leander, Historische Grammatik der hebräischen Sprache ..., 1922, p. 239 j'; F. R. Blake, JAOS 66 (1946), p. 215 note 15; idem, JNES 10 (1951), p. 243, § 3.

[13] As explanation of this phenomenon, I would prefer the opinion of Ch. Sarauw, Über Akzent und Silbenbildung in den älteren semitischen Sprachen, 1939, p. 66, especially n. 1, and of J. Cantineau, BEOIFD 2 (1932), p. 139, who consider it as a

are, to be sure, no proofs of this assumption from the alternation of such pretonic vowels with short vowels followed by a double consonant[14], since reduplication of consonants after short vowels occurs in many languages, alternating with *short* vowels followed by simple consonants[15]; nor is it borne out by Greek transcriptions as preserved in the second column of the Hexapla: Origines, it is true, transcribes *e* in open pretonic syllables by η, and since η (and ω) occur exactly in the same position as Tiberian *qameṣ*, whereas ε (and ο) structurally correspond to Tiberian *pataḥ*, both Sarauw[16] and E. Brønno[17] postulate long η and ω as against short ε and ο (and, accordingly, long *qameṣ* as against short *pataḥ*). Yet one has to beware of pitfalls: it stands to reason that, in Origines's system, these vowels only reflect differences of quality.

Origines transcribes long segol (הֶ) *by* ε. Accordingly, Sarauw[18] was forced to assume that in these forms (as to his mind everywhere) *segol* is short; for the difficulties of this assumption v. however Brockel-

---

purely phonetic fact. Cantineau loc. cit. adduced some examples from the Arabic dialect of Palmyre, exhibiting *faʿûl>fâʿûl*; later, however, Cantineau himself (Le Dialecte arabe de Palmyre, I 1934, p. 81) came to regard these cases as due to morphological assimilation of *faʿûl* to *fâʿûl* (cf. also Brockelmann, ZDMG 94, 1940, p. 349). Nevertheless, according to T. M. Johnstone, BSOAS 24 (1961), p. 250f., in the Arabic Dôsiri dialect in disyllabic words the ultimate syllable of which contains a long vowel and whose penult is a short open syllable containing the vowel *a*, there is a tendency to lengthen the penult. The unlengthened form is, however, a free variant. Though this feature seems to be quite clear (it occurs not only in *faʿûl*, like *ʿâjûz*, *gâʿûd*, but also in *khâðêt*; so also p. 293 note 1 *sâraḥt*, where the ultimate syllable, though long, does not contain a long vowel), it needs further elucidation, since it is attested in closed (!) syllables as well (*târwa*; so also before a double consonant: p. 292 note 4 *sârraḥt*).

[14] V. e.g. Bergsträsser, op. cit. (n. 8) I, p. 117, 139f.

[15] Cf. e.g. cases of reduplication in Accadian, v. W. v. Soden, Grundriß der akkadischen Grammatik, 1952, p. 109d, allegedly after secondary stress; p. 114f. as »support of the second vowel (of the imperative) by the reduplication of the third radical consonant«, in Aramaic Brockelmann, Grundriß... I, 69ff., in Maltese Arabic op. cit., p. 66z (and perhaps also op. cit., p. 66w in Classical Arabic, allegedly after stressed short vowel). In the Arabic dialect of Palmyre such a secondary gemination occurs as well. Cantineau, BEOIFD 2 (1932), 139, to be sure, regards it as parallel to pretonic lengthening, but Palmyre (n. 13) I 42 he considers it to be due to the tendency to prevent the reduction of a short vowel in an open syllable.—Bauer-Leander, op. cit. (in n. 12), p. 238i, attribute this secondary gemination in Hebrew to the analogy of *mediae geminatae* or to the tendency to preserve short vowels (if one considered pretonic open syllable as short, one would say: the tendency to preserve the quality of the vowel).

[16] Op. cit. (n. 13), p. 61.

[17] Studien über hebräische Morphologie und Vokalismus..., 1943, p. 249f. 346.

[18] P. 95ff.; Brønno, op. cit., p. 269, only states that the use of ε is remarkable.

mann, ZDMG 94 (1940), p. 343ff.[19]. Since, in all probability, *segol* in these cases is long, we may explain the use of it by Origines in one of these two ways: either Origines marks quality only or he marks both quality and quantity. In the first case, we have to assume that pretonic vowel lengthening is not mirrored in the Hexapla. Origines marked open *e* by ε, e.g. in final stressed closed syllables in verbs (as ιδαββερ »he will speak«), in nouns from roots *mediae geminatae* (as εμ »mother«) and in *segolata* (as σεθρ »covering«), thus corresponding to ˇ in Babylonian vocalization, as well as in cases of Tiberian ה ֶ (where the Babylonian vocalization again uses ˇ)[20]. Otherwise, one will have to assume that Origines's system marks both quantity and quality. Since there were at his disposal only two signs, ε and η, to mark four sounds, viz. ę, ę̂, ẹ, ệ, he used ε to mark the first three, and η to designate ệ only. Since the first assumption is simpler and explains all the data so far known, one tends, prima facie, to prefer it.

On the other hand, one is inclined[21] to infer the length of pretonic vowels from the Septuagint[22], whose transcriptions, it seems, denote differences of quantity: ε marks a short *e* (corresponding inter alia to short *ṣere* in the Tiberian vocalization and to ˇ in the Babylonian, as in nouns *mediae geminatae* like Χετ and *segolata* like Εδεμ), η long *e* (both long *segol*, like Ιεφοννη, Μανασση[23], and long *ṣere*, as in stressed closed syllables, like Ιαζηρ, and in *pretonic open syllables*, like Ησαυ, Κηδαρ). Accordingly, if this analysis is correct, we possess evidence of the prolongation of pretonic vowels in open syllables from

19 Who also hints that ε might not have marked a short vowel.—We do not, however, agree with the relevance of Brockelmann's objection that the quantity of Greek vowels has already broken down: the point is how Origines used them, and Sarauw in his brilliant paper has proved that he employed them quite consistently.—It is not clear to me what the intention of Brockelmann (op. cit., p. 346) was, when claiming that one need not accept the consequence of Sarauw's contention that the use of Babylonian ˇ for »long *segol*« would prove that *pataḥ* is long too (as if this were impossible). As a matter of fact long *pataḥ* occurs, though rarely, in the Tiberian vocalization as well (v. Bergsträsser, op. cit. [n. 8], I p. 60).

20 Thus Brønno's argumentation (op. cit., p. 196; v. also Z. Ben-Ḥayyîm, Studies in the Traditions of the Hebrew Language, 1954, p. 54 n. 61) as to the short ε in εχ is not to the point.

21 I have not analyzed the Septuagint material as thoroughly as necessary; the view propounded is, accordingly, only provisional.

22 V. especially Sarauw, op. cit., p. 59ff., who however, mixed up the transcriptions of Septuagint and Hexapla, further as to the proper nouns in the Pentateuch, exhibiting the oldest layer of the Septuagint, G. Lisowsky, Die Transkription der hebräischen Eigennamen des Pentateuchs in der Septuaginta, Diss. Basel 1940, whose conclusions, however, p. 124f., have to be corrected, since he did not realize short *ṣere*.

23 Cf. also Sarauw, op. cit., p. 97 note 1.

the 3rd century B.C. Therefore, one tends to reject Brockelmann's theory[24], accepted by Bergsträsser[25], that this lengthening exhibits an artificial pronunciation of Hebrew, after it had become extinct as a language of communication. Now, after the discovery of the Bar-Kokhba letters, we do know that Hebrew was a living language (true, in its Mishnaic form) until the first part of the second century A.D.; so the Septuagint reflects the prolongation of pretonic vowels in a living language. Nevertheless, this phenomenon *may* be due to Aramaic influence, since bilingual Jews, speaking Aramaic as their first language, might have assumed Aramaic phonetic habits and become unable to pronounce short vowels in open unstressed syllables[26].

3. Features originating in the Author's Mother Tongue and appearing in Texts written in Another Language, because of the Author's Insufficient Mastery of the Latter

An outstanding example of this phenomenon in the domain of Semitic languages is texts intended to be written in Classical Arabic by authors who, for their deficiency in the mastery of Classical Arabic, gave rise to texts teeming with features of Middle Arabic, their mother tongue. Since however the Middle Arabic features alternate freely with Classical and pseudo-Classical ones, the linguist who wants to discern the true Middle Arabic phenomena has to distinguish them from Classical and pseudo-Classical forms by careful investigation of the different groups of texts. Only if a deviation from Classical Arabic occurs quite consistently, does it exhibit, prima facie, a Middle Arabic feature, which crept into the text because of the writer's deficient knowledge of the classical language[27].

As well known, the cuneiform tablets of *Tell-el-Amarna* are written in Accadian, but the scribes, because of their deficient mastery of it, inserted not only Canaanite glosses, which translate Accadian words, but also employed Canaanite expressions and forms in the Accadian context. These deviations from correct Accadian enable us to reconstruct *to some extent* the Canaanite mother tongue of these scribes. The pitfalls of this work are, however, manifold.

As a rule, it is assumed that Canaanite nouns in *el-Amarna* have preserved the case endings, at least in the absolute[28] and before

[24] V. ZA 14 (1899), p. 343f.; Grundriß... I, p. 101.

[25] Op. cit. (n. 8), I p. 117.

[26] For pitfalls of loan words cf. also Brockelmann, ZDMG 94 (1940), p. 356.

[27] For particulars v. J. Blau, The Emergence and Linguistic Background of Judaeo-Arabic..., 1965, passim.

[28] V.e.g. Z. S. Harris, Development of Canaanite Dialects, 1939, p. 41, § 14; p. 59, § 35, and especially J. Friedrich, Phönizisch-Punische Grammatik, 1951, §§ 92$_1$; 216.

pronominal suffixes[29]. I would, however, rather propound that the use of cases is only due to archaism, whereas in living speech they had already disappeared[30]. If this assumption is correct, it means that, in some Canaanite dialects at least, the case endings had disappeared some 500 prior to standing estimates[31]. This assumption is supported by the fact that[32] in *el-Amarna* the case endings, though often used in accordance with Classical usage, are frequently misused. Now, in contemporary Middle Babylonian and Middle Assyrian the custom was to preserve the case endings[33], and Canaanite scribes were no doubt taught to write in accordance therewith. *Had the Canaanite case endings,* which exactly paralleled the Accadian one, *still been in living usage, the Canaanite scribes would not have encountered any difficulty in learning the Accadian ones.* All they would have had to do is to have added the Canaanite endings to the Accadian nouns. It is difficult to imagine that Canaanite scribes who used case endings in living speech, erred so often in adding the same endings to Accadian nouns. But, of course, this conclusion too is an indirect one, as is everything that is based on texts reflecting in one language the influence of another.

[29] E.g. *ba-di-u* »in his hand«.

[30] Cf. also El-Amarna (ed. Knudzon) 243, 13 the gloss *l[i-e]l* »at night«, without case ending in adverbial usage, as against Biblical-Hebrew *lájla.* The glosses, however, as a rule do have case endings, either in accordance with their syntactic environment (as 74, 20; 46; 79, 36 in genitive) or standing in nominative against the context (as 69, 28; 143, 11).

[31] V. Friedrich, op. cit. (n. 28), § 92 2, who thinks that in the 9th century B.C. the differentiation between nominative/accusative with the pronominal suffix of the first person singular from genitive may have been an archaizing feature.—Similarly, one will suppose that the Egyptian transcriptions of the 19th dynasty showing final vowels after absolute nouns (v.e.g. Harris, op. cit., [n. 28], p. 41f., quoting Burchardt § 173) are archaizing (as far as they reflect the same dialects). The same would presumably apply to the verb in el-Amarna. Thus e.g. the permansive, which was confused with Canaanite perfect, sometimes terminates in el-Amarna in *-a* (v.e.g. E. Ebeling, BzA 8 (1910), p. 56). Since, however, the Accadian permansive has no vocalic ending, one will interpret this *-a* as the Canaanite perfect ending. Nevertheless, it stands to reason that, as the case endings, the short vocalic suffixes disappeared in the verb as well and were kept as archaism only. The same is presumably true as to the *-a* ending of the imperfect (for which v. W. L. Moran, loc. cit. [n. 1], p. 64; Orientalia 29 (1960), p. 1ff.), which are the more difficult to be evaluated syntactically. Cf. also infra n. 46 as to the fallacy of inferring from the absence of final short vowels in verbs that they were dropped: this may be due to Accadian usage.

[32] V. F. M. Th. de Liagre Böhl, Die Sprache der Amarnabriefe, 1909, p. 33.

[33] V.e.g. v. Soden, op. cit. (n. 15), p. 80e.

4. The Problem of Parallel Development

It was A. Meillet who in a famous paper[34] treated of the problem of parallel development in comparative Indo-European grammar. He emphasized that one must not lose sight of this fundamental difficulty, which pertains to the very essence of comparative linguistics. We have dealt with this problem in Arabic dialects[35] and endeavoured to show that they are not to be derived from a *koine*, but have become more and more similar to each other, inter alia, through the »general drift«. We have also tried to demonstrate that the vestiges of *tanwîn* were preserved in Middle Arabic dialects under about the same conditions as hundreds of years later in modern Bedouin vernaculars[36]. Moreover, in a lecture[37] we have expressed the opinion that many features attributed to various »Proto-languages« may have originated in the different dialects through parallel development. Now, the same may be true as to the Canaanite and Hebrew dialects. Features attributed to »Proto-Canaanite«, because they occur in all the Canaanite dialects known to us, may have arisen in them independently. So, for instance, the well known »Canaanite« sound shift *á* > *ô* has not reached Ugaritic[38]; therefore it stands to reason that this feature did not arise in »Proto-Canaanite«, but developed in the various dialects independently[39]. Accordingly[40], assuming parallel development (and contact between the dialects), the variation between the »Canaanite« dialects was apparently greater at the beginning of their history than later.

The possibility that various dialects developed more or less along parallel lines and not necessarily together may even affect our approach to decisive problems of the history of the Canaanite dialects: one of the moot points of Hebrew vocalization is the behaviour of stressed closed syllables in verbs in contrast to nouns. Whereas in nouns these syllables contain long vowels, they exhibit short ones in verbs. Several explanations have been propounded for this phenomenon, such as: the stress was different in verbs[41]; verbs rarely stood

34 Included in his Linguistique historique et linguistique générale, I: Nouveau tirage 1958, p. 36–43.

35 V. Blau, op. cit. (n. 27), p. 12ff.

36 V. Blau, op. cit., p. 167ff.

37 Delivered at the First International Conference on Semitic Studies, Jerusalem 1965, to be published by The Israel Academy of Sciences and Humanities.

38 For the problem of the position of Ugaritic among the Canaanite dialects cf. the next §.

39 Or also by mutual contact, v. the next §.—Therefore, it is always somewhat hazardous to fix the age of a phenomenon according to its occurrence in one or even several dialects (as does Harris, op. cit. [n. 28], e.g. p. 38, § 10).

40 Pace Harris, op. cit., e.g. p. 91ff.

41 Bergsträsser, op. cit. (n. 8), I p. 115ff.

in pausal position and therefore, in contradistinction to nouns, pausal forms did not reach them[42]; or, final short vowels disappeared in verbs before they were dropped in absolute nouns, so that the vowel between the second and third radical consonants in verbs came to stand in a closed syllable and was not lengthened[43]. The last explanation is, it seems, the most plausible one[44]: verbs lost their short vocalic endings in Biblical Hebrew before absolute nouns and their, now, final vowel, standing in a closed syllable (*jirkAb* < **jirkabu*), was not lengthened, in contrast to absolute nouns (*dâḇAr*, which, at this stage, was still **dabaru* etc.)[45]. In *el-Amarna*, however, verbs did not drop their final

[42] Brockelmann, Grundriß... I, p. 106, idem, ZDMG 94 (1940), p. 336; Bauer-Leander, op. cit. (n. 12), p. 187; H. Birkeland, Akzent und Vokalismus im Althebräischen, 1940, p. 20ff.

[43] Grimme, op. cit. (n. 4), p. 51; Cantineau, BEOIFD 2 (1932), p. 141.

[44] Bergsträsser's theory fails since, because of the pausal forms of verbs, he is forced to assume alternative stress patterns of verbs (v. Bergsträsser, op. cit., I p. 162); the theory of regarding long vowels in final closed syllables of nouns as extensions of pausal forms does not hold water because of the occurrence of nouns *mediae geminatae* with short vowel (as *gan* »garden«) alongside with long pausal forms (as *gân*; cf. already Sarauw, op. cit. [n. 13], p. 69 n. 1): one would have expected a long form (as *gân*) in context as well. The occurrence of the short form *gan* < **gannu*, etc. clearly proves that the short vowel is due to the syllable being primarily closed, and one is inclined to assume that verbs exhibited closed final syllables earlier than absolute nouns of similar pattern.

[45] Cf. also *qeṭâlatḵâ* »she killed you«, where the verb with suffixes, which according to Brockelmann, Grundriss..., I p. 108o and Bauer-Leander, op. cit. (n. 12), p. 187, should have been influenced by the pausal form, has penult *pataḥ* rather than *qameṣ*, presumably owing to the closed syllable.—It stands to reason that in the imperfect short final vowels were dropped early by the impact of the apocopate, and 3rd person masculine singular of the perfect was then influenced by the imperfect devoid of final short vowel, since this vowel was felt as mark of nouns as against verbs (**jiṣḥaqu* [noun] : *jiṣḥaq* [verb] = **jaʃenu* [participle] : X; X = *jaʃẹn* [perfect]. Admittedly, nouns like *jiṣḥâq* are quite rare.—Cf. already Grimme, op. cit. (n. 4), p. 51f. By this wording Brockelmann's objection, Grundriß..., I p. 107, becomes unsubstantial).—Prima facie, one would think that *lex Philippi* contradicts the assumption of the early disappearance of final short vowels in verbs: whereas in st. cs. *i* > *a* in final stressed closed syllables (**zaqinu* > *zeqan*), presumably because the final syllable was closed early, this shift does not take place in absolute nouns (**zaqinu* > *zaqên*) and verbs (*zaqina* > *zaqẹn*), on the face of it, because the last syllable was at that time still open. This assumption, however, is fallacious. Just as nouns *mediae geminatae* like *libbu* »heart« change into *läbb* in Babylonian vocalization, λεβ in the Hexapla (cf. Χετ in the Septuagint), apparently through *lex Philippi* (in ultimate closed syllable *with main stress i* > *e*, rather than > *a*, cf. Tiberian *qẹn*, Babylonian **qän* in absolute, as against *qan* in construct), and it is only in the Tiberian system that it becomes *ẹ̄* owing to the stress, so also, through *lex Philippi*, it seems, **judabbir* becomes *jᵉdabbär* in Babylonian vocalization (v.e.g. Bergsträsser, op. cit. [n. 8], II p. 95),

short vowels before absolute nouns[46]. Therefore, if we were to consider the disappearance of final short vowels a feature that affected common »Proto-Canaanite«, we would be forced to abandon the theory of the dropping of final short vowels before absolute nouns in Hebrew verbs. On the other hand, if one presumes that the dropping of final short vowels took place at different stages in various Canaanite dialects, owing to parallel (but not entirely identical) development, there is no reason to reject the assumption that in Biblical Hebrew, in contradistinction to dialects mirrored in the texts of *el-Amarna*, final short vowels dropped in verbs earlier than in absolute nouns[47].

5. The Problem of Dialect Contact and Dialect Mixture

Similar features in related dialects may be due not only to common origin and/or parallel development, but also to dialect contact and even to dialect mixture[48]. It is in accordance with modern language theory (prevailing in Indo-European linguistics as far back as the seventies of the last century) to assume that linguistic changes spread, owing to contact between dialects, like waves over a speech area (the so-called »wave theory«). In our opinion, J. Friedrich[49] was right in claiming that, in accordance with the wave theory, the Canaanite lingual type is not the forerunner of the linguistic process, with the various Canaanite dialects splitting off from a more or less

ιδαββερ in the Hexapla and only in the Tiberian system *j^e dabbẹr*. Since ˟ stands in the Babylonian system for both Tiberian *pataḥ* and *segol*, in *qal* perfect 3rd person masc. sing. *qaṭal* and *qaṭẹl* became identical. This is the reason that in Babylonian vocalization *qaṭal* has ousted **qaṭil* even more than in the Tiberian system (v.e.g. Bergsträsser, op. cit., II p. 77). As far as *qatel* occurs in the Babylonian system, it is, it seems, due to the analogy of pausal forms: this assumption is corroborated by the fact that it is in the pause that **qatil* is relatively frequent (v. Bergsträsser op. cit., II p. 76f.). One would presume that it was through the analogy of pausal forms with vocalic afformatives (like *qaṭẹ̄la*)that *qatẹl* persisted in pause rather than in context.

[46] V. supra n. 31. It is even possible that final short vowels in verbs subsisted longer than in nouns, because (v. loc. cit.) it is only because of the apparent breakdown of the case system that one is inclined to assume that final short vowels were dropped in verbs also already at the *el-Amarna* period in living speech (pace Cantineau, BEOIFD 1 (1931), p. 96 n. 1; 2 (1932), p. 141; Birkeland, op. cit. [n. 42], p. 22: the absence of short final vowels in verbs in *el-Amarna* quoted there, corresponds to Accadian usage! Cf. supra n. 31, in fine).

[47] For another case of parallel development cf. Brønno, op. cit. (n. 17), p. 310.

[48] Cf. H. Schuchardt's well known bon mot (H. Schuchardt-Brevier, 1922^1, p. 131) that there is no language not mixed up to some extent. In general cf. e.g. H. Paul, Prinzipien der Sprachgeschichte, 1920^5, p. 390ff.

[49] V. e.g. op. cit. (n. 28), p. 1.

uniform speech (namely »Proto-Canaanite«), but itself emerged only as the consequence of the linguistic development[50]. At any rate, it is difficult to regard Ugaritic, so closely related to the Canaanite languages, as such *according to the familytree theory.* I do not claim this because of the lack of *ā́* > *ō* (and similar features) in Ugaritic, since one may consider it a late shift, which did not reach Ugarit, but because of *ð* > *d*, as against Canaanite *ð* > *z*. And one must not profess that Ugaritic *d* is poliphonic[51]. Poliphonic letters occur in alphabets which have been taken over as such by the speakers of a second language without adding new letters to it: if the second language contained additional phonemes, its speakers were forced to mark them by the existing letters which thus became polyphonic[52]. In Ugaritic, however, new letters were added at the end of the alphabet. Accordingly, it seems fallacious to consider Ugaritic *d* as polyphonic[53]. Therefore, since *ð* shifted in Ugaritic to *d* rather than to *z*, the shift *ð* > *z*, at least, must not be regarded as being handed down from »Proto-Canaanite«, but rather as occurring separately in various dialects, spreading by dialect contact and/or (v. § 4) parallel development. And it stands to reason that this may apply to several other »Canaanite shifts« as well[54].

As well known, the notion of dialect mixture has been already employed by linguists dealing with Biblical Hebrew. H. Bauer[55] even claimed that Hebrew is a mixed language; his notion of language mixture, however, was severely criticized[56], and in general correctly. One will not, it is true, concur with claims[57] that the transfer of whole paradigms from one dialect to another is unreasonable[58]; but one will

50 If this assumption is correct, there does not exist anything like »Proto-Canaanite« (and perhaps »Proto-Hebrew« either). This is the reason that I wrote these two terms between quotation marks throughout this paper.

51 The use of another sign corresponding in some words to Proto-Semitic *ð* is, it seems, an archaic feature in Ugaritic.

52 Thus in Biblical Hebrew ש marks both *šīn* and *śīn*, and in Old Aramaic e.g. *z* marks both *z* and *ð*.

53 One could, however, assume that the new letters were not added to the Ugaritic alphabet until the poliphonic use of *d* was well established. But this seems unlikely.

54 It was in the same way that modern Arabic dialects developed, v. Blau, op. cit. (n. 27), p. 13ff., and the paper quoted *supra* note 37.

55 V. e.g. Bauer–Leander, op. cit. (n. 12), passim; H. Bauer, Zur Frage der Sprachmischung im Hebräischen, 1924.

56 V. especially G. Bergsträsser, OLZ 26 (1923), p. 253ff.; B. Landsberger, OLZ 29 (1926), p. 967ff.

57 V. OLZ 26 (1923), p. 254; 29 (1926), p. 975.

58 By transfer of nouns exhibiting e.g. the form *qaṭṭâl* and denoting professions etc., this form *might* have become productive; cf. the frequent occurrence of *qâṭôl* in

hesitate to accept Bauer's view of the cardinal point of his theory of the Hebrew verbal system, viz. that the syntactic characteristics of the verbal systems of two languages mixed have been taken over in the main without alteration[59]. Moreover, in principle, the confrontation of two dialects only, Canaanite and Hebrew[60], is an oversimplification of the linguistic situation of Palestine, which was much more involved, various tribes speaking different dialects influencing each other[61]. Moreover, one must not lose sight of migrations of tri-

---

Mishnaic Hebrew, as well as of forms of *pi'el* of *mediae infirmae* like *qijjem* (attested already in late Biblical Hebrew, v.e.g. Bergsträsser, op. cit. [n. 8], II p. 151r) or of *hif'îl* of these verbs like *hôbîn* (v.e.g. Brockelmann, Grundriß ..., I p. 616, idem, ZDMG 94 (1940), p. 352; cf. already Biblical Hebrew *hôbîʃ*; no doubt due to the impact of Aramaic; cf. also U. Weinreich, Languages in Contact, 1953, p. 31ff., for the transfer of morphemes from one language to another). For the mixture of declination and conjugation systems of languages mutually intelligible v. A. Scherer apud C. Mohrmann, etc., Trends in European and American Linguistics 1930–1960, 1962, p. 229, 231. (One has to admit, it is true, that the notion of mutual intelligibility is not always quite clear, v.e.g. Schuchardt-Brevier [v. n. 48], p. 142). Cf. also for morphological mixture in the communal Baghdadi dialects H. Blanc, Communal Dialects in Baghdad, 1964, passim, e.g. p. 106 and notes 97a (belonging to p. 64) and 98a (belonging to p. 66).—Accordingly, *in principle*, even Hebrew *qâm* (instead of expected *qôm*) *might* have been borrowed from another dialect, though it may be explained as due to patterning as well: many items of the paradigms of the perfect and participle of *qal* and *nif'al* of *mediae infirmae* preserved *â* (being unstressed) or even exhibited *ă* (standing in *penult* closed syllable). The original paradigm of *qal*, perfect was perhaps: **qâmâku* > **qâmôku, qămta, qămti, *qâma* > **qôma*, etc. The participle: **qâmu* > **qôm*, **qâmatu* > **qôma, qâmîm, qâmôt*. *Nif'al*, perfect: **nasâgâku* > **nasâgôku*, etc. (and similarly the participle, along the same lines as *qal*). Now in *qal* the form with *â/a* prevailed, but in *nif'al* those with *ô*, presumably through the influence of the imperfect *jissôg* < **jissâg*.

59 V. Bergsträsser, op. cit. (n. 8), II p. III n. 1.

60 Bauer–Leander, it is true, admit other dialectal features as well, v. e.g. op. cit. (n. 12), p. 28ff., 510v, 512d. Nevertheless, they mainly content themselves with these two dialects. The same applies to some extent to Birkeland, op. cit. (n. 42), in spite of his statement, p. 14, that waves of migrations from the desert overflowed Canaan almost in every period: he immediately adds that »such restitutions«, as far as it affects Hebrew, repose upon the Israelitic migrations (which, however, also took place, in his mind, in several stages). As against Birkeland's view that the Jews constituted the nomad element, v.e.g. W. F. Albright, From Stone Age to Christianity, 1957², p. 279. As to dialects cf. also Brockelmann, ZDMG 94 (1940), p. 338; Friedrich, op. cit. (n. 28), p. 2f.; Bergsträsser, op. cit. (n. 8), I p. 11; Ben-Ḥayyîm, op. cit. (n. 20), p. 63.

61 Cf. e.g. Albright, op. cit. (note 60) p. 205, 238ff., 279. E. Schwyzer's words, Griechische Grammatik... I, 1939,¹ p. 75f., on the dialect forming factors of Greece apply, mutatis mutandis, to Canaan as well, but our actual knowledge of the dialects is even more restricted.

bes[62], as well as of the fact that a centre of (linguistic) prestige came into being comparatively late. On the one hand, the political and topographic conditions favoured dialectal partition, on the other, not only did linguistic features spread over this speech area, but literary features as well, as borne out e.g. by literary affinities between Hebrew and Ugaritic[63]. Since our knowledge of the actual linguistic features of these dialects is exceedingly scanty[64], we often grope in the dark, without knowing whether a particular feature is due to sound shift or contact between dialects. Thus[65], it is assumed that Proto-Semitic *ð* preceding *r/l* may shift to *d* in Hebrew rather than *z*: *ḥdl, ndr, qdr*[66]. They may, however, be due to borrowing, not only from Aramaic, but also from some Canaanite dialect which, like Ugaritic, has been affected by the shift *ð* > *d*[67]. The same doubts arise as to Hebrew *nṭr* < **nẓr*[68]. Here, however, the possibility of borrowing

[62] As that of Dan. Birkeland, op. cit. (n. 42), often uses the term »restitution«, meaning the introduction of forms already lost in a dialect from a dialect exhibiting a more »primitive« lingual form. (He is, however, not always quite successful when employing this term, v.e.g. Ben-Ḥayyîm, op. cit. [n. 20], p. 16 n. 5. Similarly *lajla* »night« [Birkeland, op. cit., p. 13] is not due to restitution; it represents originally, it seems, *lajl* with the adverbial ending **-ah, -aj* being preserved because standing in an open stressed penult syllable).

[63] Literary features spreading, know even less limits than linguistic ones, cf. the impact of Hebrew Bible and of Greek (v. Schwyzer, op. cit. [n. 61], p. 151) on European languages. In the case of closely related languages as Ugaritic and Hebrew, the literary influence is apt to bring with it direct linguistic impact as well, since e.g. phrases containing related, but not identical words were likely to be taken over as such, thus adding new shades of meaning to these words. (As to cases of »aberrant borrowing« between languages mutually intelligible, cf. L. Bloomfield, Language, 1933, p. 468f.).

[64] Cf. also the fact that we cannot trace Mishnaic Hebrew (exhibiting e.g. the use of demonstrative pronouns, without article attached either to the noun or to the pronoun, as *bajiṯ ze* »this house«, a feature alien to Aramaic and therefore original in Hebrew) to its ancestor in Biblical times. And what do we know e.g. about Moabitic? Cf. in general Harris, op. cit. (n. 28), p. 9ff. and also 38.

[65] I owe this remark to A. Dotan, who is about to deal with this sound shift and to show that its extension is wider than generally assumed.

[66] V. Th. Nöldeke, ZDMG 40 (1886), p. 729 n. 1; S. Fraenkel, ZDMG 70 (1905), p. 252; Brockelmann, Grundriß..., I p. 237; W. Gesenius-F. Buhl,... Handwörterbuch..., 1921[17], s.vv.

[67] Similarly, some scholars regard phenomena as being due to sound shifts, whereas others consider them loans, cf. e.g. Sarauw, op. cit. (n. 13), p. 106, 108, 109f. as against H. Bauer—P. Leander, Grammatik des Biblisch-Aramäischen, 1927, p. 147, 186y, 233f. respectively.

[68] Ancient South-Arabic *nẓr* alternating with *nṣr* does not prove anything (pace Gesenius-Buhl, op. cit. [n. 66], s.v. *nṭr*), because in the later period of that language *ẓ* is apt to become *ṣ*; v. M. Höfner, Altsüdarabische Grammatik, 1943, § 11.

becomes more likely, since, in the sense of »guarding« at least, *nṭr* has the doublet *nṣr*, thus rendering the soundshift *ẓ* > *ṭ* before *r* improbable here.

6. Plurilinear Development[69]

There exists, however, another difficulty which makes it almost impossible to succeed in reconstructing »Proto-Hebrew«, etc. We may well manage to show how a form might have developed, without being, however, sure whether the actual process took place along these lines only. We shall illustrate our case by one example:

One of the central problems of Semitic verbal formation is the question of whether or not the so-called weak verbs are to be traced back to bi-literal roots. Methodologically, Bergsträsser[70] was right in claiming that this problem can only be solved by foregoing a general decision and critically analyzing different formgroups in the various Semitic languages. Accordingly, *verba tertiae infirmae*, for example, which can in all their forms be explained as derived from tri-literal roots, are, as far as Hebrew grammar is concerned, tri-literal[71]. This is, however, by no means sure. The Hebrew verb *galâ* »was clear«, for instance[72], might have developed from »Proto-Hebrew« **galaja*, but *banâ* »built«, for instance, might have been *banâ* in »Proto-Hebrew« as well. Thus it affects Hebrew grammar too whether or not there were bi-literal roots which later developed into *tertiae infirmae*. It may well be (but this cannot be proved) that even forms that *can* be derived from tri-literal roots, actually were bi-literal in »Proto-Hebrew«[73]. Moreover, one is inclined to assume that it was the occurrence of bi-literal roots that served in some cases as a kind of catalyst, affecting tri-literal roots containing a »weak« letter, and, on the other hand, it was the existence of such tri-literal roots that transferred the bi-literal ones into the category of tri-literals. Thus, it has been claimed against the theory of bi-literal roots[74] that it does not stand to reason that e.g. **mawt* «death» and **bajn* »intervening space« are younger than the respective verbs. Moreover, why should the noun of **mît, *jimât* »to die« be **mawt* rather than **mât*?! We assume,

[69] Cf. for this expression Y. Malkiel, Philology 8 (1954), p. 187.

[70] V. OLZ 26 (1923), p. 477–81; idem, op. cit. (n. 8), II p. 3.

[71] V. Bergsträsser, op. cit. (n. 8), II p. 169.

[72] I am chosing verbs perchance only.

[73] Since our knowledge of Ugaritic morphology is so restricted, one will not venture the suggestion that the occurrence of Ugaritic *tertiae infirmae* with and without *j* is due to tri-literal and bi-literal influences respectively.

[74] V. especially Brockelmann, Grundriß..., I p. 606, who was then a partisan of the tri-literal theory.

however, that *mât* etc. was originally tri-literal: **mawita,* derived from **mawt.* Alongside with these forms there were bi-literal ones, as e.g.[75] *râm, jarûm* »to be high« (or even with short vowel, as perhaps *qăm, jaqŭm* »to stand up«). Now, by some sound shift **jamwut* e.g. developed into *jamût,* thus becoming identical with *jarûm* (and **jamwutna* e.g. into *jamŭtna,* thus becoming identical with *jaqŭmna*). Now, through analogy, the various forms of tri-literal and bi-literal verbs became mixed up. Nevertheless, all one can do is to show how the various forms *might* have developed, without being sure that this was the actual process[76].

7. We have tried to show how unlikely it is that we should actually succeed in reconstructing »Proto-Hebrew« and »Proto-Canaanite« (if they existed at all). In some cases, as in that of the history of the so-called »weak« verbs, we have only endeavoured to show that plurilinear development is probable according to what we know, without being able to show what the actual linguistic process was. In other cases, as in the transliterations of Origines and in the glosses of the *el-Amarna* tables and their deviations from »Classical« Accadian, we have tried to arrive at solutions other than the accepted ones. Yet what we have claimed for the general difficulties of reconstruction, applies to our solutions as well: one only tries to offer the simplest theory that is in accordance with the facts known, without being at all sure that the actual development was not quite different.

[75] I am again chosing verbs perchance only.

[76] Birkeland, op. cit. (n. 42), p. 103, assumes that the Isrealite nomads introduced **qawama* instead of Canaanite **qôm.* Thus he assumes that these forms emanated from two different dialects. According to our assumption, they might have existed together in the same dialect. Nevertheless, we do not regard it as necessary to explain *qâm* (instead of *qôm*) in this way, cf. *supra* note 58.

Hebrew Biblical Manuscripts in the Netherlands

By P. A. H. de Boer

(35 Hofdijk, Oegstgeest near Leiden)

The present article, which is based on personal inspection by its writer, tries to give a survey of Hebrew Biblical MSS in Dutch public libraries. Tora and Ester scrolls are not included. In De Rossi's *MSS codices Kennicottianae collationis in variis Europae partibus servati, breviter descripti, suppleti, emendati*[1] eight MSS belonging to private collections are mentioned, all of them in Amsterdam. It is uncertain whether they still exist[2]. MSS of the libraries in Utrecht, Deventer, Groningen and Amsterdam are recorded in the List of photocopies in the Institute of Hebrew MSS, Part II, Jerusalem, 1964. Here follows a description of 18 Biblical MSS.

1.

DEVENTER. Athenaeum-Bibliotheek, cod. or. 1 (former No. 6143).
Pentateuch and Targum verse by verse; *Megillot*; *Haftarot.*
Vellum. 236 ff. 43 × 32 cm, 3 col., 33 l. Quires of 8 ff., indicated by figures (birds a.o.) together with the first word of the next quire, no numbers. These indications are partly preserved because of a cut-off of the bottom of the ff. ca. XIII c. Vocalized by the original scribe. Masora parva and magna. The Haftarot are of the Azkenazi rite. Rebound.
ff. 1–23a Gen (missing 1 $_{1}$–35 $_{10}$; beginning with Targum of 35 $_{10}$); 23a–76a Ex; 76 left corner missing; 76b figure: a candlestick; 77a–114a Lev; 114b–165a Num; 165b–213a Dtn; 213b–215a Cant; 215a–217a Ruth; 217a–221b Koh; 221b–226b Est; 226b–229a Thr; 229a–236b Haftarot (incomplete).
f. 155b on a sticking-out parcel, in small characters, of the original scribe, the Hebrew text Num 29 $_{26–28}$, omitted in the column. The Targum of these verses is missing.

[1] *Variae Lectiones Veteris Testamenti*, 1784, p. xciii. Henceforth abbreviated as De Rossi I.

[2] De Rossi I, No. 643, Pentateuch cum Targ.Megh.Apht, 1344, was in 1914 in the possession of the family Lopez Suasso, according to the Catalogue of the exhibition at the occasion of the centenary of the Dutch Bible Society, Amsterdam 1914.

Photograph[3]: f. 165b. Plate I.
Literature: Catalogus der Handschriften berustende op de Athenaeum-Bibliotheek te Deventer, 1892, p. 75.

2.

DEVENTER. Athenaeum-Bibliotheek, cod. or. 2 (former No. 6144) = Kennicott 159. *The Latter Prophets*. Vellum. 58ff. 52 × 37,5 cm. 3 col., 33 l. Quires of 8ff., first quire 10ff.; indicated by a small figure in the left corner of the last folio; on f. 58b instead of the figure the first word of the next quire, עד. Vocalized by a later hand with red ink. In margin Rashi commentary in red ink. Masora parva; no final masora's. Azkenazi script. XIV or XV c.
f. 11 is damaged, a small part of the text is missing. f. 12 is smaller than the other folio's and has 2 columns.
ff. 1–13b Is, beginning with ch. 37 21; 13b–42b Ez; 42b–46b Hos; 46b–48a Joël; 48a–51a Am; 51a–51b Ob; 51b–52b Jon; 52b–54b Mi; 54b–55b Nah; 55b–56b Hab; 56b–57b Zeph; 57b–58b Hag; 58b Zech 1 1–12.

Photograph[4] f. 42b. Plate II.
Literature:
A. F. Rückersfelder[5], *Sylloge commentationum et observationum philologico exegeticarum et criticarum* 1762, p. 209–383.
B. Kennicott, *Vetus Testamentum hebraicum cum variis lectionibus*, 1776–1780. *Dissertatio generalis*, p, 84[6].

3.

GRONINGEN. University Library, MS No. 455.
Pentateuch; *Megillot*; *Haftarot*. Vellum. A + 304ff. 31,5 × 24 cm. 3 col., 24 l. Quires of 8ff., indicated by first word of the next quire on the last folio of each quire. Azkenazi script. XIII or XIV c. f. A blank; f. 1 fragment glued on paper; f. 72 damaged but text preserved; ff. 284, 303 and 304 blank. Vocalized. Masora parva. Carefully written. Rebound.
ff. 1b–53a Gen (Gen 1 6 partly missing); 53a–95b Ex (f. 67b 1 column; f. 68a top 1 column, end of ch. 14 and ch. 15 1–9); 96a–127a Lev; 127a–170a Num; 170a–208a Dtn (f. 176b ch. 4 46 missing but added

[3] By courtesy of A. C. F. Koch, Librarian of the Athenaeum-Bibliotheek, Deventer.
[4] By courtesy of Dr. A. C. F. Koch, Librarian of the Athenaeum-Bibliotheek, Deventer.
[5] Rückersfelder was professor for oriental languages and theology at Deventer from 1753 till 1787.
[6] Henceforth abbreviated as Kennicott.

at the top of the 2nd column in small characters by the same hand. f. 205a top column, along the whole breadth, end of ch. 31; ch. 32 beginning on f. 205a, continued on ff. 205b, 206a, in 2 columns. f. 208a partly 1 column in small Rashi script, partly blank). 209a–212a Cant; 212a–215b Ruth; 215b–219b Thr; 219b–227a Koh; 227a–235b Est; 235b–302b Haftarot, Azkenazi rite; poetical texts written along the whole breadth of the page.
MS at least from 1671 in the possession of the University Library of Groningen.

Literature:
H. Brugmans, *Catalogus codicum manu scriptorum universitatis Groninganae Bibliothecae,* 1898, p. 249. Handwritten observation recording the dates XV c. and, according to Prof. L. Blau from Budapest, XIII c.

4.

LEIDEN. University Library. Loose leaf in cover of MS Scaliger 4 (former No. Or. 4721).
Fragment of Ruth. Vellum. Half a folio. 21,75 × 32,5 cm. 3 col., 14 l. XII c. Square large characters. Vocalized. Masora parva. Ch. 4 20–22 in latin translation in the margin.
Recto col. A Ruth 3 10 ליהוה [until v. 13] יגאלך; col. B 3 15 בה [until v. 18] כלה; col. C 4 3 השבה [until v. 6] ויאמר
Verso col. A 4 8 הגאל [until v. 10] עדים; col. B 4 12 אשר יתן [until 4 15] טובה לך; col. C 4 19 until the end of 22.

Not recorded in previous literature.
Vide photographs[7]. Plates III and IV.

5.

LEIDEN. University Library, MS Scaliger 8 (former No. cod. or. 4725) = Kennicott 649.
Psalms. Vellum. 58ff. 23,75 × 17 cm. 1 col., 29 à 30 l. Quires of 8ff., not indicated. End XIV c. (Kennicott); XII c. (Lieftinck, but vide note 1 [Edd. of Transactions of the Cambridge Bibliographical Society]: English Hebraists are uncommon in the twelfth century). Vocalized; no masora's; coloured initials; Christian writer. Small square script. Rebound.
ff. 1a–56b Pss. i–cl.

Literature:
Kennicott, p. 108.
De Rossi I, p. xciii.

[7] By courtesy of Mz J. R. de Groot, Librarian of the University Library, Leiden, Plates III–VII.

M. Steinschneider, *Catalogus Codicum Hebraeorum Bibliothecae Academiae Lugduno Batavae*, 1858, p. 349[8].
G. I. Lieftinck, The »Psalterium Hebraycum« from St. Augustine's Canterbury rediscovered in the Scaliger bequest at Leyden in: *Transactions of the Cambridge Bibliographical Society*, II, 2, 1955, p. 97–104. With 3 photographs.

6.

LEIDEN. University Library. MS Scaliger 20 (former No. Or. 4737) = Kennicott 647.
Leviticus. Vellum. II + 67ff. + I. 12,75 × 12 cm. 1 col., 12 l. Quires of 10ff., indicated. AD 1292/93, f. 66b.
Writer חסדאי בן ישועה. Spanish square script. Vocalized. Masora parva and magna. ff. IIb and 1a geometrical figures in colour. Rebound. Photograph of f. 28b + 29a. Plate V.

Literature:
Kennicott, p. 108.
De Rossi I, p. xciii.
Steinschneider, *Catalogus*, p. 379.

7.

LEIDEN. University Library, Bibliotheca publica graeca 49 A.
Psalms. Vellum. 297ff. 22,3 × 16,5 cm. 2 col., 26 l. Quires of 8ff., one of 10 fol. XII c. Square characters. Spanish[9]? Vocalized. No masora's, no k^{e}tîb — q^{e}rê. Hebrew text not everywhere complete, comp. photograph f. 267b and 268a. Psalterium quadruplex: Hebrew, Psalterium 'iuxta Hebraeos', Septuagint, Psalterium Gallicanum.
ff. 1b–297b Psalms (1 6–2 8a missing).

Photograph f. 267b + 268a = Plate VI.
Literature:
Bibliotheca Universitatis Leidensis, Codices manuscripti, VIII. Codices Bibliothecae Publicae Graeci descripsit K. A. de Meyier, adiuvante E. Hulshoff Pol, 1965, p. 70–71.

8.

LEIDEN. University Library, N. 81 (former No. Or. 1298) = Kennicott 184.
Fragment of the Pentateuch. Vellum. 175ff. 13,5 × 10 cm. 2 col., 20 à 21 l. Quires of 8ff. and of 6ff. ca. XIII c. (Kennicott: AD 1278 [5038],

[8] Henceforth abbreviated as Steinschneider, *Catalogus*.
[9] Psalterium 'iuxta Hebraeos' might be able to prove the Spanish origin of the MS.

not found in the MS); Italian square script. Vocalized. No masora's, except final masora's in unequal extent. Some marginal notes in Greek on f. 1. Rebound.
ff. 1a–29b Gen (missing 1 1–25 2] ישבק); 29b–73a Ex; 73a–103b Lev (missing 15 2 טמא [until v. 29] יונה); 104a–149a Num; 149a–175b Dtn (missing 24 10 לעבט [until 34 12 end)

Literature:
Kennicott, p. 87.
De Rossi I, p. lxix.
Steinschneider, *Catalogus*, p. 298–299.
In former days property of J. J. Schultens.

9.

LEIDEN. University Library, Hebr. MSS. 235 (former No. Or. 6950). *Fragment of Exodus*. Vellum. Narrow strip of 2ff. Outer bifolium of a quire. Breadth of page 22,5 cm. 2 col. XIV c.? Square script.
f. 1a parts of Ex 2 16ff.; 1b parts of 3 13f.; 2a col. A parts of 9 30ff.; col. B parts of 10 3; 2b col. A 10 8f.; col. B parts of 10 14f.

Not recorded in previous literature.

10.

LEIDEN. University Library, Hebr. MSS. 244 (former No. Or. 6833[a]). *Fragment of Exodus*. Paper. 1 damaged folio. 20 × 16 cm. 1 col., 27 l. preserved. XVII c. Jemenite script. With Targum Onkelos verse by verse and the Arabic translation by Saadiah in Hebrew characters. The Hebrew and Aramaic texts have infralinear vocalization. Recto Ex 39 34 סה ערת[until v. 43; verso Ex 40 1–11.

Not recorded in previous literature.

11.

LEIDEN. University Library, Hebr. MSS. 248 (former No. cod. or. 10.868).
Fragments of Exodus. Vellum. 6ff. 23,25 × 15,75 cm. 1 col., 17 l. XV c.? Jemenite script. Supralinear vocalization.
ff. 1a–6b Ex 33 11 ואדעה [until 34 24] ושני

Not recorded in previous literature.
Photograph f. 3b. Plate VII.

12.

LEIDEN. University Library, Hebr. MSS. 249 (former No. Or. 10870). *Fragments of Genesis and Exodus.* Paper. A + B + 65ff. + some unnumbered damaged leafs sticking to the end cover. 15 × 10 cm. 1 col., 20 à 23 l. Quires of 8ff., not indicated. XVI c. North African cursive script. Original binding, leather on cardboard. Not vocalized. No masora's, no k^{e}tîb — q^{e}rê.
f. A. Gen 9 18–10 29; B + 1–34b Gen 12 1 — end of Gen (missing 37 5–38 12; 44 22–45 24); 35a–64b Ex 1 1–34 19; 65a (partially preserved) Ex 36 20–26; 65b (partially preserved) Ex 37 1–12.

Not recorded in previous literature.
Bought from a dealer in Jerusalem.

13.

LEIDEN. University Library, Warner collection No. 70 (former No. cod. or. 1195) = Kennicott 648.
Former and Latter Prophets. Vellum. 289ff. 21,25 × 17,25 cm. 2 col., 26 l. Quires of 8ff., not indicated. XIII—XIV c. Spanish square script. Rare indications of k^{e}tîb — q^{e}rê (Jer 1 5 q^{e}rê in the text, not recorded); no masora's except for short final masora. Vocalized. Numbering of folio's in Rashi script. Pericope's indicated in Rashi script, end by עד כן; Sephardic rite. Rebound. On f. 289b twice, by different hands, registration of purchase:

מקנת כספי אני אברהם
חכ״ר
קׄנׄ

On f. 1a an illegible note in Rashi script.
ff. 1b–21a Josh; 21a–41b Judg; 41b–67b I Sam; 67b–89a II Sam; 89b–115b I Kings; 115b–139b II Kings; 140a–173b Is; 174a–219b Jer; 219b–259b Ez; 259b–264b Hos; 264b–266b Joel; 266b–271a Am; 271a–b Ob; 271b–273a Jon; 273a–276a Mi; 276a–277b Nah; 277b–279a Hab; 279a–280b Zeph; 280b–281b Hag; 281b–287b Zech; 288a–289b Mal (missing first 4 words of Mal 3 18 because of cut-off of f. 289.

Literature:
Kennicott, p. 108.
De Rossi I, p. xciii.
Steinschneider, *Catalogus*, p. 288.

14.

LEIDEN. University Library, Warner Collection No. 71 (former No. cod. or. 1197) = Kennicott 646.
Complete Bible. Vellum. 514ff. 17,5 × 12 cm. 2 col., 27 l. Quires of 12ff., not indicated. XV c. (Kennicott init. XIV c.) Spanish square script. Vocalized. Masora parva and magna (and final masora's). Rebound.
ff. 1b–36a Gen; 36a–65b Ex; 65b–85b Lev; 86a–114a Num; 114a–140a Dtn; 140b–157a Josh; 157a–173b Judg; 173b–196a I Sam; 196a–213b II Sam; 213b–234b I Kings; 234b–254b II Kings; 255a–283a Is; 283a–322a Jer; 322a–356a Ez; 356a–360a Hos; 360a–362a Joel; 362a–365b Am; 365b–366a Ob; 366a–367a Jona; 367b–369b Mi; 369b–370b Nah; 370b–371b Hab; 371b–373a Zeph; 373a–374a Hag; 374a–379b Zech; 379b–381a Mal; 381b–411a Ps; 411b–421b Prov; 421b–433b Job; 433b–443a Dan; 443a–453b Ezr; 453b–457b Neh; 457b–459b Ruth; 459b–461b Cant; 461b–466a Koh, 466a–468a Thr; 468a–473a Est; 473a–490b I Chr; 490b–512a II Chr.
N.B. Megillot after Nehemiah.
Colophon on f. 512b partially erased.

זה הספר של משה בן שלמה
ענתיבי נ״ע //////////////////////
////////////! ארור גונבו וברוך
הקורא בו אמן

Literature:
Kennicott, p. 108.
De Rossi I, p. xciii.
Steinschneider, *Catalogus*, p. 288.

15.

LEIDEN. Property of W. Baars on deposit in the University Library, cod. or. No. 2.
Genesis and Exodus. Paper. 209ff. 30,25 × 22 cm. 1 col., 26–28 l. ca. XVIII c. Jemenite script. Rebound.
ff. 1–101b Gen (missing 1 1–15); 102a–209a Ex.
The masoretic text is verse by verse followed by the Targum Onkelos, with supralinear vocalization, and the Arabic translation of Saadiah in Hebrew square characters.
ff. 208–209 and ff. 35–39; 69–79; 118–124 partially in a later hand.
ff. 7–20 and 206–207 damaged with loss of text.

Not recorded in previous literature.
Bought from a dealer in Jerusalem.

16

LEIDEN. Property of W. Baars on deposit in the University Library, cod. or. 3 A + B.
Pentateuch. Paper. 131 and 160ff. 30,5 × 21,5 cm., 1 col., XIX c Square script, copied from a Jemenite MS. Biblical text surrounded with Targum and Commentary in Rashi script.
A. ff. 1a–71a Gen (missing 1 1–27); 71b–131b Ex (missing 38 30–39 20; 39 43–40 38).
B. ff. 1a–43a Lev (missing 1 1–3 7); 43b–106b Num; 107a–160b Dtn (missing 28 12–29 ; 32 42–52; 33 14–29).
Sequence of folio's in both parts greatly disturbed.

Not recorded in previous literature.
Bought from a dealer in Jerusalem.

17.

UTRECHT. University Library No. 1424 (former No. Or. 1; antea 279 x) = Kennicott 644.
Pentateuch; *Haftarot*; *Megillot*. Vellum. 248ff. 24 × 19,5 cm. 2 col., 23 l. Quires of 8ff., not indicated. XIII—XIV c. (Kennicott ex. XIII; Catalogus XVII?). Square regular script; vocalized. No masora's. A few corrections, rasurae with dots to avoid additions, made by the first hand. Final sentence: סוף דבר הכל
ff. 1b–45a Gen; 45a–81a Ex; 81a–105b Lev; 105b–141a Num; 141a–173a Dtn; 173b–226b Haftarot, according to the Sephardic rite; 226b–229a Ruth; 229b–232a Cant; 232a–235b Thr; 236a–242b Est; 242b–248b Koh.

Literature:

Kennicott, p. 108.
De Rossi I, p. xciii.
P. A. Tiele c.a., *Catalogus codicum manu scriptorum Bibliothecae Universitatis Rheno-Trajectinae*, 1887, Vol. I, p. 337.

18

UTRECHT. University Library, No. 1425 (former No. Or. 2; antea 279 y) = Kennicott 645.
The Latter Prophets. Vellum. 207ff. 20 × 26,5 cm. 2 col., 21–23 1. Quires of 6ff., not indicated. XVII c.? (Kennicott ex. XIV c.). Vocalized. Masora parva partially. Large square script.
ff. 1a–29b Is (missing 1 1–28 24a); 30a–93b Jer; 94a–159a Ez; 159a–166b Hos; 167a–170a Joel; 170a–176b Am; 176b–177b Ob; 177b–180a

Jona; 180a–185a Mi; 185a–187a Nah; 187a–189a Hab; 189a–191b Zeph; 192a–193b Hag; 194a–204a Zech; 204a–207a Mal.

Literature:

Kennicott, p. 108.
De Rossi I, p. xciii.
Tiele c.a., *Catalogus* I, p. 337.

A Concordance

between the Biblical Books and the numbers of the MSS in this Survey
(An asterisk means: incompletely preserved)

Gen	1*.3.8*.12*.14.15*.16*.17	Hos	2.13.14.18	Ps	5.7.14
Ex	1.3.8.9*.10*.11*.12*.14.15.16*.17	Joel	2.13.14.18	Prov	14
Lev	1.3.6.8*.14.16*.17	Am	2.13.14.18	Job	14
Num	1.3.8.14.16.17	Ob	2.13.14.18	Dan	14
Dtn	1.3.8*.14.16*.17	Jona	2.13.14.18	Ezr	14
Josh	13.14	Mi	2.13.14.18	Neh	14
Judg	13.14	Nah	2.13.14.18	Ruth	1.3.4*.14.17
I–II Sam	13.14	Hab	2.13.14.18	Cant	1.3.14.17
I–II Kings	13.14	Zeph	2.13.14.18	Koh	1.3.14.17
Is	2.13.14.18*	Hag	2.13.14.18	Thr	1.3.14.17
Jer	13.14.18	Zech	2*.13.14.18	Est	1.3.14.17
Ez	2.13.14.18	Mal	13.14.18	I–II Chr	14

Temple and Festivals in the Persian Diatessaron

By John Bowman

(Department of MIDDLE EASTERN Studies, University of Melbourne, Parkville, Vic.)

Ναὸς and ἱερὸν of the Greek Gospels are both rendered by ܗܝܟܠܐ in the Peshitta, so also O.S. (Sin.Pal.) except Jn 10 22 and Mt 27 51 (ܒܝܬ ܡܩܕܫܐ). In the Arabic Diatessaron[1] the word used throughout is هيكل. Not so the Persian Diatessaron[2] where كنشت[3] هيكل[4] هيكل كنشت[5] and خانه[6] are used. G. Messina, »Diatessaron Persiano«, 1951, translates هيكل, كنشت by *tempio*. P.D's underlying Syriac text[7] conforms to the Peshitta. The present writer postulates that P.D., for reasons of its own, translates ܗܝܟܠܐ by various terms. The didactic concern of the translator of P.D. is obvious in his glosses introduced by يعنى e.g. Mt 2 1 (P.D. 1 7) or Mt 2 21 (P.D. 1 10)[8] but is present in his translation itself e.g. Mt 1 16 (P.D. 1 12) »Joseph whom *they wanted* for a husband for Mary« or Lk 3 38 (P.D. 1 11) »Adam who was *created* from God«.

It is in the light of this *tendenz* that we should see his terms for the Temple. P.D. is a Persian Church document catering for the needs of its own people in the very difficult period at the end of the 13th century. The translator expected Armenians also to use it. Only a Jacobite Syrian could approximate the Armenian standpoint. In

1 Hereafter referred to as A.D.

2 Hereafter referred to as P.D.

3 (Gk. ἱερον) Mt 21 23 (P.D. 3 43); Mt 24 1a (P.D. 3 54); Mk 11 16 (P.D. 3 37); Mk 13 3 (P.D. 3 55); Mk 14 58c (P.D. 4 39); Lk 2 27 (P.D. 1 6); Lk 2 46 (P.D. 1 13); Lk 18 10 (P.D. 4 7); Lk 21 38 (P.D. 4 21); Lk 22 4 (P.D. 4 21) ܗܝܟܠܐ but Gk. <; Jn 8 2 (P.D. 3 3); Jn 18 20 (P.D. 4 38). (Gk. ναος) Mt 27 51 (P.D. 4 49); Mk 14 58 (P.D. 4 39); Lk 1 9a (P.D. 1 2); Lk 1 22 (P.D. 1 2).

4 (Gk. ἱερον) Lk 4 9 (P.D. 1 19); Lk 2 37 (P.D. 1 6); Jn 7 28 (P.D. 2 51); Jn 8 20 (P.D. 2 55); Jn 8 59 (P.D. 2 57); Jn 10 23 (P.D. 2 38); Jn 11 56 (P.D. 3 36). (Gk. ναος) Mt 27 5 (P.D. 4 50); Lk 1 9 (P.D. 1 2); Lk 1 21 (P.D. 1 2); Jn 2 21 (P.D. 3 37).

5 (Gk. ἱερον) Lk 21 37 (P.D. 4 21); Lk 22 53a (P.D. 4 3); Jn 7 14 (P.D. 2 50).

6 (Gk. ἱερον) Mt 21 12a (P.D. 3 37). (Gk. ναος) Jn 2 19 (P.D. 3 37); Jn 2 20 (P.D. 3 7).

7 Cf. e.g. Jn 10 22 (P.D. 2 38) as against O.S. (Sin Pal.) Jn 10 22. P.D. has the Marcan long ending. Surprisingly it has also Jn 8 1–11.

8 After »to the land of Israel« the gloss is »he means the province of the بيت المقدس«. Does P.D. use this term when attention is to be drawn to Jerusalem as where the Temple is?

Lk 1 9, P.D. 1 2 inserts after »the priest's office«, in the temple (كنشت) in the service of the Most High God. Temple (هيكل) can be Temple in general. However, in Lk 1 9 (A.D. 1 2) uses هيكل of Zacharias' entering the Temple and burning incense. Whereas the altar of incense in the Jewish Temple was in the ܗܝܟܠܐ, in the Jacobite Church the incense would be burned at the altar in the sanctuary during *Qurbana Qadisha*, first before the priest came out and censed the people[9]. So Zacharias is understood in Lk 1 21 (P.D. 1 2) as tarrying longer than usual at the censing of the altar in the Chancel, and cf. v. 22 as having seen the Angel in the Chancel. In both v. 21. 22 هيكل is used of the part of the Temple where the altar cf. v. 11 was[10]. In Lk 2 27 (P.D. 1 6) Simeon comes into the Temple (كنشت), whereas in Lk 2 37 (P.D. 1 6) it is said that Anna departed not from the Temple (هيكل) P.D. cannot be thinking of the Temple in Jerusalem as it was. Anna certainly would not have been allowed in even so far as Simeon. On the other hand, if we note her daily worshipping and fasting etc., she would be thought of in a Jacobite Church setting as coming up to the هيكل to receive the *bukhra* the firstborn = the Host and tarrying there daily. In Lk 2 46 (P.D. 1 13) the boy Jesus in the Temple (كنشت) is not in the هيكل[11] or Chancel, for that is *not* where the Rabbis[12] would hold discussions.

Before proceeding with examination of other references in P.D. to the Temple, it is essential to turn to the Festivals mentioned in P.D. and their order. Both P.D. and A.D. basically used the Johannine Festival framework, but with what differences. In P.D. 2 8 the Feast of Tabernacles is mentioned. Jn 7 2–13 is cited, but it is not clear that he actually went up. However P.D. sets the stage : it is Tabernacles' time. He has decided to go up, or went up. Thereafter follow 26 paragraphs *not* in a Jerusalem setting. Among these P.D. 2 10 the Woes on the Pharisees (which in A.D. Jesus delivers in Passion Week) : P.D. 2 25 Jesus' question »What say ye that I am?« and Peter's answer: P.D. 2 26 gives the first announcement of the Passion at Jerusalem and P.D. 2 28 the Transfiguration[13]. If we could under-

[9] In S. India, Cottayam Old Orthodox Seminary (Jacobite), the censing of the altar is not visible to the people as it is done behind the screen.

[10] In a Nestorian Church, the Chancel is called *Kanki* and the ܗܝܟܠܐ is the Nave.

[11] Liturgies Eastern and Western I, p. 587, edited by F. E. Brightman and C. E. Hammond, 1896, reprinted 1965.

[12] Cf. Neo-Syriac usage for Church Teachers.

[13] In A.D. the Transfiguration is mentioned in Sect 24 1–16 while the Feast of Tabernacles occurs in A.D. 27 1ff. This is the order to be expected, i.e. the Transfiguration before Tabernacles, not after, nor even during Tabernacles; while even if we were to assume that with P.D. 2 8 the Feast of Tabernacles is over, and the Transfiguration (P.D. 2 28) belongs to the next year, there is the problem why the Feast of the

stand P.D. 2 9–34 as teaching and events on the way up to Jerusalem within the Octave of the Tabernacles it would be very significant that the Transfiguration is included. P.D. 2 35 deals with the giving of sight to the man born blind. This in A.D. is set at the Feast of the Unleavened Bread A.D. 36. It is natural to see it as implying that Jesus is now in or near Jerusalem cf. Jn 9 11. P.D. 2 36 follows on with Jn 9 40–10 15. This in A.D. is in Sect. 37 and follows on His discourses set in A.D. at the Feast of Unleavened Bread (cf. A.D. 32). P.D. 2 38 now passes on to the Feast of Dedication Jn 10 22–42. It would be that P.D. wishes us to regard the Feast of Dedication as associated with the Feast of Tabernacles. With Nestorians the Feast of Dedication lasts one month e.g. in Rezayeh, Iran in 1966 it was from 30th October for 4 Sundays. In Tabriz where P.D. was compiled, snow comes by mid-November. Winter and the Feast of Dedication overlap. In P.D. 2 38 Jesus is at the Feast of Dedication in the Temple in Solomon's porch (Jn 10 23). P.D. renders Temple by هيكل here. Now if هيكل means for the Jacobite author(?) or translator from Syriac into Farsi, Chancel (see above p. 54) then here despite the difficult reference to Solomon's porch, he must have meant it to be Chancel too. We cannot expect him to know the antiquities of the Temple, apart from what the O.T. Peshitta told him. He may have thought Solomon's porch was another designation for the *Ulam* or porch of Solomon's Temple. Thinking of the Temple as a Jacobite Church, the obvious place for Christ to be was in the Sanctuary. His presence set the seal on the Dedication. Next P.D. taking its cue from Jn 10 42 has Jesus away from Jerusalem. While P.D. 2 39 40 based on Mk 10 17–22. 23–31, the rich young man and the difficulty

Dedication P.D. 2 38 = Jn 10 22–42 comes before the Johannine teachings chs. 7–8 associated with the Feast of Tabernacles: i.e. P.D. 2 50.51.52.53.54.55.56.57. It is quite unwarranted to identify the Feast mentioned in P.D. 2 50.53 as that of Unleavened Bread just because A.D. has put Jn chs. 7–8 in that setting. P.D. must not be interpreted in the light of A.D. P.D. is not primarily interested in a Calendar, nor a Lectionary, but in arranging its material to give easy access to Gospel teaching, as its 250 paragraph headings show.

P.D. does seem to be interested in Tabernacles/Dedication as well as Passover. On the relationship of Tabernacles to Dedication and vice versa cf. J. Van Goudoever, Biblical Calendars, 1959, ch. XXV, p. 210–14. The Jacobite Feast of Dedication of the Church begins cf. Goudoever, op. cit., p. 212, with the Sunday closest to the first day of November; while it only lasts eight days, on the 14th September there was the Exaltation of the Cross, the lessons for which as Goudoever points out are more for a pilgrim festival and a festival of Dedication than a festival of the Cross. That the Greeks celebrated the Feast of the Dedication of the Temple or the Holy Sepulchre on the 14th September is significant. We may allow that Jacobites could possibly have once given more than eight days to the Feast of Church Dedication as do the Nestorians now.

of a rich man entering the kingdom of heaven, might still be thought of as having their setting in Judea (cf. Mk 10 1), this cannot apply to P.D. 2 40.41.43. In these latter paragraphs He passes through Samaria (cf. Lk 9 51–56; Jn 4 4), converses with the Samaritan woman (Jn 4 5–38) and evokes the belief of the Samaritans in Him (Jn 4 39–44)[14]. However, in P.D. 2 41; Lk 9 53 is cited that His face was as *going to* Jerusalem; and in P.D. 2 44.45.46, Lk 9 57–58. 59–60. 61–62 are quoted: »I will follow thee whithersoever thou goest«, and the other who said: »suffer me first to go and bury my father«, and the third who said: »but first suffer me to bid farewell to them that are at my house«. We are to understand these as said when He is on the way to Jerusalem. Then in P.D. 2 47 He is back in Jerusalem. This is introduced by the words: »And after these things there arrived the time of the Feast in Judea« cf. Jn 5 1. It is here that P.D. 2 47 the healing at the pool of Bethesda with its five porches, of the man who had been infirm 38 years. If this typifies the Jewish people and their trust in the Law, then P.D. is paralleling this with the Samaritan woman at the well P.D. 2 42, and contrasting in the paragraphs that follow the Jewish response with that of the Samaritans. But what is the Feast of Jn 5 1? The fact that P.D. 2 50.51.52.53.54.55.56.57 cites Jn 8 12–20. 21–32. 33–59, clearly indicates the Feast of Tabernacles. P.D. 2 50 begins with Jn 7 14 'But when the time of the Feast was finished' (cf. Messina, op. cit., p. 169), 'Jesus entered the هيكل كنشت and taught.' Messina renders هيكل كنشت by *"tempio (bis)"*. With respect one would suggest that he has overlooked the *izāfeh*[15], and the meaning demanded is the هيكل of the كنشت. Again P.D. thinks of the Christ as in the Chancel of the Temple thought of as a Jacobite Church (cf. above). But when did Jesus appear there? In Jn 7 14 Pesh. has ܟܕ ܕܝܢ ܦܠܓܘ ܝܘ̈ܡܬܐ which could mean: they divided the days of the Feast, and refer to the *hol ha-Mo'ed*. After all, at Tabernacles, there are the first and second day of the *Hag* proper and the עצרת or מועד שמיני the eighth day. The Gk. τῆς ἑορτῆς μεσούσης could be a paraphrase of the Aramaic to make it understandable to those not acquainted with Jewish technical terms as to the Feast of Tabernacles. If وچون روزگار عيد پراخت is »quando il tempo della festa volse alla fine«, what feast is finished, and what does روزگار عيد refer to? Is the Feast that of Dedication of P.D. 2 38, are we to imagine that P.D. 2 39–46 and 47.48.49 happened in the eight days of Hanukkah? The events could be thought of as being compassed in that time. Or, have we to think back to P.D. 2 8 which cites Jn 7 2–13 on the Feast of Tabernacles, and are

[14] A.D. 21 cites Jn 4 4–44 much earlier in the Ministry namely between the visit to the region of Tyre and Sidon (cf. Mk 2 31) and His going to Galilee (Jn 4 43).

[15] Cf. the construct relationship in Hebrew or Arabic.

we asked to think of P.D. 2 9–54 as happening within that time? After all it is only in P.D. 2 53 that Jn 7 37 is cited with the mention of the great day, the last of the Feast (of Tabernacles). The difficulty of imagining time for all the events recorded between P.D. 2 9–54 within the eight days of Tabernacles is removed if we remember that P.D. is thinking of the four weeks of the Feast of Dedication in Syrian Churches. Being a Harmony of the Gospels he has apparently to give prominence to Tabernacles, but as a Churchman of the Church of the East, the Feast of the Dedication of his Church is in his mind. This for him took the place of both *Hag-Sukkoth* and Hanukkah.

Before proceeding to examine what P.D. makes of Jesus' next and last visit to Jerusalem, that of Passion Week, let us see what are the Feasts in A.D. The Feast of Passover and Unleavened Bread assumes the position in A.D. that Tabernacles and Dedication are given in P.D. This different attitude is reflected in their respective identifications of the Johannine 'Unknown Feast'. We have in A.D. during the Ministry[16] of Jesus 3 Passovers, the last of which He attends; A.D. 18 24 cites Jn 6 4 in the story of the feeding of the 5,000 that the Passover was at hand. P.D. omits this Festival reference. A.D. while following the Synoptic convention that Jesus attended only the Passover immediately before His death, does contrive to have Him be present at the Feast of Unleavened Bread apparently the year before His death. This for A.D. was an important occasion. However, this was not the first Feast during the Ministry when Jesus visited Jerusalem. After mentioning the Passover which He did not attend A.D. 18 24 citing Jn 6 4, A.D. cites in Sect. 22 9, Jn 5 1 'And after that was the feast of the Jews, and Jesus went up to Jerusalem'. The whole of Jn 5 is cited there and then in A.D. No indication is drawn by A.D. as to what that Feast was. A.D.'s next Feast is that of Tabernacles, cf. A.D. 28 1–32 drawing on Jn 7 2–31. It was only 'when the days of the Feast of Tabernacles were half over, Jesus went up to the Temple, and taught (A.D. 38 15, cf. Jn 7 14). *Nothing* of the teaching of Jn 8 9 is in A.D. associated with that Feast. Then A.D. 30 31 says: 'And after that, the time of the Feast of Unleavened Bread of the Jews arrived, and Jesus went out to go to Jerusalem'. This Feast of Unleavened Bread seems to find its Gospel source in Jn 5 1a which is now utilized for a second time by A.D. and this time the 'Unknown Feast' is identified with the Feast of Unleavened Bread. In P.D. Jn 5 1 is associated with Tabernacles/Dedication, but here in A.D. with the Feast of Unleavened Bread and the Cleansing of the Temple. Is it A.D.'s solution to the problem of how to harmonize Jn 2 and the

[16] Both A.D. and P.D. cite Luke that Jesus at 13 years old was *at the Passover* at Jerusalem, but this is not included here.

cleansing of the Temple with the Synoptic cleansing of the Temple at the end of the Ministry? But this Feast of Unleavened Bread is not at the end of the Ministry, though it attracts to itself features associated with the last journey to Jerusalem[17], and events and teaching in the Synoptics set in the last week[18]. In addition, it has assumed in A.D. the place given to Tabernacles in John's Gospel and in P.D. A.D. 34 46–48 (Lk 19 47.48) informs us that Jesus (still in Jerusalem at the Feast of the Unleavened Bread at which He cleansed the Temple) was teaching every day in the Temple; the chief priests and the elders, sought to destroy Him, but could not with the people hanging upon Him to hear Him. A.D. is using these verses as an introduction to Jn 7 31–11 57. Within this large slab of Johannine material only Mt 22 41–46 is intruded (between Jn 7 52 and Jn 8 12 cf. A.D. 35 17–22). It is important to note that A.D. 35 1 (Jn 7 37) identifies 'the great day which is the last of the Feast' because of its setting here, as the last day of Unleavened Bread, not that of Tabernacles as P.D. Actually, the last day of the seven days of Unleavened Bread is a special day, just as the eighth day at Tabernacles. The Johannine material (Jn 7 37–8 59) which in P.D. 2 53–57 is given a Tabernacles' setting is here in A.D. 35 1–36 9 associated with the Feast of Unleavened Bread. A.D. 35 17–20 = Mt 22 41–44 is however in P.D. 3 51 part of the teaching of Passion Week. Interesting too is the fact that A.D. 36 10–47 = Jn 9 1–38 on the

17 E.g. the second prediction of His death, A.D. 30 40–45 = Mk 10 32. 33b. 34a, and Lk 18 31b. 33.34, cf. P.D. 3 30 = Mk 10 32–34 Lk 18 33; the request of the Mother of James and John A.D. 30 46–52 = Mt 20 20. 21a and Mk 10 35–40, cf. P.D. 3 31 = Mt 20 20–28 Mk 10 35–45; Zaccheus at Jericho A.D. 31 15–24 = Lk 19 1–10, cf. P.D. 3 32 = Lk 19 10; blind Timaeus A.D. 31 25–35 = Mt 20 29b. 34a Mk 10 46b. 47a. 48b. 49 Lk 18 35–39a. 42b. 43, cf. P.D. 3 33 = Mk 10 46–52 Lk 18 35–43.

18 The Widow's mite A.D. 32 12–15 = Mk 12 41. 42a. 44a Lk 21 3, cf. P.D. 3 53 = Mk 12 41–44 Lk 21 1–4; the cursing of the unfruitful fig-tree A.D. 32 22–26 = Mt 21 17 Mk 11 12–15a. 19a Lk 9 11, cf. P.D. 3 42 = Mt 21 18 Mk 11 12–14 (for the sequel on the fig-tree cf. A.D. 33 1–5 = Mt 21 20b Mk 11 19–23, in P.D. 4 5 Mk 11 20–24); between the cursing of the Fig-tree and its withering away A.D. inserts Jn 3 1–21 which in P.D. 2 58 comes immediately after the last day of the Feast (Tabernacles). Further A.D. 33 28–60 (= Mt 21 46 Mk 11 28b. 29a. 30b.32b 33 Mk 12 3b. 4. 5a. 6a Lk 20 2a. 6b. 9b. 13. 14b. 17b) inserts here the question of His authority, P.D. 3 43 (Mt 21 23–27 Lk 20 1–8); the parable of the two sons told by their Father to work in the vineyard, P.D. 3 40 (Mt 21 28–32); the householder and the vineyard entrusted to husbandmen and how they treated His son, P.D. 3: 45 (Mt 21 33–41 Mk 12 1–9 Lk 20 9–16), and the stone that the builders' rejected P.D. 3 46 (Mt 21 42–44); also A.D. 34 1–8 on tribute to Caesar or no (Mt 22 15–18b. 19. 21 Lk 20 20b. 26) cf. P.D. 3 48 (Mt 22 15–22 Mk 12 13–17 Lk 20 20–25) and the Sadducees' question on the woman and the seven levirs, A.D. 34 9–24 cf. P.D. 3 49 (Mt 22 23–35 Mk 12 18–27 Lk 20 27–40) as well as His summary of the Law, A.D. 34 25–34 (cf. P.D. 3 50 Mt 22 36–40 Mk 12 28–34a).

opening of the eyes of the man born blind, possibly has an allusion to baptism especially v. 7 صبغة شيلوحا. If so, it may be significant that in A.D., Jn 9 is associated with the Feast of Unleavened Bread = Passovertide, the great season for Baptism in the Early Eastern Church. In P.D. Jn 9 1–39 occurs in the Tabernacles period as does the Feast of Dedication P.D. 2 38. In A.D. after the Feast of Unleavened Bread, the next Feast mentioned is the Feast of Dedication A.D. 37 25ff. = Jn 10 22. Transition from Unleavened Bread to Dedication is abrupt, the result of A.D. using only Johannine material here and giving the Johannine Tabernacles' teaching a Passover setting. A.D. may wish to underline that Passover and Dedication are for him the most important Feasts; it is besides a Temple cleansed at the previous Feast of Unleavened Bread (Passover Season), that Jesus is present in at the Feast of Dedication.

In both A.D. and P.D. the next Feast at Jerusalem that is mentioned, and which Jesus attends is the Passover before His Crucifixion. In A.D. since much of the Synoptic material associated with the last journey to Jerusalem has been used up in connection with A.D.'s Feast of the Unleavened Bread of the previous year, little remains but the anointing by Mary at Simon the leper's house at Bethany, A.D. 39 1–17[19]. P.D. however can combine both the Synoptic and Johannine accounts e.g. the stories about Zaccheus and blind Bartimeus at Jericho, and also the Resurrection of Lazarus as well as the anointing of Jesus at Simon the Leper's house. With the Entry, P.D. has the Cleansing of the Temple. P.D. is not only more impressive here but is a better Harmony of the material. Whereas P.D. has two poles, Tabernacles and Passover which bring much of the Gospel material into their individual orbits, A.D. has but one pole in two stages, Unleavened Bread and Passover. In P.D. 3 37 Jesus enters Jerusalem and casts out those teaching in the Temple. Jerusalem[20] itself is called بيت المقدس an expression which recalls O.S. Jn 10 22 and Mt 27 51 of the Temple; but this should not be stressed as it is here probably influenced by a Muslim Arabic term[21]. But the term

[19] Made up of Jn 12 1.2 Mk 14 3a Jn 12 9–11.3a Mk 14 3b Jn 12 3b.6 Mk 14 4 Mt 26 9 Mk 14 5b Mt 26 10a Mk 14 6b Jn 12 7b.8a Mk 14 7b Mt 26 12 Mk 14 8b.9.

[20] بيت المقدس is used to translate ܐܘܪܫܠܡ in P.D. thus: P.D. 1 7 Mt 2 1 coming of the wise men; P.D. 1 10. Mt 2 21 gloss on the land of Israel in the statement as to where St. Joseph took the B.V.M. and the Infant Christ from Egypt; P.D. 3 4, Mk 3 22; P.D. 2 8, Mk 7 1 scribes from Jerusalem; P.D. 3 37, Mt 21 10; Mk 11 1 Jesus' coming up for the Entry into Jerusalem; P.D. 4 49 uses بيت المقدس (citing Mt 27 53) for Jerusalem.

[21] بيت المقدس usually in Muslim Arabic stands for the Temple. In. P.D. امامان is used for the chief priests, an example of an adoption and adaption of a Muslim term.

P.D. uses of the Temple in Mt 21 12a (Pesh. ܗܝܟܠܐ ܕܐܠܗܐ) is خانه خدا House of God. For P.D. this is *not* the Cleansing of the هيكل. P.D. in using Jn 2 19 has 'destroy this *house*' خانه (Gk. ναὸν, Pesh ܗܝܟܠܐ ܗܢܐ A.D. هيكل). P.D. has in Jn 2 20 that the Jews said اين خانه this house (Gk. ὁ ναὸς, Pesh. ܗܝܟܠܐ) was 46 years in building. In Jn 2 21 P.D. has 'but He was referring to هيكل تن خوش the Temple of His body' (Gk. περί τοῦ ναοῦ τοῦ σώματος αὐτου Pesh ܗܝܟܠܐ ܕܦܓܪܗ). P.D. cites Mt 21 12a خانه من My house (Gk. ὁ οἶκός μου Pesh ܒܝܬܝ) shall be called خانه نماز (Gk. οἶκος προσευχῆς Pesh ܒܝܬ ܨܠܘܬܐ). P.D. 3 37 citing Mk 11 16 regarding His not allowing anyone to carry a vessel through the Temple, the Farsi is در كنشت (Gk. δια τοῦ ἱερου O.S. ܒܓܘ ܗܝܟܠܐ). It is significant that the Persian Diatessaron here clearly distinguishes between Temple when applied to Jesus' body and when used of the Temple building, so much so as to change in Jn 2 20 Pesh ܗܝܟܠܐ to house. House could be much wider as witness the use of Holy House (بيت المقدس) as synonym for Jerusalem. In the Jacobite Syrian Church the *Bukhra* the Host is only in the هيكل the Chancel. Finally, there is the rending of the Temple Veil. Mt 27 51, P.D. 4 49. It is described as در كنشت 'in the Temple'. True Gk. has τοῦ ναοῦ O.S. ܐܦ̈ܘ ܬܐܪܐ ܕܬܪܥܗ ܕܡܕܒܚܐ Pesh. ܐܦ̈ܝ ܬܪܥܐ ܕܗܝܟܠܐ A.D. وجه باب الهيكل But كنشت can be used of the Temple as a whole e.g. P.D. 3 54 paragraph heading عمارت كنشت (the building of the Temple) or Mt 24 1a Mk 13 1b; if so the Temple كنشت is not the Chancel.

The present writer is not convinced that the Persian Diatessaron is a Diatessaron which even claims for itself connection with Tatian's Diatessaron. It is Diatessaric rather than the Diatessaron, if the latter name is reserved for Tatian's Diatessaron or descendants thereof. It is of the thirteenth century, at least in its Persian dress, and though the Syriac behind does show through, it is written for those who know only Farsi[23] and for the upbuilding of the Persian Church of its own day. And yet some old traditions may be preserved along with some not so old. One possibly old tradition is the place of the Footwashing in P.D. 4 23 which *comes after* the Sacred Repast (P.D. 4 22). In A.D. 44 not only does the Footwashing come before, and indeed if A.D. is not being very clumsy, it is on a night other than that when He kept the Passover with His disciples[24]. It is as if A.D. is deliberately indicating that the Footwashing and the Last Supper are to be kept separate. P.D.'s order reminds us of *Aphraates*: *De Paschate*[25] where

[22] در كنشت could be rendered door of the Temple. در means both »door« and »within«.

[23] Messina: Notizia su un Diatessaron Persiano Tradotto dal Siriaco, 1943, p. 20, 21.

[24] N.B. according to A.D. 44 34–40 the arrangements for the holding of the Passover Meal had not been made till after the Footwashing had taken place.

[25] Aphraates, op. cit., II Patrologia Syriaca, 1904, p. 532.

the Footwashing comes after the Supper; it is there associated with the Institution of Christian Baptism[26]. While P.D. does not expatiate yet the word used in the Farsi here for the washing of the feet could indicate baptism. What is clear in P.D. is that the emphasis on the sacramental, e.g. the Ministry of Christ starts in P.D. 1 20 with His baptizing, followed closely (P.D. 1 23) by the miracle of the Water into Wine. A.D. does *not* include Jesus' baptising (A.D. 6 5) till after the miracle at Cana (A.D. 5 22–33) which latter is itself followed by the proclaiming the acceptable year of the Lord in Nazareth. P.D. as we have seen emphasizes Tabernacles, the Feast associated with *water*, and not only so, P.D. brings together Gospel stories and sayings emphasizing water, and lumps them with the season of this Feast: P.D. 2 35 the man born blind, P.D. 2 42 the Samaritan woman at Jacob's well, P.D. 2 53 the rivers of living water and P.D. 2 58 the night speech with Nicodemus. It is not that P.D. separates being baptized from the death of Jesus. It is rather that as a Churchman, the Feast of Tabernacles or Dedication, the Church Feast per se, was important. Entrance to the Church fellowship was by baptism, which in his time was no longer so closely tied to the Passover Season.

There was a Feast called Nusardil[27], 50 days after Ascension among the »Assyrians« around the Rezayeh (Urmi) plain. At Nusardil much water is splashed or sprinkled. One[28] version of its origin is that it commemorates the baptism of 1,300,000 persons with Ghengis Khan converted by Mar Shukha-el-Eshoo the Nestorian bishop of the time. The bishop could not baptize each one individually, so threw water over them. Ghengis came to the area just 70 years before the Diatessaron was written in Persian. The baptism of Ghengis and his men was associated with a season of the year nearer Tabernacles than Passover. Did this event lead to a rediscovery of the prime importance of baptism in a Church that had become almost »ethnic« and moribund, and is it reflected in the Persian Diatessaron?

[26] While in Theodore, Gospel of John, CSCO Scriptores Syri III, 1940, p. 257, the Footwashing is associated with a making ready to receive the baptism of the Spirit. Isho'dad the Nestorian on Jn 13 10 denies that the Footwashing has anything to do with baptism. Cf. The Commentaries of Isho'dad of Merv. ed. and translated by M. D. Gibson, I and II, 1911.

[27] Nusardil in Urmi (Rezayeh in 1966 was on 17th July).

[28] This is the explanation given by the Nestorian priest at Geogtapa in the Urmi plain.

A Fundamental Manuscript for an Edition of the Babylonian Onqelos to Genesis: MS 152 of the Jewish Th. Seminary of New York.

by Alejandro Díez-Macho

(Colegio San Miguel, Rosellón 175, Barcelona, 11)

This MS consists of 131 folios in vellum, measuring 24 × 17.5 cms. The text is written in continuous lines, as often happens in Oriental manuscripts, and has 22 lines to each page. The state of conservation is excellent for the major number of the folios, but there are some illegible pages; e.g. the first and the last (folio 131b); it is also difficult to read: 8b, 9a, 19–20a, 60b, 107b. The exterior margin of folio 16 has been cut away. Usually the vowels and the consonants are clear, although sometimes it is difficult to distinguish the above-the-line *pataḥ* from *šᵉwa'*. Some pages have a splendid appearance. The scribe was a Yemenite as far as one can judge from the typical character of the script, which is exactly the same as that of MS Eb 30 (MS 506, ff. 3–4, of the Jewish Theological Seminary). This kind of writing is like that of MSS 131 and 229 and other ancient Yemenite MSS. One of the proofs that the copyist is Yemenite is the frequent confusion of –̈ and –: which occurs in all the ancient Yemenite MSS[1]: MSS 131, 229, 508A of the Jewish Theological Seminary of New York, etc.: Gen 8 7 הערב (for הערב), יבשת (for יבשת), 8 11 ותבא (for וַתָּבו)[2], 9 4 תאכלו (two vowels –: and –̈ on the same consonant), 9 6 שפך (two vowels –: –̈ for the same consonant), 9 12 ויאמר (*sic* for ויומר), etc.

The calligraphy is most careful, and the final letters, and sometimes letters which are not final, are stretched out to reach the margin, just as in MS 131. The scribe, therefore, is a professional, but the MS was not written in a very distant epoch. We would date it in the 13th century, although the texts, not only the Aramaic, but the Hebrew too, are copied from much more ancient MSS. In the calligraphy, we do not find any signs of special antiquity, the ה for example, has its vertical line on the left separated.

[1] For an explanation of this fact see my article: Nuevos MSS. bíblicos babilónicos, Estudios Bíblicos, 16 (1957), p. 251ff.

[2] In the MS coming from Sufut-Kale.

The MS contains Gen 4 12–48 11[3]. Following upon the Hebrew text is the Targum of Onqelos, and following that is the Arabic translation of Saʿadya; the three texts are separated by a full stop placed on the top left-hand corner of the last word. This is the way in which texts were separated in ancient Yemenite MSS. Apart from the Arabic text, which does not show vowels, the other two texts show vowels according to the supralineal system. One finds a simple supralineal system of vowels, which shows the same vowels as one finds in Yemenite MSS: $\overset{\curlyvee}{\_\_}\ \overset{<}{\_\_}\ \overset{\cdot\cdot}{\_\_}\ \overset{\cdot}{\_\_}\ \overset{:}{\_\_}\ \overset{\shortmid}{\_\_}$. There are no *dageš* nor *maqqeph*. The first exist in Babylonian, but they are not found very often; the second do not exist in simple or ancient Babylonian.

The accentuation in the MS is reduced to the supralineal *atnaḥ* which sometimes is not a tonic accent and which has the same form as in Babylonian. Usually the Yemenite scribes do not transcribe Babylonian accents written with letters[4]. They are usually contented with the $\overset{\wedge}{\_\_}$ or the $\overset{\top}{\_\_}$ or else they add, as in MS 131, Tiberian accents.

The *šewaʾ*, especially the mobile *šewaʾ*, occur frequently in MS 152. These can be found in Babylonian MSS, but what one does not find in these MSS are quiescent *šewaʾ*, which are clearly in our MS additions of the Yemenite copyist.

This simple punctuation causes us to believe that our MS derives from a Babylonian original which was punctuated according to the simple system, that is to say, it derived from an ancient Babylonian MS.

The text, both in consonants and vowels, is written by the same hand in the whole MS, if we make exception of a few pages which are vocalized by a different hand as far as one can judge from the different »ductus« of the vowels and by the pattern of vocalization which sometimes is more Yemenite and other times more Babylonian than in the rest of the MS. These few pages vocalized by a different first hand are always on the back of the MS, which for reasons that we do not understand, were left without vowels by the first *naqdan*.

Besides this first ordinary or extraordinary hand, other hands have intervened in MS 152, but all of them Yemenite, as can be seen by the writing employed in the correction, the black ink, the kind of corrections made and this characteristic coarse method of correcting ancient MSS which later Yemenite experts always employed. But

[3] The MS T.-S B 10 5 from the Cairo Geniza contains part of chapter 3 and the part of chapter 4 lacking in MS 152. This MS contains Onqelos to Gen 3 16–7 4. I have published this MS with a preliminary study in my article: Un manuscrito babilónico de Onqelos en el que se confunden los timbres vocalicos *pataḥ* y *qameṣ*, Sefarad 19 (1959), p. 273–282.

[4] There are few exceptions; for instance, MS K f. 4 of the Jewish Theological Seminary of New York.

amongst all these various Yemenite correctors one has particular importance: the one whom we will call the second hand. This one tried to correct the Targum and the Hebrew according to the Yemenite system[5].

Turning to evaluate the text of MS 152, we must begin by making a fundamental distinction between the Targumic text of Onqelos and the Hebrew text.

a) MS 152, textual basis for a future edition of the Targum of Onqelos to Genesis

Our respected teacher, Paul Kahle, always considered the edition of Onqelos in its genuine Babylonian tradition as a scientific »desideratum« in this matter. Unfortunately, the Babylonian fragments of the Geniza of Cairo were too fragmentary to make it possible with them to edit the whole Onqelos. Because of the lack of genuine and complete Babylonian MSS, Kahle used to advise that we should take as a basic text the MS Or. 2363 of the British Museum, which is practically complete and, although Yemenite, has a number of Babylonian traits. Another Yemenite MS, also in the British Museum, MS Or. 1467, shows even more signs of the Babylonian system, although second hand has tried to change the Babylonian punctuations in favour of the typical Yemenite punctuations. But this is a MS in which is lacking the first two books of the Pentateuch and part of Leviticus. Because of all this, Kahle advised that the MS Or. 2363, should be taken as a basis and to use for the critical apparatus Or. 1467. Kahle believed that these MSS were very old, of the 11th century. I think they are not older than MS 152.

On the basis of these ideas, Sperber prepared the critical edition of Onqelos, taking as his basic text MS 2363 shown as letter »y« in his critical edition of Leiden, 1959.

Sperber, in his prologue to his edition of Onqelos, does not distinguish accurately between Yemenite and Babylonian MSS. His presentation of the MSS, Or. 2363, Or. 1467 and Or. 2228–30 of the British Museum and MS 84 Socin of Halle as »Manuscripts with Babylonian Vocalization« (p. V) in 1959 is ambiguous and might cause the reader to think that his edition is an edition of the Babylonian Onqelos, even if he adds (p. VI) that MSS Or. 2228–30 and MS Socin 84 represent Babylonian and Yemenite textual tradition. This would be misleading. These MSS, used by our friend, have of what is Babylonian first the vocalic signs. As is well known, the Jews of the Yemen took these from the Jews of Mesopotamia and they have kept them up to the present day, although already in the 11th century they began to conceal beneath these Babylonian signs a Tiberian punctua-

[5] To know the work of Yemenite revisers see Nuevos MSS . . ., p. 253 f.

tion. Further they have, as we have said about MSS 2363 and 1467, some remains of genuine Babylonian punctuation, as a result of which Kahle preferred these MSS to others which were then known.

We do not wish to suggest that Sperber did not know the difference between Yemenite and Babylonian MSS: on p. XVII of his prologue he points out the importance of the Hebrew MS 448 of the Vatican precisely because it conceals beneath Tiberian signs a Babylonian punctuation in the first hand, as Sperber himself pointed out to the present writer and as I have shown in various works[6]. But would it not have been desirable if he had specified more clearly the Yemenite character of his MSS »with Babylonian vocalization«?

This kind of clarity was vital in an edition of Onqelos which came out in 1959, because at that time one already knew of a series of Babylonian MSS, Babylonian not only in the vocalic signs above the line, but also in the punctuation, MSS which may be found in the library of the Jewish Theological Seminary of New York, a place where Sperber worked many years.

Of the existence of these Babylonian MSS, which made possible the edition of almost the whole of Onqelos in a better Babylonian tradition, we gain an account for the first time in 1954[7], as the result of our investigations in the library of the Jewish Theological Seminary of New York where we went to carry on our research urged thereto by Sperber's advice and help.

In the Prologue of the Polyglot Bible of Madrid, published in Madrid in 1957, we announced our intention of editing the Babylonian Targum of Onqelos on the basis of the following MSS: for Genesis, MS 152, for Leviticus, Numbers and Deuteronomy, MS 133a, both MSS to be found in the Jewish Theological Seminary of New York; for Ex 3 22–8 15, the MS 153 from the same centre, together with fragments K 1 and K 2–3 from the same centre, and the Babylonian fragments already known by Kahle coming from the Geniza of Cairo, and other fragments which we discovered in the University Library of Strasbourg[8]. For Deuteronomy MS 131 of the JThS preserves a

[6] Specially in a large study: Un importante manuscrito targúmico en la Biblioteca Vaticana, in: Homenaje a Millás Vallicrosa, I 1954, p. 375–463; cf. also VT 8 (1958), p. 126–133.

[7] Cf. Estudios Bíblicos 13 (1954), p. 207–210; cf. also Nuevos MSS . . ., p. 235–277.

[8] Biblia Polyglotta Matritensia, Prooemium, 1957, p. 10. To the above materials it should be added now the MSS uncovered by our friend I. Yeivin, *Qiṭʿe Miqra babliyyim-temaniyyim bmifʿal ḥašifat »Ginze Teman« šel Yehudah Levi Nahum bHolon*, Kiryat Sefer 40 (1965), p. 561–568. He describes 16 new fragmentary MSS, those of the Pentateuch containing Onqelos. The MSS were copied in Yemen but they derive from Babylonian MSS. Most of them show Tiberian, or not typically Babylonian, punctuations.

better Babylonian Onqelos than MS 133a which shows some Yemenite deviations.

This material which makes possible the publication of Babylonian Onqelos — except for certain parts of Exodus — does not appear in Sperber's edition; he simply ignores it. Only on p. XV of the prologue does he mention the fragments from the Geniza, whose vocalization he promises to study in the final volume of »The Bible in Aramaic« which is the general title of Sperber's edition of the Targumim.

These deficiencies which we have pointed out can be explained by remembering that the edition of the Targumim by Sperber was prepared with European MSS and in Europe before the author emigrated to New York and many years before we discovered in that city the Babylonian MSS of Onqelos which we have mentioned.

Sperber's work was then already finished, and to use these MSS as a basic text or in critical apparatus would have meant beginning the work again.

Turning in particular to MS 152, it contains in 131 folios, the consonantal and vocalic text, genuinely Babylonian, of the Onqelos to Genesis. Until the discovery of this MS, we only knew a few wretched fragments of the Babylonian Genesis.

The only thing in the Targum of MS 152 which is not genuinely Babylonian is the use of the furtive *pataḥ*, but this *pataḥ* — which might well be an addition of the Yemenite copyist[9] as occurs in MS 131 from the Jewish Theological Seminary — is found also — genuine or imported, and probably the last — in certain Babylonian MSS which come from Mesopotamia. In the final folios of MS 152, one can find the simple *š^ewa*' in the word אבהון but such a simple *š^ewa*', which is normal in the avocalic gutturals of the Yemenite system, is found often in genuine Babylonian MSS[10].

We now proceed to offer the transcription of the Onqelos to Chapter 39 to Genesis, making note of the corrections introduced by the second Yemenite hand, which usually affect the treatment of the gutturals, the punctuation of the conjunctive *waw* before *š^ewa*', or before labials, the change of *maqtal* into *miqtal*, and the vocalization of *kol* (in Babylonian always *kol*, never *kôl*), etc. In the edition which follows we point out the most frequent corrections introduced by the

[9] Cf. Nuevos MSS ..., p. 263; cf. also A. Díez Macho–S. Spiegel, Fragmentos de piyyutim de Yannay en vocalización babilónica, Sefarad 15 (1955), p. 312 and footnote 11b.

[10] Cf. my article: Nuevos mss. importantes, bíblicos o litúrgicos, en hebreo o arameo, Sefarad 16 (1956), p. 16s.; Fragmentos de piyyutim ..., p. 292; Nuevos mss. ..., p. 247–251, 257s. Cf. too I. Yeivin, *Qiṭ'e Miqra babliyyim-temaniyyim ḥadašim bbet ha-sefarim ha-leummi wha- universitai*, Kiryat Sefer 34 (1964), p. 564.

Yemenite corrector in the Aramaic text, and some (like *et* > *at*) in the Hebrew text.

There belongs also to the second Yemenite hand the frequent addition of two accents: a tiny vertical stroke above the line, which reminds one of the *zaqeph*, and the below the line *atnaḥ*.

The silent *šᵉwa*ʾ are additions by the Yemenite copyist: the »Vorlage« of Babylon lacked them. This explains why the Yemenite copyists sometimes added them, sometimes, omitted them.

Transcription of Onqelos, Gen 39

1 ויוסף יתחת למצרים וזבניה פוטיפר רבה דפרעה רב קטוליא גברא מצראה
מיד ערבאי דאחתוהי לתמן׃ 2 והוה מימרא דייי בסעדיה דיוסף והוה גבר מצלח
והוה בבית רבוניה מצראה׃ 3 וחזא רבוניה ארי מימרא דייי בסעדיה וכל דהוא
עביד ייי מצלח בידיה׃ 4 ואשכח יוסף רחמין בעינוהי ושמיש יתיה ומנייה על ביתיה
וכל*דאית ליה מסר בידיה׃ 5 והוה מעידן דמני יתיה בביתיה ועל כל*דאית ליה
ובריך [2 ובריך] ייי ית בית מצראה בדיל יוסף והות ברכתא דייי בכל [2 בכל]
דאית ליה בביתא ובחקלא׃ 6 ושבק כל דליה בידא דיוסף ולא ידע עימיה מדעם
אלהין לחמא דהוא אכיל והוה יוסף שפיר בריוא ויאי בהזוא׃ 7 והוה בתר פתגמיא
האלין וזקפת איתת רבוניה ית עינהא ביוסף ואמרת שכוב עמי׃ 8 וסריב ואמר
לאיתת רבוניה הא רבוני לא ידע עימי מא בביתא וכל [2 וכל] דאית ליה מסר
בידי׃ 9 לית דרב בביתא הדין מיני ולא מנע מיני מדעם אילהין יתיך בדיל דאת
אתתיה ואיכדין אעביד בשתא רבתא הדא ואיחוב קיי׃ 10 והוה כד מלילת עים
יוסף יום יום ולא קביל מנה למשכב לותה למהוי עימה׃ 11 והוה כיומא הדין
[2 הדין] ועל לביתא [2 לביתא] למבדק בכתבי חשבניה ולית אינש [2 אינש] מאינשי
ביתא [2 ביתא] תמן בביתא׃ 12 ואחדתיה*בלבשיה למימר [2 למימר] שכוב עמי
ושבקיה ללבשיה בידה וערק ונפק לשוקא׃ 13 והוה כד חזת ארי שבקיה ללבשיה
בידה וערק לשוקא׃ 14 וקרת לאינשי [2 לאינשי] ביתה ואמרת להון למימר חזו
איתי [2 דאיתי] לנא גברא עבראה [2 עבראה] לחיכא בנא על לותי למשכב עמי
וקרית בקלא רמא׃ 15 והוה כד שמע ארי ארמית קלי וקרית ושבקיה ללבשה
לותי וערק ונפק לשוקא׃ 16 ואחיתתיה ללבשיה לותה עד דעל רבוניה לביתיה׃

* וכל 2 m.
* ואחדתיה 2 m.

17 ומלילת עימיה כפיתגמיא האלין למימר על לותי עבדא עבראה דאיתיתא לנא
לחיכא בי׃ 18 והוה כד ארמית קלי וקרית ושבקיה ללבשיה לותי [2 לותי] וערק
לשוקא׃ 19 והוה כד שמע [estas 3 voc. d. 2 m] רבוניה ית פתגמי אתתיה דמלילת
עמיה למימר [2 למימר] כפתגמיא האלין עבד לי עבדך ותקיף רוגזיה׃ 20 ודבר
רבוני יוסף יתיה ויהביה בבית אסירי אתרא דאסירי מלכא אסירים והוה תמן בבית
אסירי׃ 21 והוה מימרא דייי בסעדיה דיוסף ונגד ליה חסדא ויהביה לרחמין בעיני
רב בית אסירי׃ 22 ויהב רב בית אסירי בידא דיוסף ית כל אסיריא דבבית
אסירי וית כל דעבדין תמן ממימריה הוה מתעביד [מתעביד quizá leg.]׃ 23
לית רב בית אסירי חזי ית כל סורחן בידיה [2 בידיה] בדמימרא דייי בסעדיה
ודהוא עביד ייי מצלח׃

The most frequent corrections of the second hand

2nd h.		1st h.	2nd h.		1st h.
ואמר	<	ואמר	את	<	את
ועבד	<	ועבד	כל	<	כל
ארי	<	ארי	וּ	<	וּ
אמרת	<	אמרת	ו במף	<	ו במף
אקטל	<	איקטל	מקטל	<	מקטל
קין	<	קין	יש	<	יש

The Hebrew Text of MS 152

The evaluation of the Hebrew text of MS 152 is not simple, because one cannot assert that it is a Yemenite text, although there are many Yemenite forms. Nor can one assert that it is purely Babylonian, although there are constant Babylonian punctuations. Nor can one say, without clearing up many points first, that it is a mixed Hebrew text, in part Babylonian, in part Yemenite, since one can affirm this of the vocalic text, but it does not appear to be applicable to the consonantal text. Only after an extremely detailed study of MS 152 can we come to any decision about the quality of the Hebrew text.

A: The vocalization of Hebrew Text

a) Babylonian features of the Hebrew Text.

1) בֿן, אֿת when Tiberian text has אֶת־ y בֶּן־ and Yemenite בֿן, אֿת.

2) כֹּל for Tiberian כָּל־ and Yemenite כֹּל.

3) במף + וֹ for Tiberian במף + וּ and Yemenite במף + וֹ; vg. Gen 5 29 וֹמֹעצֿבוֹן (BH. וּמֵעִצְּבוֹן); 5 30 6 1 וֹבֿכות (BH. "וּב); 6 16 וֹפֿתח (BH. "וּפ); 6 19 וֹמכל (BH. וּמִכָּל־); 7 2 וֹמן (BH. וּמִן); 7 10 וֹמי (BH. וּמי); 8 14 וֹבחדש (BH. "וּב); 8 16 וֹבניך (BH. "וּב); 9 12 וֹביניכם (BH. "וּב); 9 12.13.15.17 וֹבין (BH. "וּב); 10 2 וֹמגוג (BH. "וּמ) ... etc.

4) ְ + וֹ for Tiberian ְ + וּ and Yemenite ְ + וֹ; vg. Gen 6 15.16 וֹשלשים (BH. "וּשְׁ); 6 18 7 7 וֹנשי (BH. וּנְשֵׁי); 6 19 וֹנקבה (BH. "וּנְ, 2nd h. וֹנקבה); 7 24 8 3 וֹמאת (BH. "וּמְ); 9 1 וֹרבו (BH. "וּרְ); 9 2 וֹבכל (BH. וּבְכָל־, 2nd Yemenite h. וֹבכל); 9 23 וֹפנהם (BH. "וּפְ); 10 3.4.6.7 (*bis*) וֹבני (BH. "וּבְ); 10 6 15 וֹכנען (BH. "וּכְ; 2nd h. "וֹכ); 10 7 וֹדדן (BH. "וּדְ; 2nd h. וֹדדן); 10 19 וֹצבים (BH. "וּצְ); 10 21 וֹלשם (BH. "וּלְ); 10 25 וֹלעבר (BH. "וּלְ); etc.

5) Conversive *waw* of the Imperfect does not weaken the vowel of the 2nd. consonant of the verb: vg. Gen 5 30.32 ויוֹלד (BH. וַיּוֹלֶד); 6 6 ויִנחם (BH. וַיִּנָּחֶם; 2nd Yemenite h. ויִנחם); 8 10 ויחל (BH. וַיָּחֶל; 2nd Yemenite h. ויחל); 8 12 וייחל (BH. וַיִּיָּחֶל; 2nd h. Yemenite וייחל); 9 1 ויברך (BH. וַיְבָרֶךְ; 2nd h. Yemenite ויברך) ...

6) There is no *maqqeph*; therefore the final vowel of the word united in Tiberian by *maqqeph* remains unchangeable: vg. Gen 6 9 התהלך (BH. הִתְהַלֶּךְ־; 2nd h. Yemenite התהלך); 24 35.36 ויתן (BH. וַיִּתֶּן); 25 8 ויאסף (BH. וַיֵּאָסֶף); etc.

7) Hebrew words with Babylonian vocalization: Gen 5 29 עצבון (BH. "עִצְּ); 6 3 וֹעשרים (BH. "וְעֶ; Yemenite "וֹע); 9 5 דמכם (BH. דִּמְכֶם; 2nd h. Yemenite "דמ); 9 6 בצלם (BH. בְּצֶלֶם; 2nd h. Yemenite בצלם); 8 21 לב (BH. לֵב; 2nd h. Yemenite לב); 24 45 לבי (2nd h. Yemenite לבי); 9 3 אשר (BH. "אֲ); 7 22 בחרבה (BH. בֶּחָרָבָה); 24 21 דרכו (BH., 2nd h.

Yemenite ״דַ֯ר״); 24 32 רֹגליו (BH. and 2m. Yemenite ״רַ֯״); 25 8.17 וַ֯יָּמׇת (BH. וַיָּמָת).

8) Words without »*pataḥ furtivum*«. Gen 8 9 מׇנוּח (BH. מָנוֹחַ); 8 11 נֹח (BH. נֹחַ).

9) Vocalization of words under the influence of pausal accents: Gen 6 7.17 השַׁ֯מַ֯ים (BH. הַשָּׁמָיִם), but 7 3 השמַים[11] (BH. הַשָּׁמַיִם; 2nd h. Yemenite השמ֯ים); 7 4 ל֯יל֯ה (BH. לָיְלָה; 2nd h. לַיְלָה); 8 1 ·המ֯ים (BH. הַמָּיִם; 2nd h. Yemenite המַים); 8 2 ·השמ֯ים (BH. הַשָּׁמָיִם; 2nd h. Yemenite השמַים); 9 20 כ֯ר֯ם (BH. כָּרֶם; 2nd h. Yemenite כ֯רַם).
But we find also words which show ‑ַ‑ by the first hand and ‑֯‑ by the second Yemenite hand. This is further evidence to prove that the MS derives from Babylonia: in fact, it is fairly common in the Babylonian tradition to find major disjuntive accents (responsible for ‑ַ‑ vocalization instead of Tiberian *pataḥ* or Yemenite ‑֯‑) where Tiberian tradition offers minor disjuntive accents.

10) First person sg. Imperfect Qal אקטל: Gen 9 5 אדרֹש (BH. ״אֶדְ״; 2nd h. Yemenite ״א֯ד״); *ibid.* אדרֹשנו (BH. אֶדְרְשֶׁנּוּ); 24 49 ואֹפנה (BH. וְאֶפְנֶה); 24 7 אתֹן (BH. אֶתֵּן); 24 14 ואשת֯ה (BH. וְאֶשְׁתֶּה).

b) Yemenite vocalizations which are found also in Babylonian MSS which do not come from the Yemen[12]

Down below we turn our attention to vocalizations which up till now would have been unhesitatingly considered as Yemenite, because they are used in Yemenite phonetics. But on finding such punctuations in other MSS which certainly come from Babylonia areas outside the South of Arabia, the problem arises of deciding if these vocalizations were added by the Yemenite copyist or if they were already in the Babylonian apograph.

1) Vowelless א, ע punctuated with *šᵉwa'*.

This is usual in our MS 152 for the Hebrew Text: כ֯א֯שר, א֯שר, א֯ני, א֯ררט; Gen 24 2 ואשביע֯ך, 9 א֯דניו, 10 ע֯שרה, 31 ת֯עמד, and it is also usual

[11] This deviation probably is due to a major disjuntive accent in Babylonian tradition.

[12] Cf. Nuevos mss. importantes..., p. 16–18. See punctuations of this kind in my article: Un manuscrito yemení de la Biblia babilónica, Sefarad 17 (1957), p. 245–248; cf. I. Yeivin, *Qiṭ'e Miqra ... bHolon*, p. 561–568.

punctuation in different non Yemenite MSS, several of them very old; for instance, this is usual vocalization in MSS of Mišna and *piyyutim*: MS. T.-S H 17$_1$ of the IX–X cent., edited by G. Dawidowicz, Liturgische Dichtungen der Juden, 1938, p. 13 (Hebrew section): עֲצרת; MS T.-S B 2$_6$ עָלה, אֲרי; MS T.-S 4$_8$ (Ka 14): דְעַלְתא, אֲנשים, לַעֲשות, וַעשׂי, תַעביד, עֲבַרתון; T.-S B 4$_2$ (Ka 3) עֲבַדתו, אֲשר, אֲריחהי, אֲדני; MS T.-S B 4$_3$ (Ea 3) עֲ, וַאתא, לַאתר; עֲ and עֲ; T.-S B 4$_{12}$ (Ea 7): עֲ אֲ and עֲ אֲ; MS T.-S B 4$_{18}$ (Ea 13): אֲשר, תַעשׂו, etc. . . .

2) Use of the »Verdünnung«

In the Hebrew text of our MS the »Verdünnung« is regularly used; vg. 8 $_{20}$ מִזבח; 24 $_{38}$ מִשפחתי (but 24 $_{40}$ מִמִשפחת).

In other MSS non Yemenite: T.-S H 17$_1$, p. 1 (Hebrew section) of Dawidowicz's book מִשכנו; p. 13 (Hebrew) בְמִכתבו; MS T.-S B 4$_{19}$ (Ea 18) מִלחמה and T.-S B 4$_{41}$ (Kb 10) מִקדשי.

3) Words vocalized in a different way as the usual Babylonian vocalization. In our Hebrew text: 8 $_9$ רַגלה; 6 $_{12}$ דַרכו; אַל (once double vocalization אַל (אַל is the Babylonian pointing); 8 $_{14}$ עֶשרים; 9 $_3$ לְאכלה; 7 $_2$ שִבעה (for שִבעה); 8 $_{11}$ עֵת (for עֵת). In sources non Yemenites we find, for instance, in T.-S H 17$_1$, op. cit., p. 12 (Hebrew) אֵש (intead of אֵש); T.-S B 4$_5$ כל־, לב, אֵל־; MS T.-S B 4$_2$ (Ka 3) רַגליכם (for רגליכם), אַל (for אַל); MdO, p. 199 שִבעה.

4) Punctuation of the *waw* before *šᵉwa'* or labials (וּ and וּבמף). Such a type of vocalization together with the classical Babylonian (וּ) is found in the Hebrew text of MS 152. It is found, too, in non Yemenite MSS, vg.: T.-S B 2$_6$ ״ומלו, ונפקו and ונפקו; T.-S B 4$_5$ (Ka 11) '; MS T.-S B 4$_{41}$ ובאחוות; T.-S B 4$_{18}$ (Ea 13) וצבאו and ובשר, ופקדיהם.

5) Furtive pataḥ, for instance נֹחַ; 24 $_{21}$ חצליח.

There are then, in MS 152, many punctuations which seem influenced by Yemenite, which can be explained supposing either that they were already in the apograph, or that the same apograph was influenced by Tiberian phonetics — as in the case of the MSS which were punctuated in the complicated Babylonian system — or else because the apograph came from Babylonian schools in which the punctuation was different from the classical Babylonian punctuation, for example, Babylonian schools in Palestine, Syria or Egypt[13].

c) Punctuations which we do not find outside the Yemenite tradition

There are punctuations which we do not find outside the Yemenite tradition. One might suppose that these punctuations were not copied but supplied by the Yemenite copyist, according to the system to which he was accustomed. If the Babylonian apograph was defective, it might well be that many words were written defectively in the original, and that the copyist vocalized them in Yemenite system.

But this explanation, which explains sufficiently that sometimes some words have Babylonian vocalization and at other times have Yemenite vocalization, does not explain why אֶקְטל or אֱקַטל should have been written in the original apograph always in a defective way, since these verbal forms are not usually defective words, or at least they are not always defective. Therefore, if אקטל and אקטל almost always take a Yemenite form, the answer is that the Yemenite copyist not only has supplied the defective vocalization of the apograph but that on other occasions he has changed it.

It does not help to insist that there are Babylonian originals which are very defective, which have very few vowels. This is true, but when such a lack of vowels does exist, the words which most show this are particles like ו, את, כל etc., and not verbal forms like אקטל, אקטל. If the Yemenite influence were to be explained by the defectiveness of the apograph, we ought to find most Yemenite influence in the particles את (for את), ו or ו (for ו), כל (for כל) etc. which very often do not show vowels; and where we ought to find that least Yemenite influence would be in the verbal forms. Since the contrary is the case, we are forced to conclude that the Yemenite influence of MS 152 is not owing always to the vocalic defectiveness of the apograph.

In conclusion, if not all the *yemenisms* are found in Babylonian MSS from outside the Yemen, and if not all the *yemenisms* can be explained by the hypothesis that the copyist in those cases supplied according to the Yemenite system the vowel which was lacking in the Babylonian apograph, we are left to think that the only possible explanation of the punctuation of the Hebrew text of MS 152 is, that in great part, it is copied from a Babylonian original, and that on the other hand, a great part is supplied, and on occasion changed, to fit

[13] On the existence of Babylonian Centres outside of Mesopotamia see: Fragmentos de piyyutim . . ., p. 318f.

in with Yemenite phonetics. Therefore, the vocalic text of MS 152 is in part Babylonian, in part Yemenite. It is more or less Babylonian or more or less Yemenite according to whether the punctuation detailed in section b) above were already in the apograph or have resulted from changes or additions of the copyist.

B: Consonantal Hebrew Text

The important matter for biblical textual criticism is not that the vowels of MS 152 should be often, or in a great part, Babylonian. When all is said and done, differences in vocalization are nearly always phonetic variations, which have a purely historical value. It is of little importance to recover the phonetics of the biblical text which was normal in the Mesopotamian Academies, since we cannot be sure that it is the original phonetics of the Hebrew text[14]. But what is of extraordinary importance is to know if the consonantal text of MS 152 is a Babylonian consonantal text; it is the consonantal text which principally determines the sense of the text.

From what we have said above, it can be deduced that MS 152 is the copy of a »Vorlage« of Mesopotamia. It would be absurd that a Yemenite copyist should copy a Tiberian consonantal text and add to it so many Babylonian vowels — which were neither in the Tiberian consonantal text nor in any Yemenite text — as one finds in MS 152.

Once agreed that the scribe copied a Babylonian apograph, the question is: did he limit himself to making certain vocalic changes while transcribing faithfully the original consonantic text, or did he change too the basic Babylonian consonantal text. In order to clarify this point, which is the really important point, we are going to follow two paths: first compare the consonantal and orthographic texts of MS 152 with the Babylonian masora of Sufut-Kale (this was published by Ginsburg in vol. III of his edition of »The Massorah«). If MS 152 follows the norms of the Babylonian Masora, it will be a Babylonian text. Afterwards, we shall look and see if MS 152 presents the text which different Masoretic sources attribute to the *Madinḥae*, or Oriental, in a determined number of the words of Genesis.

[14] The Babylonian Jews preserved in special points of phonetics, an older pronunciation than that used by Palestinian Jews; for instance, they used the pattern *maqtal* (not *miqtal*); they pronounced open *qameṣ*; on the contrary, the *qameṣ* was closed in Palestine even from the beginning of Christianity, etc.. About the traditional significance of the phonetics of contemporary Yemenites, see S. Morag, Notes on the vowel System of Babylonian Aramaic as Preserved in the Yemenite Tradition, Phonetica 7 (1962), p. 217–239.

a) The Consonantal Text of MS 152 and the Masora of Sufut-Kale

We have examined with great care all the Masoretic Babylonian rubrics of the MS of Sufut-Kale in so far as it concerns Genesis. Unfortunately, this MS is only conserved for Gen 5 29–10 27.

	MS 152	*BH*³	*Babylonian Masora*
1) Gen 6 7	(15)נחמתים	נחמתי	נחמתי
2) 6 19	(16)להחיות	לְהַחֲיֹת	להחית ב׳׳ חס׳׳ בענ׳׳
3) 8 3	(17)וישבו	וַיָּשֻׁבוּ	וישבו של׳׳ וחס׳׳
4) 8 4	אררט	אֲרָרָט	אררט ג׳ דק׳׳ במיקפץ
2nd h.	אררט	ד׳	פומא;אררט דממלכות (Jer 51 27)
			דק׳׳ בפיתחא
5) 8 9	וישלח	וַיְשַׁלַּח	No Masora
6) 8 10	ויחל	וַיָּחֶל	ויחל ז׳ דק׳׳ מערבאי
2nd h. Yemenite	ויחל	ט׳	אמרין ויחל קדמ׳׳ דק׳׳
			קדמ׳׳ ויחל ;תינינא ויחל דק׳׳
7) 8 10	ויסף	וַיֹּסֶף	ויסף שלת דק׳׳ וחס׳׳
8) 8 12	(18)ויסר	וַיָּסַר	כולה באוריתא ויסר
			בר מן ג׳ ויסר
			ויסר חס׳׳ יסיר של׳׳
9) 8 17	הוצא כת׳׳	הַוְצֵא	היצא והוצא
	היצא ק׳׳	היצא ק׳׳	כת׳׳ ופולג׳׳
10) 8 20	הטהרה	הַטְּהוֹרָה	הטהרה חס׳׳
11) 8 20	ויעל	וַיַּעַל	ויעל
2nd h. Yemenite	ויעל		
12) 8 21	מנעוריו	מִנְּעֻרָיו	מנעריו ג׳ דק׳׳
		ג ב חס׳׳	(No remark on חס׳׳ של׳׳)

15 Perhaps a contamination from following עשיתים. In codices 5 and 8 listed by Kennicott, also נחמתים.

16 Thirty one codices of Kennicott list show full spelling (scriptio plena) להחיות; the rest, defective spelling (scriptio defectiva).

17 All codices listed by Kennicott, except 13 and 244, show defective spelling.

18 The first hand puts [sign] but afterwards changes it into [sign]. In I Sam 15 6 ויסר for Tiberian וַיָּסַר; MdO, p. 187.

	MS 152	*BH*³	*Babylonian Masora*
13) 9 18	שם וחם	שֵׁם וְחָם	שם וחם
14) 9 7	וסבתא	וסבתה	וסבתא בׄ דק״
	2nd h. Yemenite וסבתה		
15) 9 19	וצבים כת״	וּצְבִיִם	וצבים

If the preceding table is examined, it will be seen that the only real variant between MS 152 and the Masora of Sufut-Kale is the first, which, although it is attested in another two MSS, is probably an error of the copyist, because of the attraction of the verb עשיתים.

The second variant is purely orthographical, and may be found in many MSS.

3 and 9 are not even orthographical variants, since it is possible in the Babylonian Masora to write them with full and defective spelling.

4 is a vocalic variant (not a consonantal variant), but as for the reading in 152, although it is different from the Masora of Sufut-Kale, it is not very probable that it is an occidental vocalization since all the occidental MSS punctuate אררש, and the Masora itself recognizes the following punctuation אררש for Jer 51 27.

5: the Masora says nothing about this variant of MS 152 with relation to BH, but according to the codex No. 1 in Madrid, in Gen 28 5, there is a parallel case, in which the Eastern MSS read וישלח for וַיִּשְׁלַח.

6: refers to the vocalic text, and even so, it seems there is concordance, not only consonantally, but vocalically, between the reading of MS 152 and the Masora.

7: agrees with the Masoretic note which refers to the defective lettering; it differs only in vocalization.

8: this is badly vocalized by Ginsburg. He reads[19]: כולה אוריתא וַיָּסַר בר מן ג וְיָסֹר ... וְיָסֵר חס׳ יָסִיר של׳ whereas one can read the original in the photographs of the codex of Sufut-Kale (f. 4b) as follows: כולה אוריתא ויסר בר מן ג ויסר ... ויסר חס׳ יסיר של׳

If one reads the Masora in this way, it agrees with the reading of MS 152, so far as it concerns the defective writing, and it even agrees with the first punctuation of the MS so far as concerns vocalization.

[19] The Massorah, III p. 219.

10 & 11: Here MS 152 agrees with the Masora and disagrees with BH.

12: MS 152 disagrees (full spelling) with the Masora (which is defective), but the Masora here refers to the number of times when the word occurs, and it does not decide, as it normally decides, if it must be written full or defectively.

BH here agrees with the Masora.

13: MS 152, BH and the Masora agree, but one should notice that the transcription which Ginsburg offers of this passage of the Masora (p. 222, Gen 9 18) is mistaken. He puts שם חם instead of שם וחם which is in the copy of the text on p. 261 of vol. III of »The Massorah« and in folio 5b of the photographs of the MS[20].

In 14, MS 152 and the Masora are in agreement. They differ from BH.

In the reading 15, which the Tiberian Masora refers as particular to the *madinḥae*[21], our MS 152, and BH also, offer the Babylonian reading.

To sum up, apart from Gen 6 7 and 6 19, MS 152 does not suggest any discrepancies which affect the consonantal text in respect of the Babylonian Masora; even the second of these two discrepancies has to do with the full and defective orthography, a point in which there is discrepancy in other Babylonian MSS[22].

In Gen 8 21, there is also a variant of full or defective writing, but one cannot assert that the writing of MS 152 is not equally as Babylonian as that of the Masora.

As far as BH is concerned, it differs in various vocalizations from the Babylonian Masora. Its consonantal text only differs in full and defective writing in Gen 8 20 and 9 7.

From all of which it may be deduced that for the moment nothing prevents us considering the consonantal text of MS 152 as Babylonian. It does not seem likely, then, that the Yemenite copyist has altered the consonantal text of the Babylonian »Vorlage«. One may say also that MS 152 offers us a consonantal text of a Babylonian MS which, it is quite clear, differs very little from the consonanted text of BH, which is considered as a Palestinian or Western text.

[20] P. Kahle put at my disposal the photostats of the Sufut-Kale MS of Masora. On the Masora of Sufut-Kale and on new fragments of Babylonian masora showing substantial agreement with that masora, see G. E. Weil, Quatre fragments de la Massorah Magna babylonienne, Textus 3 (1963), p. 74–120.

[21] Hebrew Bible, ed. C. H. Ginsburg, Gen 10 19.

[22] On differences in »plene« or defective spelling in Babylonian MSS see my article: Un manuscrito protobabilónico de los libros poéticos de la Biblia, Estudios Bíblicos 18 (1959), p. 350–356.

b) The consonantal text of MS 152 and *madinḥae* readings referred to in Tiberian Masora

	Ms 152	*BH*[3]	*Madinḥae*
Gen 4 22	תובל קין	תובל קין	תובלקין
Gen 10 19	וצבים כת	וּצְבֹיִם	וּצְבֹיִם כת וּצְבוֹיִם קר [ירושלמי וּצְבֹיִים כת]
Gen 10 21	הגדול	הגדול	הגדול [מערבאי חס הגדל]
Gen 10 26	חצרמות	(23) חצרמוח	חצרמות
Gen 31 47.48	גלעד	(24) גלעד	גלעד
Gen 12 8 13 3 etc.	בית אל	בית־אל	ביתאל
Gen 14 1.4.5.9.17	כדר לעמר	כדרלעמר	כדרלעמר
Gen 41 45.50 46 20	פוטיפרע	פוטי פרע	פוטיפרע
Gen 23 6 26 16	ממנו	מִמֶּנּוּ	מִמֵּנּוּ

Whit reference to the variants immediately above, they throw little light upon the subject we are discussing, since they almost all refer to the writing in one or two separate words of compound names. For Ginsburg, the writing in one word of such compound names is a sign of Orientalism, whilst for Delitzsch-Baer it is exactly the opposite[25]. Variant 3 is Oriental. Variant 9 does not affect the consonantal text, it affects the vocalic text, and the vocalization is Western, not Oriental.

But, even if there were variants in the text of MS 152 with respect to the Masora of the *madinḥae*, it should be noticed again that the Babylonian Masora itself is not uniform. MS 508A of the Jewish Theological Seminary of New York, although it is a Babylonian MS, differs in many ways from other Babylonian texts, as we have proved in a study dedicated to that MS[26]. Nevertheless, one cannot deny that »The discrepancy is usually rare, even when one is dealing

[23] In the critical apparatus: Sic L., Bomberg 1524/25 et Or; plerique Occ חצר־מות.

[24] In the critical apparatus: Sic L, Bomberg 1524/25 c Or; al גל עד.

[25] Cf. my article: Onqelos Manuscript with Babylonian Transliterated Vocalization in the Vatican Library, VT 8 (1958), p. 118 note 3.

[26] See my article: Un manuscrito protobabilónico..., p. 350–356.

with full and defective writing, between Babylonian texts and Tiberian texts, especially in the Pentateuch«[27], an observation which I. Yeivin has confirmed recently in his study of Babylonian or Yemenite Babylonian MSS in the collection of Yehudah Levi Nahum[28].

[27] Ibid., p. 350.

[28] *Qiṭ'e Miqra* . . ., p. 561. Unfortunately we have not been able to compare Hebrew and Aramaic text of MS 152 with the corresponding texts of MS א (p. 561 s.) of the study of I. Yeivin. This MS contains Gen 9 17–10 22 17 9–18 3 (Hebrew text and Onqelos). It offers a Babylonian text copied in Yemen.

Indications of Antiquity in the Orthography and Morphology of the Fragment Targum

By Malcolm C. Doubles

(St. Andrews Presbyterian College, Laurinburg, North Carolina)

In his book »The Cairo Geniza«, the late Paul E. Kahle closes his discussion of the Aramaic Targums in the following manner:

> »In the Palestinian Targum of the Pentateuch we have in the main material coming from pre-Christian times ....«[1]

In spite of this well-known opinion on the part of Kahle, there is no unanimity on this matter in the scholarly world. Furthermore, subsequent attempts to demonstrate the validity of this thesis have invariably met with cogent criticism. A. Diez Macho has published his examination of the many phenomena in the Codex Neofiti I which induced him to conclude that »The PT (Palestinian Targum), even if it in its present recension, preserved in the Ms. Neofiti I, seems to belong to the first or second century A.D., is on the whole a prechristian version«[2]. However, this article produced an immediate rejoinder from P. Wernberg-Møller who, citing the same phenomena, demonstrated the possibility of another conclusion[3].

Furthermore, the painstaking labors of A. Vööbus have led him to adopt a position in support of this thesis, as well as another of the theses advanced by Kahle, namely, the dependence of the Syriac Peshitta on a Palestinian Aramaic Targum[4]. However, the trenchant criticism of this work by M. H. Goshen-Gottstein is evidence of the difference of scholarly opinion relative to this approach to the Palestinian Targums[5].

[1] Paul E. Kahle, The Cairo Geniza, 1960², p. 208.

[2] A. Diez Macho, The Recently Discovered Palestinian Targum: Its Antiquity and Relationship with the Other Targums, Congress Volume Oxford, 1959, Suppl VT 7, (1960), p. 236.

[3] P. Wernberg-Møller, An inquiry into the validity of the text-critical argument for an early dating of the recently discovered Palestinian Targum, VT 12 (1962), p. 312–330.

[4] A. Vööbus, Peschitta und Targumim des Pentateuchs. Neues Licht zur Frage der Herkunft der Peschitta aus dem altpalästinischen Targum. Handschriftenstudien (Papers of the Estonian Theological Society in Exile, 9), 1958.

[5] JSS 6 (1961), his review of Vööbus' book, p. 266f.

One of the principal problems which has plagued researchers in this subject has been the paucity of Aramaic texts which can be dated definitely in the last century B.C. — first century A.D. Prior to the discoveries at Qumran only the following were known: »A few very short inscriptions in Jerusalem, a few Aramaic words in the New Testament and Josephus, the Aramaic bill of sale from 134 C.E., the Ta'anith Scroll (1st. Cent. C.E.) and the few Aramaic words and sentences to be found in Tannaitic literature«[6].

E. Y. Kutscher has described the Aramaic of the *Genesis Apocryphon* discovered in Cave I at Qumran, and has noted how it enters a »virtual vacuum of Aramaic texts in Palestine before the rise of Middle Aramaic (about 500 C.E.)«[7]. In this situation, Kutscher states that although it is true that Targums are of very early origin, it has not been possible so far to fix their date or to state how much earlier they are than the Talmudic period (200–500 C.E.).

In addition to the *Genesis Apocryphon*, other Aramaic material such as the Targum to the Book of Job and the Book of Enoch have been discovered at Qumran. Their publication will provide further Aramaic material to be used to reconstruct the language of Palestine in the first century A.D.

The discovery of this material at Qumran provides comparative material not here-to-fore available, and invites a study of the language of the Targums in terms of the Qumran texts. Kutscher dates the *Genesis Apocryphon* on the basis of its language to the first century B.C.[8]. Concerning the date of the Job Targum, v. d. Ploeg has suggested that it may well represent a stage of Aramaic between that of the Book of Daniel and that found in the *Genesis Apocryphon*[9].

This paper will be an attempt to study certain phenomena in one tradition of the Fragment Targum in the light of this material from Qumran. Primarily the excellent study by Kutscher on the *Genesis Apocryphon* will be used to demonstrate the Aramaic language at Qumran in the immediately pre-Christian years, and certain examples of this language in the Fragment Targum, in contrast to the expected »Middle Aramaic«, will be noted.

[6] E. Y. Kutscher, The Language of the Genesis Apocryphon, Scripta Hierosolymitana 4 (1958), p. 3.

[7] Ibid.

[8] Ibid., p. 22.

[9] J. van der Ploeg, Le Targum de Job de la Grotte 11 de Qumran, Premiere Communication, 1962, p. 7: »... On peut dire que l'araméen de notre targum présente certaines déviations de l'araméen classique (= d'empire), qui le placent entre l'araméen de Daniel et celui de 11 QGenAp«.

MS Vaticanus 440

The text of the Fragment Targum which will be used in this paper is that of the MS Vaticanus 440. Unless there is a note to the contrary, the Fragment Targum forms cited in the body of this paper will be those of this manuscript.

MS Vat. 440 is a codex containing the Hebrew text for the last two books of the Pentateuch, with Targum Onkelos, the Haftorah and Megilloth, and in the last part the Jerusalem Targum. The Aramaic of the Fragment Targum proceeds verse by verse, with only a Hebrew word or two to indicate the verse in question. The manuscript comes from the 13th century[10]. This text of the Fragment Targum was made known to the scholarly world by M. Ginsburger who, in Appendix II (p. 74–90) of his work »Das Fragmententhargum«, printed the variants of MS Vat. 440 (and Codex Leipzig 1) from the printed text of the Fragment Targum as this latter is found in the Bomberg Bible (Venice 1517/18)[11].

However, Ginsburger's presentation of the text of this extremely important manuscript contains some 2,000 errors and is completely unreliable. I owe my thanks to the late Paul E. Kahle for making available to me his photographs of the Fragment Targum portion of MS Vat. 440, which I have used in my study and which I am preparing for publication.

At the time of the publication of his work, Ginsburger noted that the Fragment Targum was preserved in two different recensions, one of these found in MS Paris 110 and the other in MS Vat. 440, with which latter text Codd. Nuremburg 1, Leipzig 1, and the printed version agreed by and large[12]. A more careful examination confirms Ginsburger's opinion relative to the priority of MS Vat. 440 in any discussion of this tradition of the Fragment Targum. The mater lectionis used to indicate the final *ā* sound, the widespread use of the plene spelling indicating the early unpointed character of the text, the forms with *Waw* which are probably Hebraisms from post-Biblical times, the archaic spelling of certain words, and the spelling of the relative pronoun *d'* confirm Ginsburger's opinion and provide the material for the comparative study offered in this paper.

[10] Assemani, Bibliothecae Apostolicae Vaticanae, Catalogue I, p. 400.

[11] M. Ginsburger, Das Fragmententhargum, 1899.

[12] Ibid., p. xii.

Points of Comparison between the Fragment Targum and the Aramaic of Qumran

I. Final ה and Final א

Characteristic of the orthography of the Vatican manuscript of the Fragment Targum is its frequent use of final ה instead of final א. In these cases the Leipzig codex usually parallels the Vatican text, and in some cases has final ה where the latter text corresponds to the printed version with final א. This use of ה is generally associated with texts written at a date centuries earlier than that often assigned to the Palestinian Targum(s).

The following examples of feminine nouns in the absolute state reveal this phenomena: Gen 6 3 19 24, תתובה; Gen 12 2 49 7 Dtn 32 21, (Bomberg Bible and Nuremburg MS 1: Gen 3 22 Dtn 28 50)[13] אומה; Gen 36 39, בישה; BN: Ex 19 5, סגולה. Where comparison is possible, and in general, all of the texts of Targum Onkelos as their readings are presented in Sperber's edition prefer א to ה for this feminine absolute ending[14]. In contrast to Targum Onkelos and in agreement with the *Genesis Apocryphon*, the Fragment Targum uses both א and ה for this ending while the Jerusalem inscriptions prefer ה[15].

Quite frequently, this use of final ה by the Fragment Targum is revealed in the sign for the status emphaticus, in both the singular and plural numbers. In the singular, such examples as the following are found: Gen 8 22, שורבה; Gen 18 1–2, מלאכה; Gen 47 21, Ex 10 28 15 24, עמה; BN: Lev 3 9, שלימה; BN: Lev 24 11, ברה; Num 23 24, אריה. In the plural, Gen 27 29, אומייה; Gen 35 9, 48 22 Ex 13 19, טבייה; Gen 49 22, כוויה; Ex 14 20, ליליה; Ex 14 25, גלגלייה. Like the Targum Onkelos, the *Genesis Apocryphon* seems to prefer final א for this determinate state of the noun, in contrast to the Jerusalem inscriptions, Samaritan Aramaic, and the Palestinian Talmud, which prefer ה[16].

In Gen 38 15 the pronominal suffix, 3rd person fem. sg., is spelled with final ה rather than א: »Her face«, אפהה. The general use of final א in this form compares to that of regular »Targumic« Aramaic usage as well as to the use of the *Genesis Apocryphon*, which also has only one instance of this form with final ה[16].

This preference is likewise apparent in the spelling of some proper nouns: Gen 26 35, רבקה; Gen 46 28, גושנה; Gen 50 2, בלהה.

Occasionally, the Peʿal perfect 3rd masc. sg. of a verb with a weak third radical reveals this tendency: Gen 44 19, Ex 12 42, חמה;

[13] References to readings from the Bomberg Bible of 1517/18 and to MS Nuremburg 1 will henceforth be abbreviated B and/or N respectively.

[14] A. Sperber, The Bible in Aramaic, I 1959.

[15] Kutscher, op. cit., p. 26–28.

[16] Kutscher, op. cit., p. 26–28.

Gen 50 1, בכה; Ex 14 34, רמה. Except for verbs ל״א, the *Genesis Apocryphon* employs final ה in forms such as these, whereas Targum Onkelos has a universal preference for final א[16].

There are examples where infinitives also show this use of final ה in the Fragment Targum, a situation found neither in Targum Onkelos nor in the *Genesis Apocryphon,* but in the Palestinian Talmud and Midrashim[16]. For instance, Gen 28 12, למבסרה; Gen 38 25, למתוקדה; Ex 10 29, למיתכלייה.

Sometimes participles in the Fragment Targum are found with final ה where final א is normally expected. Thus, Gen 15 12, Dtn 32 35. עתידה; Gen 49 22, שתילה; Gen 50 1, מקבעה; BN: Lev 23 29,ציימה.

This widespread use of ה as mater lectionis at the end of a word is a definite indication of the western character of the Aramaic of the Palestinian Targum(s). Certainly we must now recognize the fact that the Fragment Targum parallels Galilean Aramaic and Samaritan Aramaic (but not Christian Aramaic) in its use of ה as mater lectionis. In addition, this fact would seem to require an acceptance of the fact that much of the material in these Targums comes from sources independent of Targum Onkelos, which are as old or older than the official Targum, inasmuch as often this orthographical variation is found where Targum Onkelos and the Fragment Targum parallel one another. One might raise the question whether both the Fragment Targum and the *Genesis Apocryphon* do not reflect western Aramaic under the influence of eastern Aramaic already moving toward the regular use of א at the end of a word[17].

II. The Relative Pronoun די

In its use of the relative pronoun די, the Vatican manuscript of the Fragment Targum exhibits a definite preference for writing the pronoun as a separate word. In the manuscript, the particle may stand alone, or it may be joined in its full form to the succeeding word. In general, the preference is for the pronoun to stand alone, but there are enough exceptions to warrant attention. Of course, when the shorter form ד is used it is always joined to the following word. The self-standing form of the relative pronoun is used in Biblical Aramaic and is generally considered the more ancient way of writing it[18].

In the *Genesis Apocryphon,* this notation of the relative pronoun is used between sixty and seventy times, and in only six cases is the relative formed by ד joined to the succeeding word[19]. In a slight

[17] Contra Kutscher, op. cit., p. 28.

[18] G. Dalman, Grammatik des jüdisch-palästinischen Aramäisch, 1905², p. 116.

[19] Kutscher, op. cit., p. 6.

contrast to this, the Targum of Job found in Cave 11 at Qumran always employs the self-standing די form for this pronoun[20].

It is of interest in this connection to note, however, that this form of the relative pronoun is not restricted to the Palestinian Targum(s). Sperber notes that in almost every occurrence of the pronoun in Targum Onkelos, at least one of the manuscruipts or printed versions spells it די, in contrast to the shorter form joined to the following word, which is the form usually considered to be »Targumic Aramaic«[21].

The effect of this situation is to cause one to raise a question of alternatives similar to that raised earlier. If this way of spelling the relative pronoun is to be recognized as that used in Palestine prior to the rise of »Middle Aramaic«, then another argument for the early character of Targum Onkelos is made, and the further argument may be made that the Fragment Targum must stem from the same general time, at least on the basis of this particular criterion. On the other hand, if this sort of argument is impossible, then the form of the relative pronoun as די cannot be considered significant in determining the date of a text, in spite of its general use in early texts and its defective spelling in »Middle Aramaic«.

III. The Western Character of Certain Verbal Forms

In common with Christian Aramaic and the Aramaic of the *Genesis Apocryphon*, the Fragment Targum preserves some forms of the verb which are apparently restricted to western Aramaic. Their presence in the Qumran material attests to the antiquity of these forms in relation to »Middle Aramaic«, where they are no longer found.

For instance, in Num 11 26, the printed edition (B) of the Fragment Targum has the Pe'al imperfect 3rd masc. pl. of the verb as יקוצון, when the normally expected Aramaic form would be יקצון. This compares with יכולון in the *Genesis Apocryphon*[22].

In the same manner, the Pe'al imperative masculine plural appears in several places in a form similar to one recorded by Kutscher from the *Genesis Apocryphon*[23]. In Gen 35 9, the printed version B and N of the Fragment Targum record the form כבושו, and in Num 9 8, all the Fragment Targum versions have the reading שמועו[24].

[20] v. d. Ploeg, op. cit., p. 7.

[21] Sperber, op. cit., p. viii–ix.

[22] Kutscher, op. cit., p. 13.

[23] Ibid., p. 13.: תקוצו.

[24] But for additional appearances of this form in the targums, cf. Dalman, op. cit., p. 277.

This western use of *Waw* is also reflected in several participial forms found in the Fragment Targum. The Paʿel participle, masc. sg., is formed by V in several places in a manner showing this influence. In Gen 35 9, we find מבורך instead of מברך, and in Ex 12 42, מזומן instead of מזמן. Thus it appears that this is simply another characteristic of western Aramaic dialect, perhaps under the influence of post-Biblical Hebrew.

It is interesting to note the influence of the *Waw* in certain Aphʿel preformatives. In the manuscript V, the Aphʿel perfect 1st c. sg. appears as אוקמית in Gen 44 18, and the Aphʿel imperfect 1st c. sg. appears in Gen 12 3 as אוברך. This interesting spelling may very well be quite instructive in regard to the pronunciation of the Aphʿel in western Aramaic.

It is evident that the appearance of forms such as these cannot force the conclusion that an early date must be assigned to the Fragment Targum. However, their appearance in the Qumran material indicates that it is not necessary to attribute the presence of these forms to error. They are rather the indication of the western character of the Fragment Targum, and may quite possibly be morphological residue from a time before the standardization of »Middle Aramaic« when the language was still influenced by Hebrew.

IV. Nouns Parallel in the Fragment Targum and Qumran

The manuscript (V) spelling of the city »Damascus« parallels that spelling found at Qumran. Thus, in Gen 14 15 15 2 Num 34 15, in V we find דרמסק, instead of the דמשק of the Masoretic Text and the other Aramaic versions[25]. The only difference in the Fragment Targum rendering and that found at Qumran (in both the *Genesis Apocryphon* and the Isaiah Scroll) is that the Targum employs *Samek* where the scrolls have *sin*.

The archaic spelling of the word »Head« is found several times in the Fragment Targum manuscripts. In Gen 40 17 44 18, V has ראש where BN have ריש. In Gen 1 14, N has ראשי with the *Aleph* corrected to *Yodh* by a later hand, while VB have ריש. Kutscher records the spelling of this word in the Qumran material as ראיש, the middle form between ראש and ריש[26].

Here again we see apparently archaic forms in the Fragment Targum which when taken alone do not seem to have any great significance. However, when these instances are placed alongside others, one begins to question and to ask if there may not be some

[25] Kutscher, op. cit., p. 22.

[26] Ibid., p. 25–26.

importance to be attached to such a wide variety of archaic phenomena.

V. An Archaic Verbal Spelling

The Fragment Targums preserve an interesting and archaic spelling of the verb »to displease«. The changes from the archaic and original spelling to the more accepted »Middle Aramaic« spelling can be seen in the comparison of the manuscript forms with the printed versions.

In Num 16 15, the manuscripts V and N of the Fragment Targum preserve the verb spelled in this manner: ובעש and אבעשית, while the printed version B has corrected this spelling to ובאש and אבאשית respectively. The second occurrence of this verb in this verse is preserved by Targum Onkelos with the spelling אבאישית. Additional occurrences of this verb in the Book of Deuteronomy preserve the archaic spelling in every text of the Fragment Targum. In Dtn 15 10, יבעש is found, and in Dtn 28 54 there is תבעש. In both of these verses Targum Onkelos has אי instead of ע[27].

It is quite instructive that medieval manuscripts of a targum often said to be late in origin and dependent upon Targum Onkelos should not only preserve such an archaic spelling for this verb but also should preserve exactly such an archaic form in three verses where all manuscripts and versions of Targum Onkelos testify to a later spelling of the word.

Apparently, this phenomenon raises several questions. For one, is there any significance to the fact in certain Fragment Targum words *'Ayin* has not been changed to the »Middle Aramaic« *Aleph* expected in these words? For another, if the Fragment Targum has been extracted from and is based upon Targum Onkelos, why is this dependence not apparent in the spelling of a word such as the one treated above? Furthermore, if the practice of writing the Targum to the Pentateuch began as late as is often stated to be the case, why does this archaic spelling of a word even appear in a Pentateuchal targum when this form of the word is evidently attested in no other Aramaic texts?[29]

[27] P. Wernberg-Møller, Prolegomena to a Re-examination of the Palestinian Targum Fragments of the Book of Genesis, JSS 7 (1962), p. 256 f. for a discussion of this word as used in the targums.

[28] Kutscher, op. cit., p. 7f.; cf. note 34, p. 8.

[29] Dalman, op. cit., p. 48, lists this word as Galilean Aramaic as opposed to the »Targumic« מרע, but even in his listing the nominal form is spelled ביש (Samaritan בהאש), both of which would be later spellings of this word. Dalman does not list the verbal form.

VI. Interchanges of *Yodh, He,* and *Aleph* to Represent the Sound (e:) at the End of a Word

Just as the *Genesis Apocryphon* sometimes indicates the final (e:) sound by the letter ה, so also does the Fragment Targum from time to time[30]. In addition, sometimes one text of the Targum will employ א where the others have ה or י.

a. This phenomenon may be seen in the following examples of the Peʿal:

1. Perfect 3rd masc. sg.: קרא in V but קרי in BN in Ex 12 42;
2. Imperfect 3rd masc. sg.: יהא in BN but יהי in V in Gen 35 9 and 49 2[31];
3. Participle masc. sg.: קשה in V but קשי in BN in Gen 44 18;
4. Infinitive: למהתא in V but למהתי in BN in Gen 44 4 and למברא in BN but למברי in V in Ex 12 42.

b. The following forms in the Ithpaʿel are also found:

1. Imperfect 3rd masc. sg.: יתגאה in BN but יתגאי in V in Gen 49 17;
2. Participle masc. sg.: מתגאה in V but מתגאי in BN in Ex 15 1.

The appearance of these forms would seem to indicate that at some time in its transmission, the language of the Fragment Targum had not been completely standardized and some variation was still possible. At this point, there can only be posed the question, what light does the Aramaic of the Qumran material cast upon the development of a standardized representation of the final (e:) sound and does this have any bearing on the origin of the language of the Fragment Targum?

VII. Plene Spelling

Plene spelling with *Aleph* and *Waw* is the general practice of the Qumran scrolls[32]. This characteristic is also found in the Fragment Targum manuscripts V and L. These two texts not only employ *Aleph* and *Waw*, but also *Yodh.*

Frequently VL use *Yodh* to indicate *Hireq* where BN have only the pointing. Often the same is true in the case of *Sere*, and sometimes in the case of *Seghol.* (תיהוי, איפשר, מיהוי).

In a number of words, V has *Waw* to indicate *Holem* where BN have the defective spelling with only the pointing. In some words, BN use *Waw* to indicate *Sureq*, where V simply has the vocalization. Rarely is the reverse true.

30 Kutscher, op. cit., p. 25.

31 This is in addition to those examples cited by Dalman, op. cit., p. 71 and 354.

32 Kutscher, op. cit., p. 26.

In several places, V uses *Aleph* to indicate *Kames* where BN have the defective spelling with the pointing. Occasionally, the reverse is true.

Finally, it is quite in accordance with the usage of V to employ יי and וו for consonantal *Yodh* and *Waw*, where BN have י and ו. Very occasionally is the reverse true.

It would appear that the significance of this phenomenon lies not in any demonstration of an early date for the Fragment Targum, but rather is an indication of the unvocalized character of this Targum at one point in its history[33]. That this type of plene spelling is common to the Qumran scrolls simply demonstrates that no longer can a text with this spelling automatically be classified as coming from the period of »Middle Aramaic«. Thus at this point, the manuscript of the Fragment Targum makes it possible at least to consider a date of origin prior to the Medieval Age.

Results of such comparison

It would seem to be the conclusion of such a process of comparison that one cannot automatically date the Fragment Targum to the era of Middle Aramaic. Certainly there are a number of linguistic phenomena which raise questions about such a procedure.

That the Fragment Targum was unvocalized at one point in its history is apparent from the plene spelling common both to MSS Vat. 440 and Leip. 1 and to the Cairo Geniza texts[34]. It is significant that for the first time the Qumran scrolls have yielded numerous pre-Christian Palestinian texts which have exactly this phenomenon common to them. Thus an origin in the intertestamentary period is not impossible.

The use of *He* as mater lectionis at the end of many words, and the full spelling of the relative pronoun די, common both to the Vaticanus text and to some of the Cairo Geniza texts, indicate a time of origin prior to the standardization of this ending and pronoun. Now it is exactly the Aramaic of Qumran which reflects this same period of transition. Must it not be considered significant that only in these unofficial targums is this ambivalence of ending found elsewhere? It would appear that whatever date of origin is assigned to the Fragment Targums, it must explain this apparent relic from an early transitional period.

[33] Certainly the vocalization of the Fragment Targum manuscript V is no more reliable than the texts of Targum Onkelos with sublinear pointing, cf. Sperber, op. cit., p. viii. Does this apply also to BN?

[34] P. E. Kahle, Masoreten des Westens, IV/2 1930.

Finally, the preservation of ancient spellings and forms in these texts likewise requires attention.

Thus, a study of the morphology and the orthography of the Fragment Targum provides another line of evidence indicating the possibility of an early date for the Targum. Although such a study cannot prove an early date for the Targum in the present state of knowledge, it does add another link to the chain of arguments for such a date. Furthermore, this type of study can shed some light on the origin and relationship of the Fragment Targum and Targum Onkelos. In conclusion, it seems to be increasingly possible to argue that the linguistic evidences for a late dating for the Fragment Targum may simply be the unconscious reflection of the time of Medieval copyists, while the actual date for this Targum must be determined by the survivals of ancient morphological and orthographical forms, together with other evidences from different lines of investigation.

Isaiah 52 13–53 12: the Servant of the Lord

By G. R. Driver

(University of Oxford)

This section of the Old Testament, describing the sufferings of the Servant of the Lord, one of the most famous in the Bible, has been abused as much as it has been used by theologians to find their own doctrines in it or to read the New Testament into it; the purpose therefore of the present article is to try to find out exactly what the Hebrew text means.

The following notes on the text are therefore submitted with a view to preparing the way for the translation which follows them.

V. 13. The poet begins the description of the Lord's servant by saying that יַשְׂכִּיל 'he will prosper', to which objection has been taken on the ground that in fact he is gravely ill-treated and that the time to speak of his success and prosperity is at the end of the poem. Further, השׂכיל is inappropriate to the Servant's circumstances, inasmuch as it expresses not plain success or prosperity, for which הצליח is the proper word (s. 53 10), but success as the result of wise or clever provision[1], i.e. worldly success, which is out of the question. The suggestion has therefore been made to alter this verb into יִשָּׂקֵל, 'he will be lifted up' and to see a reference to his ill-treatment in it as also in the following three verbs; but the suggestion insolves tampering with the consonantal text[2]. This difficulty may be avoided by re-vocalizing the verb as יִשָּׂכֵל 'he will be bound'; the Acc. *šakkīlu* 'bandage, scarf' (as something tied round the head), the Hebr. שִׂכֵּל 'crossed' e.g. the hands[3]' (Gen 48 14) and the Arab. *šakala* 'bound, tied (a beast's feet or legs)' lends colour to such an emendation. Then the following verbs will refer to the lifting up of the Servant after being bound as a form of punishment, such as hanging[4]. The *double entendre* thus implied in the following clause, namely 'he shall be exalted and lifted up and shall be very high' is similar to that which Jesus uses when he says 'I, if

[1] Cf. S. R. Driver, Samuel[2], p. 149.

[2] J. Morgenstern, VT 11, p. 313.

[3] Gen 48 14.

[4] Cf. Thr 5 12 (as a form of torture), Gen 41 13 Josh 8 29 Esth 2 23 7 9.10 9 14 (as a mode of execution).

I be lifted up from the earth, will draw all men unto myself'[5], which may indeed be based on a recollection of this very passage. Thus the link between the beginning and end of the poem is preserved, though not exactly in the form usually desiderated[6].

V. 14. Obviously the text here is rhythmically defective, lacking two beats to bring it into conformity with the preceding and following lines. Neither the early Vss. nor the Scrolls throw any light on the gap; but the Targ.'s כמא דסברו ליה בית ישראל יומין סגיאין 'as the house of Israel waited for him many days' points a way to restoring the MT. The first difficulty lies in עליך 'at thee', since the pronoun has no antecedent; and all the Vss. evade it by reading עליו 'at him'. However, on the ground that difficilior lectio potior, it may be retained, and as antecedent עַמִּי 'O my people', reflecting the Targ.'s בית ישראל 'house of Israel' may be inserted; for, though interpreting the clause wrongly, the Targumist has seen that Israel must be the object of the address. Then an original abbreviated רב׳ ימ׳ standing for רַבִּים יָמִים 'many days' has been misread as רבים 'many people', possibly misled by this word in the following verse; the same error has been made by the Massoretes in לא־רַבִּים יחכמו 'it is not the great that are wise', where the parallel זקנים as well as the metre show that רַבֵּי יָמִים 'aged' must be read; the LXX's οἱ πολυχρόνιοι and the Vulg.'s *longaevi* (cf. Pesh. and Saʿad.) support this simple emendation. The error here is clearly due to the fact that the phrase is unique; but it will have been helped by the use of abbreviations for such common words as those here used, and especially by the habit of not writing out terminations[7]. Moreover, a contributory cause may have been the fact that the adj. רב precedes the noun; the idiom, however, though rare is permissible as shown by רבים בנים 'many sons', רבות בנות many daughters and רבות עתים 'many times'[8]. The construction is probably due to Aramaic influence, which is especially marked in poetry[9]. The meaning then is that, as the nations were once appalled at the disaster which had befallen the prosperous Israelites, so now they would be amazed at that which would overtake the servant of the Lord.

The following clause, which is bracketed in the R.V., is certainly out of place and ought to come after v. 2 of the following chapter[10].

[5] Gen 12 32.

[6] S. Mowinckel, He that Cometh, p. 205.

[7] Job 32 9; s. Textus 1, p. 114–117, and 4, p. 78f.

[8] I Chr 28 5 Prov 31 29 Neh 9 28.

[9] Cf. C. Brockelmann, G.V.G.S.S., II p. 202f. The Syr. *saggîʾ* 'many' regularly precedes the noun which it qualifies (Th. Nöldeke [tr. Crichton], Comp. Syr. Gr., p. 168).

[10] K. Marti, Jesaja, p. 345–347.

V. 15. Although רבים in the last verse means 'many', force is added if here it is translated 'mighty', in spite of the Vss., in parallelism with kings; for the author of the poem delights in playing on the varied meanings of the words that he uses (s.n. on 53 10).

V. 1–2. In v. 2 an antecedent is required for the pronoun in לפניו 'before him'; this in perhaps מי 'who', which may then be translated 'has anyone ...?' to bring out this point. Otherwise, the Lord must be the antecedent term.

V. 14. Scroll A has משחתי for the MT's משחת, which looks like a forma mixta of נִשְׁחָת and מָשְׁחָת, which ought perhaps to be read[11]. That משחתי is meant to be read מָשַׁחְתִּי 'I marred'[12] is out of the question; the final *-î* must be taken as the so-called *ḥireq compaginis*[13], which Scroll A has also elsewhere in this book[14].

V. 15. The LXX render יזה גוים רבים by θαυμάσονται ἔθνη πολλά, reading the intrans. יִזּוּ instead of the trans. יַזֶּה which the MT has; and this is surely the preferable reading, although no other ancient Vs. has it. The objection that this translation of the verb imports an emotional element which the cognate Arab. *nazâ* 'leapt' has not got is incorrect; for this means not only 'leapt up' but also 'leapt for joy' (Freytag) as will as for eager desire (Lane) and anger (Dozy). The reason, of course, must be sought in the context; and none can be given to show why it may not mean also 'leapt for surprise, grief' or any other emotion. The idea that the verb is used elliptically to mean 'he shall sprinkle (ritual water) over' i.e. perform purificatory rites on behalf of many nations[15], is fantastic and has nothing to commend it; it implies a misuse of the verb, is not supported by any ancient Vs. and introduces a technical rite of the cult which is alien to the spirit of the poem.

V. 3. The meaning of חדל אישים is probably not 'rejected of men' (R.V.) but 'shrinking from men'. The Vss. offer little help; but Saʿad.'s מנקטע מן אלנאס 'cut off from men' and the S.-Arab. *ḫdl* 'desisted' and Arab. *ḫadilu(n)* 'abstaining from aiding, holding back from going with (a person)' (Lane)[16] suggest that the translation given above is approximately correct. Possibly, too, contamination with a verb

[11] Cf. Is 59 3 Thr 4 14 and Is 63 3 for similar alternative forms (s. E. Kautzsch [tr. A. E. Cowley], Hebr. Gramm. § 51 h).

[12] A. Guillaume, JBL 76, p. 42.

[13] Cf. Is 45 5 47 8. 10; s. A. Rubinstein, Biblica 35, p. 475.

[14] E.g. Is 49 41 (מתעבי for מתעב).

[15] H. S. Nyberg, ap. C. R. North, Second Isaiah, p. 228 f.

[16] Cf. E. Ullendorff, VT 6, p. 196, and S. D. F. Goitein in JPOS 14, p. 141.

connected with the Arab. *haḏala* 'was frustrated, lacked means and assistance; hung back and was separated from the flock/herd' (Freytag), which is in harmony with the meaning here assigned to the word, may be suspected[17].

Further, the meaning of ידוע חלי cannot be 'acquainted with grief' (R.V.; for, if taken from ידע 'knew', it must mean 'known by grief'); and the LXX's εἰδὼς φέρειν μαλακίαν and Sa'ad.'s באלאמראץ מערוף 'known for sicknesses' are but attempts to evade the difficulty. If, however, it is translated 'submissive under sickness'; the verb is the Hebr. יָדַע = Arab. *wadu'a'* was quiet, submissive'[18] which has now been recognized in a number of passages[19], and the difficulties disappear[20]. The Gr. γενόμενος ὑπηκόος μεχρὶ θανατου and δια τῆς ὑπακουῆς τοῦ ἑνός might be cited in illustration of the present interpretation of the Hebrew verb[21].

V. 4. That נגוע 'stricken' is rightly translated *leprosus* by Jerome, though possible, is improbable. That those addressed only considered him 'stricken' is against such a view; for a leper must have been visibly such. A general sense is therefore preferable. In either case it refers to something different from the connotation implied in 'struck down' or 'stricken to death', where the reference is to being struck down by an unjust judicial sentence.

V. 5. The various translations of מחולל 'wounded' (LXX, Vulg.) or 'killed' (Pesh.) or 'profaned' (Aq. and Targ., in which it is applied to the sanctuary) or 'sickened' (Sa'ad.) are interesting, as showing that 'pierced', as the word may be rendered, is taken by only one of the ancient interpreters as necessarily importing the death of the Servant; and the same point may be made on 'wounded' (A.V., R.V.) and 'pierced' (B.-D.-B.). That 'the strong verbs »pierced« and »crushed« are probably metaphors expressing the fatal ravages of leprosy' (Skinner)is a flight of fancy, and the attempt to support the suggestion

[17] Cf. Is 2 22 Job 19 14; s. D. W. Thomas, Suppl VT 4, p. 11f.

[18] Cf. Syr. *yd'* (Pesh. at Ps 119 158 and Ezr 4 13).

[19] E.g. Gen 18 21 Judg 8 16 16 9 Hos 9 7 Is 9 8 Jer 14 18 31 18 Ps 14 4 35 15 53 5 138 6 Job 9 5 20 20 21 19 37 7 Prov 5 6 9 13 10 9 13 20 14 33 19 9 Dan 12 4 Sir 7 20. The sense is not equally certain in all these passages.

[20] Reiske, Jobus 5, p. 76; Michaelis, NOEB. 7, p. 20f.; Kennicott, RSPOT. p. 222; Thomas, JTS 35, p. 298–306; 36, p. 409–12; 37, p. 59f.; 38, p. 404f.; 39, p. 273f.; 41, p. 43f.; 42, p. 64f., and JTS, N.S. 4, p. 23f.; 5, p. 56; 6, p. 226; 12, p. 50f.; 15, p. 54f. and TRP 5, p. 12; Driver, JTS 38, p. 48f.; 41, p. 162, and O.B.L. I, p. 137, and JQR, N.S. 28, p. 119f., and ap. Gemser, Sprüche Salomos, [1963], p. 111f.; Buttenwieser, Psalms, p. 478.

[21] Phil 2 8 and Rom 5 19 (Allen, Vox Evangelica, p. 24–28).

by referring to the piercing of Rahab[22] serves only to show the preposterous evidence that a theologian can produce! Neither מחולל nor מדכא per se imports the death of the victim; indeed, the whole context suggests that these and the other expressions used to describe the sufferings of the Servant refer to physical ill-treatment and not to his death at the hands of his fellow-men.

V. 7. The force of והוא 'and he' is to introduce an antithetic notion[23], here 'though oppressed, yet he humbled himself'. Clearly נאלמה 'dumb' belongs rhythmically and in sense with כרחל לפני גוזיה, and its omission by one Hebr. MS is accidental, while the following ולא יפתח פיו is a vertical dittograph from the end of the preceding verse and, being hypermetrical, must be deleted (Lagarde).

V. 8. Many translations have been proposed for מעצר וממשפט לקח 'by oppression and judgement he was taken away' (R.V.). For example, it has been thought to mean that he was carried off to execution after an oppressive i.e. unjust sentence, or that he was so carried off 'without hindrance and without right' or that he was taken by God to Himself so as to be far from i.e. to escape unjust condemnation and execution. The $\sqrt{}$*'ṣr*, however, in the Semitic languages hardly connotes oppression, and whether the phrase can mean 'unhindered' is almost equally uncertain; for the root imports being shut up, closed, detained rather than hindered. Possibly the best explanation is 'after detention/arrest (cf. Pesh.'s and Sa'ad.'s 'after imprisonment') and after sentence'[25] or perhaps rather 'without protection (of kin) and without due legal procedure', which the Arab. *'uṣru(n)* 'asylum, refuge', *'aṣîru(n)* 'dependent on the family' and *'a'ṣiru* 'kinsmen' suggest; this use of the root seems to occur also in עצור ועזוב 'protected by the clan and destitute of a clan's protection' i.e. 'kinsman and (unprotected) guest', meaning 'every man'[26].

Clearly 'who considered his generation' or the like is an unsatisfactory translation of את־דורו מי ישוחח, inasmuch as 'generation' barely makes, indeed does not make, sense in the context; this, however, can be won if the Hebr. דּוֹר is taken as meaning the same thing as the Acc. *dûru* 'lasting state' and the Arab. *dauru(n)* 'role (in life)'

[22] Is 51 9.

[23] Cf. Gen 48 14 (s. Joüon, Gramm. de l'Hébr. Bibl., § 171 f.).

[24] Skinner, Isaiah, II p. 143.

[25] Volz, Festschrift Budde, p. 182 (cf. II Kings 17 4 Jer 33 1 39 15 53 8).

[26] Yahuda, ZA 16, p. 240–58; cf. Vollers, BASS 5, p. 222, and Mowinckel, op. cit., p. 198.

and *aldârâni* 'the two states (i.e. this life and the next)[27], namely 'plight, fate'[28] or the like [29].

What exactly נגזר מארץ חיים 'he has been cut off from the land of the living' means is also not clear, namely whether the servant has been cut off, i.e. removed, from human society by imprisonment or by execution; for the following expressions are equally ambiguous. The second clause in this line is corrupt, as נֶגַע למו 'a blow for him' at the end is not possible, and נֻגַּע (Oort) or rather נִגַּע (Vitringa; cp. Scroll A's נוגע) 'he got himself smitten' may be read. The LXX's ἤχθη εἰς θάνατον suggests that they may have taken למו as an abbreviation for or a corruption of למות[30] and so have read נָגַע לַמָּוֶת 'he came near to death' (Houbigant) Alternatively, if נֻגַּע לַמָּוֶת or נֻגַּע 'he was stricken to death' is read, this is equally ambiguous, as it may mean only 'he was grievously stricken'; for 'to death' is a well known Semitic idiom for 'grievously, severely' (s. 53 12).

V. 9. No subject is expressed for וַיִּתֵּן 'and he gave'; it must then be the indefinite sg. 3rd person (cf. the indefinite pl. ויתנו in Scroll A and one Hebrew MS, de Rossi), unless the verb is read as the pass. וַיֻּתַּן 'and it (sc. his grave) was appointed' with one Hebrew MS (Kennicott). Which is read makes no essential difference to the sense. The parallel רשעים 'wicked' suggests that עשיר, which if kept must be altered to the pl. עשירים (Scroll A), 'rich' is not intended; it must then be a forgotten Hebr. עשיר 'rabble' which the Arab. *ġutru(n)* 'rabble, refuse of mankind' will support[32]; another suggestion worth mentioning is the Arab. *ʿatîru(n)* 'stumbling; corrupt, untruthful', even though it does not offer quite so appropriate a sense[33] and requires a plural form. Either interpretation is preferable to altering the text to עשי רע 'evildoers' (Böttcher); for all the Vss. support the consonants of the MT. The following בְּמֹתָיו 'in his deaths (sic)' is also improbable, and the Pesh.'s 'in his death' (cf. LXX and Vulg.) has suggested altering it to בְּמוֹתוֹ 'in his death', which has little point. The most favoured conjecture is בָּמָתוֹ 'his cairn, tomb' or the like (ibn Ezra)[34]; possibly a

[27] So in JTS 36, p. 403, and JBL 53, p. 285; cf. Nyberg, ZDMG, NF 17, p. 332.

[28] Cf. Ps 24 6.

[29] Possibly also in Discipline 3 14 4 15, where בדורותם may mean 'in their (appointed) destinies' rather than 'in their (respective) societies' (Brownlee, Discipline, p. 13); but 'in their generations' is not impossible (W.-Møller, Discipline, p. 67 f.).

[30] Driver, Textus 4, p. 94.

[31] Cf. Job 20 6 Est 4 14 II Chr 3 11. 12 for the preposition.

[32] R. North, Bibl 35, p. 1.

[33] Reider, VT 2, p. 118.

[34] Cf. Ez 43 17, where the same difficulty occurs.

preferable suggestion is to read בֵּית (=ב׳)־מוֹתוֹ 'his tomb' on the analogy of the Acc. *bît mûti* 'house of death' = 'grave'[35].

V. 10. The interpretation of both clauses in ויהוה הפץ דַּכְּאוֹ הֶחֱלִי אִם־תָּשִׂים אשם נפשו presents difficulties, and translations like 'yet it pleased the Lord to bruise him; he hath put him to grief; when thou shalt make his soul an offering for sin ...' (R.V.) are to all intents and purposes nonsense, and attempts to elucidate what they mean are a waste of time, so that emendation becomes necessary. The Vss., though almost equally at sea, throw out hints which may serve as pointers to the original text and its meaning.

The LXX's καθαρίσαι 'to purify', which has a long priority over the Vulg.'s *conterere,* seem to show that the verb may be not the pure Hebr. דכא 'crushed' but an Aramaizing Hebr. דכה/דכא = זכה 'was pure, innocent, justified'. This verb is assumed again by several Vss. (whether rightly or wrongly is difficult to say) in לא דכאו עד היום הזה 'they have not shown themselves contrite' (Theod.) or they have not shown themselves innocent to this day' (Aq., Symm., Theod.); and the noun must be read in לשׁון־ שקר ישׂנא דַכָּיו 'a lying tongue hates its crushed ones', which is almost nonsense and must be corrected to דָכוּי or לשׁון־ שקר ישׂנא דִכּוּי 'a lying tongue hates innocence' or 'vindication' (LXX, Vulg., Pesh., Targ.), i.e. the slanderer dislikes seeing his victim cleared of his slanderous accusations[36]. An objection that has been brought against assuming דִּכָּא = זִכָּה 'declared innocent' or the like here is that דִּכָּא 'crushed' has just occurred in this very passage[37]. The objection, however, is very nearly a commendation of this interpretation of the verb; for the use of homonyms in totally different senses is characteristic not only of Exilic and post-Exilic literature[38] but also of this very poem, which has נענה 'was afflicted' and 'showed himself submissive', הפגיע 'inflicted' and 'interceded', נגע 'struck down' physically and judicially, possibly רבים 'many' and 'great' and חָפֵץ 'was pleased' beside חֵפֶץ 'business, cause'[39].

Then החלי 'he made sick', which cannot be paraphrased *in infirmitate* (Vulg.), is a solecism, is inappropriate to the picture and in any earl cannot stand without an object; and the 2nd person in תשים 'thou shalt make' is intolerable. Sense can be made by following Begrich in interchanging two letters and reading הֶחֱלִים אֶת־שָׂם אשם נפשו 'he

[35] Van Hoonacker, Rev Bibl N.S. 6, p. 526; cf. C.R. North, op. cit., p. 231. Cf. Acc. *bît mûti* and Syr. *bêt mîte'* 'house of the dead' for 'sepulchre, tomb.'

[36] Jer 44 10 and Prov 26 28; s. JTS 41, p. 174f., and JRAS 75, p. 168.

[37] C. R. North, op. cit., p. 231.

[38] Cf. Torrey, Second Isaiah, p. 199–203, where 28 instances in II Isaiah are listed.

[39] Cf. JTS 36 , p. 404 on *kesef* (Js 55 1–2), and ZAW 55, p. 68f. on *nefěs* (Is 58 10)

healed him who made himself an offering for sin'[40], which follows naturally on the preceding clause as here interpreted. The Targ.'s בדיל לנקאה מחובין 'in order to cleanse him of sins' hints at this interpretation of the clause, while חָלַם Q. 'was healthy' and Hi. 'restored to health' is established well enough in the O.T. to call for no detailed justification[41]. The construction of את with an anarthrous participle can be justified by several similar instances, if justification is needed[42]; but the pronominal suffix with נפשו 'his soul' in effect provides the necessary determination.

V. 11–12. In v. 11 the first clause is rhythmically defective, lacking one beat, and the verb has no object; the LXX supplies φῶς, whence אור has long been conjecturally restored (Houbigant), and its restoration has now been confirmed by Scroll A, which has this very word. The verb, however, is not ראה 'saw' but ראה = רוה 'was drenched, sated' as the parallel שׂבע 'was full, satisfied' shows; this verb, which has now been recognized in a number of passages[43], can take the term describing that with which the subject is filled, as here, in the accus. case[44]. The objection that ראה = רוה 'was drenched, flooded; filled tight' is an unsuitable verb to use with אור 'light' will not bear scrutiny[45]; for רוה is used here as elsewhere in parallelism with שׂבע 'was satisfied, surfeited'[46], and ראה with the same parallel verb may be similarly used in a metaphorical sense e.g. with various abstract notions as its object[47]. The same figure of speech, too, occurs elsewhere, as in 'the knowledge of a wise man shall abound as a flood'[48]. Finally the corresponding Syr. *rwâ* 'drank to satiety, was intoxicated' is freely used in a metaphorical sense, when the object with which

40 Stud. z. Deuterojesaja, p. 58.

41 Job 34 4 (Q.) and Js 38 6 (Hi.).

42 E.g. Js 64 4 Ez 2 2 16 32 (?) Ps 146 9.

43 E.g. Is 28 7 Jer 31 14 Thr 3 1 Ps 36 9 40 13, 50 23 60 5 91 16 Job 10 15 20 17 33 21 Prov 7 18 23 31 Koh 2 1 Sir 31 28; cf. I Macc 6 34.

44 Schultens ap. Dathe, Jobus, p. 45–6; Zweifel ap. Geiger in Jüd. Zeitschr. 4, p. 283; Derenburg, ibid., 5, p. 191; Geiger, ibid., 9, p. 120–123 (cp. Urschrift, p. 414); Ružička in ZA 25, p. 121; Ball, Job, p. 196; Torczyner, Hiob, p. 138, and Lash. w-Sef. 1, p. 45; de Vaux in Rev Bibl N.S. 48, p. 594; Driver in JTS 36, p. 151–153, and Anal. Bibl. et. Orient. II xx, p. 351, and Bibl 32, p. 187–188, and JSS 9 p. 348–349; Seligman in Tarbitz 27, p. 132; cp. Jer 31 14 for the accus. case.

45 C. R. North. op. cit., p. 233f.

46 Jer 31 14 and Thr 3 15.

47 Job 10 15 (affliction) and Ps 1 23 91 16 (salvation).

48 Ecclus 31 13 (16), where the Hebrew text is missing (Gr. ὡς κατακλυσμός, Vulg. *tanquam inundatio*); cf. 'floods of golden light' (Tyndall).

the subject is filled may be error, love, fear of God, and so on[49]. The objection rests on too narrow a view of the meaning of the root and of its possible semantic development. It is also not supported by incorrectly taking יראה in parallelism with בדעתו ; that מעמל נפשו and בדעתו on the one side and יראה and ישבע on the other are chiastically parallel terms is as clear as daylight and ought not to require restatement.

That החלה 'made sick' can mean also 'pierced, wounded', as Symm.'s τραυματισμός here suggests, even though the dictionaries may admit such a meaning (B.-D.-B.), is against the analogy of the Semitic languages and therefore cannot be accepted; and such a sense is nowhere necessary. So the copyist of the Scroll A of Isaiah, thinking this the sense, has ויחללהו 'and he pierced him' for the MT's החלי 'he made sick' (!).

The Hebr. חלה conceals several distinct verbs, as the cognate languages show. These are (1) Bab. *ḫalû* 'to be sick' and Aram. חֲלָא 'suffered'; (2) Arab. *ḥalā* 'adorned' and *ḥaliya* 'was adorned'; (3) Aram. חֲלֵי and Arab. *ḥalâ*, *ḥaliya* 'was sweet, pleasant', (4) Ugar. *ḫly* 'was alone' and Arab. *ḫalâ* I 'was alone, vacant, disengaged', II 'ceased from, abandoned (an affair)', IV 'evacuated (a place)', V 'disengaged oneself (from an affair), left the society (of one's fellow-men)'; and (5) Eth. *ḫalláya*, 'cared, cared for, thought of'.

The first three verbs are well enough known and therefore call for no consideration beyond a notice that some of the meanings commonly ascribed to them belong to one or other of the last two verbs. Thus חלה 'was sick', when used in connection with wounds, may well refer not to the actual injury or wound but to the consequent fever and ill-health[50]. Next the supposed חלה 'was sick in mind, anxious' is cognate not with *ḥalâ* 'suffered' but with *ḫalláya* 'cared'[51], as the context of the five passages in which it occurs clearly shows[52].

Other passages, where חלה 'was sick' is linguistically impossible, can and must be subsumed under *ḫalâ* 'was alone; was empty, emptied himself out'. The causative theme appears in חלה את־פני יהוה 'appeased, propitiated the Lord', meaning properly 'made the Lord's face free / unique i.e. secured his favour uniquely for himself'[53], as the corresponding Arab. 'let your father's face be free unique (*yaḫlu*) for you'[54] and many similar expressions show[55]. The passive form of the same verb occurs in 'thou too art left alone (חֻלֵּיתָ) 'i.e. removed from human society and become like us' i.e. numbered with the dead[56]. This verb may also be restored in two passages where ignorance of it has resulted in mis-vocalization. The first may be read חָלְתָה היא שָׁנְתָה ימין עליון 'is it (sc. God's hand) disengaged, has the Most High's right hand

[49] Payne Smith, Thes. Syr. II, 3840 f.

[50] II Kings 1 2 (injury due to falling from a window; cf. Josephus, Ant. Jud. IX 2 i 19, where it is rendered νοσήσας in agreement with the Vss.), and II Kings 8 29 (ill-health due to wounds received in battle).

[51] Eitan, HUCA 12/13, p. 82f.

[52] I Sam 12 8 Is 57 10 Jer 5 3 (where the accent must be shifted) Am 6 6 Prov 23 35.

[53] E.g. II Chr 32 12 (and passim).

[54] Qur'ân 12 9.

[55] Cf. Margoliouth in Hastings' 'D.B.' III 29.

[56] Is 14 10.

desisted / ceased to act?'[57]; and the second is וְיָחֵלּוּ ... מִמַּשָּׂא מלך [ו]שׂרים 'and they shall desist ... from setting up king [and] princes'[58] (cf. Theod.'s διαλείψουσι and Vulg.'s *quiescent*). The same root will explain רעה חוֹלָה 'unique', not 'sick disaster'[59] and הֶחֱלֵיתִי מכותך 'I have made thy smiting unique' i.e. given thee an unprecedented smiting' and נַחְלָה מכותך 'thy wound is unique / unprecedented'[60].

What verb is meant remains uncertain when Samson, suggesting various ways by which he may be outwitted, says וְחָלִיתִי 'then shall I become weak' (R.V.) like any other man[61]. That he will become sick or feverish as after a wound cannot be meant, and חלה 'was sick' does not seem applicable to a diminution or loss of miraculous muscular strength; and in fact both translations are ruled out by 'like any other man'. Weakness is not a characteristic mark of all men. Two possible explanations of the verb, however, suggest themselves in the light of the foregoing discussion. The verb intended by the writer may be that cognate with the Arab. *ḥalâ* 'was pleasing, sweet' and the post-Bill. Hebr. חלה 'mollified' as in הרי בניך מרים חַלֵּה אותן 'lo! thy sons are cruel; mollify them'[62]; Samson will accordingly have meant 'then I shall become amenable/tractable' i.e. as easy to manage as other men. Alternatively, the verb may be identical with the Arab. *ḫalâ* 'was alone; was empty, emptied himself out', when Samson will have meant 'then I shall be emptied out (sc. of my strength)' or 'left alone' i.e. defenceless, so as to become physically like other men[63]. Which verb is meant can hardly be decided, especially as the ancient Vss. throw no light on the problem.

Another verb commonly referred to the √*ḥlh* occurs in (מאד) הָחֳלֵיתִי 'I am (sore) wounded', as it is commonly but wrongly translated (R.V.); for 'I have been made (very) sick', which is the correct translation[64], is a remark which is barely conceivable in the mouth of a man who has been fatally wounded in battle. Further, these three passages cannot be separated from וַיָּחֶל מאד 'and he was greatly distressed' (R.V.)[65] in the account of Saul's death where this translation yields a very dubious sense; the verb here must be referred to the √*ḥll* and read וַיּוּחַל 'and he was pierced (sc. by arrows)' or 'wounded (by the archers)', as the LXX's ἐτραυματίσθη and Vulg'.s *vulneratus est* show. This Hebr. חלל Hi. 'pierced', Ho. 'was pierced' may then be identified with the Arab. *ḫalla* I 'penetrated', V 'pierced with successive thrusts of a lance or spear'. Similarly הָחֳלֵיתִי 'I have been made sick' may be vocalized הוּחַלּוֹתִי 'I have been pierced, wounded', which the Vulg.'s *vulneratus sum* in all three passages supports and which perfectly fits the context. Further, in the last passage the LXX render מאד by εἰς τὰ ὑποχόνδρια 'in the soft under-belly', which also suits the context extremely well; this מאד (however vocalized) can be easily explained as cognate with the Arab. *ma'ada* 'was soft', with which the Arab.

[57] Ps 77 11 (where the MT has חַלּוֹתִי and שְׁנוֹת, neither of which makes sense); cf.: Syr. *šnâ* 'departed, receded', which explains the last verb.

[58] Hos 8 10 (MT וַיָּחֵלּוּ).

[59] Koh 5 12. 15; s. Eitan, loc. cit., p. 63.

[60] Mi 6 13 and Nah 3 19.

[61] Judg 16 7. 11. 17.

[62] Jastrow, Dictionary II, 467.

[63] Eitan, op. cit., p. 2.

[64] I Kings 12 34 = II Chr 18 33 35 23.

[65] I Sam 31 3.

ma'du(n) 'soft, fresh', *ma'adu(n)* 'flank, belly' and *mi'datu(n)* 'stomach' are connected as words derived from a strengthened form of the same root.

All forms of the √*ḥlh* must be kept distinct from the √*ḥl'* which occurs once or twice. The first passage is תַּחֲלֻאֶיהָ אשר חלה יהוה בה־ 'its extreme prostration which the Lord let loose upon it (sc. the land of Israel)'[66]. Clearly the verb is not חלה Q. 'was sick' (B.-D.-B.), partly because this verb hardly suits the accompanying noun and partly because this causative form does not occur elsewhere[67]. It too is clearly cognate with the Arab. *ḫallā* 'left alone, let go, dismissed, let loose', with which the LXX's ἀπέστειλεν 'sent' (cf. Pesh.) and Targ. Ps.-Jon'.s גרי 'let loose' exactly agree. Equally clearly תחלאים has no connection with חלה 'was sick', if only because of its final letter, but must be referred to the Arab. *ḫala'a* 'prostrated on the ground, scourged, took the skin off (a person); forced (a woman)'[68]; it occurs only twice again, where the context shows that it describes symptoms of famine or starvation[69], while the intensive pl. form suggests 'extreme, utter prostration', here again that caused by hunger, as its true meaning. This explanation of the Hebrew word tallies nicely with the final symptoms which Procopius[70] describes in his account of one of the sieges of Rome by the Goths, when the inhabitants of the city had only nettles to eat, which they boiled to prevent the pungent herbs from stinging their lips; but they soon found this diet insufficient, their flesh withered away and took on a livid hue[71], giving them a ghostly appearance; and many, even as they walked along chewing nettles, were suddenly seized by death and fell to the ground (ἔθνησκόν τε καί ἐκ τοῦ αἰφνιδίου ἐς γῆν ἔπιπτον). The second passage is that describing the malady of which king Asa died. One account is that חאה את־רגליו 'he was diseased in his feet' (R.V.) while the other has וַיֶּחֱלֶא ... ברגליו 'and he was diseased? ... in his feet' (R.V.)[72]. The Vss. offer no help, all having colourless verbs denoting illness, whereas the different forms of the verb (חלא, חלה), although they may be nothing but variations of the same verb, suggest different roots. Such a disease of the feet, longstanding and terminating fatally at an advanced age, can hardly have been other than senile gangrene[73], as the Chronicler seems to have thought; for, while this disease is painful, it is also malodorous, so that the king is said by him to have been laid after death' in the bed which he (?) had (had) filled with sweet odours and divers kind of spices by the apothecaries' art; and they prepared very great quantities of resinous substances for him', i.e. they buried his

[66] Dtn 29 21.

[67] The Pi. is cited only once again in an obviously corrupt passage (Ps 77 11), and the Pu. where it is cited comes from a different root (Is 14 10).

[68] So Venema ap. Michaelis, Jerem. Vatic., [1793], p. 143; cf. Scharbert, Der Schmerz im Alten Testament, p. 37f.

[69] Jer 14 18 16 4.

[70] In the 'History of the Wars (Gothic War)', VII xvii 13–18.

[71] Cf. Thr 5 10 (cf. Syr. *kmîr* 'black').

[72] I Kings 15 23 = II Chr 16 12.

[73] Short, The Bible and Modern Medicine, p. 28. Neither dropsy (Epstein, Medizin im Alten Testament, p. 148) nor gout (Preuss, Biblisch-Talmudische Medizin, p. 191f.) nor some disease of the genital organs on the assumption that רגלים is here a euphemism for them (Humbert in RHPR 44, p. 4) suit the symptons as) her interpreted.

body in such preparations to drown the stench as the bodies of Saul and his sons were treated with such stuffs as preservatives before being transported to Jabesh Gilead[74]. This Hebr. חלא must then be equated with the S.-Arab. *ḫl'* 'was foul, defiled' and the classical Arab. *ḥali'a* 'was covered with pustules', whence *tiḥli'u(n)*, *tiḥli'atu(n)* 'dirty black marks on the skin' is derived, while the Acc. *ḫalû* 'black moles on the skin' and the Soc. *ḥal'eh* 'dirt' may also be compared[75]. The same Hebrew root may be recognized again in כנחשת רועו יחליא 'his wickedness is foul as verdigris on copper'[76] and in חֶלְיָה 'sooty deposit' left by fire on the bottom of a kettle or cauldron[77]. Briefly, the root describes dark-coloured, dirty-looking patches on metal or the human skin, pustules (on the lips) and so on[77a], and thus agrees with the suggestion that the disease here meant is gangrene; for in this disease the skin is badly discoloured and in its advanced stages *bullae* may be formed, in consequence of the development of putrefactive gases, under it. That the Chronicler goes on to speak of the disease as a חלי 'malady' is immaterial; he is simply using a general term to describe a specific condition for which an exact term has ceased to be necessary. The same thing may be said of the author or compiler of Kings, when he uses חלה 'he was diseased' to describe the king's condition, unless this is a variant form of or an error for חלא 'he was gangrenous'[78].

The second clause of this verse is rhythmically defective, lacking one beat, while the first clause of v. 12 has one beat too many; there too צדיק עבדי cannot be translated 'my righteous servant' (R.V.), which is grammatically impossible. If then צַדִּיק 'righteous' is transferred from after יצדיק and is put before it as צֶדֶק 'righteousness', the verb gains an object parallel to the restored אור 'light' in the parallel clause; the line may then be rendered literally 'after/through the travail of his soul he shall be sated with light, by his suffering he shall be filled with i.e. win full justification'[79]. Thus דעת 'humiliation'

[74] I Sam 31 3; cf. Am 6 10 (s. ZAW 66, p. 314f.).

[75] V. Soden, Akkadisches Handwörterbuch, I 314, and Leslau, Ethiopic and South Arabian Contributions to the Hebrew Lexicon, p. 20.

[76] Ecclus 12 10 (LXX ἰοῦται, Vulg. *aeruginat*).

[77] Ez 24 6. 11. 12 (LXX ἰός, Vulg. *rubigo*, Targ. ויהומתא 'filth, sediment'; s. Ehrlich, Randglossen, V. p. 94.

[77a] Also חֳלִי 'sores' (Js 1 5).

[78] The sufferer from senile gangrene normally does not live long (cf. Galen, Opera Omnia VII *de tumoribus* § 8, who says that the necrosis, unless it is healed διὰ ταχέων, spreads ῥᾳδίως and causes death), commonly dying in a couple of months; but Sir George W. Pickering, Regius Professor of Medicine, says in a private communication (dated on 31 March 1966) that 'it is unusual for gangrene to spread like this over the course of a year when it is due to arterial restriction, but it is possible. I have seen cases like this'. Further, the compiler of Kings says nothing of the duration of the disease, and the statement of the author of Chronicles that Asa was attacked by the disease in the 39th. year and died of it in the 41st. year of his reign ought not to be pressed too hard; it may indicate but a little over a year, and even this may be an exaggeration of the period (if it is not actually fictitious) characteristic of the Chronicler's work.

catches up ידוע חלי 'humbled by suffering' in v. 3; for 'knowledge' here is off the point, whatever sense may be read into it, as something parallel to 'the travail of his soul' is required. Accordingly, the alteration of בדעתו[80] into ברעתו 'by his evil fate'[80a] becomes needless.

V. 12. In the first line יְחַלֵּק 'he shall allot a share' must be read יֵחָלֵק 'he shall receive a share' to bring out the contrast with אֲחַלֵּק 'I will allot as a share'; but whether the alteration of בָּרַבִּים to בְּרַבִּים is a gain is not clear although in this form it agrees with the parallel term.

Unfortunately the Massoretes seem to have confused חָלַק 'received a share' and חִלֵּק 'divided, distributed shares' in their vocalization of the MT; for the post-Bibl. Hebr. חִלֵּק 'distributed' is decisive as against the Syr. *ḥlaq* 'distributed' in favour of this interpretation (rather than vice versa) of the two themes. Accordingly the Q. 'took a share' as read in six passages may be accepted as the norm[82] and must be corrected to Pi. in the eight places when the context requires 'divided, distributed'[83]; similarly the Pi. may be accepted in the five passages where it means 'divided, distributed shares'[84] but must be corrected to the Q. in the three where 'received a share' is the sense required by the context[85].

In the second clause the force of הערה למות נפשו 'he poured out his soul unto the death' (R.V.) is again uncertain and equivocal. The Vss. take this to mean that he was delivered up to death, which does not necessarily imply that he was put to death, although it may have this force. Saʿadyah, however, has גרר למות נפסה 'he laid bare/exposed his soul unto death', which may be the sense also in אל־תער נפשי 'do not empty out my soul (i.e. deprive it of defences)/, do not lay my soul utterly bare'[86], where death is not mentioned.

The use of לַמָּוֶת or לָמוּת 'to death' as expressing a superlative degree and so meaning 'utterly' or the like[87] has been detected in a number of passages of the Old and of the New Testaments[88]. In the

[79] Cf. Torrey, op. cit., p. 421f., and Driver, Orient. et Bibl. Lovan. I., p. 134f., and Judaean Scrolls, p. 256f., 443.

[80] Cf. דעת 'chastisement' (Dan 12 4).

[80a] Ritschl ap. Dillmann; s. Ehrlich, Randglossen, IV p. 192.

[81] Bertholet, ThLZ 48 20.

[82] Josh 18 2 22 8 I Sam 30 24 II Sam 19 30 Job 27 17 Prov 17 2.

[83] Dtn 4 19 29 25 (cf. 32 8) Josh 14 3 I Chr 29 25 II Chr 23 18 Neh 9 22 Job 39 17.

[84] Ex 15 9 Judg 5 30 Is 9 2 53 12(1) Prov 16 19.

[85] Gen 49 27 Ps 68 13 (cf. Judg 5 30) Is 53 12(2).

[86] Ps 141 8.

[87] Torrey, Second Isaiah, p. 423, and Thomas, VT 3, p. 219–22.

[88] E.g. Judg 16 16 Jon 4 9 Ps 18 5–6; Mat 26 38 and Mk 14 34.

same way 'to death' is used in other Syriac, as also in Arabic, literature; and the Engl. 'tired to death' and similar expressions show how widespread the idiom is[89].

Finally Scroll A's לפשעם 'for their transgressions', though supported by no ancient Vss., has sometimes found favour, although the alteration is not in any way necessary; the object too for whom or which intercession is made is elsewhere not the offence but the offender[90]. Yet a variation on את־פשעים 'with transgressors' in the previous clause is attractive[91].

The poem may now be translated

13 Lo! my servant shall be bound and lifted up,
he shall be raised aloft, very high.
14 As once men were aghast at you,
[O my people, for many days],
15 So now mighty nations shall be startled
and kings shall purse their mouths in disgust at him;
for they shall see what had never been told
and shall ponder things never heard before.
1 Can anyone have believed what we have heard,
and to whom has the power of the Lord been revealed?
2 Yet in his sight he shot up like a sapling,
like a root in parched ground;
he had neither beauty nor majesty to attract our gaze,
no form that we could delight in him,
14 his form so disfigured as to lose all likeness to a man,
his beauty marred beyond human semblance.
3 He was despised, one who shrank from men's sight,
A man tormented and humbled by suffering;
An object from which men turn their gaze,
despised and held of no account by us.
4 Yet himself he bore our sufferings
and our torments he endured,
while we accounted him smitten,
struck down by God and afflicted.
5 Yet for our transgression he was pierced,
bruised for our guilty deeds;
his chastisement was health for us
and by his scourging we were healed,
6 All of us had gone astray like sheep,
each of us had gone our own way;
but the Lord laid upon him
the punishment of us all.

89 Cf. II Kings 20 1 = Js 38 1, where King Hezekiah is said to be sick למות but does not die.

90 Gen 23 8.

91 Cf. Sellin, ZAW 55, p. 209.

7 Though hard pressed, he submitted himself
and did not open his mouth
like a sheep that is led to the slaughter,
like a ewe that is dumb before the shearers.
8 Without protection, without justice he was taken away;
and who gave a thought to his plight,
that he was cut off from the world of living men,
struck down for my people's transgression,
9 (that) a grave was appointed for him with the wicked,
his burial place with the rabble,
although he had done no violence
nor had spoken an untrue word?
10 But the Lord was pleased to give him the victory
and restored him who had made himself an offering for sin;
so, enjoying long life, shall he see his children's children,
and in his hand shall the Lord's cause prosper.
11 After his pains he shall be flooded with light,
through his humiliation he shall win full justification;
so shall my servant justify many,
himself bearing the penalty for their guilt.
12 Therefore I will allot him a portion with the great
and he shall take a portion of the spoil with the mighty,
because he has exposed his life even to death
and let himself be counted with transgressors,
because himself he has borne the sin of many
and made intercession for transgressors.

Two questions remain and call for an answer.

First, did the Servant die? Here the curious point calls for notice that no phrase is used which unambiguously implies his death. The text says that he was 'pierced', which is not necessarily fatal[92], that he was dumb 'like a sheep led to the slaughter', a figure of speech describing his refusal to answer questions, that 'he was taken away', i.e. arrested, that 'he was cut off from the land of living men' which may refer only to solitary confinement away from the society of men, that 'he was stricken to death', which may mean morely that he was grievously ill-treated, and that 'his grave was appointed' in such and such a place, which does not necessarily imply that he was ever laid in it. Contrariwise, the text says that after his sufferings 'he shall be flooded with light', which may mean simply that he will recover from the ill-treatment, when he will suddenly be enlightened and understand the purpose of his sufferings, that 'he will prolong (his) days' and that 'he will see children's children' i.e. that he will recover his health and live long enough to see grand-children, and that 'the Lord's cause will prosper in his hand'; and that finally he will be

[92] Cf. II Kings 18 21 = Is 36 6.

richly rewarded because 'he exposed his life to (the risk of) death'. The first group of expressions are frankly equivocal and cannot be used to prove one thing or the other; the last group can hardly be taken in any other than their literal sense. That a poet may have imagined the death and resurrection of an ill-treated fellow-Jew in Babylon during the Exile and have conceived of him after such a resurrection as looking down from heaven on his children's children (who cannot be his 'spiritual children'; for 'seed' is a purely physical term in the Old Testament) is barely, indeed is not, credible. That the passage is quoted in the New Testament as foretelling the sufferings of Christ does not mean that every word and phrase in it must be forcibly assimilated to the use made of it by writers adapting its language to a purpose which the original writer may not and indeed cannot have had in mind. The picture is surely that of one who, having been mistakenly thought wrong and been accordingly maltreated, is by Divine providence eventually proved right and restored to his former position of influence in the society in which he lives to enjoy a ripe old age, honoured by all men.

The second question is: Who was the Servant? This is one to which many answers, as imaginative as they are improbable, have been given. That 'he' is the personified community gives a vagueness to the picture which robs it of much of its force and appeal. If he had been some well-known figure already dead, why should the poet have lost a significant point by withholding his name? No harm can have been done by revealing it. The simplest solution and the most obvious would seem to be that he was some unknown Jew, whether teacher or preacher or prophet, whose message inflamed and alarmed his fellow-countrymen or perhaps the Babylonian authorities against him; for Jews might resent his denunciation of their apostasy or fear that he would embroil them with the Babylonians and bring down dire punishment on themselves, while the Babylonians might regard him as a dangerous fanatic urging rebellion on his fellow-exiles[93]. In either case he was successful in his mission, whatever it was, and was restored to favour with his fellow-men, Jews or Babylonians, and richly rewarded for the faithful fulfilment of the task which God had laid upon him. His name will never be known but his memory will live for ever in one of the noblest passages of Hebrew literature.

In conclusion, I offer this examination of a famous passage as a small tribute to the memory of a great teacher and an outstanding scholar

זריז בכ״ד ספרים

whose works have thrown a flood of light on the Hebrew language and whose teaching has inspired pupils from many lands.

[93] Cf. Judaean Scrolls, p. 216, 314, 348–50.

A Letter of Hārūn ar-Rashīd to the Emperor Constantine VI

By D. M. Dunlop

(Middle East Institute, Columbia University, New York, N. Y.)

The following enquiry is based on a document which might well have come from the archives of the ʿAbbāsids, and perhaps did so at one point. Its actual source is unknown to me. It was printed separately with a brief introduction and testimonia from highly respectable Egyptian authorities under the title *Risālah Abī ar-Rabīʿ Muḥammad b. al-Laith ilā Qusṭanṭīn malik ar-Rūm* in 1355/1936 at Cairo by al-Ustādh Asʿad Luṭfī Ḥasan from a larger work of his, *Kitāb al-Islām*, where doubtless the immediate provenance of the *Risālah* is fully explained. This I have been unable to see (but cf. Postcript). Asʿad Luṭfī Ḥasan sub-titled his edition *hiyā ar-risālatu 'llatī baʿatha bihā 'l-Khalīfat al-ʿAbbāsī Hārūn ar-Rashīd*, 'it is the letter sent by the ʿAbbāsid Caliph Hārūn ar-Rashīd'. Since Hārūn reigned from 170/786 to 193/809, the Constantine in question should be the Byzantine Emperor Constantine VI (reigned 780–797), and, as we know from Ṭabarī[1], Abū ar-Rabīʿ Muḥammad b. al-Laith, stated to be the actual writer of the Caliph's letter, was a contemporary. On the face of it therefore there is no reason to doubt the authenticity of the *Risālah*.

The work consists of about ninety pages of text (p. 19–110). Much of it is taken up with a theoretical statement of the claims of Islam vis-à-vis Christianity, courteous in tone, though sometimes sharply polemical. This is by way of preliminary to the last part of the *Risālah* in which the Commander of the Faithful summons Constantine to Islam, in order to ensure his welfare in this life and the next. If he is concerned only for this world, he is advised to accept the necessity of paying tribute (*jizyah*) (p. 100). A formal demand of this kind made to a Byzantine emperor is, so far as my information goes, unparalleled. The *Risālah* then describes the advantages which formerly accrued to the Byzantines 'in the days of the ransom' (*aiyām al-fidyah*) and the disadvantages under which they now suffer, showing how the different classes are affected and going into some detail: the Byzantine generals, who today are awaiting armies from every pass (p. 101), the agriculturists and proprietors, who to-

[1] Annals, *sub anno* 187 / 803 (III, ii, 668).

day are prevented from cultivating their lands (p. 102), the merchant class, who are no longer able to trade with the Muslims as formerly and have lost their profits (p. 103), the clergy, who now have to urge their flocks to fight their fear and to oppose the pacific command of Christ about turning the other cheek (p. 103f.), and the country people who, instead of enjoying security and leisure, are faced with the prospect of seeing their wives and children led captive, their flocks and herds destroyed, their trees and produce ruined and their homes abandoned, all of which disasters happened in the previous state of war (p. 104f.). The Commander of the Faithful has long been astonished that by abandoning an arrangement so favourable to yourselves, you have endangered your future, especially since you have in doing so broken the most solemn oaths, taken publicly by the authority of your patricians and bishops (p. 105f.). God will assuredly punish such conduct, and the Commander of the Faithful will be the instrument of God's vengeance. His resolution to attack you, unless you now pay the *jizyah*, is fixed. This *Risālah* is his messenger to you preceding his soldiers and the herald announcing the arrival of his armies (p. 108). The authenticity of the *Risālah*, which is not in doubt, will, I take it, have been sufficiently established if the circumstances in which it was sent and the approximate date can be ascertained.

Further, the *Risālah* makes somewhat extensive use of the Old and New Testaments, and this is interesting, especially in view of the date, presumably towards the close of the 8th century A.D., a long time before the famous Arabic translation of the Old Testament by Saʿadiah Gaon (died 942), and earlier than the *Kitāb ad-Dīn wa'd-Daulah* (Book of Religion and Empire) of ʿAlī b. Rabban aṭ-Ṭabarī (ʿAlī Ṭabarī)[2], which was completed at the court of al-Mutawakkil (Caliph 232/847–247/861) and contains numerous Arabic Bible quotations. The *Risālah* of ʿAbd Allāh b. Ismāʿīl al-Hāshimī (to which the well-known *Apology of al-Kindī* is the reply), represented as having been written at the court of Hārūn's heir al-Ma'mūn, contains only Qur'ānic quotations. We cannot think of Muḥammad b. al-Laith providing his quotations for himself, as might have been done by a John of Damascus, if he is the author of the Arabic polemical works which circulate under his name. As a Muslim of Iranian stock, (see below), no convert from Judaism or Christianity, it is next to impossible that Muḥammad b. al-Laith knew the original languages, and Syriac also is very unlikely. These Biblical quotations appear to be almost the earliest[2a] which we have in a Muslim author. What then is their origin?

The *Risālah* thus offers two problems, one historical, the other literary. I would hope that the attempted solutions of both might have

[2] Transl. A. Mingana, 1922; text ed. Mingana, 1923. [2a] See below.

been of interest to my late teacher, Prof. Kahle, who as well as being a great Biblical scholar, was eminently at home in the history of Islam.

According to Ṭabarī and many other authors[3] the Byzantine Emperor Nicephorus I, shortly after his accession in 802, denounced the existing treaty with the Arabs and refused to pay tribute, thereby arousing the Caliph's indignation and precipitating an attack upon himself. In the words of Ṭabarī[4], 'When Nikfūr (Nicephorus) began to rule and the Byzantines submitted quietly to him, he wrote to ar-Rashīd; "From Nicephorus, king of the Greeks, to Hārūn, king of the Arabs. To proceed[5], the queen who was before me (sc. Irene, reigned with Constantine VI 780–790, alone 797–802) put you in the place of the rook (*rukhkh*, castle at chess) and herself in the place of the pawn. She sent to you of her wealth many times what you should have sent her. But this was women's weakness and folly. So when you read my letter, restore the moneys you have received from her, and pay a ransom for yourself by which you may be released from the reckoning. If not, the sword is between us and you." When ar-Rashīd read the letter, he was transported by rage, so that none might look at him, much less address him. The company scattered, fearful of saying or doing anything. The vizier was at a loss whether to give him advice, or leave him to act alone. (The Caliph) then called for pen and ink, and wrote on the back of the letter: "In the name of God, the Merciful, the Compassionate, from Hārūn, Commander of the Faithful, to Nikfūr (Nicephorus), dog of the Greeks. I have read your letter, o son of an unbelieving mother. You will see the answer rather than hear it".' On the same day, Ṭabarī tells, Hārūn set his armies in motion. The Caliph's rage which has echoed down the centuries seems disproportionate, even for an irascible man upon the denunciation of a treaty. What was the agreement which had been broken? In 165 / August 781—August 782, during the lifetime of his father, the Caliph al-Mahdī, Hārūn had led in person a huge army to the sea of Marmora. The ruler in Byzantium was then the Augusta Irene, acting for her son, Constantine VI, who was still a boy. The Arab invaders got into difficulties, and it became mutually advantageous to call off hostilities. Envoys passed between Hārūn and the Empress, according to Ṭabarī[6] 'for seeking peace, reconciliation and the payment of ransom' (*fī ṭalab aṣ-ṣulḥ wa'l-muwāda'ah wa-i 'ṭā' al-fidyah*), to which Hārūn agreed, adding that the money proposed

[3] Ṭabarī, Ibn al-Athīr, Suyūṭī, and among the moderns Sir W. Muir, E. H. Palmer, Ameer Ali, Philip Hitti, S. F. Mahmud, J. J. Saunders, etc. all give the story.

[4] III, ii, 695.

[5] The Arabic words so translated (*ammā ba'du*) mean literally 'but afterwards' and are customary after the preliminaries of letters, etc.

[6] III, i, 504.

should be paid, and that guides and markets should be provided for the Muslims on the march back. The amount mentioned was 70,000 or 90,000 dīnārs[7], to be paid in Nīsān (April) and Ḥazīrān (June) every year. A truce was arranged for three years, and the prisoners taken by the Arabs, to the number of over 5000, were handed over. More than 2000 prisoners had already been killed in cold blood. It would appear that the money payment, though due at regular intervals over a period of years, was represented as ransom (*fidyah*) for the prisoners (and may have been initially agreed to in order to save as many lives as possible), not tribute (*jizyah*). Yet it is to be noted that the latter term 'tribute' appears in the narrative of Ṭabarī, and again in a poem which he quotes describing the event[8].

According to Theophanes for the same event (A.M. 6274 / A.D. 782)[9], Hārūn advances to the Bosporus, where he can apparently effect nothing. A Muslim victory is won by a subordinate commander, but the Arabs are checked by the Domesticus, and on the prompting of a deserter seek peace. The Augusta and Hārūn then exchange many gifts, and they agree that she will pay (tribute) to the Arabs every year (*stoikhēsantes kai* ⟨*phorous*⟩ *kata kairon* [Latin version, *per singulos annos*] *telein autois*). We learn from the *Risālah* itself that Hārūn prevailed on his father to accept the ransom[10]. The fact of the tribute (apparently there so called) is confirmed in Byzantine official records[11].

But it was not this arrangement of 782 that was broken by Nicephorus in 802, for it had been broken long before, before even the expiration of the stipulated three years' term. This is plain from Ṭabarī, who again gives the circumstances[12]. 'Then began the year 168 / 784–785, the events of which included the breach by the Byzantines of the peace which had run between them and Hārūn b. al-Mahdī as we have previously mentioned, an act of treachery on their part, in Ramaḍān of this year. Between the beginning of the peace and the treachery of the Byzantines and their breach of it was a period of thirty months. 'Alī b. Sulaimān who at that time was governor of al-Jazīrah and Qinnasrīn sent Yazīd b. Badr b. al-Baṭṭāl with a raiding party against the Byzantines. They took booty and were victorious'.

[7] The uncertainty is evidently dependent on the reading of some Arabic text. 'Seven' and 'nine' when written in words are easily confused.

[8] Ibid., 505.

[9] Ed. De Boor, p. 456.

[10] P. 110.

[11] G. Ostrogorsky, History of the Byzantine State, transl. J. Hussey, 1957, p. 162 n. 1, citing F. Dölger, Regesten der Kaiserurkunden des oströmischen Reiches, p. 340.

[12] III, i, 521.

Ramaḍān, A.H. 168 when the Byzantines denounced the treaty corresponds to March, A.D. 785. Thirty months from then takes us back to August or September, 782, for the inception of the agreement, which plainly the Byzantines broke just before the April payment in the third year was due. Irene was still acting as regent for her son (till 790)[13]. Al-Mahdī was still Caliph, till later in 785, when he was succeeded briefly by his elder son al-Hādī.

The very short Caliphate of of al-Hādī and the early years of Hārūn (from 786) afforded no opportunities for attempting to coerce the Byzantines. But in 181/797–798 war was renewed on a large scale. Hārūn, now Caliph, once again headed the Muslim armies. For some reason details are lacking in our principal sources, Ṭabarī and Ibn al-Athīr, but we read that the Caliph subdued the fortress of aṣ-Ṣafṣāf[14] ('the Willows') near al-Maṣṣīṣah (Mopsuestia in Cilicia), and one of his generals reached Ancyra (Ankara). Information is scanty also on the Greek side, but it can scarcely be doubted that Constantine's lack of success against the invading Arabs was a contributory cause of his tragic deposal by his mother's orders, which happened not long after his return to Constantinople (August, 797)[14a].

Irene, upon assuming supreme power, made peace with the Arabs, and the tribute was renewed[15]. It was this tribute which, paid apparently during successive years of her reign, was denounced by Nicephorus. Evidently the *Risālah* was sent to Constantinople at some point in the sequence of events which has just been traced. But before saying more on this, the writer has a claim on our attention. Muḥammad b. al-Laith is mentioned once by Ṭabarī, in the passage already cited[16], as having been the first to lay a complaint against the Barmecides. This he did in the form of another *risālah*. Hārūn sent for Yaḥyā b. Khālid, the head of the family, and asked him if he knew Muḥammad b. al-Laith, and what he thought about him. Yaḥyā, who had heard about the memorial, replied that he did and that Muḥammad b. al-Laith was suspected as a heretic. He was thereupon imprisoned for a time, till after the disgrace of the Barmecides.

[13] Sir John Glubb, The Empire of the Arabs, 1963, p. 281, ascribes the initiative in 785 to Constantine, who was still a minor.

[14] Ṭab., III, ii, 646. Muir gives Ephesus, which may be due to conjectural emendation of the text of Ibn al-Athīr, The Caliphate, ed. 3, p. 479.

[14a] Mas'ūdī (Tanbīh, Egyptiàn ed., 1938, p. 142 = transl. p. 227–228) reports the course of events somewhat loosely, saying that Constantine when he grew up (*nasha'a*) broke the peace, was then attached and defeated by Hārūn, and, returning to Constantinople, was blinded by his mother's orders.

[15] Again confirmed in the records, Ostrogorsky, Hist. of the Byz. State, p. 162, citing Dölger, Regesten, p. 352.

[16] III, ii, 668, sub anno 187.

Yaḥyā's charge was no doubt an attempt at self-defence, but there was some colour for it in the high Iranian origin of Muḥammad b. al-Laith, as leading to sympathy for Zoroastrianism. He was perhaps also open to suspicion as being a sympathiser with the devotees of mysticism[17]. The *Fihrist* says that he was of noble Persian ancestry, but says nothing about the mystical interest. More particularly to our purpose, the *Fihrist* mentions among his works one which may well be the same as the *Risālah*, calling it *Jawāb Qusṭanṭīn ʿan ar-Rashīd*[18]. This may signify 'Reply to Constantine for ar-Rashīd', which appears to be a mistake. There is at all events no indication in the *Risālah* that it is a reply to anything except, from the Caliph's standpoint, a vexatious situation.

Asʿad Luṭfī Ḥasan in his introduction describes Muḥammad b. al-Laith as 'the chief scholar of his time and the most eloquent of the stylists of his age' (*kabīr ʿulamā' zamānihi wa-ablagh fuṣaḥā' awānihi*), a description which perhaps would be difficult to substantiate. On the other hand, D. Sourdel's characterization of him as '*personnage de peu importance*'[19] scarcely does justice to his rôle as the writer of the *Risālah*. On at least one occasion he was connected with great events involving directly a Caliph and an Emperor.

When then was the *Risālah* written? During the Caliphate of Hārūn, i.e. not before 170/786, but after 790, when Constantine assumed sole power, since Irene is not addressed or even mentioned as ruling, and before 797 (blinding and deposition of Constantine). Hārūn is on the point of war, or says he is (*Risālah*, p. 108, see above). His great and successful expedition was made in 181/797. Some time before this date is indicated, probably not very long. With a date 795 or 796 we should not be far from the actuality. As against this kind of dating for the *Risālah*, the only point to be made is that it seems a little strange that Hārūn should have such a distinct impression of the initial 'ransom' of 782, more than a dozen years before. But after all he negotiated it, and certainly in view of this and the subsequent happenings, his anger at the Byzantines becomes more understandable.

We now come to the Biblical quotations contained in the *Risālah*, apparently the earliest Muslim work in which such quotations are used. Exceptional is a single passage (John 15 23 ff.) in the *Sīrah* of Ibn Isḥāq (ed. Wüstenfeld, 1858, 149 f.), which follows the Syro-Palestinian version[19a]. The numerous Scriptural quotations in the later

[17] Cf. as-Sulamī, Ṭabaqāt aṣ-Ṣūfīyah, ed. J. Pedersen, index.

[18] Ed. Flügel, p. 120.

[19] Le Vizirat ʿAbbāside de 749 à 936, I 1959, p. 112.

[19a] See A. Guillaume, The version of the Gospels used in Medina *circa* 700 A.D., Al-Andalus 15 (1950), p. 289 ff.; J. Schacht, Une citation de l'Évangile de St. Jean dans la *Sīra* d'Ibn Isḥāq, ibid. 16 (1951), p. 489–490.

Kitāb ad-Dīn wa'd-Daulah of ʿAlī Ṭabarī, already referred to, are no doubt due to his early education as a Christian, before he was converted to Islam. If it could be shown that he knew Hebrew, this would probably mean that he belonged to a family originally Jewish, as stated by some[20]. In spite of appearances we can say with some certainty that ʿAlī Ṭabarī did not know Hebrew. In two passages where he seems to quote the original Hebrew (*Kitāb ad-Dīn wa'd-Daulah,* 81 and 84, Book of Religion and Empire, 95 and 98), what he had in front of him was evidently the Septuagint version, as a third passage shows (*Kitāb ad-Dīn wa'd-Daulah,* 67, Book of Religion and Empire, 78), probably in Arabic and possibly in the translation of Ḥunain b. Isḥāq[20a]. At all events, as Mingana pointed out, the *Kitāb ad-Dīn wa'd-Daulah* has been a storehouse of Biblical texts in Arabic, which have been used by later Muslim writers[21]. This has not been the case with the *Risālah,* so far as I am aware. ʿAlī Ṭabarī also refers to a certain Marcus the translator (Mārqus or Mārqūs at-Tarjumān) who made a translation (*tarjamah,* p. 67) or commentary (*fassara,* p. 81, *tafsīr,* p. 84), or both, of at least some Biblical books, including the Pentateuch probably and Isaiah[22], from Syriac into Arabic (text 81, transl. 95 where *leg* books of Syriac). An Arabic version by Marcus was therefore probably before ʿAlī Ṭabarī, as well as the Syriac Peshiṭṭā[23].

All this is different in the *Risālah,* where no indication of the source of the Biblical quotations is given. Sometimes the same scriptural passages are adduced by both the *Risālah* and the *Kitāb ad-Dīn wa'd-Daulah.* There is no question of borrowing. We give some examples.

Deuteronomy 33 2

Risālah, 96–97. *wa-min dhālika fī ākhir at-Taurāt* : ʿ*jā'a Allāh tabāraka wa-taʿālā min Sīnā' wa-ashrafa min Sāʿīr wa'stabāna wa-'staʿlana min jibāl Fārān wa-jā'a ʿan yamīnihi ribwāt al-qiddisīn*'. ʿA. Ṭabarī, 74. *qāla Mūsā fī hādha's-sifr fī'l-faṣl al-ʿishrīn* : ʿ*inna'r-Rabb jā'a min Ṭūr Sīnīn wa-ṭalaʿa lanā min Sāʿīr wa-ẓahara min jabal Fārān wa-maʿahu ʿan yamīnihi ribwāt al-qiddisīn*'.

Isaiah 21 6.9

Risālah, 93. *wa-min dhālika qaul Ashʿayā an-nabī' ʿalaihi as-salām* : ʿ*qīla lī aqim baṭāran* (*leg naṭṭāran*) *mā tarā bikhabrī? qāla arā rākibain baʿīrain muqbilain aḥaduhumā yaqūlu li-ṣāḥibihi saqaṭat Bābil wa-asnāmuhā al-manḥūtah.*' ʿA.

[20] E.g., M. Steinschneider, Die arabische Literatur der Juden, 1902, p. 32ff.

[20a] Cf. Masʿūdī, *Tanbīh,* Egyptian ed., p. 98 = transl., p. 159.

[21] See his Remarks on Ṭabarī's Semi-Official Defence of Islam, Bulletin of the John Rylands Library 9 (1925).

[22] Cf. the passages quoted above.

[23] Mingana, introd. p. xviii.

Ṭabarī, 82. *ar-Rabb qāla lī hākadhā : ʻ mḍi fa-aqim ar-rabī'ah ʻalā'l-manẓarah li-yukhbira bimā yarā fa-kāna 'ladhī ra'ā rākibain aḥaduhumā rākib ḥimār wa'l-ākhar rākib jamal....idh aqbala aḥad ar-rākibain wa-huwa yaqūlu hawat hawat Bābil wa-takassara jamīʻ ālihatihā al-manjūrah'.*

Ḥabakkuk 3 3,6

Risālah, 94. *wa-min dhālika qaul Ḥabbaqūq* al-*mutanabbi' fī zamān Dāniyāl : ʻ jā'a Allāh min as-samā' wa'l-Qiddīs min jibāl Fārān wa'mtala'at min taḥmīd Aḥmad wa-taqdīsihi wa-masaḥa'l-arḍ bi-yamīnihi wa-malaka riqāb al-umam'.* ʻA. Ṭabarī, 103. *qāla Ḥabbaqūq an-nabī' ʻalaihi as-salām : ʻ inna Allāh jā'a min at-Taiman wa'l-Qaddūs min jabal Fārān laqadi 'nkasafat as-samā' min bahā' Muḥammad wa-'mtala'at al-arḍ min ḥamdihi .... qāma famasaḥa 'l-arḍ thumma ta'ammala 'l-umam wa-baḥatha ʻanhā'.*

Psalm 149 4–8

Risālah 94–95. *wa-min dhālika qaul Dāwūd ʻalaihi as-salām fī'z-Zabūr : ʻ. . . min ajal ann' Allāha 'ṣṭafā lahu ummatahu wa-aʻṭāhu an-naṣr wa-saddada aṣ-ṣalihīn bi'l-karāmah yusabbiḥūnahu ʻalā maḍājiʻihim wa-yukabbirūna Allāh bi-aṣwāt ʻāliyah bi-aidīhim suyūf dhāt shafratain li-yantaqima Allāh min al-umami 'ladhīna lā yaʻbudūnahu thumma yuqayyidu mulūkahum bi'l-quyūd wa-ashrāfahum bi'l-aghlāl'.* ʻA. Ṭabarī, 78. *wa-qāla fī'l-mazmūr al-mi'ah wa't-tāsiʻ wa'l-arbaʻīn: ʻ min ajl anna 'r-Rabba 'rtāḥa li-shaʻbihi wa-taṭawwala ʻalā 'l-masākīn bi'l-khalāṣ fal-yataʻazzazi l-abrār bi'l-karāmat wa-yusabbiḥūnahu ʻalā maḍājiʻihim wa-yukrimū Allāh bi-ḥanājirihim li-anna fī aidīhim as-saif dhā 'sh-shafratain lil-intiqām min ash-shuʻūb wa-taubīkh al-umam wa-ithqāl mulūkihim bi'l-quyūd wa-ʻilyatihim wa-mukramīhim bi's-salāsil'.*

A number of other passages might be adduced from the *Risālah.* It must suffice here to say that they are close enough to the text of the Old Testament to allow us to think that the author was working with a version, not a paraphrase. His Arabic version contained books from the three main divisions of the Old Testament, and may have included the Pentateuch, the Major and Minor Prophets, and the Psalms.

His New Testament quotations tell a different story. They are comparatively few, and are taken exclusively, so far as I have been able to determine, from St. John's Gospel *plus* the beginning of the Lord's Prayer and a single Beatitude, which is misquoted.

John 14 28

Risālah 89–90. *wa-akdhaba'l-Masīḥ ʻalaihi as-salām kalāmahum ḥaithu yaqūlu : ʻ lau kuntum tuḥibbūnanī lafariḥtum ḥaithu adhhabu ilā ilāhī fa'inna ilāhī aʻẓamu minnī'.*

John 20 17

Risālah 90. *ʻ anā adhhabu ilā ilāhī wa-ilāhikum'.*

John 16 5 *with* 15 26–27 *and* 16 13, *cf.* 14 26

Risālah 93. *min dhālika mā qad shahida bihi 'Isā 'alaihi as-salām 'indakum wa-bayyanahu fi'l-Injīl lakum idh qāla li'l-ḥawāriyīn : 'anā adhhabu wa-saya'tīkum al-Baraqlīṭ rūḥ al-ḥaqqi 'lladhī lā yatakallamu min qibal nafsihi innamā yaqūlu kamā yuqālu lahu wa-huwa yashhadu 'alayya wa-antum tashhadūna li'annakum ma'ī min qabl an-nās bi'l-khaṭī'ah* (*leg bi'l-badī'ah*) *wa-kull shai' a'adda Allāh lakum yukhbirukum bihi'*.

This is not a Scripture passage, but a combination of several ideas from St. John's Gospel, chapters 15–16.

Cf. Matthew 5 7

Risālah 108. '*ṭūbā li'lladhīna yarḥamūna an-nās fa'inna ūlā'ika aṣfiyā' Allāh wa-nūr banī Ādam*'.

Matthew 6 9 = *Luke* 11 2

Risālah 98. '*yā abānā 'lladhī fi's-samā' taqaddasa 'smuka*'.

Cf. John 15 14

Risālah 98. *qāla'l-Masīḥ li'l-ḥawāriyīn* : '*antum ikhwatī*'.

The result of an examination of these New Testament passages (there is another on p. 98 which I cannot identify: '*a'ṭi* (imper.) *kull man āmana bī sulṭānan yud'ā lahu*', and yet another, exceptionally, on p. 77, in the first part of the *Risālah* : *qāla li-man 'jtama'a ilaihi min al-ḥawārīyīn* : '*bi'l-waḥī ukallimukum w'al-amthāl aḍribu lakum*') is not such as to lead to the conclusion that Muḥammad b. al-Laith had a complete copy of the New Testament before him in Arabic. There is no evidence that he even had St. John's Gospel. Perhaps rather he depended on some informant.

In view of the somewhat extensive Old Testament quotations, it is natural to raise the question of a possible pre-existent Arabic version of the Hebrew Bible before Sa'adiah Gaon. This has recently been strongly denied by M. Zucker[24], but his discussion is open to some criticism in detail, and he has not removed the possibility that the work of Aḥmad b. 'Abd Allāh b. Sallām mentioned in the *Fihrist* included exactly such a version. The passage is too long to quote here, but can be read in the Arabic *Fihrist*[25] and soon conveniently in an

[24] 'Al Targum Ras''ag leTorah, 1959.

[25] Ed. Flügel, p. 21–22. The passage was studied by I. Kratchkovsky in an article: O perevode Biblii na arabskiĭ yazik pri Khalife al-Ma'mūne (On the translation of the Bible in Arabic at the time of the Caliph al-Ma'mūn), Christianskiĭ Vostok 6 (1918), p. 189–96, not included in Kratchkovsky's Izbrannie Sochineniya (Selected Works), 6 vols., 1955–60. Cf. G. Graf, Geschichte der christlichen arabischen Literatur, I 1944, p. 88 n. 2.

English translation of the *Fihrist* by Bayard Dodge, which it is hoped will be published in the 'Records of Civilization' series at Columbia. Aḥmad b. ʿAbd Allāh b. Sallām knew some Hebrew, confirming his Jewish origin, which is otherwise likely. Is he the source of the quotations of the Old Testament, even of the New Testament, in the *Risālah* of Muḥammad b. al-Laith? This is not impossible, since we note that he was apparently a freedman of Hārūn[26], and if so, the two might well have been in contact.

Postcript

I have now been able to see the *Kitāb al-Islām* of al-Ustādh Asʿad Luṭfī Ḥasan mentioned above (1350/1932), in which the author mentions that a photographic copy of the *Risālah* was used by Aḥmad Farīd Rifāʿī for the latter's book *ʿAṣr al-Maʾmūn* (3 vols., 1346/1928), but he does not say where the copy was taken from. The *Risālah* is printed in extenso in Rifāʿi's book, II p. 188–236, with some footnotes and is stated to be from a manuscript of the *Kitāb al-Manẓūm wa'l-Manthūr* of Ibn Ṭaifūr (ibid., I p. 406), who died in 280/893, i. e. a good early source (Brockelmann, Geschichte d. arab. Litteratur, I p. 138).

[26] *Fihrist*, ibid.

Soferim — Massoretes, »Massoretes« — Nakdanim

By R. Edelmann

(Rosenørns Allé 65, Copenhagen)

It is a commonly accepted fact that the term »Massorah« is being used as a designation for practically the whole field of what may be understood as »Philology of the Hebrew Bible«, especially as far as what concerns the biblical text as it appears in writing (and in print too, for that matter), i.e. its orthography and its graphic peculiarities, but also its pronunciation, the various systems of vowel signs and the so-called »accents«, and the like; further, the various rules, treatises and collections thereof, like the Diḳduḳe ha-ṭeʿamim (DT), etc. By »Massorah«, finally, is also understood the *Massorah marginalis* (MP and MM) and *finalis* as well as collections of these, like »Okhlah we-Okhlah«[1]. The use of this single designation for all these, among themselves disparate, objects of old scribal activities originates from Eliah Levita and seems also to have been coined by him[2]. The older literature, in our case, the literature from the heyday of the »Massoretes«, however, seeks to differentiate between all the various activities that now are covered by the same term »Massorah«. This literature has a special elaborate terminology attached to each of these single activities. The **סופר** the scribe (e.g. DT, p. XXXIV, cf. Kahle, M.d.W., I 1927, p. 60, and elsewhere) **כתב** wrote the consonantal Bible text proper[3] (ibid. and in the colophons of many old MSS, e.g. Tshuf. 36 (DT, p. XXXVI, cf. Kahle, op. cit., p. 58), which was *written* by Solomon ben Buyaʿa, the same **סופר** who according to the existing statements also wrote the consonantal text of the Aleppo Codex (A). The additions to the consonantal text, i.e. the vowels (**הניקודים**), the »accents« (**הטעמים**), and the Massorah (**המסורות**)[4] were

[1] Cf. also K. Levy, Zur masoretischen Grammatik, 1936, p. 7, and G. E. Weil, Initiation à la Massorah, 1964, p. 33 n. 2.

[2] Cf. inter alia W. Bacher, A contribution to the history of the term »Massorah«, JQR 3 (1891), p. 785f.; cf. also I. Levy, Neuhebr. u. chald. Wörterbuch, III p. 179.—As for the spelling of the word, see also E. Ben-Jehuda, Thesaurus totius hebraitatis, s.v. מסרה, מסורה and מסרת.

[3] In some cases **כתב** seems to have a less restricted meaning, viz., that the scribe has brought the codex into its final form (see below, note 5).

[4] Cf. K. Levy, op. cit., p. י.

made by specialists in these matters. The word נקד meant: to provide a manuscript with vowel signs and »accents«, and מסר meant: to add the Massorah marg. and fin. (מסורת, pl. מסורות) (e.g. Tshuf. 36 [see above], which was provided with vowel signs and »accents« by Ephraim b. Buyaʿa [DT, p. XXXVII] and elsewhere). In many cases, it is true, all stages of the preparation of a MS might have been executed by one and the same man[5], but the awareness of the different character of each of them and of their function was expressed in the terminology used. Thus the specialists in the various fields had a designation of their own, as we conveniently can find them listed together in the text which has been edited by K. Levy, op. cit., p. יד:

[5] Twice in L (fol. 474ª and fol. 479ª) the colophons state that Samuel b. Jacob כתב ונקד ומסר the Codex (cf. A. Harkavy u. H. L. Strack, Catalog der hebr. Bibelhandschriften... in St. Petersburg, 1875, p. 269f.). Now, on fol. 491ª there is a colophon in the form of an acrostic poem giving the name Samuel ben Jacob twice. In the third stanza the poet writes: עשיתי המקרא נחמדת תאותי. By this expression he, according to the special terminology used in such cases (see the text above), might refer to his providing the MS with vowels etc. only. How this may be, at any rate a detailed and painstaking paleographic comparison between the main consonantal Bible text and the additional text of the MS is urgently needed.—As for the Cairo Codex (C), Moshe ben Asher in the colophon (cf. Kahle, Cairo Geniza, 1959, plate 7, and Der hebr. Bibeltext seit Franz Delitzsch, 1961, pl. 17) uses the word כתבתי, which at the first view would indicate that he had written the consonantal text of the MS only. On the other hand it might be possible to interpret some expressions used furtheron in the same colophon (כשהבינו [= כמו שהבינו] עדת נביאים... המבינים כל נסתרות והמשפירים סוד חכמה... לא כיחדו דבר ממה שניתן להם ולא הוסיפו מאמר על מה שנימסר להם והעצימו והגדילו המק[רא]... בטעמי שכל בפירוש דיבור בחיך מתוק ביופי מאמר...) and later in the »copyright« declaration (...דבר ששג'נו בו בכתב או בניקוד או במסרת או בחסר או ביתר...) so, that the scribe meant to say that he was the writer also of the vowel signs (נסתרות and סוד חכמה, because by providing the words with vowel signs their meaning is revealed), of the Massorah (על מה שנימסר להם), which is counting the words and the letters (including the חסירות ויתירות), and of the »accents« (טעמי שכל, פירוש דיבור, חיך מתוק, יופי מאמר, by these expressions indicating the functions of the »accents« as both punctuation and musical signs, as regulators of the diction and cantillation of the text). Cf. also Kahle, Cairo Geniza, p. 91–105. Whether this is so or not, the colophon at any rate presents some difficult problems. See also below in the main text. I here only want to add that it from the colophon clearly appears that the Cairo Codex originally has been one part only of a complete Bible MS, as suggested by U. Cassuto (cf. Kahle, Cairo Geniza, p. 94). The notes on p. 581, 582 and 583 of the Codex (Kahle, Hebr. Bibeltext, plates 11, 12 and 13), giving it as a MS of the Prophets only, are all written by hands different from the colophon, apparently at a time when the two other parts of the whole Bible MS were lost. A careful study of these problems, including also a paleographic comparison of the colophon with the main text of the Codex is needed.

בעלי הקריאה והניגונים והטעמים והמסרות ואנשי הדדקדוק, i.e. »specialists in the pronunciation (הקריאה, they knew the vowels and their rules), in the cantillation and the diction (i.e. the punctuation) (הניגונים והטעמים), in the מסורת (i.e. the Massorah marg. and fin.), and the grammarians (אנשי הדקדוק)[6], (i.e. those who wrote the treatises like DT, אל כלאם פי אלשוא[7], סדר הסימנים[8], etc.)«. Also the term נקדן is found in these old documents[9]. His functions seem mainly to have consisted in providing a Bible text with נקודות and טעמים, that is to say he was a specialist in the pronunciation of the words (the vowel system and its rules) and in the cantillation and diction (the »accents« and their rules) and in the grammar, just as we know him from medieval France.

The differentiation within the scribal terminology must reflect a differentiation within the activities of the scribes. We are led to assume that they divided the work between themselves, which involved that a specialist in one field was less proficient in another one. This was obviously the case with the writer of the Leningrad Codex B 19a (L) Samuel b. Jacob. The publication of this Codex together with its MP has proved to be very useful. Its peculiarities and the problems which it offers, through its MP[10] and also otherwise, have given rise to a zealous occupation with »massoretic« studies during the last two or three decades.

[6] Cf. K. Levy, op. cit., p. יד.

[7] Ibid., p. ד.

[8] N. Allony, ed., סדר הסימנים, HUCA 35 (1964), p. אf.

[9] Cf. K. Levy, op. cit., p. י.

[10] Cf. A. Rubinstein, Singularities in the Massorah of the Leningrad Codex (B 19a), JJS 12 (1961), p. 123f.; F. Pérez Castro, La masora del Códice de Profetas de el Cairo, Sefarad 23 (1963), p. 227f.; and A. Rubinstein, The problem of errors in the Massorah parva of Codex B 19a, Sefarad 25 (1965), p. 16f. Cf. also A. Sperber, Problems of the Massora, HUCA 17 (1943), p. 293f.—In some instances, however, the notes given in the MP may prove not to be errors, but refer to that part of the Bible only where the note is found, as e.g. to the Pentateuch or even to a part of it, or the like. It also goes without saying that the Massorah follows the lexicographical and morphological principles of the time and may therefore bring words together which according to our interpretation do not belong together. In this connection it should be noted that the fact that a MS was considered a »model codex«, as A apparently was, did not prevent it from displaying errors. A (Textus 1, plate) has to תמצאן (Dtn 31 21) the MP ב̇ וחס, which is an obvious error (L has ל̇). It is possible that this error may have arisen by confusion with תמצאון I Sam 9 13 where it appears twice (L has ב̇). The Massorete, arriving at Dtn 31 21, remembered that the form תמצא(ו)ן appears twice, but finding it defective there, he adds וחס. Or does the note mean: The word appears twice (the other one being תמצאינה Jer 50 20), but (ו) (here) it is defective? In both cases it would appear, as it does from many other instances, that the Massora originally was concerned with the consonant text only, as its origin goes back to a time long before the vowel signs were introduced. See also below in the text (p. 122).

In the colophon of this Codex (fol. 479ᵃ)[11] the scribe states that he has prepared the Codex using the carefully corrected manuscripts (הספרים המוגהים המבואר[ים]) (plural!) of Aaron b. Moses b. Asher as his *Vorlagen*. We are not able to make out which MSS Samuel b. Jacob had before him when he wrote this Codex, nor which use he has made of them, although we can make certain inferences about that. At any rate he cannot have used the Aleppo Codex (A). This becomes clear when the MP of L is compared with the MP in those parts of A that have been published by I. Ben-Zvi in facsimile[12]. This fact also appears from a comparison between the main consonantal text of L with the corresponding text of A with regard to the פתוחות and סתומות[13]. But from the wording of the colophon in addition to the obviously selective nature of L[14] which moreover, at any rate in the MP, shows so many errors and discrepancies between the MP and the text[15], a few factors can be deduced, which might be able to help us better to discuss the problems with regard to the old makers of Bible MSS and to understand the nature of their work.

The use of the plural in the colophon of L does not necessarily mean that Samuel b. Jacob has collated the same MSS for the whole Codex including the main consonantal text *and* the vowels and »accents« *and* the Massorah. It can even as well be assumed that he used different MSS for each of these three components of a Hebrew Bible codex.

The assumption that Samuel b. Jacob has collated different MSS for each part of his work may be supported by the fact that a codex was not always, in all its components, executed by one scribe, as we have seen in the case of Solomon b. Buyaʿa (see above). This means that a scribe who wanted to prepare a complete codex himself would use those *Vorlagen* he had at his disposal, eventually making certain amendments according to his knowledge, but would be more careful in the selection of the *Vorlagen* within the field where he was a specialist. As for L, Samuel b. Jacob seems to have been a specialist in the setting of vowels, »accents«, and the other signs only, and the Aaron b. Asher codices which he mentions in the colophon might therefore have been used by him mainly for this part of his work. This assumption may be supported by two facts, firstly: L agrees

[11] Strack, DT, p. IX n. 6.

[12] I. Ben-Zvi, The Codex of Ben-Asher, Textus 1 (1960), 12 plates. Cf. also Kahle, Cairo Geniza, p. 111.

[13] Cf. M. Goshen-Gottstein, The authenticity of the Aleppo Codex, Textus 1 (1960), p. 27.

[14] Cf. Strack, DT, p. XXVI.

[15] See above, note 10.

widely with the BA school just in this part[16] as against the other parts (see above); secondly: it appears that the activities of the various schools of scribes of that period, including BA, BN, the school which is represented by the Cod. Reuchlinianus (not even 100 years younger than L)[17] and others were mainly concerned with the elaborate systems of vowels, »accents« and other signs and their rules. This is at any rate the case with the *Ḥillûfîm* between BA and BN, where there is no reference to the consonantal text. The same can be said about the »massoretic« treatises: DT, etc. The »Massoretes« were נקדנים like their French colleagues (cf. above).

Also the Cairo Codex seems to originate from two different scribes (like Tshuf. 36, see above). A careful palaeographical investigation of the hand of the main consonantal text compared with that of the rest of the Codex is needed, so much more so as the interpretation of the colophon with regard to whether Moses ben Asher has executed the whole work, including the highly artistic illuminations[18] or the main consonantal text only is unsettled, although it looks as if the illuminations originate from the same hand as the colophon and the Massorah fin., viz. from Moses ben Asher, who also provided the Codex with vowel signs and »accents« but who does not seem to have written the main consonantal text as well[19].

The »Massoretes» (נקדנים) were, to all appearances, professional scribes, who produced Bible codices on order from wealthy people[20]. They accomplished their work according to their knowledge and ability and with a higher or lower degree of accuracy. Much depended also on which MSS they chose for their *Vorlagen*. Naturally enough they attached much importance to the calligraphy, as can be seen not only from the written Bible text, which in many cases originates from the hands of, likewise professional, סופרים, but also from the artistic way in which the additional components of the MSS are written and arranged. In some cases, as in C[21] and L[22], the illumina-

[16] Cf. F. Pérez Castro, Corregido y correcto, Sefarad 15 (1955), p. 3f.

[17] This group of MSS very often differs in its punctuation from both BA and BN. This is especially to be seen in the cases where the *Ḥillûfîm* expressly state that BA and BN do not differ.—The Cod. Reuchlinianus is mentioned only because it is the best known of the whole group, described and classified by me in P. Kahle, Masoreten des Westens II, 1930, p. 52*–60*.

[18] Cf. Kahle, Hebr. Bibeltext, p. 95f. and plates.

[19] Cf. above, note 5.

[20] C was made on order from Ja‘vez b. Solomon ha-Bavli (Kahle, Hebr. Bibeltext, pl. 16) and L on order from Mevoraḥ b. Josef ibn Ozdad ha-Kohen (Harkavy-Strack, Catalog, p. 269).

[21] Cf. above, note 18.

[22] Fol. 465ᵃf., cf. Harkavy-Strack, Catalog, p. 264.

tions and the »massoretic« text are interwoven in such a way that the decorative aim seems to be prevalent. This developed further during the following centuries into the richly decorated Bible MSS, in which the illuminations are made only from Massorah and »massoretic« texts. The accuracy and reliability of such material must obviously be of little value, but it is also questionable whether the owner of such a MS was interested in this material in an other way than as traditional material for the decoration of a Bible codex. The content of this material was of importance for the professional scribe and the student only, and these had other sources at their disposal, viz. model codices and learned »massoretic« treatises and collections.

Several model codices are known to have existed down the ages, from the time of the Second Temple on till about the end of the Middle Ages. Their common feature was the fact that they were מוגה, corrected[23]. The characteristics of each of these model codices, as far as the available sources permit it, have still to be established in detail and compared among themselves and with other codices like A and others of corresponding reputation. The results of such a task might prove to be helpful for the determination whether the many existing divergent Bible MSS can be classified according to »schools« or are products of the professional »Massoretes» through the centuries. At any rate it will appear that the text of the Pentateuch generally is the best preserved part of the Bible.

In this connection it might be worthwhile mentioning that Maimonides, when he collated the BA codex in order to prepare a Torah scroll fit for liturgical use in the synagogue, was looking only and exclusively for the consonantal text of the Pentateuch part of what was then considered to be a model codex (שהיה בירושלים מכמה שנים להגיה ממנו הספרים ועליו היו הכל סומכין)[24]. He was interested neither in the vowels, »accents« and other signs, nor in the Massorah, but only in the graphic presentation of the sections (פתוחות and סתומות) of the Pentateuch text and of the two »Songs« of Moses: Ex 15 2–21 and Dtn 32 1–43[25]. He wanted guidance in these matters from this special codex, because it was considered reliable as a model codex in general, including the consonantal text, unlike *all other MSS*, which were highly incorrect in these matters »as even the Massoretes (בעלי המסרת,

[23] As for L, Samuel b. Jacob states in his colophon (see above) that he collated carefully corrected MSS of Aaron b. Asher, and that also this his codex is carefully corrected (והוא מוגה באר היטב). Referring to what has been the result of thorough investigations into his codex, these words must be considered as merely a professional recommendation for his work.

[24] Jad ha-Ḥazakah, II, Ahavah, Hilkot Sefer Torah, VIII, 4. Cf. M. Goshen-Gottstein, op. cit., p. 17f.

[25] Jad ha-Ḥazakah, l.c., VIII, 3.

not ordinary scribes) who write and make lists (שכותבין ומחברין) in order to indicate the פתוחות and the סתומות differ in these matters, (a fact which becomes manifest) through the disagreement of the MSS which are being relied upon (שסומכין עליהם) «[26].

From authoritative hand we here have a statement about the בעלי המסרת, their function and their divergencies, a statement which corroborates what is known about them and what can be inferred from other sources. From the list quoted above (p. 117f.), which belongs to the period that is here dealt with, we know that the functions of the בעלי המסרת must have been different from those of the other persons counted in that list. Maimonides mentions them as those who deal with how the consonantal text of the Bible is to be written. That means that they are, so to say, the theorists of the scribes (סופרים), and just that corresponds with what Massorah in the classical, original meaning of the word is in relation to the consonantal text of the Bible. Only after the introduction of all the auxiliary signs into the Bible MSS the נקדנים also became »Massoretes«, and these signs were to a certain degree included in the Massorah. It is, however, rather unclear in what the massoretic activities of the »Massoretes« consisted or, to say it in other words, what the word מסרת meant in their usage, viz. whether they themselves had acquired the statistical, massoretic knowledge, like the Massoretes of the earlier period, which they then applied when they wrote their MSS or whether they compiled the massoretic notes from the MSS which they used as *Vorlagen*. This would account e.g. for the peculiarities of the Massorah in L, which, apart from the numerous errors (see above), also shows many signs of being a compilation[27], as well as for the fact that in many MSS (like in L) the text and the Massorah do not go together. Actually it is not possible to speak about *the* Massorah, but rather about the Massorah of each single MS. This applies even to the oldest part of the period dealt with here. The Pentateuch MS Tshuf. 17[28] has a statement which Firkowitsch, it is true, has manipulated in his notorious way. But if not the whole of it is invented, this far can be taken into consideration: »This codex of the Torah of the Lord (which) is perfect (Ps 19 8) with the Massorah of my father ... « (עם מסורת אבי...). This means that we here have a Pentateuch codex with a Massorah which is compiled by a certain person and not merely written by him. In such case, as we have seen above, the wording would have been something like זה ספר... שכתב ושמסר אבי. At any rate,

[26] Ibid., VIII, 4.—I suggest that the consonantal text of Tshuf. 36 be compared with that of A, both having been written by the same scribe, Solomon b. Buya'a, cf. above.

[27] E.g. to אֶת(אֲשֶׁר) Prov 3 12 the MM on fol. 410 mentions BA as against the בעל טבריה.

[28] DT., p. XXXIV, and Kahle, M.d.W., I p. 60f.

we can here see an argument for the existence of various individual collections of Massorah already in early times, which lead us back to a still earlier period. On this I hope to be able to publish a fuller study within the not too distant future.

The present concentrated essay is intended as the prolegomena to this study, but also to be a contribution to the Memorial Volume for Paul Kahle, who through his bringing to light of so much new material and through his active work has given rise to zealous studies and intense discussions within wide circles.

Neue Belege für das phönizische Hermes-Emblem

Von Otto Eißfeldt

(Halle/Saale, Steffens-Str. 7)

In dem Aufsatz über Christus-Monogramm und phönizisches »Hermes-Emblem« von 1945[1] habe ich die Möglichkeit erwogen, daß das meistens aus einem acht-, seltener aus einem sechsstrahligen Stern bestehende Hermes-Emblem »wenn nicht auf die Entstehung, so doch vielleicht auf die Verbreitung und Deutung des Christus-Monogramms von Einfluß gewesen ist«[2]. Dabei spielten phönizische Bleisarkophage[3], die — mit vielen Verschiedenheiten im einzelnen — auf ihrer dem Kopfe der Leiche entsprechenden oberen Schmalseite eine viersäulige Tempelfront mit syrischem Giebel, auf der unteren Schmalseite aber einen acht- oder sechsstrahligen Stern aufweisen[4], eine erhebliche Rolle. Jene Tempelfront und dieser mehrstrahlige Stern sind nämlich den auf zwei Seiten des aus dem 30 km nordnordöstlich von Baalbek gelegenen Fiki stammenden achtseitigen Altars[5] dem Jupiter Heliopolitanus und dem Hermes beigegebenen Symbolen[6] so auffallend ähnlich, daß zwischen der Tempelfront und dem Strahlenstern der Bleisarkophage einerseits und den auf dem Altar aus Fiki[7] anderseits Beziehungen bestehen müssen, daß also auch bei den auf den Bleisarkophagen angebrachten Motiven der Tempelfront und des Strahlensterns die Deutung auf Jupiter Heliopolitanus und Hermes sehr nahe liegt. Dussaud bemerkt auf S. 46 seiner Anm. 7 genannten Arbeit zu den auf dem Altar von Fiki an fünfter und sechster Stelle dargestellten Gottheiten Jupiter Heliopolitanus und

[1] ZDPV 67 (1945), S. 163–182 (= Kleine Schriften, II 1963, S. 542–557).

[2] 1945, S. 179 (1963, S. 555).

[3] Vgl. dazu 1945, S. 171–173 (1963, S. 548–550).

[4] Vgl. Abb. 6–10.

[5] Vgl. Abb. 1 nach MUB 21 (1937/38), Taf. XXVI, 3.

[6] Vgl. Abb. 2 nach Syria 23 (1942/43), S. 47, Fig. 7.

[7] Vgl. S. Ronzevalle, Jupiter Héliopolitain. Nova et Vetera, MUB 21 (1937/38), S. 1–181, S. 87–142, Taf. XXVI–XLII und R. Dussaud, Temples et Cultes de la Triade Héliopolitaine à Ba'albeck, Syria 23 (1942/43), S. 33–77, Taf. III–IV, S. 45–49 mit fig. 6 auf S. 46 und fig. 7 auf S. 47; R. Mouterde, L'astrologie à Héliopolis-Baalbek. Jupiter Heliopolitanus Rex et Regulus, BMB 13 (1956), S. 7–21, Taf. I, S. 16–18; H. Seyrig, Nouveaux monuments de Baalbek et de la Beqaa, BMB 16 (1961), S. 109–135.

Hermes dieses: »Jupiter héliopolitain (5) est représenté au-dessus d'un naos à fronton et à quatre colonnes que flanquent deux taureaux. Quant au dieu-fils (6), son 'terme', particulièrement historié, pose sur un socle qu'accostent deux animaux peu distincts et que décore un astérisque sur lequel nous reviendrons pour écarter son identification avec le foudre«, und S. 73 fährt Dussaud nach Erwähnung und Abbildung eines zum Heiligtum des Hermes auf dem bei oder in Baalbek gelegenen Hügel Scheich ʿAbdallah[8] gehörenden Grenzsteins (Abb. 3), der unter dem im Genetiv stehenden Namen des Hermes (Ἑρμου)[9] einen sechsstrahligen Stern zeigt, so fort: »Au-dessous du nom divin de la borne de Sheikh ʿAbdallah, a été gravée une sorte d'étoile à six branches... Ce caractère astral est d'une valeur trop générale pour servir à caractériser une divinité. Cependant, le rapprochement, entrevu par M. Schlumberger, avec l'astérisque du cippe octogonal de Fiki... s'impose, et aussi avec le signe semblable d'un plomb de Baʿalbeck. Ce même symbole nous paraît figuré également sur plusieurs sarcophages en plomb du cycle dionysiaque«.

Als Symbol des Hermes, der um die Wende der Zeiten vor allem als Theopompos, als Geleiter der Seelen zu Gott, geglaubt wurde, wäre aber die Übertragung des Strahlensterns auf Christus schon denkbar. Indes geht es jetzt nicht um eine Wiederaufnahme dieser Frage, sondern nur um die anspruchslose Mitteilung, daß sich seit 1961 das Material an phönizischen Bleisarkophagen aus den ersten christlichen Jahrhunderten, das für die Behandlung jener Frage außerordentlich wichtig ist, sehr erheblich vermehrt hat. Hinzu kommt, daß Münzen, die jetzt in oder bei den meisten Bleisarkophagen gefunden worden sind, ihre sichere Ansetzung ermöglichen, und zwar dahin, daß neben solchen, die aus dem 2. oder 3. Jh. n. Chr. stammen, einige ins 1. Jh. n. Chr. zurückreichen und damit die 1945[10], als nur Sarkophage aus dem 3. Jh. n. Chr. bekannt waren, ausgesprochene Vermutung, daß sie eine längere Vorgeschichte haben müßten, in erfreulicher Weise bestätigen.

[8] Zu Hermes und zu seinem Heiligtum auf dem Scheich ʿAbdallah vgl. D. Schlumberger, Le Temple de Mercure à Baalbek-Héliopolis, BMB 3 (1939), S. 25–36, Taf. I–III; O. Eißfeldt, Tempel und Kulte syrischer Städte in hellenistisch-römischer Zeit, Der Alte Orient 40 (1941), S. 53–60, und G. Lankester Harding, Baalbek, a new guide, 1963, S. 6–7, Nr. 11; S. 22–23.

[9] Zu dem eben erwähnten und abgebildeten (Abb. 3, nach Syria 23, 1942/43, S. 73, Fig. 17) Grenzstein eines Hermes-Heiligtums ist zu vergleichen die Rückseite (Abb. 4, nach Seyrig, MUB XXXVII, 1961, Taf. XXII) eines 262 n.Chr. von dem Priester Drusus in dem auf der Nordspitze des Libanon gelegenen *Maqām er-Rabb* errichteten Sockels, die Νέμεσις und darunter ein Rad, das Symbol dieser Göttin, zeigt. Vgl. H. Seyrig, Némésis et le temple de Maqam er-Rabb, MUB 37 (1961), S. 261–270. Taf. XXII. XXIII, samt Einlegblatt: „Note rectificative".

[10] 1945, S. 176 (1963, S. 553).

Wie J. Hajjar, Un hypogée romain à Deb'aal dans la région de Tyr[11], mitteilen kann, ist ein Bauer aus dem 14 km südöstlich von Tyrus gelegene Deb'aal[12] im Juni 1961 bei der Anlage einer Zisterne auf die Decke eines Hypogäums gestoßen, das dann auf Anordnung des Generaldirektors der Libanesischen Altertümerverwaltung Émir Maurice Chéhab von J. Hajjar in fünfwöchiger Ausgrabungsarbeit gründlich erforscht worden ist und, da es zwei Jahrtausende unbekannt und daher unausgeraubt geblieben ist, eine überreiche Ausbeute ermöglicht hat: zwei Steinsarkophage, neunundzwanzig aus tyrischen Werkstätten stammende Bleisarkophage und eine Fülle von Grabbeigaben, darunter, wie schon angedeutet, viele Münzen, die eine sichere Ansetzung der Sarkophage ermöglichen. Von dem Hypogäum als ganzem, seinem 6,30 zu 4,75 m großen Mittelraum mit je vier Loculi an der Nord-, der West- und der Südseite und dem Eingang im Osten ermöglicht die Abb. 5[13] eine Anschauung. Im übrigen werden nur die Schmalseiten der fünf Bleisarkophage hier im Bilde wiedergegeben. Denn wenn auch die Deckel der Bleisarkophage und ihre Längsseiten viele sepulkrale Symbole aufweisen, deren erneute Untersuchung an Hand des jetzt erschlossenen Materials sich lohnen würde, so gehören die auf den Schmalseiten angebrachten Motive als Ausdruck des Glaubens, die Seele des in dem Sarkophag Liegenden werde durch den Hermes Theopompos zu Jupiter Heliopolitanus als dem obersten Gott geführt werden, doch offenbar besonders eng zusammen[14].

Der in Loculus 2 gefundene Bleisarkophag F. 367[15] aus dem Jahr 63–64 n. Chr. weist auf dem Kopfschmalende vier korinthische Säulen auf, die einen von belaubten Zweigen gebildeten und achtblättrige Rosetten als Akroterien zeigenden syrischen Giebel tragen. Solche Rosetten sind weiter in den zwei seitlichen Interkolumnien und an der oben mit einem gedrehten Stab abschließenden Basis angebracht. Das Fußende des Sarkophags wird von einem Stern, dessen acht Strahlen in Efeublätter endigen und an ihrem Schnittpunkt ein Medusenhaupt zeigen, gebildet. Je ein Efeublatt füllt die Zwischenräume zwischen den Strahlen.

Der aus Loculus 3 stammende Bleisarkophag F. 382[16], der nach Ausweis von Grabbeigaben nicht vor 136 n. Chr. datiert werden kann, ist auf seiner Kopfschmalseite mit zwei nach rechts schreitenden Pan-

[11] BMB 18 (1966), S. 61–104, Taf. I–XXIII. 2 Falttafeln.

[12] Vgl. R. Dussaud, Topographie historique de la Syrie Antique et Médiévale, 1929, S. 25, und Hajjars Bemerkung dazu auf S. 61, Anm. 1.

[13] Nach Hajjar, S. 63.

[14] Vgl. 1945, S. 174 (1963, S. 551–552).

[15] Hajjar, S. 69–70, Taf. III–IV, unsere Abb. 6.

[16] Hajjar, S. 73–75, Taf. V, unsere Abb. 7.

Gestalten und einer zwischen ihnen angebrachten achtblättrigen Rosette geschmückt. Darüber und darunter erscheinen zwei Mischkrüge mit Weinblatt samt Traube zwischen ihnen. Auf der Fußschmalseite kehrt die Verzierung mit Mischkrügen, Weinblättern und Trauben wieder. Aber die Rosette ist durch ein Medusenhaupt ersetzt, und an die Stelle der Pan-Gestalten sind Weinblätter und Trauben getreten.

Die Kopfschmalseite des in Loculus 6 zu Tage gekommenen Bleisarkophags F. 424[17] aus dem Jahre 94–95 n. Chr. ist geschmückt mit vier auf einem Strickstab stehenden jonischen Säulen, deren Schäfte aus Perlen und Scheiben gebildet sind, und einem aus belaubten Zweigen bestehenden syrischen Giebel, über den sich noch ein Bogen aus Efeublättern wölbt. Die seitlichen Interkolumnien sind mit Lorbeerbüscheln gefüllt und das mittlere noch dazu mit einem Medusenhaupt über ihnen. Das Fußschmalende aber zeigt einen Stern mit acht, in Lorbeerblätter endigenden und Halbmondschilde (lunae peltatae) einschließenden Strahlen.

Die Kopfschmalseite des aus dem Jahre 63–64 n. Chr. stammenden, in Loculus 6 zu Tage gekommenen Bleisarkophages F. 383[18] weist diesen Schmuck auf: Vier auf einen Strickstab stehende gedrehte Säulen tragen einen von belaubten Zweigen gebildeten syrischen Giebel. Während die seitlichen Interkolumnien mit Lorbeerbüscheln gefüllt sind, zeigt das mittlere oben ein Medusenhaupt und darunter Lorbeerblätter. Die Fußschmalseite weist einen achtstrahligen Stern aus Strickband auf, dessen Strahlen in Efeublätter auslaufen, während die Zwischenräume zwischen ihnen mit Lorbeerbüscheln ausgefüllt sind und ihr Schnittpunkt von einem Blüten-Medaillon überdeckt wird. Der Bleisarkophag F. 399[19] aus Loculus 11, dessen Alter sich nicht genau bestimmen läßt, von dem aber hier mitgeteilt sein mag, daß in ihm außer Resten eines Grabtuches auch Lorbeerblätter, die auf den Toten gelegt waren, gefunden worden sind[20], zeigt auf dem Kopfende eine von vier korinthischen Säulen gebildete Tempelfront mit syrischem Giebel aus belaubten Zweigen, dem ein Efeublatt und zwei Mischkrüge als Akroterien dienen. Während das mittlere ohne Verzierung geblieben zu sein scheint, sind die seitlichen Interkolumnien durch Lorbeerbüschel ausgefüllt. Das Fuß-

[17] Hajjar, S. 80–81, Taf. VIII, unsere Abb. 8.

[18] Hajjar, S. 84–85, Taf. XI, unsere Abb. 9.

[19] Hajjar, S. 88–89, Taf. XIII, unsere Abb. 10.

[20] Vgl. dazu Hajjars Bericht, S. 71 Anm. 1: »Ces restes de suaire ainsi que ceux trouvés dans la tombe 11 (cf. infra) seront communiqués au Professeur H.-J. Hundt, du Römisch-Germanisches Zentralmuseum à Mayence, qui a bien voulu se charger d'en faire l'étude. Le résultat de ses recherches paraîtra, s'il le juge utile, dans l'un des prochains volumes du B.M.B.«.

schmalende zeigt sechs aus Strickband gebildete Strahlen mit sehr kräftigen Blumenrosetten an ihren Enden und eine ebenso kräftige Rosette über dem Schnittpunkt der Strahlen.

Die glückliche Auffindung und vorbildlich schnelle Veröffentlichung eines stattlichen und gut erhaltenen Tyrischen Hypogäums aus römischer Zeit hat also das uns für die Erforschung der Tyrischen Kunstgeschichte der römischen Zeit zur Verfügung stehende Material[21] sehr erheblich vermehrt, wobei vor allem auf die Sepulkralkunst dieses Zeitraums erwünschtes Licht fällt. Wer hätte es zu hoffen gewagt, daß drei Jahrtausende nach der Heranziehung des berühmten Erzgießers Hiram aus Tyrus durch Salomo, von der I Reg 7 13–50 so eindrücklich Kunde gibt, im Gebiet von Tyrus ein Fund gemacht werden würde, der zeigt, daß die Tyrischen Metallkunsthandwerker das auf Salomo folgende Jahrtausend hindurch ihre guten Traditionen bewahrt und ausgebaut haben!

[21] Ein bereits 1937 in der 3 km östlich von Tyrus gelegenen, aus dem 2. Jh. n.Chr. stammenden Nekropole von *El-Awatin* zu Tage gekommenes Hypogäum, dessen Wände mit gut erhaltenen Malereien aus dem Gebiet der griechischen Mythologie bedeckt sind — Alkeste und Herakles, Tantalus, Sirenen und dergleichen — ist inzwischen, wie M. Dunand, Tombe peinte dans la campagne de Tyr, BMB 18 (1966), S. 5–51, Taf. I–XXV, zu berichten weiß, im Museum zu Beirut wieder aufgebaut.

Die israelitischen Propheten in der samaritanischen Chronik II

Von Georg Fohrer

(Erlangen, Geisbergstr. 12)

I.

Der im Jahre 1963 erschienenen Edition und Übersetzung des samaritanischen Werkes »Memar Marqah« von J. Macdonald hat P. Kahle eine Einführung vorangestellt, die sein langwährendes Interesse auch am samaritanischen Schrifttum seit seiner philosophischen Dissertation von 1898 »Textkritische und lexikalische Bemerkungen zum samaritanischen Pentateuchtargum« bezeugt. Daher dürfte es angemessen sein, an dieser Stelle auf einen anderen samaritanischen Text einzugehen, der — wieder als Beiheft zur Zeitschrift für die alttestamentliche Wissenschaft — gleichfalls von Macdonald erstmalig ediert und übersetzt wird und dessen Veröffentlichung Kahle gewiß ebenso begrüßt hätte wie diejenige von »Memar Marqah«. Es handelt sich nach der Klassifizierung von Macdonald[1] um die samaritanische »Chronik II«, eine Version des unter dem Titel ספר הימים bekannten Werkes, von dem bisher nur die als Grundlage dienende Version der Josuageschichte bekannt war[2].

Macdonald charakterisiert das Werk folgendermaßen (unter Auflösung der Abkürzungen): »*Sepher ha-Yamim* as a title refers to a work which exists in more than one version, *e.g.* Chronicle II or the Joshua part of Chronicle II. Chronicle II may have existed originally as a Book of Joshua, which is in no way connected with *Sepher Yeshoshua* (Chronicle VI), but may have contained large tracts of the Biblical Text. Chronicle II, as represented by MS H 1, is basically a very old chronicle of unknown date, possibly *derived* from a pre-Masoretic Text version of the Biblical Text possessed by one or more

[1] J. Macdonald, The Theology of the Samaritans, 1964, S. 44–49, der insgesamt sieben samaritanische Chroniken anführt.

[2] Vgl. vor allem D. Yellin, Das Buch Josua der Samaritaner (hebr.), Jerusalem 6 (1902), S. 138–155; M. Gaster, Das Buch Josua in hebräisch-samaritanischer Version, ZDMG 62 (1908), S. 209–279, 494–549; Ders., On the Newly Discovered Samaritan Book of Joshua, JRAS 1908, S. 795-809; Ders., The Sameritan Hebrew Sources of the Arabic Book of Joshua, ebd. 1930, S. 567–599; A. D. Crown, The Date and Authenticity of the Samaritan Book of Joshua as seen in its Territorial Allottments, PEQ 96 (1964), S. 79–100.

north Palestinian (Samarian) families. There are several clear indications that it is fundamentally a substantial excerpt from the Biblical Text which could have been held by northern as well as southern Israelites ... To the original text underlying Chronicle II as we now know it was later added, perhaps after the 4th century A.D. reorganization of life and worship, some of the material in non-biblical classical Hebrew«.

Einige einführende Bemerkungen über die Eigenarten des Werkes scheinen geboten zu sein:

1. Die Chronik II umspannt die Zeit der alttestamentlichen Bücher Josua bis Könige. Für deren Darstellung hat der »Chronist« auszugsweise den Text jener Bücher unter gelegentlicher Heranziehung von Abschnitten aus den Chronikbüchern verwendet. Während dabei Josua von samaritanischen Familien anscheinend als ein in gewissem Maße heiliges Buch betrachtet wurde, unterscheidet sich der Richterteil der Chronik II so stark vom kanonischen Richterbuch, daß er anscheinend alte Traditionen aus einer nördlichen Quelle verarbeitet hat. Den Samuel-, Königs- und Chronikbüchern sind vor allem solche Auszüge entnommen, die das persönliche Leben der Könige betreffen oder von besonderem Interesse für den Norden waren; dagegen sind politisch-militärische und jerusalemische priesterlich-kultische Mitteilungen ausgelassen oder zusammengefaßt worden. Auf die Behandlung der Prophetenerzählungen wird später einzugehen sein.

2. Das allmählich hinzugefügte Material läßt sich, wie Macdonald zeigt, auf zwei Quellengruppen zurückführen: a) eine in sich wieder geschichtete profane, pro-davidische Quelle und b) eine oder mehrere priesterliche, anti-davidische Quellen.

3. Der Chronik II lassen sich mancherlei interessante geschichtliche und religionsgeschichtliche Anschauungen entnehmen. So wird durch die — in einigen Fällen gar nicht abwegige — Gleichsetzung von שפט und מלך ein Königtum für die einheitliche israelitische Gemeinschaft seit der Zeit Josuas mit einer Sukzession der »Richter«-Könige bis Simson angenommen. Der Bruch — das samaritanische Schisma bzw. der »Abfall« der anderen Israeliten — ereignete sich, als Eli den Kultus von Sichem nach Silo verlegte. Damit fand eine Spaltung in zunächst zwei, nach der Übernahme des Kultus von Silo in Jerusalem, der Spaltung des Königtums und der Bildung von götzendienerischen Gruppen in immer mehr Teile statt. Die Samaritaner wollen dabei sogleich eine eigene, von den Nordisraeliten unterschiedene Gruppe gewesen sein, die stets am wahren Glauben und Kultus festgehalten hat. Da übrigens nach ihrer Ansicht das wahre Betel, wo Jakob sein Traumerlebnis hatte (Gen 28 10ff.), auf dem Garizim lag, werden die beiden Staatsheiligtümer Jerobeams I. in

Dan und Samaria lokalisiert. Beachtenswert ist, daß die synchronistischen Angaben für die judäisch-israelitischen Könige durch synchronistische Angaben über die samaritanischen Hohenpriester ergänzt werden.

4. Kennzeichnend für die Art und Weise, in der geschichtliche Gestalten und Ereignisse beurteilt werden können, ist die Erklärung für den Widerstand Samuels gegen die Errichtung — im Sinne der Chronik II genauer: die Wiedererrichtung — des Königtums. Auch nach der Chronik II forderten die Ältesten wegen des üblen Verhaltens seiner Söhne von ihm: »Gib uns einen König, daß er uns regiere!« (I Sam 8 1ff.). Dann aber fährt sie fort: »Da erkannte Samuel, daß seine Söhne nicht Herrscher in seinem Volke an seiner Stelle werden könnten; denn sie forderten einen König an Stelle seiner Söhne, der über sie herrsche. Da war Samuel sehr besorgt und bedrückt« (I Sam § G: K*–L*). Er suchte die Vertreter des Volkes von ihrem Verlangen abzubringen, indem er ihnen die einschneidenden Rechte vortrug, die ein König geltend machen würde (I Sam 8 10ff.) — natürlich zu dem eigennützigen Zweck, das Volk dadurch so zu erschrecken, daß es doch mit seinen Söhnen vorlieb nähme. Als ihm dies mißlang, hatte er nach der Erhebung Sauls immerhin die Genugtuung, daß dieser »nichts tat außer auf Anordnung Samuels; alles, was der ihm befahl, tat er« (I Sam I: § A*). Eine derartige Darstellung läßt erwarten, daß auch die Propheten nicht ungeschoren bleiben.

II.

1. In der Tat sucht man in der Chronik II nach den im alttestamentlichen Text erwähnten Propheten oft vergeblich. Die Erwähnungen sind ausgelassen und nicht in die Chronik übernommen worden. So fehlen:
die von der Debora handelnden Verse Jdc 4 4–9, der Name der Debora in 4 10ff. und das Deboralied 5;
die Erwähnung des prophetischen Mannes Jdc 6 8 in der allerdings ohnedies stark zusammengestrichenen Gideonüberlieferung;
die Samuel als Propheten verstehenden Abschnitte I Sam 9–10;
ein großer Teil der Saul-David-Überlieferung mit der Erzählung von Sauls »prophetischer Rolle« in I Sam 19, der Erwähnung des Propheten Gad in 22 5 und von Propheten überhaupt in 28;
die erneute Erwähnung des Propheten Gad in II Sam 24 11 mit der ganzen Überlieferung über die militärischen und religiösen Maßnahmen und Handlungen Davids in II Sam 19–24;
die ganze Erzählung von der symbolischen Handlung des Ahia von Silo I Reg 11 29ff.;

die Erwähnung des »Gottesmannes« Semaja in I Reg 12 22 (mit dem ganzen Abschnitt 12 21–24);
die Prophetengeschichten in I Reg 13–14 und die Erwähnung des angeblichen Propheten Jehu in 16 7. 12;
die Erwähnung von Propheten in II Reg 17 13, wobei allein dieser Vers aus dem fortlaufenden, interpretierten Zitat von 17 7–16 ausgelassen worden ist;
die gesamten Jesajalegenden in II Reg 18–20, wobei zudem für die Darstellung des Feldzuges Sanheribs gegen Juda der Text von II Chr 32 herangezogen wird — unter anderem vermutlich deswegen, weil dort Jesaja nur einmal genannt wird und sein Name leicht zu tilgen war.

Zumindest ein Teil der angeführten Verse oder Abschnitte ist offensichtlich zu dem Zweck ausgelassen worden, die Erwähnungen oder Erzählungen von Propheten zu beseitigen. Das gilt auch für den größten Teil der Überlieferung von Elia und Elisa, auf die unter 3. einzugehen ist.

2. Der Prophet Natan durfte in der Chronik II ebenfalls nicht erscheinen und mit David in Verbindung gebracht werden, zumal die ursprüngliche Chronik und die Erweiterungen aus profanen Quellen den König keineswegs negativ beurteilen, wie dies in den priesterlichen Erweiterungen geschieht. Daher ist es nicht Natan, der ihm nach anfänglicher Zustimmung den Bau eines Tempels mit einem Jahwewort untersagt (II Sam 7). An seine Stelle tritt vielmehr der samaritanische Hohepriester, der den David durch einen Brief, in dem er auf die alleinigen Rechte des von Gott erwählten Berges Garizim pocht, so erschreckt, daß der König den schon begonnenen Bau einstellen läßt und die ihn fragenden Vertreter des Volkes unter Hinweis auf das von ihm vergossene Blut auf seinen Sohn Salomo vertröstet (II Sam § B: A*–N*).

Die Erzählung vom Vorgehen Natans gegen David nach dessen Verfehlung mit der Batseba in II Sam 12 1ff. ist ausgelassen worden. An ihrer Stelle finden sich Überlegungen über die Schuld Davids, Mitteilungen über seine Opfer und die Genealogie Davids (II Sam § D: A*–P*).

3. Ist also ein sehr großer Teil der Prophetenüberlieferungen von der Chronik II ausgelassen worden, so werden im Gegensatz zu dieser Methode zwei Propheten mehrfach angeführt: Elia und Elisa. Freilich geschieht dies nicht so, daß die von ihnen handelnden Erzählungen ganz oder großenteils aus den Königsbüchern übernommen worden wären. Vielmehr werden sie wie in den vorher genannten Fällen zum überwiegenden Teil ausgelassen. Wo dies nicht oder nicht ganz geschieht oder wo Elia oder Elisa sonst erwähnt werden, sind sie in einer Weise dargestellt und beurteilt worden, daß die überhaupt nicht er-

wähnten Propheten von sich sagen könnten, sie seien wesentlich besser davongekommen als jene beiden. Soweit wie möglich soll dies im Folgenden an der Übersetzung der in Frage kommenden Abschnitte oder Sätze gezeigt werden. Dabei werden die aus dem Alten Testament stammenden Textteile durch kursiven, die samaritanischen Erweiterungen oder Bemerkungen durch gewöhnlichen Druck gekennzeichnet.

a) »Und *der Tisbiter Elia aus Tisbe in Gilead* nannte sich in jenen Tagen selbst einen Propheten und (behauptete), daß der Herr mit ihm spräche. Und Elia kam *nach Zarpat*, das zu Sidon gehört, zum Hause *einer Witwe. Da sagte er zu ihr: 'Bringe mir doch in einem Gefäß ein wenig Wasser, daß ich trinke'. Als sie dann hinging*, um für ihn Wasser *zu holen, rief er ihr zu: 'Bringe mir doch einen Bissen Brot mit'. Da antwortete sie* ihm: *'Bei dem Herrn, deinem Gott, ich habe nicht* einen Bissen, *sondern nur eine Handvoll Mehl und ein wenig Öl*, und ich will es verwenden *für mich und meinen Sohn, daß wir es essen und sterben'. Aber er sagte zu ihr: 'Fürchte dich nicht, geh und tue, wie du gesagt hast*; dann werde ich selber essen und auch ihr. Wenn du mir davon zu essen gibst, *wird das Mehl nicht zu Ende gehen und das Öl nicht abnehmen'. Da ging* die Witwe *und tat nach* seinen *Worten*. Elia aber riß das Ganze an sich und aß es, dann ging er von der Witwe fort. Und nach dem Weggang Elias hungerte der vaterlose Sohn der Frau zu Tode. — Dieser Elia hatte einen anderen Namen, der war Chananja. Alle Tage seines Lebens war er heimatlos und flüchtig vor dem König Ahab, dem Sohn Omris, und seinem ganzen Volk. Chananja ging und floh vor Ahab, dem Sohn Omris, und seinem ganzen Volk über den Jordan, um sich jenseits des Jordans auf seiner Ostseite versteckt zu halten. Doch er versank im Wasser des Jordans und starb« (I Reg 12–22: § J).

Eindeutig soll der Schluß der I Reg 17 7ff. nacherzählten Anekdote den Elia als einen üblen Schurken hinstellen, der eine schutzlose Witwe mit einer wertlosen Verheißung betrügt und dadurch den Tod ihres Sohnes verursacht. Die zweite Notiz geht nicht auf eine alttestamentliche Überlieferung zurück. Die Gleichsetzung Elias mit Chananja kann auf einer Verwechslung mit dem Chananja von Jer 28 oder dem Chanani von I Reg 16 7 beruhen[3].

b) Die weitere Eliaüberlieferung wird von der Chronik II nicht berücksichtigt. Die meisten Erzählungen und Anekdoten sind einfach ausgelassen worden. Auch die Erzählung von Nabots Weinberg ist gekürzt. Die Chronik II bringt lediglich I Reg 21 1–16, während der

[3] Für die teilweise abweichende Darstellung in MS H 2 und in der samaritanischen Chronik VI kann auf die ausführliche Darstellung Macdonalds in der Chronik II verwiesen werden.

mit v. 17 beginnende Abschnitt über das Auftreten Elias fehlt. Das entspricht dem üblichen Verfahren des Chronisten, wie es sich oben aus 1. ergeben hat. Ungeachtet dessen wird bei der Schilderung der Revolution Jehus nach der Ermordung und Zerfleischung der Isebel die auf Elia zurückgeführte Ankündigung ihres Endes nach II Reg 9 36 zitiert, jedoch mit einer bezeichnenden Änderung der Einleitung: »So war es gemäß dem *Wort Elias*, des Zauberers...« (II Reg — II Chr § B).

c) Ebenso fehlt der größte Teil der Elisaüberlieferung in der Chronik II, oder die Erzählungen sind wie II Reg 3 4ff. in einer solchen Weise zusammengestrichen bzw. neu gefaßt worden, daß Elisa ausgeschieden wird. Nur mehr zwei Erzählungen erwähnen ihn.

In der Erzählung von der Blendung der Aramäer II Reg 6 8ff. erwidert einer der Diener des Königs von Aram auf dessen Verdacht des Verrats an den König von Israel mit dem erweiterten v. 12: »*Nein, mein Herr König, vielmehr sagt Elisa in Israel dem König von Israel* alle *Worte, die du in deiner Schlafkammer sprichst*, denn er ist ein Wahrsager, Zauberer, Totengeistbefrager und Wahrsager« (II Reg — II Chr § A: II Reg 6 12 und B*).

In der anschließenden Erzählung von der Hungersnot in Samaria II Reg 6 24ff. hört der König von Israel sich die Klage und Beschwerde der Frau an, deren Sohn gekocht und gegessen worden ist, und zerreißt seine Kleider (v. 30). Die Chronik II fährt fort: »Dann suchte der König einen Boten zum Wahrsager Elisa, um ihn mit dem Schwert zu töten, weil er dieses Unheil hingewälzt hatte. Aber Elisa und all seine Schüler flohen vor dem König von Israel und wohnten in einem anderen Land« (II Reg — II Chr § A: E*–F*).

d) Dem allen entspricht das Gesamturteil über Elia und Elisa: »In jenen Tagen fanden sich Elia und sein Diener Elisa ein. Sie nannten sich selbst Propheten und sprachen zu der ganzen Versammlung Israels Worte auf Befehl des Herrn, die der Herr nicht befohlen hatte; er hat nicht mit ihnen geredet« (I Reg 12–22 § M: P*–Q*).

4. Nach dem Vorbild des Urteils über Elia und Elisa hat ein späterer Schreiber ganz kurz drei weitere Propheten eingeführt: »In seinen Tagen[4] erschienen Hosea, Joel und Amos. Man sagte über sie in ganz Israel, daß sie Zauberer seien« (II Reg — II Chr § F: B*).

5. Nur viermal werden Propheten weder unerwähnt gelassen noch abwertend beurteilt.

Bei der Schilderung der Thronfolgestreitigkeiten in I Reg 1 nennt die Chronik II in v. 8 und 10 den Natan, allerdings ohne die Bezeichnung »Prophet« (I Reg 1–11: § A). Immerhin weist auch die Septuaginta die Bezeichnung in v. 10 nicht auf.

[4] Gemeint ist Jerobeam II.

Ferner wird für die Zeit des Joas, dargestellt nach II Chr 24, der dort in v. 20 eingeführte Sacharja beibehalten, wenn auch unter Änderung des Textes: »Aus dem Volke kam ein Mann mit Namen Sacharja; der wies sie zurecht, aber sie hörten nicht auf seine Stimme« (II Reg — II Chr § E: A*).

Weiter wird im Anschluß an II Reg 14 25 berichtet: »*Jona, der Sohn Amittais, der aus Gat-Chepher war,* lebte in jenen Tagen« (II Reg — II Chr § F).

Schließlich wird für die Zeit des Königs Josia noch Jeremia erwähnt: »In seinen Tagen erschien Jeremia. Er war der Sohn des Priesters Hilkia. Er wohnte in der Stadt Anatot im Lande Benjamin bei Jebis[5]; es ist die Stadt, in die der König Salomo den Priester Abjatar vertrieben hatte, als er ihn als Priester absetzte. Im 13. Jahre der Regierung Josias begann er von sich zu behaupten, daß er ein Prophet des Herrn, des Gottes Israels, sei. Aber viele Männer von den Judäern verschworen sich gegen ihn und steinigten ihn zu Tode« (II Reg — II Chr § N: F*–I*).

III.

Es stellt sich somit heraus, daß die Chronik II mit den Prophetennotizen oder -erzählungen in drei verschiedenen Arten verfährt. Jede von ihnen läßt sich auf einen bestimmten Kreis zurückführen:

a) Der ursprüngliche »Chronist«, der das alttestamentliche Material ausgewählt und zusammengestellt hat, ist über die Erwähnungen von Propheten einfach hinweggegangen. Er hat sie ausgelassen und dafür in Kauf genommen, daß er den Text verstümmeln oder umschreiben mußte.

b) Die profanen Erweiterungen nennen dagegen einige Propheten ohne positive Würdigung, aber auch ohne herabsetzende Bemerkungen. Ihre Verfasser haben sich damit begnügt, die Bezeichnung »Prophet« auszulassen oder — wie im Falle Jeremias — von der bloßen Behauptung, es habe sich um einen Propheten gehandelt, zu sprechen. Bei diesem Verfahren wird also ebenfalls kein Prophet als solcher anerkannt.

c) Die priesterlichen Erweiterungen — und ihnen folgend der spätere Schreiberzusatz — erwähnen einige Propheten, jedoch unter starker Abwertung und Herabsetzung; danach hat es sich nicht um wirkliche Propheten, sondern um Wahrsager, Zauberer usw. gehandelt. Es ist interessant zu sehen, daß dem sowohl das Urteil des assyrischen Königs Sanherib über die judäischen Propheten entspricht: »... die Männer, die euch sagten: 'Wir sind Propheten vom Herrn

[5] Gemeint ist Jerusalem.

für euch', haben euch durch dieses Wort verleitet, denn sie waren Wahrsager, Zeichendeuter, Zauberer und Orakelbefrager, sie waren keine Propheten« (II Reg — II Chr § L: FF*–GG*), als auch die Aufzählung von Wahrsagerei, Zeichendeuterei, Zauberei und Befragen von Totengeistern unter den Sünden der Zeit des Königs Manasse nach II Chr 33 6 (II Reg — II Chr § N). So kann man geradezu fragen, ob das abwertende priesterliche Urteil über die Propheten nicht einer derartigen Aufzählung entnommen worden ist — was dann freilich um so grotesker wirkt, als Manasse die in solcher Weise charakterisierten Propheten, die eigentlich nach seinem Geschmack hätten sein müssen, in Wirklichkeit zusammen mit anderen religiösen und politischen Opponenten gegen seine Politik blutig verfolgt hat (vgl. II Reg 21 16).

Wie läßt sich das verschiedenartige, im Grunde aber doch einheitliche Verfahren in den Schichten der Chronik II erklären? Einen Hinweis bietet die Fortsetzung der soeben zitierten Worte Sanheribs über die Propheten: »haben sie euch heute aus meiner Gewalt und aus der Gewalt meines Volkes gerettet, wie es Mose, der Sohn Amrams, im Lande Ägypten in bezug auf den Pharao und all seine Diener getan hat, als er eure Väter mit starker Hand und ausgerecktem Arm aus dem Lande Ägypten führte?« (II Reg — II Chr § L: HH*–JJ*).

Diese Abwertung der Propheten im Vergleich mit Mose führt auf die richtige Spur. Wie Macdonald gezeigt hat, erkennen die Samaritaner lediglich Mose als Propheten an, außerdem sekundär und auf dem Wege über Mose noch Aron und Mirjam[6], so daß sie selbstverständlich alle anderen Ansprüche ablehnen. Das Prophetentum Moses ist zudem gekennzeichnet durch die völlige Kenntnis des göttlichen Willens, den Besitz übernatürlicher Macht, die Einbeziehung des wahren Priestertums und das Verfügen über die Weisheit. Angesichts dieses Prophetenverständnisses, das sich von demjenigen des Alten Testaments tiefgreifend unterscheidet, ist es erklärlich, daß die Samaritaner und also die Chronik II den Anspruch der alttestamentlichen Propheten grundsätzlich zurückweisen müssen — sei es, indem man sie gar nicht erwähnt, ihnen die Bezeichnung »Prophet« vorenthält oder ihnen verurteilenswürdige Betätigungen zuschreibt. Ebenso wird erklärlich, daß gerade Elia und der mit ihm verbundene Elisa in den priesterlichen Erweiterungen der Chronik II aufs Korn genommen und in geradezu ehrenrühriger Weise charakterisiert werden. Einmal sind sie die Propheten des israelitischen Nordens, über die eine umfangreiche Überlieferung in den alttestamentlichen Geschichtsbüchern vorliegt und die für den Norden, an dem die Chronik ja in besonderem Maße interessiert ist, von großer Bedeutung

[6] J. Macdonald, The Theology of the Samaritans, 1964, S. 204–211.

waren. Ferner wird Elia in einem Teil der Überlieferung als ein neuer, zweiter Mose, also in samaritanischer Sicht als eine Art Konkurrent oder Gegenspieler des allein als Prophet anerkannten Mannes hingestellt[7]; daher ist ihm eine besonders schroffe Ablehnung zugedacht worden. Dies alles zeigt wiederum, daß die Chronik II nur im Gesamtzusammenhang der samaritanischen religiösen und theologischen Auffassungen gelesen und verstanden werden kann.

[7] Vgl. G. Fohrer, Elia, 1968².

Ein persischer Titel im Altaramäischen

Von W. B. Henning*

(7 Eton Court, Berkeley, California)

Waidranga[1], der langjährige persische Oberkommandierende an der Südgrenze Aegyptens, führt in einem in das 8. Jahr des Darius (= 416 v.Chr.) datierten Dokument, zusätzlich zu seiner Bezeichnung als »General« (*Rab-Ḥailā*), den sonst unbekannten Titel *Hptḥpt'* (הפתחפתא)[2]. Nach der berühmten Beschwerdeschrift, die die Juden von Yeb (Elephantine) wegen der Zerstörung ihres Tempels an Baguwahya[3], den Gouverneur von Judäa, richteten, bekleidete er aber das Amt eines *Frataraka* im 14. Jahre des Darius (= 410)[4]. Mit Recht hat man aus dieser Abfolge geschlossen, daß die Veränderung eine Beförderung bedeutete[5]. Es darf als feststehend erachtet werden, daß der *Frataraka* in der Rangordnung dem Satrapen zunächst stand; wenn also der Satrap ein Land, der *Frataraka* eine Provinz regierte, so dürfte der *Hptḥpt'* der Vorsteher eines Kreises gewesen sein.

Abgesehen von der Gleichsetzung des Wortendes mit dem überaus häufigen altiranischen *pati* »Herr« sind zur Erklärung des neuen Titels (der durch zweimaliges Vorkommen vor dem Verdachte der Verschreibung gesichert ist) bisher nur negative Bemerkungen geliefert worden. B. Geiger bei Kraeling (S. 228): »but then, *hptḥ-* can hardly be connected with *hapta* 'seven', on account of the guttural«; W. Eilers (AfO 17, 12, S. 333): »*haftaχᵛa* 'Siebentel' wäre sinnlos«[6]. Es scheint jedoch, daß der Titel noch zu Beginn des 3. nachchristlichen Jh. in Persien in Gebrauch war; um das erkennen zu können, ist freilich ein etwas kühner Sprung vonnöten.

* Der Verfasser ist am 8. 1. 1967 verstorben.

[1] Die stete Schreibung mit *-y-* empfiehlt diese Lesung trotz elam. *Mi-ut-ra-an-ka*, worin E. Benveniste, J. A. 1954, S. 306, diesen Namen erkannt hat. Viell. haplologisch aus **Waida-dranga-* »das Wissen befestigend«.

[2] E. G. Kraeling, The Brooklyn Museum Aramaic Papyri, Nr. 8 Z. 2 und 3.

[3] Dies ist die richtige Aussprache für *Bigwai*/Βαγώας im Altpersischen, vgl. meine Bemerkungen zu *Ztwhy*, *'rtwhy* und *Wrwhy* bei G. R. Driver, Aramaic Documents of the Fifth Century B.C., abridged edition, S. 57, 71, 75.

[4] A. Cowley, Aramaic Papyri of the Fifth Century B.C., Nr. 30 Z. 5 (vgl. Nr. 27 Z. 4 und mit Artikel, *prtrk'*, Nr. 31 Z. 5).

[5] E. G. Kraeling, a.a.O., S. 228.

[6] Weitere Bemerkungen sind mir nicht zu Gesicht gekommen.

In den *Res gestae* (*Kārnāmag*)[7] des Begründers des sassanidischen Reiches, Ardaschir S. d. Pābag, ist viel von einem Fürsten namens *Haftānbuxt* die Rede, der das südliche Küstengebiet der Persis beherrschte und Ardaschir viel zu schaffen machte; er hatte sich einen Drachen oder »Wurm« (*kirm*) zugelegt, der den Grund seines Daseins bildete und göttliche Verehrung genoß. Wenn uns auch *Haftānbuxt* als Eigenname entgegentritt, so haben wir doch angesichts der steten Verwirrung von Name und Titel in der iranischen Tradition ohne weiteres das Recht anzunehmen, daß es sich ursprünglich um einen Titel handelte. Dafür, daß H. seit langem unbesehen als Eigenname gilt, ist gewiß die »sprechende Etymologie« der Wortform mitverantwortlich: als »Von-den-Sieben [d.h. Planeten]-erlöst« kann sie in gefälliger Weise als Ausfluß des »altorientalischen Gestirndienstes« gebucht werden.

J. Marquart, der Hauptkritiker der Quellen der iranischen Geschichte, hat als einziger erkannt, daß die überlieferte Form falsch ist. »Ursprünglich wohl«, so schrieb er kurz in einer Anmerkung[8], »*Haftānpāt* 'von den Sieben (Planeten) beschützt', woraus sich auch Firdausīs هفتواد am leichtesten erklären ließe«. Marquart, der also im Banne der obenerwähnten Etymologie blieb, machte diesen Vorschlag gewiß in erster Linie wegen der in der persischen Sekundärüberlieferung[9] gebräuchlichen Form, *Haftwād* (oder *Haftwāδ*), die in der Tat in Betracht gezogen werden muß; denn wenn in jener Version des Kn., welche den persischen Werken zugrunde lag, *Haftānbuxt* gestanden hätte, so wäre kein Mensch auf den Gedanken verfallen, anders als geradeso zu lesen. Dazu kommt, daß die arabische Umsetzung bei Ṭabarī[10], wenn auch hoffnungslos verderbt, immerhin noch zeigt, daß das Original nicht auf *-buxt* endigte.

Marquart war zwar auf dem richtigen Wege, jedoch stand die für das Ur-*Kārnāmag* vorauszusetzende Schreibung dem Überlieferten näher als er dachte; statt *-p't* endete sie auf *-b't*, welches (da -'- und -*ḥ*- im Pehlewi identisch sind) sich von *-bwḥt* nur durch Wegfall von -*w*- unterscheidet.

[7] Abgekürzt Kn. Gemeinhin gebe ich doppelte Zitate: Kapitel (römische Ziffer) und Paragraph nach der Ausgabe von D. P. Sanjana, Seite und Zeile nach der von E. K. Antia. Nöldekes Übersetzung (Bezzenbergers Beiträge, Bd. IV) ist mir z.Zt. nicht zugänglich.

[8] J. Marquart, *Ērānšahr*, 44 A. 1, mit Hinweis auf handschriftliche Verwechslung von *bwḥt*, *bḥt*/*b't* und *p't* in einem andren Namen.

[9] Firdousi, *Mujmal at-Tawārix* (S. 60 ed. Bahar), *Nuzhat-al-Qulūb* (übers. Le-Strange S. 138) etc.

[10] I 817 Z. 5, ann. b (die Schreibungen mit Hilfe der ihrerseits verderbten Kn.-Form zu emendieren ist verlorne Liebesmüh'; zu beklagen ist, daß in dem Kairiner Neudruck, II 39 Z. 14, nur die künstlich hergestellte Form, unter Fortlassung der Varianten, erscheint). Vgl. Nöldeke, Tabari, 11 A. 1.

1. Überliefert	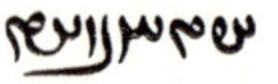	*Haftānbuxt*
2. Marquart	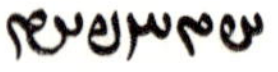	*Haftānpāt*
3. Echte Form	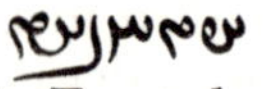	

Daß aber Nr. 3 die echte Form darstellt, ergibt sich aus einer im Kn. selbst implicite enthaltenen Volksetymologie: H. hatte *sieben Söhne* (VI 14 = S. 28⁷). Obwohl ebendiese Etymologie im Schahname explicite zu finden ist (*Haftwād* hieß, so »weil er sieben Söhne hatte«)[11] und einen überklugen Lexikographen die nichtexistierende Vokabel *wād* »Sohn« in das persische Wörterbuch einzutragen verführt hat[12], ist ihr Mitspielen im Kn. nicht klar erkannt worden, weil das Pehlewi-Wort, das dem Verfasser des Kn. vorschwebte, früher nicht sehr geläufig war: nämlich *'wb't* (Pehl. Psalter), *'wb'tk* (Buch-Pehl.) »Generation, Nachkommen«. Allerdings kennen wir nicht seine genaue Aussprache[13] (*ōbāt*? / *ōβāt*? *aβāt*?). Ob aber der ganze Name bzw. Titel *Haftōbāt* oder *Haftōβāt* oder *Haftaβāt* (später mit *-βād*/*-vād*) war, ist von geringem Gewicht: Dieser Art war jedenfalls die Form, die der Verfasser des Kn. beabsichtigte[14]. Das persische *Haftwād* ist ihre vollkommen richtige Fortsetzung.

Marquart hat auch zur Lokalisierung der im Kn. erzählten Ereignisse wichtige Beiträge geliefert[15]. Haftobat (wie ich der Kürze halber schreiben werde) war ein Räuber- und Piratenhäuptling, der

[11] Ed. Tehran VII S. 1948 V. 496 (bei Firdousi hat H. auch noch eine Tochter, aber »Töchter rechnete er nicht als jemanden«).

[12] Ein noch weniger vertrauenswürdiges Wort ist *buxt*/*būxt* »Sohn«, worauf sich Darmesteter, Ét. Ir., II, 82 verließ; wie man z. B. aus dem *Farhang-i Rašīdī* ersehen kann, ist es aus *Buxt(-i) Naṣṣar*, der Verballhornung von Nebukadnezar, abstrahiert worden.

[13] Schon im Mittelalter war sie in Vergessenheit geraten, wie Neryosengs Fehllesung *'nb'tk* beweist, vgl. *Škand-gumānī-vazār* XIV 7, S. 196, ed. de Menasce (mit Stellennachweis); dort zufällig im Kompositum mit *haft* »sieben«, *haftanbādaa*, dessen Pehlewi-Schreibung, in Wests Ausgabe S. 247 geliefert, abgesehen vom *-k* mit der oben gegebenen Form Nr. 3 identisch ist.

[14] Man darf nicht außer acht lassen, daß unser Kn.-Text auf einer einzigen Handschrift beruht; alle umlaufenden Hss. sind Abschriften jener noch existierenden alten Hs. (die als *MK* bekannt ist): die sog. Varianten in den Ausgaben sind daher nur als Schreibfehler zu bewerten.

[15] Aus ihr ergibt sich aufs klarste, daß die Geschichte von Haftobat und seinem *kirm* nicht (wie das die etymologiefreudigen Perser unvermeidlicherweise späterhin annahmen) als Ätiologie des Namens der östlich angrenzenden Provinz *Kirmān* gedacht war. Im Kn. bezieht Ardaschir aus jener Provinz, sowie aus *Makuristān* (später *Mukrān*) und *Pārs*, seine Truppen (vor dem Auftreten des H.) IV 12 = S. 22⁹ und schickt dorthin eine Armee zum Kampf gegen die *Bāriz* (nach seiner Beseitigung) IX 2 = S. 40¹¹. Von einem Zusammenhang mit Haftobat, der VI 3 = S. 26¹⁰ ausdrücklich nach *Pārs* verlegt wird, ist noch keine Rede.

den südlichen Teil der Persis und die Küsten des persischen Golfes unsicher machte; bis nach dem Indusgebiet schickte er seine Leute auf Piraterie (*pad hēnīh*[16] VI 4 = S. 26 pu.). Sein (ältester) Sohn, der *Īrahistān*[17], das Hinterland von Sīrāf (*hodie* Tāhirī), dem nachmalig berühmten Haupthafen von Persien, für ihn verwaltete, brachte ihm im Notfalle Hilfstruppen von Arabern und Omanitern[18] auf dem Seewege. Er selber hauste in einer in einem unidentifizierbaren Gau[19] gelegenen Festung, deren Namen ebenfalls strittig ist[20]. Sie lag jedenfalls nicht sehr weit von der Küste ab; denn dorthin (*bār-i drayāb*, VI 25 = S. 31⁹) gerät Ardaschir auf der Flucht nach einem mißlungenen Eroberungsversuch. Von da erreicht er »das Dorf, welches man *Mānd*[21] nennt« (VII 1 = S. 31 u.), wonach die bei den islamischen Geographen erwähnte Wüstenei *Māndistān* sowie heutzutage der sie begrenzende Unterlauf des alten *Sikkān*[22], *Rūd-i Mānd*, benannt sind. Ardaschirs Operationsbasis ist das offensichtlich sehr nahe gelegene *Ardašīr-xurreh* (*hodie* Fīrūzābād), das naturgemäß häufig erwähnt wird, zweimal (VIII 18 = S. 40^3, IX 1 = S. 40^9) auch unter seinem, ursprünglichen Namen, *Gōr*[23]; sogar das von A. gegrabene Flußbett welches das Wasser aus dem Talkessel von Gōr ableitete und dem Sikkān zuführte, ist genannt, *Rūd*[*-i Wa*]*rāzag* (IV 17–18 = S. $23^7/^8$) = *Rūd-i Burāze* im Fārsnāme des Ibn Balxī. Man darf daran erinnern, daß in der sassanisidischen Provinzialeinteilung das ganze Ge-

[16] Für die Einengung des Sinnes auf Seeräuber vgl. armen. *hēn*.

[17] *'lḥst'n* VI 15 = S. 28^{10} für *'ylḥst'n* siehe Marquart, *Ērānšahr*, S. 43f., der eine unnötig starke Änderung wollte; vgl. Pehl.-Vendidad III 23 (S. 13 Z. 19 ed. Spiegel) *zufr rōstāg čēgōn 'ylḥst'n* »ein tiefliegender Distrikt wie z.B. *Īrahistān*«.

[18] *Myčnyk'n* VI 15 = S. 28^{11} für *Myčwn-*, siehe Marquart (ebd.), dessen Emendation angesichts *Myčwn* Gr. Bd. 208^5 wieder zu weit geht.

[19] Marquart, a.a.O., S. 44. Viell. ursprünglich *Gōčihrān/Gōzihrān*, d.h. Gebiet eines Γωσίθρης (vgl. Nöldeke, Tabari, S. 4–7).

[20] Pehl. *Gulār*, Tabarī *'l'r*, siehe Marquart, a.a.O. A. Egtedâri (Iqtidārī) hat in seinem nützlichen Werke *Lāristān-i kuhan* (»Das alte L.«), 1955, S. 46, auf den gegenwärtigen Ortsnamen *Gilār* hingewiesen, der gut *Gulār* fortsetzen könnte. *Gilār* liegt nach dem *Fārsnāme* 1½ *farsax* südl. v. *Bīdšahr*, welches selbst 6 fars. sw. von *Gūyum* liegt; nach dem *Farhang-i Juγrāfiyā'ī* 54 km. von *Gūyum*.

[21] Dieser für das Verständnis der Vorgänge wichtige Name ist sogar Marquart entgangen.

[22] In dieser Form nicht nur bei Plinius (*Siccanas*) und Arabern, sondern auch in Pehlewi, *Sk'n* Gr. Bd. 88^{12} (von Marquart, *Wehrot*, S. 177, anders aufgefaßt). Vgl. W. Tomaschek, Küstenfahrt Nearchs, S. 60.

[23] Verschrieben *Gwb'l*, statt *Gwbl* (daß es sich um *Ardašīr-xurreh* handelt, ist von Marquart, a.a.O., S. 146, zwar erkannt worden, trotzdem suchte er den Namen anders zu erklären). Dies ist die richtige Schreibung für *Gōr* aus *Gaβr* »tiefliegendes Tal« (vgl. manich. mpers. *gbr*; die ursprüngliche Bedeutung ist »Gebärmutter«); *Gwl* dagegen (vgl. Marquart, Provincial Capitals, S. 19 § 44) ist von der späteren Aussprache beeinflußt.

biet bis Sīrāf und bis in die Nähe von Lār zum Distrikt Ardašīr-xurreh gerechnet wurde. Mitten in seiner südlichen Hälfte, genau im Zentrum des Dreiecks Sīrāf-Lār-J̌ahrum, befindet sich heute das große Dorf *Haftovān*[24] (*Haftavān*), in dessen Namen[25] gewiß die Erinnerung an *Haftobāt* (*Haftvād*) fortlebt; es ist auf allen besseren Karten markiert[26], aber, weil abseits der Karawanenstraßen, in den älteren Quellen nicht erwähnt.

Es bedarf dieses Blickes auf die Lokalgeographie, um den Grund für die unverhältnismäßige Ausführlichkeit der Haftobat-Geschichte, ja für ihre Erwähnung überhaupt, verstehen zu können. Am nördlichen Rande des Kreises, in dem H. sein Wesen trieb, lag nämlich der Sitz des heiligsten Feuers des Sassanidenreiches, des *Ādur-Farnbāg*. Gewiß, so dürfen wir annehmen, war der Verfasser des Kn. ein Magier jenes Hauptfeuers der zoroastrischen Priesterschaft. Nur so erklären sich die im Vergleich mit allen anderen Quellen einzigartige Vertrautheit des Kn. mit der unmittelbaren Nachbarschaft sowie das religiöse Moment im Kampfe gegen Haftobat, in dessen Gebiet durch seine Beziehungen zum indischen Küstenland wohl ein Nāga-Kult, der den Magiern ein Dorn im Auge war, eingedrungen war. Nicht umsonst auch berichtet uns das Kn., daß Ardaschir, ganz am Anfang seiner Laufbahn, sowie er auf der Flucht vor dem parthischen Großkönig die Meeresküste und damit Sicherheit erreicht hatte[27], als Allererstes sich zum »Hofe« des Farnbāg-Feuers begab, um seine Huld zu gewinnen[28].

Über die Örtlichkeit, die das heilige Feuer beherbergte, das Dorf *Kāriyān*, hat eigentlich schon G. Hoffmann (vor 85 Jahren) alles Nötige beigebracht[29]. Das noch heute existierende Dorf liegt nach Muqaddasī eine Tagesreise, nach dem *Farhang-i J̌uyrāfiyā'ī* 42 km sw. (wahrscheinlich wnw.) von *Gūyum*; die Entfernung von dem oben ge-

[24] So nach Egtedari, a.a.O., S. 19.

[25] Wohl Kürzung von *Haftobātān*/*Haft(o)vādān* »dem H. gehörig«. Vgl. Namen wie *Burāzǰān* (von *Burāze*, s. oben), *Kirmānšāhān* usw.

[26] Auch bei Wilson, Persian Gulf. Nach The Times Atlas 27° 46′ n. Br., 53° 18′ ö. L.

[27] Um diesen Augenblick zu verewigen, gründete er dort die Siedlung *Buxt-Ardašīr* (IV 8 = S. 21[12]), d.h. »A. ist gerettet«, die naturgemäß an der Küste der Persis zu suchen ist (es war A. prophezeit worden, daß er, sobald sein Auge auf die See fiele, vor dem Parther nichts mehr zu fürchten hätte). Der Name ist zweifellos der Ahnherr des heutigen *Būšir* (Bushire, Bushehr), wenn auch dieser (ebenso wie andre Kn.-Namen) sonst in den älteren Quellen nicht vorkommt. Marquart, *Ērānšahr*, S. 42, verlegte freilich *Buxt-A.* an die gegenüberliegende Seite des Meeres, was den Sinn der Kn.-Geschichte zerstört.

[28] Diesen Punkt hat G. Hoffmann, Syrische Akten persischer Märtyrer (1880), S. 287f., mit Recht hervorgehoben.

[29] A.a.O., S. 284ff.

nannten *Haftovān* dürfte 70 km (in der Luftlinie) kaum überschreiten[30]. Sogar die Lösung der einzigen ernstlichen Schwierigkeit, der Behauptung des Ind. Bundahischn, daß Vištāspa das Feuer nach Kabul gebracht habe und es »noch jetzt dort weile«, hat Hoffmann richtig vorausgeahnt[31]. Das Auftauchen der vollständigen Version des Bundahischn (*Gr. Bd.* 125^{2-3}) zeigte zwar, daß »*Kāvulistān*, das Land *Kāvul*« verderbt war, aber der neue Text bot gleichfalls Schreibungen, die nicht leicht zu verstehen waren[32]. Einzig und allein die Mutter-Handschrift (*TD*) des *Gr. Bd.*[33] hat das Richtige:

rōšn-kōf īg pad K'lnyk'n[34] *deh*

»Berg *Rōšn*[35], der beim Dorfe *Kārnīkān* (liegt)«; daß *Kāriyān* (viell. eig. *Kārriyān*) das ältere *Kārnīkān* (urspr. »dem *Kāren* gehörig«?) fortsetzt, steht außer Frage.

Wir können nun untersuchen, wie aram. *Hpthpt'* und Haftobat sich zueinander verhalten. Bei dem letzteren sind wir keineswegs verpflichtet, dem Verfasser des Kn. in der Schriftanalyse Glauben zu schenken; denn wenn er auch um die richtige Aussprache Bescheid wußte, so folgte er in der Orthographie einem seit Jahrhunderten schulmäßig festgelegten Schriftbild, dessen Ursprung ihm unbekannt war: er sah es als *ḥpt-'wb't* an, wir aber dürfen getrost annehmen, daß es ursprünglich als *ḥptḥw-b't* gemeint war. Damit gewinnen wir den Anschluß an die aramäische Form, die dementsprechend aus dem von Eilers verworfenen **haftax^{u}wa-* »Siebentel« (Aw. *haptahva*, Altpers. **haftauva-*) sowie *pātā*, Nom. sg. von *pātar-* »Schützer, Wächter«[36],

[30] Genaue Distanzen kann ich nicht liefern, weil die Geographen erst kürzlich die Lage von *Gūyum* (von der *Kāriyān* abhängt) geändert haben: auf allen früheren Karten lag es ein gutes Stück westlich vom 54. Längengrad, aber 1959 hat es seinen Platz östlich von ihm gefunden (und ist gleichzeitig südlich verlagert). The Times Atlas gibt an: 28° 3′ n. Br., 54° 2′ ö. L. (*Kāriyān* ist nicht markiert, wohl aber das ihm ganz nahe *Hārm*, 28° 13′ n. Br., 53° 43′ ö. L.). *Gūyum* (arabisiert *Ǧūyum*, besser *Ǧuwaim*) darf nicht mit dem gleichnamigen Ort nördl. v. Schiraz verwechselt werden; wohl urspr. **gau-dam-* »Kuh-hausen«.

[31] A.a.O., S. 286.

[32] Siehe A. Christensen, L'Iran sous les Sassanides², S. 165.

[33] Diese kann ich dank dem freundlichen Entgegenkommen von Mrs. Meherbanu B. Anklesaria und der Großzügigkeit meines früheren Schülers Peshotan K. Anklesaria benutzen.

[34] Man sieht leicht, wie »*kavārvand*« und »*kanārang*« aus *k'lny-* zustande gekommen sind.

[35] Viell. entsprechend dem *Kūh-i Yāsīn*, an dessen Abhang Kāriyān nach dem *Far.-i Ǧ.* liegt.

[36] Ein ziemlich sicheres Beispiel von *pātā* in תיפתיא aus altiran. *tāyu-pātā* (Nom. sg.) »der die Diebe bewacht (auf sie achtgibt)«, vgl. mein Manichäisches Bet- und Beicht-Buch, S. 90 Anm. 1, Anders hierüber H. W. Bailey, Annali (Ist. Univers. Or., Napoli) 1, S. 115.

zusammengesetzt ist. Aus **haftaxᵘwapātā*[37] wurde beim Übergang zum Mittelpersischen zunächst **haftaxwpāt*, worin *-p-* früh stimmhaft wurde[38], also **haftaxwbāt*, welches von der Pehlewi-Schreibung repräsentiert wird. Daß daraus in der späteren Aussprache **haftaubāt*, schließlich **haftōbāt* o. dgl. wurde, kann auf verschiedene Weise erklärt werden[39] und ist auf jeden Fall im Einklang mit der Tatsache, daß mittelpersische Bruchzahlen gegenüber altiran. *-axᵘwa-* bloßes *-ō-* (oder *-ū-*) aufweisen[40].

Wenn nun der achämenidische Kreishauptmann den Titel »Schützer des *Siebentels*« führte, so darf man wohl annehmen, daß die Einteilung der Provinzen in *sieben* Kreise als der Normalfall angesehen wurde; sie mag ein Vorbild in der iranischen Kosmologie, nach welcher die Welt in sieben Erdteile (*karšvar-*) zerfiel, gehabt haben. Ganz ähnlich teilte man in spätsassanidischer Zeit das ganze Reich in *vier* »Richtungen« (*pādgōs*), deren Verwalter *pādgōsbān* »Schützer[41] des *P.*« heißen, und dementsprechend die Provinzen in »*Viertel*« (*tas(s)ōg*), deren jeweilige Anzahl freilich häufig dem Namen Hohn sprach[42].

[37] Bloßes *ḥ* für *xᵘw/xʷ* ist eine Kürzung, die wir dem aramäischen Schreiber nicht verdenken können; vgl. übrigens *ḥrzmy* (חרזמי, zweimal bei Cowley) »Choresmier«, von *Xᵘwārazmi-*, vgl. H. H. Schaeder, Iranische Beiträge, S. 68 [266].

[38] Dies ist allerdings schwer zu beweisen, weshalb denn die von Marquart restaurierte Schreibung auf den ersten Blick anziehend erscheint (vgl. oben S. 139). Für die Konsonantengruppe *-xwp-* weiß ich kein andres Beispiel. Stimmhaftwerden in der Kompositionsfuge wird in der Orthographie manchmal angezeigt, z.B. bei *'ndym'ng'l'n* statt *-k'l'n* (vgl. mein Mitteliranisch, S. 45). Vgl. Μασαβάτης gegenüber aram. Mspt (מספת), vgl. meine Anmerkung bei G. R. Driver, a.a.O., S. 81.

[39] Z.B. durch Konsonantenhäufung.

[40] In Pehl. *haftōtak* (oder *haftūtak*) »Siebentel« ist, wie *srišōtak* im Vergleich mit aw. *ϑrišva* zeigt, *-tak* ein zusätzliches Element, so daß *haftō* = aw. *haptahva-*; ebenso *panǰōtak* »Fünftel«, *aštōtak* »Achtel«. Außerhalb des Pehlewi mit *-ka*-Suffix, manich- mpers. *pnjwg* = *panǰōg* »Fünftel« (JRAS, 1945, S. 149 Recto Z. 1) und *tswg* = *tas(s)ōg* »Viertel« (ebenda Verso Z. 23; Sogdica S. 24 Z. 6, vgl. S. 25; daraus arab. *ṭassūǰ*, pers. *tasū* usw.). Nirgends ist eine Spur des altiran. *h/x* erkennbar, welches ja auch in den (nur elamitisch bezeugten) altpersischen Formen nicht sichtbar wird, daher viell. in einem Dialekt der Persis ausgefallen war (mpers. *whyšt'w*, selten *whyštw*, »Paradies«, das mit *dwšwx* »Hölle« kontrastiert, verdient besondere Beachtung). Das mittelpers. Material ist bei der lebhaften Besprechung der altpers. Bruchzahlen vernachlässigt worden (vgl. zuletzt O. Szemerényi, Stud. Indo-Eur. Num., S. 75 Anm. 40; K. Hoffmann, KZ 79 (1965), S. 247 ff.; G. Cameron und I. Gershevitch, JNES 24 (1965), S. 183 ff.). Nach *tswg* ist elam. *ṣa-iš-ma-kaš* = *čāçuvaka-* (nicht = *čašu-*); *pnjwg* entspricht elam. *pan-su-ma-*[*kaš*], nicht aber *pan-su-kaš*.

[41] Nominalformen von *pā-* »schützen« wurden für territoriale Amtsbezeichnungen bevorzugt, wie ja schon *xšaϑrapāvan-* »Satrap« (wörtl. »Landesschützer«) zeigt; schon deshalb ist *pātar-* wahrscheinlicher als *pati-* in *Hptḥpt'*.

[42] In Babylonien z.B. hatten die Provinzen bis acht »Viertel«, gelegentlich auch bloß drei (vgl. M. Streck, Die alte Landschaft Babylonien, I, S. 14 ff.).

Dereinst aber hatte man jedenfalls in der Persis die achämenidischen Gepflogenheiten beibehalten, als das Land nach der griechisch-makedonischen Eroberung seine Freiheit wiedergewann. Daher finden wir in der Persis, der Hochburg des religiös-politischen Konservativismus, jene nur aus Oberägypten bekannten achämenidischen Titel, den *Frataraka* und den *Haftax*^{u}*wapātā*, beide innerhalb der arsakidischen Periode, den einen ganz an ihrem Anfang, den andern in ihren allerletzten Tagen[43].

Nur zögernd bringe ich hier zum Schluß eine Art Beweis dafür, daß vielleicht noch im 6. Jh. der erste Teil von Haftobat richtig als »Siebentel« aufgefaßt wurde; freilich fließt er aus einer Quelle, auf die der Historiker sich noch weniger gern verläßt als auf das Kn. In einer dem Fabelbuch Kalila wa Dimna beigefügten Geschichte, die, wie Nöldeke gezeigt hat[44], ursprünglich auf Pehlewi geschrieben war, begegnet ein König, in dessen Namen **Hawṭaβād*[45] wir unschwer unseren Haftobat wiedererkennen. Das Schloß dieses Fürsten lag beim Berge *Anōšag-bād*, und

> »am Fuße des Berges ist ein Loch, und ein Siebentel des Windes dieser 3½ Regionen kommt aus dem Loche .... «[46].

Es verlohnt sich nicht, hier weiter auf diese höchst seltsame Geschichte einzugehen. Wir dürfen aber die Vermutung äußern, daß sie im wesentlichen aus einer Volksetymologie des Namens, *Siebentel* + *Wind* (Pehl. *wāt*, später *wād*, pers. *bād*), herausgesponnen worden ist. Es ist interessant zu beobachten, welche Mühe sich die Perser gegeben haben, sich das ihnen Sinnlose sinnvoll zu machen.

43 Der Umstand, daß die christliche Kirchenprovinz Persis in sieben Bistümer zerfiel (vgl. E. Sachau, Zur Ausbreitung des Christentums in Asien, S. 58), könnte eine früh-sassanidische Siebenteilung widerspiegeln.

44 Th. Nöldeke, Die Erzählung vom Mäusekönig und seinen Ministern, 1879.

45 In der alten syrischen Übersetzung *hwṭb'd*, daneben *hwṭ'b'd, hwṭ'bt'*, auch *hwṭ'bd* (Schulthess, K. u. D., 2, S. 241 Anm. 628). Das, wie es scheint, nur in einer einzigen Hs. der arabischen Versionen vorliegende *hwṭb'r* (weshalb Nöldeke, a.a.O., S. 8, *hû-tabâr*) hat m.E. keinen unabhängigen Wert; es ist wohl erst aus dem Syr. transliteriert.

46 Nöldeke, dessen Übersetzung des Syrers S. 24 hier zitiert ist, bemerkte, daß der Verfasser nur die Hälfte der aus sieben *karšvar* bestehenden Welt als bewohnt zu betrachten scheine. Im Arabischen: »ein Siebentel aller Winde, so in den 3½ Regionen der Welt wehen«.

ΒΛΕΠΕΤΕ Philippians 3 2

By G. D. Kilpatrick

(27 Lathbury Road, Oxford)

During the years when he lived in Oxford it was my privilege to discuss many problems of text and interpretation with Professor Paul Kahle. Like others I owe much to the stimulus and encouragement that he provided. In particular his wide range of interest and readiness to consider various possibilities when we were considering a problem were particularly instructive.

Does βλέπετε in Phl 3 2 mean »look at« or »beware of?« To settle the question we must look at the evidence. Particularly important are the instances of βλέπειν with the accusative, but to begin with let us look at all the evidence for the use of the word.

We find the following constructions in the New Testament:

(1) Transitive:

(a) with the accusative: Mt 5 28 7 3 11 4 13 17 14 30 15 31 18 10 24 2 Mk 4 24 5 31 8 23.24 13 2.9 Lk 6 41.42, 7 44 8 16 10 23 (2), 24 11 33 24 12 (v.l.) Joh 1 29 5 19 11 9 20 1.5 21 9.20 Act 4 14 8 6 9 8 12 9 13 11 Rm 7 23 8 24.25 I Cor 1 26 10 18 II Cor 10 7 12 6 Phl 3 2 (3), C 2 5 4 17 H 2 9 10 25 II Joh 8 Rv 1 11.12 5 3.4 11 9 16 15 17 8 18 9.18 (v.l.) 22 8.

(b) passive: Rm 8 24 II Cor 4 18 4 H 11 1.3.

(2) Intransitive: Mt 6 4.6.18 12 22 13 13 (2) .14 (2) 15 31 Mk 4 12 (2) 8 18 13 23.33 Lk 7 21 8 10 (2) Joh 9 7.15.19.21.25.39 (3) .41 Act 1 9 2 33 9 9 22 11 (v.l.) 28 26 2 Rm 11 8 I Cor 13 12 Rv 3 18 9 20 22 8.

(3) With prepositions:

(a) εἰς Mt 22 16 Mk 12 14 Lk 9 62 Joh 13 22 Act 1 11 3 4.

(b) κατὰ Act 27 12.

(c) ἀπὸ Mk 8 15 12 38 Lk 21 30; cf. Act 22 11 (v.l.).

(4) With dependent clauses:

(a) ὅτι II Cor 7 8 H 3 19 Ja 2 22.

(b) no example of accusative and infinitive.

(c) with ἵνα I Cor 16 10 C 4 17 II Joh 8.

(d) interrogative πῶς Lk 8 18 I Cor 3 10 E 5 15.

(e) μή Mt 24 4 Mk 13 5 Lk 21 8 Act 13 40 I Cor 8 9 10 12 G 5 15 C 2 8 H 3 12 (μήποτε) 12 25.

It may be said at once that the only passages where βλέπειν seems to mean »beware« are in (3c) and 4(e) and even in 4(e) we may translate after the pattern of »look, lest you fall«. Indeed we may argue that the precautionary element resides in the ἀπό and the μή. In no case is βλέπειν used with the accusative demonstrably with the meaning »beware of«.

We find a similar state of affairs in the Apostolic Fathers:

(1) Transitive:

(a) with the accusative: Bar 1 3.7 5 10 10 11 II Cl 20 1 I Eph 6 1 Mg 6 2 Pap 3 2 Did 3 4 H 1 4 2 2 5 3 9 4 10 4 (2) .9 11 3 16 2 17 5 18 6 22 5 43 1 (2) 51 2 (2) 52 8 (3) 53 1 (2) 54 1 61 2 62 1 63 1 69 4 (2) 72 6 73 2 79 5.7 73 1 84 4 (2) 86 2 77 1 90 5.

(b) passive: I Cl 28 1.

(2) Intransitive: I Cl 25 4 I Tr 9 1 H 29 3 50 6.7 78 2.

(3) With prepositions:

(a) εἰς: Bar 16 10 H 1 5.

(4) With dependent clauses:

(a) ὅτι: H 30 2 33 6 35 5 36 9 39 11 43 21 51 4 59 4 72 4.

(b) accusative and infinitive: Bar 4 14.

(c) no example with ἵνα.

(d) interrogatives ποῖος H 91 6.
πόσος I Cl 56 16 H 72 1(2).
πῶς Bar 10 11.
τίς Bar 13 6.

(e) with μή H 50 5 68 5.
μήποτε H 17 6 9 18 7 60 2 65 2 105 5.

Here too there is no example of βλέπειν used with the accusative demonstrably with the meaning »beware of«. In this construction the meaning seems to be in the New Testament, the LXX and the Apostolic Fathers »see, look at, consider«. Without giving details we may report that the usage in the LXX is similar to that in the New Testament and the Apostolic Fathers. Preisigke-Kiessling support this as does Mauersberger's Polybios-Lexikon. Indeed a clear example anywhere of βλέπειν with the accustive meaning »to beware of« is still to be found.

We may relate this to one or two examples. Mk 4 24, βλέπετε τί ἀκούετε, is not »beware of what you hear«, but »consider what you hear«. Mk 13 9, βλέπετε δέ ὑμεῖς ἑαυτούς, does not mean »beware of yourselves«. We can see the development of this in the well-known expression in the papyrus, BGU 1079.24 (i A.D.), βλέπε σατὸν [= σαυτὸν] ἀπὸ τῶν Ἰουδαίων, »beware of the Jews«. We may also recall I Cor 1 26 βλέπετε γὰρ τὴν κλῆσιν ὑμῶν.

If the Apostle wanted to express this kind of meaning, he had ways of doing it as with ἀπέχεσθαι ἀπό I Th 4 3 5 22.

The interpretation of βλέπετε at Phl 3 2 is particularly important as scholars have argued that there is a total lack of connexion between

3 1 and 3 2 and have gone on to infer either that a passage has been lost between these two verses or that 3 2ff. is a fragment of another letter. In considering these suggestions the meaning of τὰ αὐτά in 3 1 and of βλέπετε in 3 2 is particularly important, but while the reference of τὰ αὐτά has been frequently debated that of βλέπετε has been taken for granted. With the meaning suggested by the evidence »look at, consider« the connexion of 3 2 with what has gone before is not as abrupt as is usually assumed.

A Study of the Relationship between *A Genesis Apocryphon* and the Pentateuchal Targumim in Genesis 14 1–12

By G. J. Kuiper

(Theological Seminary, Johnson C. Smith University, Charlotte, North Carolina)

Shortly after the publication of part of the text of *A Genesis Apocryphon*[1], the late Professor Paul E. Kahle raised the question whether this Aramaic scroll from 1Q might not be »an early specimen of a written Aramaic Pentateuch Targum from Palestine«, an ancient representative of the Palestinian Targum tradition[2]. M. Black, after a study of the published columns of the scroll from Qumran, put forward the tentative conclusion that it »is almost certainly our oldest written Palestinian Pentateuch Targum ...«[3].

It is the purpose of this inquiry to examine this hypothesis on the basis of a critical study of the narrative in Gen 14 1–12 in *A Genesis Apocryphon* (GA, columns XXI.23–XXII.1) and the Pentateuchal targumim (Targum Onkelos [O], Targum Pseudo-Jonathan [PJ], Ms Neofiti I [N], and the Fragmentary Targumim [FTgg])[4], subjecting

1 N. Avigad and Y. Yadin, A Genesis Apocryphon, A Scroll from the Wilderness of Judaea .... Columns II, XIX–XXI, 1956.

2 M. Black, The Recovery of the Language of Jesus, NTS 3 (1957), p. 310. In his The Cairo Geniza, 1959², p. 198, Kahle preferred to call it a »Midrash book«, noting the midrashic material characteristic of both the Genesis Apocryphon and the Palestinian Targum tradition.

3 NTS 3, op. cit., p. 313.

4 For O the edition by A. Sperber has been used: The Pentateuch according to Targum Onkelos ,The Bible in Aramaic, I 1959; for PJ the Add. MS 27031 of the British Museum (the ed. of this MS by M. Ginsburger, Pseudo-Jonathan, 1903, is often not reliable), with variants noted from the ed. princ. in Biblia Rabbinica.... At the command of Zuan Bragadin (1590/1); concerning the discovery and nature of N cf. A. Diez Macho, The Recently Discovered Palestinian Targum: Its Antiquity and Relationship with the Other Targums, Suppl VT 7 (1959), p. 222–245; for the FTgg the ed. princ. in the Biblia Rabbinica, 1517/8 (Bom); MS 110, Paris, Bibliotheque Nationale (Par); MS 440, Rome, Biblioteca Apostolica Vaticana (Vat); Codex Norimbergensis 1, Nürnberg, Stadtbibliothek (Nor); Codex Lipsiensis 1, Leipzig, F. Delitzsch Bibliothek (Lips); and quotations in ancient authors given in M. Ginsburger, Das Fragmententhargum, 1899, p. 91ff. The passage does not occur in the Cairo Geniza Fragments of the FT ed. by P. Kahle, Masoreten des Westens, II: Das Palästinische Pentateuchtargum..., 1930. I am indebted to M. Black, and M. C. Doubles, for the use of photostatic copies of some of these MSS and edd.

these texts to a linguistic analysis and a comparison of their interpretive materials. Both the fact that only five of the twenty columns of GA have been published so far, and the limits of this passage of twelve verses will make the conclusion only a tentative working hypothesis.

The examination of the relationship between GA and the Pent. tgg necessitates a prior consideration of the relations among the Pent. tgg, particularly with regard to PJ. I will briefly give my own conclusions in this respect, reached on the basis of a study of representative passages from the Pentateuch, and some supporting evidence from Gen 14 1–12, together with references to currently-held opinions. After this consideration, I will turn to the investigation of GA in relation to the Pent. tgg.

I.

It is undisputed that O differs from all the Pal. tgg (PJ, N, CG, FTgg) in its generally literal translation of the Hebr. text, whereas the Pal. tgg have longer or shorter midrashic additions[5]. It is, therefore, to the verses-proper that our critical attention must be turned to ascertain some working hypotheses of Pent. targumic relationships. Kahle argued that O originated and evolved in Babylonia from the third century on; that it became the official targum there, written in the literary »Reichsaramäisch«; and that it was taken from there to Palestine when the two countries had been united under Arab suzerainty, firmly establishing itself in Palestine subsequent to 1000 and replacing the earlier Pal. Tg, which had translated the Hebr. into the Aram. spoken in Palestine[6]. Some scholars have concluded that O itself is based to some extent on the Pal. Tg tradition[7], but among those who hold this opinion even G. Dalman, followed more recently by E. Y. Kutscher, admits that its language is not that spoken by Judean Jews, but that it differs from that of the P. Talmud and the

[5] The Cairo Geniza, op. cit., p. 192–195.

[6] Ibid.; Masoreten des Westens II, op. cit., p. 1*.

[7] W. Bacher, Kritische Untersuchungen zum Prophetentargum. Nebst einem Anhange über das gegenseitige Verhältniss der pentateuchischen Targumim, ZDMG 28 (1874), p. 59f., and Targum, The Jewish Encyclopedia 12, p. 59, cf. p. 61, »... the nucleus of the Palestinian Targum is older than the Babylonian, which was redacted from it.« Further, M. Ginsburger, Das Fragmententhargum, op. cit., p. XIV; G. Dalman, Grammatik des Jüdisch-Palästinischen Aramäisch..., 1905², p. 12f.; P. Grelot, Les Targums de Pentateuque. Étude comparative d'après Genèse, IV, 3–16, Semitica 9 (1959), p. 86f.; P. Wernberg-Møller, Prolegomena to a Re-examination of the Palestinian Targum Fragments of the Book of Genesis Published by P. Kahle, and their Relationship to the Peshitta, JSS 7 (1962), p. 262ff.; and G. Vermes, Haggadah in the Onkelos Targum, JSS 8 (1963), p. 169.

B. Talmud and is closer to Bibl. Aram., moreover that this tg is »eine gelehrte und künstliche Nachbildung des hebräischen Originals«[8]. Others have maintained that the Pal. Tg used O in its composition[9].

A study of the verses-proper in the tgg reveals the overwhelming evidence that the renderings of all Pal. tgg, including PJ, differ from those of O. Often all Pal. tgg agree with each other in a common translation different from O[10]; but many times the Pal. tgg reflect differences among themselves, all of which are unlike O[11]. The evidence does not permit us to hold that the general nature of any of the Pal. tgg (e.g. the FTgg or PJ) is a composite of a pre-Onkelos Pal. Tg and O[12]. The overwhelming evidence is that all the Pal. tgg render

[8] Dalman, op. cit., p. 13, cf. also p. VIIf., 40f.; E. Y. Kutscher, The Language of the Genesis Apocryphon, A Preliminary Study, 1957, p. 9f. Cf. Wm. B. Stevenson, (Revised by J. A. Emerton), Grammar of Palestinian Aramaic, 1962², p. 97f.

[9] E.g. J. Bassfreund, on the basis of the late midrashim in PJ and FT, Das Fragmenten-Targum zum Pentateuch, sein Ursprung und Charakter und sein Verhältnis zu den anderen pentateuchischen Targumim, MGWJ 40 (1896), p. 163, 405.

[10] E.g. in v. 3, »All these were united in the valley of Siddim...« (כל־אלה חברו אל־עמק השדם), the verb is rendered in PJ, N, Bom, Vat, and Nor: א(י)תבחרו (PJ, Vat, and Nor having the אית, prefix, characteristic of Pal. Aram. Cf. Dalman, op. cit., p. 402f.), and in O: אתכנשו, the Pal. tgg choosing the same root as the Hebr.; the noun »Siddim« is translated in PJ, N, Bom, Vat, Nor, and Levita: פרדיס(י)א. »the gardens,« a noun occurring only in the Pal. tgg, not in O (E. Brederek, Konkordanz zum Targum Onkelos, BZAW, 1906, p. 176; and J. Levy, Chaldäisches Wörterbuch über die Targumim, 1959, II p. 287) and in O: חקליא, »the fields.« The latter variant occurs again with the same evidence in v. 8 and 10. Cf. also v. 10, »And the valley of Siddim had many pits *full of* (מליין/מליא, PJ, N, Vat, Bom, Nor, Lips; or) *producing* (מסקן, O) bitumen;« and in v. 2 and 8 the orthography of »Zoar«.

[11] E.g. in the numerals *twelve, thirteenth,* and *fourteenth* in v. 4f.: PJ has the »worn-away forms,« i.e. forms in which the ע of עשׂ/סר, »ten«, has been lost, a characteristic orthography of Pal. Aram. (Stevenson, op. cit., p. 102): תרתיסירי...תיליסירי...בירביסרי; also in PJ the א of ארבע has become a י, an orthographical peculiarity of the Pal. tgg, not found in O (Dalman, op. cit., p. 97f., 126) N reads: תרתין עשרה...תלת עשרי...ארבעה עשרי: in תרתין N has the longer form (ibid., p. 102, 124f.) of תרתי, against O, where characteristically for O the *ai* is given up for an *a*: תרתא (ibid., p. 91, 126); N has עשרה in the first instance, characteristic of Pal. Aram., O having עסרי three times (Emerton in Stevenson, op. cit., p. 101).

[12] A. Geiger thought that both FT and PJ are a synthesis of O and a recension of the Pal. Tg (Urschrift und Übersetzungen der Bibel in ihrer Abhängigkeit von der inneren Entwicklung des Judenthums, 1857, p. 451–480); Kahle held this as a tentative hypothesis for PJ (Das palästinische Pentateuchtargum und das zur Zeit Jesu gesprochene Aramäisch, ZNW 49, 1958, p. 110). Ginsburger supposed the Pal. Tg in PJ to be a recension other than FT (Die Fragmente des Thargum jeruschalmi zum Pentateuch, ZDMG 57, 1903, p. 80), and Grelot identified this recension as N (Semitica 9, op. cit., p. 88).

differently from O and that they generally reflect vocabulary, orthography, and syntax of Pal. Aram., even when they evidence different streams of the Pal. Tg tradition.

Secondly, there is agreement with O in all the Pal. tgg, but this agreement is seen to be minor when correctly estimated in the perspective of the predominant difference between O and the Pal. tgg. There is agreement with O not only in PJ, but also in N, the FTgg, and sometimes in several Pal. tgg[13]. It is remarkable that in the cases where some Pal. tgg agree with O, PJ often concurs with those Pal. tgg which do not accord with O[14]. This agreement with O, found in all the Pal. tgg, must be assessed correctly as minor against the predominant disagreement between the Pal. tgg on the one hand and O on the other[15]. The evidence is clearly against the thesis that some Pal. tgg (e.g. PJ or FT) may be revisions of O in accordance with a pre-Onkelos Pal. Tg tradition[16]. Another explanation has to be found for the minor agreement between O and all the Pal. tgg. The remarkable evidence, in passages where some Pal. tgg agree with O while others do not, that PJ concurs with the latter, reinforces the conclusion that PJ is one of the Pal. tgg.

Thirdly, we consider the circumstances of this minor agreement between one or more Pal. tgg and O. This agreement varies from verse

[13] In PJ, e.g. in v. 11, »the goods«: רכש is rendered by O and PJ: קני(י)נא, »the possessions«, and N: ממונהון, »their wealth«. In N, at v. 10, both N and O read לטורא, »to the mountain«, and PJ uniquely renders לטווריא, »to the mountains«, not only making the meaning generally easier (»they fled to the mountains«), but also using the noun טַוְרָא which occurs only in the Pal. tgg (Levy, op. cit., I p. 298). In v. 9 the FTgg: Vat (ארבעה) and Par (ארבעא), as well as N, agree with O: ארבעה in, »four kings«, using the fem. abs. st. with the masc. noun. PJ has the constr. st. ארבעת.

[14] E.g. in v. 9, O and N translate the Hebr. שנער, »Shinar«, with בבל, »Babel«; PJ, Bom, Vat, and Nor, however, with פונטום, »Pontus.« A. Diez Macho has also called attention to this important fact, noting e.g. that in Dtn 5 6–21, PJ corresponds with CG versus Par and perhaps N which agree with O. (Suppl VT 7, op. cit., p. 239).

[15] For example in v. 11, to which we referred above with regard to PJ and O rendering alike »the possessions«, we find that in the whole clause PJ predominantly follows the Pal. tg, »And they took (PJ, N: ונס(י)בו, a Pal. Aram. usage; O does not use נסב for the Qal of לקח, Brederek, op. cit., p. 61; O: ושבו, »and they captured«) every possession (cf. above of Sodom and Gomorrah; PJ spells uniquely with ו: דסדום ועמורה, possibly characteristic of Pal. Aram.; cf. H. Odeberg, The Aramaic Portions of Bereshit Rabba, with Grammar of Galilaean Aramaic, 1939, II p. 154, 156, 27) and all their food (PJ, N: מזונ(י)הון, which does not occur in O, Brederek, op. cit., p. 162; O: מיכלהון) «. PJ represents a Pal. tg here, generally in accord with N, with only one agreement with O.

[16] As Dalman, op. cit., p. 32f., 44.

to verse and from tg to tg. M. C. Doubles in his study »The Fragment Targum« has noted that the agreement with O is more marked in Nor and Bom than in Vat and Lips[17]. A study of the whole of N, PJ, and CG parallel to that of the FTgg is necessary to determine the variation in this agreement. These minor similarities between O and the Pal. tgg, however, appear to be explained most easily by the fact that the Pal. tgg were copied by scribes who knew O[18].

Fourthly, we need to ask whether the hypothesis of such influence from O through scribal copying adequately explains the passages where we find agreement between O and the Pal. tgg in which the midrashic additions or substitutions of the Pal. tgg occur in O as well. This striking evidence[19], found throughout the Pent., of such agreement between O and the Pal. tgg particularly when O has incorporated the midrashic addition or substitution of one or more of the Pal. tgg, means that O knew the Pal. tg tradition and used this tradition in its own composition. It appears to me that this conclusion explains most adequately these minor agreements with O in the otherwise unique Pal. Pent. Tg tradition. If this thesis is correct, PJ is not a Pal. tg revised under the influence of O[20], and FT does not consist of marginal variants from the Pal. Tg to O or to a recension of the Pal. Tg already influenced by O[21]. Instead the minor agreements

[17] A Critical Re-examination of the Editio Princeps, Das Fragmententhargum, by M. Ginsburger, in the Light of Recent Discoveries (St. Andrews University, unpublished doctoral dissertation, 1962), p. 33*.

[18] Grelot has pointed out that the oral tradition of O has possibly influenced the MSS of the Pal. tgg: »Il a donc pu y avoir contamination latérale des textes, non seulement par alignement intentionnel, mais surtout par reminiscences involontaires aboutissant à modifier telle expression ou telle orthographe« (Semitica 9, op. cit., p. 63).

[19] In our passage the following evidence is in point. In v. 7, »and they came to En-mishpat« (ויבאו אל־עין משפט), PJ renders, »and they came to the place *where* the judgment *was decreed* (Ithp. פלג)«: ואתו לאתרא דאיתפליג דינא, and O reads: »and they came to the valley of *the decree of* (noun פילוגא) the judgment«: ואתו למישר פילוג דינא. O has an abbreviated form of the addition of PJ; the Hebr. word עין, »spring«, in the proper noun *En-mishpat* is translated freely as in PJ, but by a different noun. In v. 6, O renders »the valley of Paran«: מישר פארן for MT, »El-paran«: איל פארן, following PJ, Bom, Vat, Nor, in interpreting *El* as *valley*. Cf. also in v. 5, »the Rephaim«.

[20] As held by: Bacher, The Jewish Encyclopedia, op. cit., XII, p. 59ff.; Z. Frankel, Einiges zu den Targumim, ZRIJ 3 (1846), p. 120; T. Jansma, Twee Haggada's uit de Palestijnse Targum van de Pentateuch, 1950, espec. p. 4–7; and A. Diez Macho, Suppl VT 7, op. cit., p. 239.

[21] The former has been held by: Bacher, ZDMG 28, op. cit., p. 59; Bassfreund, MGWJ 40, op. cit., p. 405; Kahle, ZNW 49, op. cit., p. 110; and Jansma, op. cit., p. 5f.; and the latter by Ginsburger, Pseudo-Jonathan, op. cit., p. XIVf.

between O and the Pal. tgg are examples of the dependence of O on the Pal. Tg tradition.

Fifthly, the Pal. Pent. Tg tradition, which includes PJ, is a varied as well as a unified tradition. These tgg represent one tradition because of their common basis in the Hebr. text and their inception and further development in Palestine. Yet their independent development in separate localities, over periods of time, brought about different recensions or streams in this tradition. Grelot has noted the differences between N and Par and concluded that we have here two recensions of the Pal. Pent. Tg[22]. Ginsburger concluded that PJ and FT[23], and also the MSS of the FTgg, e.g. Vat and Par[24], represent separate streams of this tradition. Doubles has identified four such families of the Pal. Pent. Tg tradition: N, CG, Par, and Vat-Lips-Nor-Bom[25]. Now we must add PJ as another such family, which, besides N, is the only Pal. tg covering the whole Pent[26]. These five families need to be studied as separate streams of the Pal. Pent. Tg tradition in the analysis of Pal. Aram. and exegesis. This total Pal. tradition must be considered next to the authoritative, Babylonian Targum Onkelos, which was written in official literary Aram., depends at least in part on this Pal. tradition, and may have influenced this tradition through the memory of O on the part of scribes copying the Pal. tgg. The marginal readings in N appear to be variants from the MT, all Pent. tgg, and even GA[27].

With these working hypotheses regarding Pent. targumic relationships it is possible to turn to an examination of GA and the tgg.

[22] Grelot, Semitica 9, op. cit., p. 85.

[23] Pseudo-Jonathan, op. cit., p. XVII; Fragmententhargum, op. cit., p. XIV; and ZDMG 57, op. cit., p. 80.

[24] Neue Fragmente des Thargum jeruschalmi, ZDMG 58 (1904), p. 377.

[25] M. C. Doubles, Toward the Publication of the Extant texts of the Palestinian Targum(s), VT 15 (1965), p. 25. I think that it is unlikely that any of the FTgg are, strictly speaking, marginal variants from one recension of the Pal. Tg to the PJ recension of the latter, as was held by Zunz, Die gottesdienstlichen Vorträge der Juden, historisch entwickelt. Ein Beitrag zur Alterthumskunde und biblischen Kritik, zur Literatur- und Religionsgeschichte, 1892², p. 69–75; and Frankel, ZRIJ 3, op. cit., p. 120.

[26] A new edition of the sixteenth cent. MS of PJ is necessary, not only to provide it with a critical apparatus of variants from the ed. princ. of 1591, but also to overcome the errors in Ginsburger's ed. of the MS.

[27] In our passage mgg variants are from the MT: v. 5 (also O and PJ) and 9 (also O and the FTgg); from O in v. 4; from PJ in v. 7; from O and PJ in v. 8; from Bom, Vat, Nor in v. 6 (2x) and 10; from FT quotations in v. 1 (Levita, Aruk) and 12 (Levita); and from the GA (!) in v. 4.

II.

In GA, as in the tgg, the Aram. paraphrase follows the Hebr. verse by verse, though this is most marked in columns XXI and XXII, and contains verses-proper and free midrashic additions[28]. M. Black has called attention to the agreement of fact of GA »with the pre-Onkelos Palestinian Pentateuch Targum«[29]. The study of Gen 14_{1-12} reveals the following characteristics of GA in relation to the tgg and the Hebr. text.

In the verses-proper there is agreement in GA with all the Pal. tgg as well as with the Hebr. text. The agreement with one tg is particularly marked with N, but is also found with PJ[30]. There is accordance with N and PJ, and with all the Pal. tgg[31]. As is the case in all tgg,

[28] Cf. Black, NTS 3, op. cit., p. 310f., and M. R. Lehmann, 1Q Genesis Apocryphon in the Light of the Targumim and Midrashim, RQ 1 (1958/59), p. 252.

[29] Op. cit., p. 311.

[30] *With N*: In v. 4, in »twelve«, GA and N follow the Pal. Aram. orthography: עשרה (Emerton in Stevenson, op. cit., p. 101f.). In the same verse MT: מרדו is rendered by GA and N: מרדו בה, »they rebelled against him« (cf. LXX Codex Eugenii in Holmes and Parsons: συναπέστησαν ἀπ' αὐτοῦ, listed in: The Old Testament in Greek..., ed. A. E. Brooke and N. McLean, 1906, I, I; LXX Cod. Vat: ἀπέστησαν.). In v. 8–9 there is factual, and to some extent, verbal agreement between GA and N. The MT has: ...ויערכו אתם מלחמה...את כדרלעמר, »and they arranged against them the battle line... against Chedorlaomer...«, translating אִתָּם, *with them* as in Judg 20 20 (cf. עם in this meaning in II Chr 13 3), and אֵת as probably being the same preposition repeated preceding the kings against whom the battle is to be fought: *against* Chedorlaomer... (at Judg 20 20 there is misunderstanding among the versions about אתם: Pesh. ܟܠܗܘܢ ܗܠܝܢ ܥܒܕܘ ܩܪܒܐ: all of these made war; Bohairic-Lag., Ethiop.: παρετάξαντο εἰς πόλεμον: they arranged themselves (or: their troops) for battle; and the LXX, which is redundant: παρετάξαντο αὐτοῖς εἰς πόλεμον: and they arranged their own troops, themselves, for battle). N has לקבלתהון...ית, translating specifically, »against them«, followed by the sign of the direct object. This explicit reading is also found in GA: at Hebr: אתם the ms of GA is illegible, but Hebr: את is rendered לקובלי: *against him*. GA agrees with N factually, and to an extent verbally. Cf. further v. 7, »in Hazazon-Tamar«, and v. 11, »of Sodom and Gomorrah«.

With PJ: In v. 4, in »twelve«, GA follows Pal. Aram., omitting the final ן in תרתי (Dalman, op. cit., p. 102, 124f.; cf. Mmg: תרתי!) as also in PJ: תרתיסירי, characteristic of Pal. Aram. (Stevenson, op. cit., p. 101). Cf. also the orthography of *Sodom* and *Gomorrah* in v. 2. 8. 11, resp. XXI 24. 31. 33, where the preponderance of the *o* vowel is probably characteristic of Pal. Aram. (Odeberg, op. cit., II, p. 154; cf. also Kutscher, op. cit., p. 22f.).

[31] *With N and PJ*: In v. 4, *in* in »in the thirteenth year«, is expressed by the accus. of time in MT: ושלש עשרה שנה, followed in this by O and Nmg. (Gesenius Hebrew Grammar, ed. E. Kautzsch and A. E. Cowley, 1956², p. 374) This adverbial accus. is frequent in Eastern Aram., e.g. B. Talm., but uncommon in Western

GA occasionally follows literally the Hebr. text[32]. Thus there is every indication of accord between GA and the Pal. tgg in the verses-proper.

There are a few instances of correspondence between GA and O. The remarkable fact is that where GA corresponds with O, it generally corresponds also with one or more of the Pal. tgg[33].

In many instances there are unique readings in GA in the verses-proper[34]. This phenomenon, also found in each Pal. tg, is character-

---

Aram., which uses ב, e.g. *Ber. Rab.* (Max L. Margolis, A Manual of the Aramaic Language of the Babylonian Talmud, 1910, p. 74; Odeberg, op. cit., p. 87. PJ), N, and GA follow the Western Aram. syntax and have ב. Cf. also v. 12 (XXI 34).

With all the Pal. tgg: Most important is the rendering of *Gebal* in GA, PJ, and N, for *Seir* in v. 6 (XXI 29). גבלא is peculiar to the Pal. tgg, not occurring in O, and is found in Sam as well (Levy, op. cit., I p. 123; Black, NTS 3, op. cit., p. 312; and Avigad and Yadin, op. cit., p. 29). To be noted also is the preference of די rather than ד in GA, both in the genitive construction (v. 3, XXI 25) and for the relative pronoun (v. 5, XXI 28), which runs through the whole GA so far published. די occurs in Bibl. Aram., the ancient portions of the B. Talm., as an archaic use in *Ber. Rab.*, in 11QtgJob, and in such older documents as Megilla Ta'anith, Gamaliel's letters in Tosephta, Sanhedrin 2 6, the divorce form in J. Gittin IX 3, the form in J. Jebamoth 14b, and significantly also in the Pal. tgg; ד, on the other hand occurs in the B. Talm., and generally in O. Hence, GA represents ancient usage here, in common with the Pal. tgg, incl. PJ and 11QtgJob, as opposed to the B. Talm. and O (H. Bauer—P. Leander, Grammatik des Biblisch-Aramäischen, 1962, p. 85f.; Margolis, op. cit., p. 18; Odeberg, op. cit., II p. 7; J. v. d. Ploeg, Le Targum de Job de la Grotte 11 de Qumran (11QtgJob), Première Communication, 1962, p. 7; Dalman, op. cit., p. 116; and Sperber, op. cit., I p. viiif. Examples of די in the Pal. tgg are PJ, CG, Nmg, Vat, at Ex 19 4; Bom and Nor at Gen 14 5; N at Gen 8 1; Par at Gen 4 10; and Lips at Dtn 34 10. Cf. espec. the discussion by M. C. Doubles, »Indications of Antiquity in the Orthography and Morphology of the Fragment Targum«, in this vol.).

32 *With the Hebr. text*: In v. 1 (XXI 23), »Goiim«, v. 3 (XXI 25), »the valley«, and »Siddim«, v. 5 (XXI 27f.), »the Rephaim...the Zuzim...the Enim«, and in v. 1f. the constr. st. in the descriptions, »the king of....«

33 *With O alone*: In v. 1, GA renders *Shinar* (שנער) as בבל (so N-interlinear variant; in v. 9 N also has בבל).

With O and PJ: In v. 5, »and they destroyed«, is ומחו (MT: ויכו); in v. 12, »and he dwelt«, is ותבו (following MT: וישבו).

With O, PJ, and FT: In v. 5, GA agrees with O, PJ, Bom, and Nor in rendering »the Rephaim in Ashteroth-Qarnaim«, as »the Rephaim *who were* (די/ד,) in Ashteroth-Qarnaim«.

With O, PJ, and N: In v. 8, »and they went out«, ונפק(ו) (MT: ויצא); and in v. 10, »and they fled«, ועדק(ו) (MT: וינסו). Cf. also v. 2 (XXI 25), »Zeboiim«.

34 In v. 3 (XXI 25), GA reads: אזדמנו, »they met«, (MT: חברו) using a verb not found in O for Hebr. חבר (Brederek, op. cit., p. 149) which does occur however in the Pal. tgg, e.g. CG at Lev 22 27. Cf. also v. 5 (XXI 27), where GA renders freely, as characteristic of the Pal. tg tradition, »... the king of Elam commanded to all his associates«.

istic of independently and freely developing tgg. It is significant that most unique readings of GA are related to a Palestinian context in language or tradition[35], providing further evidence of the relationship of GA to the Pal. tg tradition.

[35] In v. 2 and 10 (XXI 24, 32; cf. v. 8) GA spells »Gomorrah«: עומרם (MT and tgg: ע(ו)מרא/ה), for which the explanation may be found in the preference of Pal. Aram. to add a final ן to words, and the characteristic of the Pal. tgg to alternate final ם and ן (Dalman, op. cit., p. 102; cf. Kutscher, op. cit., p. 23f.). In v. 2 (XXI 25) the orthography שמיאבר in GA for שמאבר in MT and the tgg, is similar to the Pal. Aram. of *Ber. Rab.*, in which יא is used for *e* (Odeberg, op. cit., II, p. 153). In v. 4 (XXI 26f.), »they served«, MT: עבדו , is rendered in GA: הווא יהבין מדתהון, »they continued paying their tribute«, using the noun מדא, not used in O, but occurring amongst others in *Ber. Rab.* (Brederek, op. cit., and Jastrow, op. cit., p. 797). To be noted also is the use of ל to the exclusion of ית as the sign of the direct object, both with the pron. suff. (e.g. XXII 9) and prefixed to a noun (e.g. XXI 28). Both ל and ית are used in these ways in the Pal. tgg (e.g. Lev 22 27 in PJ, N, CG, Par, Bom: ל) as well as Christ. Pal. Syr. (»CPA«; F. Schulthess, Grammatik des Christlich-Palästinischen Aramäisch, ed. E. Littmann, 1924, p. 88), and the Pal. Talm. and Midrashim (Dalman, op. cit., p. 110, 226). The use of ית in the tgg may be a slavish imitation of the Bibl. Hebr. את (Dalman, op. cit., p. 110) or may have been a usage of Old Aram. (F. Rosenthal, Die Aramaistische Forschung seit Th. Nöldeke's Veröffentlichungen, 1964, p. 201, who cites Nöldeke, Syr. Gram.², p. 217 n. 1). The usage of GA is thus found in Western Aram., though the use of ל to the exclusion of ית is peculiar to GA and may point in the direction of Eastern Aram. (Kutscher's argument, op. cit., p. 21, that this use of ל with suffixes is an earlier usage is questionable, as these forms occur seldom in older Aram.—cf. W. Baumgartner, Lexicon in Veteris Testamenti Libros, co-ed. L. Koehler, 1953, p. 1089—and are not found in the older Aram. in the B. Talm.—cf. Margolis, op. cit., p. 84—). In v. 5 (XXI 29) GA significantly has a מ above the line at לזוומיא (with מ above), having changed Zuzmaiah to Zamzummiah, reading, »...and he destroyed the Rephaiah who were in Ashterah-Qarnaim and the Zamzummiah who were in Ammon...«, for Hebr., »... and he smote the Rephaim in Ashteroth-Qarnaim, the Zuzim in Ham....». Avigad and Yadin have noted that GA identified »the Zuzim« with »the Zamzummim« of Dtn 2 20, the name that the Ammorites gave the Rephaim, the tall people who lived in Ammon before them. Having made this identification, »the Zuzim in Ham« (MT) are no longer a separate people, but are the same as the preceding »Rephaim«. Accordingly, MT: בְּהָם, »in Ham«, is understood as בָּהֶם, »among them«, referring to the preceding Rephaim, who lived in Ammon according to Dtn, and is translated in GA: די בעמן, »who were in Ammon« (Avigad — Yadin, op. cit., p. 35. Cf. LXX: ἔθνη ἰσχυρὰ ἅμα αὐτοῖς, »and the mighty people *with* them«, Pesh: ܘܥܫܝܢܐ ܕܥܡܗܘܢ »and the strong ones who were *with* them«, and the Vulg.). It is significant that the same tradition is expressed in the tgg, possibly in two ways. First, N, Bom, Vat, Nor, Levita render MT, »in Ham«, as דבהון (די בהון), and MT, »the Zuzim«, as ויית זיותניא, »and the bright (noble) ones among them«. As in GA, the reference is to a group among the Rephaim, and not to a separate people of the Zuzim as in

In GA, as in the Pal. tgg, we find midrashic additions. Among the shorter additions some agree with the tgg[36], and others have affinities to Palestinian traditions, as has been noted in the discussion of the unique renderings. GA also includes unique, longer additions, another characteristic of the Pal. tgg[37]. In the presentation of midrashic additions, some of which coincide with those in the Pal. tgg, while others are unique and often reflect likeness to Palestinian traditions, the nature of GA is revealed as the same as that of the Pal. Pent. Tg tradition.

Finally, there is the question of the relationship to the book of Jubilees in some of the unique readings of GA. In v. 1 (XXI. 23), for MT, »And it was *in* the days *of* Amraphel ..., Ariok..., they did ...«, GA alone substitutes, »*Before* these days there came Amraphel ..., Ariok ..., *and* they made ...«, correcting the grammar[38] and indicating a new sequence of events, in which »before these days«, puts Chedorlaomer's action at least before Abram's move to Hebron[39], making a difficult reading[40]. The reading in Jubilees 13 22, »And *in*

---

the Hebr. Secondly, PJ and O speak of »the strong ones«: וית תקיפיא דבהמתא »and the strong ones who were in Ham«. »in Ham« adheres to the Hebr. text, though the fem. emph. ending is given in Aram.; but the interpretation of »Zuzim« as »the strong ones« identifies this group with »the strong ones« of Dtn 2 20, i.e. the Zamzummim, the Ammonites' name for the giant Rephaim. PJ and O thus relate the same tradition as GA. We may safely conclude here that the same tradition of interpretation lies behind GA on the one hand and the Pal. tgg of N and FTgg on the other; and furthermore that O as well as PJ follows this Pal. tradition, different from the Hebr. text. Cf. also v. 10 (XXI 33), »in pits«, and v. 11f. (XXI 33f.), נכסיא, »goods«, as Pal. Aram.

[36] In v. 5 (XXI 28f.): די (ד׳), in »*who were* in Ashteroth-Qarnaim, ... in Ham, ... in Shaveh Qiriathaim« (GA, O, PJ, N, FTgg).

[37] E.g. GA ends v. 3 (XXI 25f.) with the addition, »and the king of Elam and the kings who were with him prevailed over the king of Sodom and over all his associates, and they placed tribute upon them«. Cf. such additions as PJ in v. 1 explaining Amraphel, »he is Nimrod, who commanded that Abram be thrown in the fire«.

[38] The grammar of the Hebr., in which »Amraphel etc.« is both the possessive, indicating the time, as well as the subject of the verb (due probably to a mistranslation of an Akk. original *inūma*, »when«, as »in the days of«; cf. E. A. Speiser, Genesis, The Anchor Bible, 1964, p. 101), is impossible. Cf. Vulg.: *in illo tempore*.

[39] So Avigad—Yadin, op. cit., p. 33.

[40] The sequence of events in the narrative is: Lot's departure from Abram (Gen 13 11–13), God's command to Abram to survey the land and promise of it to him and the innumerable descendants whom he will have (Gen 13 14–17), andAbram's moving to Hebron where he builds an altar (part of his survey of the land) (Gen 13 18). The difficulty is that at the end of Chedorlaomer's military action an escaped person comes to Abram at *Hebron* (Gen 14 13).

this year came Chedorlaomer, ... Amraphel, ... and slew ...«[41] is the easier compared with GA, in that in the former the military action of Chedorlaomer occurred in the same year as Abram's move to Hebron. In a cautious way we would ask whether the relationship between Jubilees, »in form a midrashic targum on Genesis«[42], and GA is not one in which Jubilees, representing the easier reading, is a further development of, and depends upon GA, the latter representing the harder reading[43]? In v. 10 (XXI. 32f.) we find a Pal. tradition (*Ber. Rab.*) in GA, which also occurs in Jubilees[44]. Though we need to know more about the origins of Jubilees, we may cautiously infer that the origins of Jubilees are possibly to be found in Pal. traditions, perhaps in the tradition represented by GA.

The common nature of GA and the Pal. tgg is evidenced clearly in v. 1 (XXI. 23). GA renders: אריוך מלך כפתוך for MT: אריוך מלך אלסר (Arioch king of Ellasar). כפתוך has been identified by Avigad and Yadin as most probably referring to Cappadocia. This spelling, which is not found elsewhere[45], is thought to be due to a confusion of כפתוך with כפתור (Caphtor). In a number of passages the Biblical *Caphtor* or *Caphtorim* is translated as *Cappadocia* or *Cappadocians* in the tgg, Pesh., LXX, and Vulg. But it is not clear why GA spells כפתוך in confusion with the Hebr.: כפתור, when the latter is rendered in Aram. as קפודקיא or קפוטקיא. As reasons for this identification are given the renderings in Symmachus (Ἀριὼχ βασιλεὺς Πόντου) and Vulg. (*Arioch rex Ponti*) in this verse, and the explanation in Gen. Rab. 41_4 of אילסרים, a kind of pistachio which grows in Asia Minor and particularly in the forests of Pontus, by their place of origin, Ellasar[46].

Information from the Pal. tgg now confirms this identification of כפתוך as *Cappadocia*. Nmg at Dtn 2 23b reads כפדכייה for *Cappadocia*, the only known instance outside GA of the spelling with two Kaph's[47].

41 R. H. Charles, The Apocrypha and Pseudepigrapha of the Old Testament in English, II 1913, p. 33.

42 C. C. Torrey, The Apocryphal Literature, 1953, p. 126.

43 GA lists the kings in a different order in v. 1, putting Chedorlaomer first, in agreement with Jubilees 13 22, which is probably based on this implied order in v. 4f. Cf. Avigad—Yadin, op. cit., p. 34.

44 This tradition, that the king of Sodom did not fall into a pit but escaped, removes the contradiction in the continuation of the narrative in v. 17, where the king of Sodom comes to greet Abram, after the latter had been victorious over Chedorlaomer and his allies. It occurs also in *Ber. Rab.* 41 5–7 and Jubilees 13 22.

45 The tgg, Talmudim and Midrashim have קפודקיא and קפוטקיא only. Cf. M. Jastrow, A Dictionary of the Targumim, the Talmud Babli and Yerushalmi, and the Midrashic Literature, 1950, p. 1398, and J. Levy, Wörterbuch über die Talmudim und Midrashim, IV 1963, p. 351. But cf. below Nmg at Dtn 2 23b.

46 Avigad—Yadin, op. cit., p. 9, 34.

47 O reads קפוטכאי at Gen 10 14 in the Lisbon (1491) Bibl. Hebr. Cf. Sperber, op. cit.

The existence of both spellings of *Cappadocia* in the Pal. tg tradition of N and Nmg (קפודקיא and כפדכייה) confirms the identification of כפתוך in GA as *Cappadocia*.

Furthermore, at v. 1, Nmg reads: דפונטוס, for N: דאלסר, in: מלכא דאלסר. In v. 9, the only other occurrence of אלסר in the MT, N itself translates: דפונטוס and Nmg: דאלסר. This identification of *Ellasar* with *Pontus*, also found in Symm. and Vulg., further substantiates the reading *Cappadocia* in GA, because at one time, parts, and later, all of Pontus was included in Cappadocia[48]. PJ reads: דתלסר in both passages, and the FTgg in v. 9: דאלסר (Bom, Vat, and Nor). PJ and these FTgg however have דפונטוס with reference to Amraphel, the king of Shinar, referred to immediately preceding, in v. 9, and PJ alone in v. 1[49]. This reading *Pontus* in the Pal. tg tradition lying behind PJ and FTgg may be an interpolation at the wrong king, in which case it can be taken with reference to MT, *Ellasar*[50]. Thus all the Pal. tgg extant at v. 1 and 9, PJ, FTgg (Bom, Vat, Nor, and the quotations in Aruk and Levita), N, and Nmg, support the thesis that כפתוך in GA refers to Cappadocia. Hence, the Pal. tgg, in their identification of *Ellasar* with *Pontus* verify the reading of *Cappadocia* in GA[51]. GA shares with these Pal. tgg[52] the spelling of *Cappadocia* (Nmg, Dtn 2 23b) and the tradition of *Cappadocia-Pontus* for *Ellasar* in Gen 14 1 (PJ, N, Nmg, FTgg). The Pal. tgg, including PJ, and GA reflect a common tradition of orthography and interpretation at this point.

It is clear that GA is a targumic text. Following the Hebr. text, the Aram. translation inserts midrashic material. It parallels the free translations of the Pal. tgg and is unlike the literal translation of O in which we find very few additions (and these are minor) to the Hebr. text. In the study of this passage in GA and the Pal. tgg, many unique renderings have been found in GA. This is a characteristic of the Pal. tgg also, and is a reflection of the free and separate development of

48 The Interpreter's Dictionary of the Bible, III 1962, p. 841.

49 At Gen 14 1, quotations from the FT are found in Aruk: פנטוס, and Levita: פנטס. It is not clear whether these quotations refer to MT *Ellasar*, or to *Shinar*.

50 The Pal. tgg, however, read *Pontus* for MT *Shinar* in some passages: at Gen 10 10: PJ, Par, and Nmg; at Gen 11 2: Bom, Vat, Par, Nor, and Nmg; at Gen 14 1: PJ; and at Gen 14 9: PJ, Bom, Vat, and Nor.

51 *Gen. Rab.* 42 4 explains אלאסר as אנטיוכס. M. R. Lehmann has noted that this midrash may be referring to the same location as GA at Gen 14 1, because Antioch was in the vicinity of Mount Taurus, which formed the Southern border of Cappadocia. (RQ 1, op. cit., p. 261).

52 PJ shares the tradition of the Pal. tgg and differs here in the verse-proper from O. At v. 1, PJ reads, »Pontus«, with Nmg and FTgg, versus O, »Ellasar«. Even the identification of MT, »Shinar« as »Pontus« is made in PJ and the other Pal. tgg, but is absent from O.

the individual Pal. tg as an independent translation of the Hebr. text. Even more significant is the affinity to Pal. Aram. and Pal. traditions in these unique renderings of GA, which supports the hypothesis that GA is a Pal. tg. The occasional close agreement with the Hebr. text is found in all Pal. tgg and points to the nature of the tgg as translations of the Hebr. text. Agreement of the renderings of GA is found with all the Pal. tgg extant for our passage, PJ, N, and the FTgg, but is particularly marked with N. GA appears to be a Pal. tg related to N. Where GA reflects accord with O, it does this nearly always with one or more of the Pal. tgg. It is difficult to understand dependence on O in the same passages in different tgg, which present the general character of having developed independently and freely. It is also difficult to explain this fact in these tgg as influence from O through the copying of the Pal. tgg by scribes who remembered O, though this is not impossible. It is more likely that O depends in these instances on the Pal. tg tradition, and that *this* tradition, and not O, is represented in GA and the Pal. tgg in these examples. This evidence in GA supports the same conclusion reached with regard to agreements between O and the Pal. tgg. Our conclusion is the tentative thesis that GA is a unique recension of the Pal. Pent. Tg tradition, to be placed next to those of PJ, N, CG, Par, and Vat-Lips-Nor-Bom; that this recension is related to N; and that it, as well as the other Pal. Pent. tgg, lies behind the authoritative translation of O. The significance of the identification of GA as a Pal. tg, to be dated no later than the first century A.D., lies in the contact it gives us with Palestinian Jewish interpretations and the Palestinian Aramaic of the first centuries B.C. and A.D[53].

[53] Lehmann, RQ 1, op. cit., p. 249–263, who has concluded that GA probably represents the pre-Onkelos Pal. Tg tradition.

The Shiloaḥ Inscription Reconsidered

By G. Levi Della Vida *

(Via Po, 9 Roma)

Although it is no longer unique as it was at the time it was found, in 1880, the Shiloaḥ inscription still remains the most significant among the inscriptions in Old Hebrew, nor has its position been impaired by the discovery of the Gezer calendar, the Silwān epitaph and the Samaria and Yavneh-Yam ostraca (the Lakish ostraca being set apart because of their character of »letters«). Beside being »the only monumental inscription on stone«[1], it is related to a historical event mentioned in the Bible, namely the opening, of a tunnel through which the water of the »Virgin's Spring« was made to flow into the pool of Shiloaḥ/Siloam on the southeastern spur of the Temple Hill in Jerusalem. This impressive achievement, for which credit is given to the king of Judah Hezekiah (715–686 B.C.), is mentioned or hinted at in II Kings 20 $_{20}$ II Chr 32 $_{3-4.30}$ and Sir 48 $_{17}$. The sixline text is sufficiently perspicuous, in spite of a couple of gaps due to the breaking off of the stone and of lack of agreement among scholars about the exact meaning of some words. The remarks which follow wholly disregard the philological discussion of the text; however, in order to make understanding easier, it has been thought advisable to add a translation which essentially reproduces the one which was given by G. A. Cooke more than sixty years ago[2] and also takes into account the most recent translation by W. F. Albright[3]:

> [1][...] of the boring through. And such was the event of the boring through. While [the miners were swinging?] [2]the axe each towards his fellow and while there were still three cubits to be bored through [there was hear]d the voice of each cal[3]ling to his fellow, for there was a split (?) in the rock on the right [and on the left?]. And on the day of the [4]boring through the miners struck, each confronting his fellow, pick against pick, and [5]the water flowed from the spring to the pool for 1,200 cubits. One hund[6]red cubits was the height of the rock above the heads of the miners.

* Der Verfasser ist am 25. 11. 1967 verstorben.

[1] This connotation is given by Röllig in H. Donner — W. Röllig, Kanaanäische und aramäische Inschriften, 1962–1965, II p. 186 (No. 189). One will find there the essential bibliography on the subject.

[2] A Text-Book of North-Semitic Inscriptions, 1903, No. 2, p. 15.

[3] J. B. Pritchard, Ancient Near Eastern Texts relating to the Old Testament, 1950, 1955², p. 321*b*.

Besides the questions which arise from the literal interpretation of the wording, some other no less important remain, which have been the reason for an impressive number of essays[4]. In the first place, attention has been called to the odd circumstance that the script, which is carved on the right wall of the tunnel, covers only the lower part, a little less than one half, of a broad surface which had been smoothed previously as though to receive a much longer text. Actually, some scholars have surmised that the present inscription contains only the latter part of a report, the former part of which was never carved at its proper place.

Another unsolved problem refers to the authorship of the inscription. It has been commonly assumed that the workers who cut through the tunnel were responsible for it[5]. But a still more mysterious riddle arises from the stylistic set-up of the text. Even if no other Old Hebrew monumental inscription has been known so far, as was remarked above, a sizable amount of monumental inscriptions in Phoenician and Aramaic is now available (to which the Moabite stele of Mesha may be added) and they yield a correct notion of the epigraphic style as was currently employed in the Near East from the 9th to the 7th century B.C., a style which presents a considerable uniformity, and which we should expect to see also used, with no substantial difference, in a Hebrew inscription of the same age. In all records of the same nature, be they Phoenician, Aramaic or Moabite, one constantly meets the name of the person who set them up, generally a king or a ruler; if their content is religious, the name of one or more deities is always mentioned; furthermore, the circumstances under which the events recorded in the text took place are never passed under silence. Our text differs entirely from this pattern: it opens abruptly with a hint at the boring through of the water-tunnel[6], and proceeds by relating the queer story of the unexpected meeting

[4] A detailed discussion of the different viewpoints, together with an extensive bibliography, can be found in D. Diringer, Le iscrizioni antico-ebraiche palestinesi, 1934, p. 81–102, a work which is brought up to date by S. Moscati, L'epigrafia ebraica antica, 1951, see p. 40–43.

[5] After many others, this is mantained by A. Lods, Histoire de la littérature hébraïque et juive, 1955, p. 330–331. Such appears to be also Röllig's opinion. However, one ought rather to think of their employer, since it is unlikely that a gang of ordinary workmen would be so educated as to know how to compose a flawless piece of literary prose or would have money enough as to hire somebody to do it for them.

[6] A number of parallels from the Near East has been assembled by J. A. Montgomery, A Critical and Exegetical Commentary on the Books of Kings (ICC), 1950, p. 511, and one from the area of the Roman Empire (Lambaesis in North Africa, »Corpus Inscriptionum Latinarum« VIII 2728) is mentioned by Cooke, p. 16.

of the voices of the workers belonging to the two gangs which were advancing from opposite ends. No personal name is ever mentioned, no reference whatsoever is made to the immediate antecedents of that astonishing event[7].

Several explanations of such oddities have been propounded, but none of them possesses the slightest degree of probability (see Diringer, p. 94–95). A new explanation, which appeared to me so obvious that I doubted at first whether it might not have been already offered in some book or article which I might have overlooked, has been given by me, very cursorily indeed, in a review of the above mentioned book by Donner and Röllig (Rivista degli Studi Orientali 39, 1964, p. 311–312). Since I strongly suspect that it may have escaped the attention of most of those who are interested in that subject, I have thought that it may not be out of place to present it anew in a slight expanded form.

Attention has been called above to the fact that the style of the Shiloaḥ inscription contrasts in the crudest manner with the style of all North-Semitic inscriptions of a historical or religious content which are known so far. Obviously, this text does not represent a document of a sacral character, nor one proceeding from a public authority. Cooke defined it properly as a text which »reads like a good prose passage out of the O.T.«, and Albright stated that »the language is perfect classical Hebrew prose«. The acknowledgement of certain stylistic peculiarities leads to the conclusion that (I quote from my own review) »we are not dealing with a text which was conceived and written as an epigraphic item, but rather with the copy of a literary narrative, which may have been either a chronicle or an archival record (which is more or less the same). Every unbiased reader of the Shiloaḥ 'inscription' cannot avoid the impression that he finds himself in presence of a passage from a book which, in the style of a perfect historiographer, recounts the strange occurrence which accompanied the boring through of the tunnel«.

The above mentioned passage II Kings 20 20 links the cutting of the channel (*t*^{e}*ʿālāh*) and the digging of the pool (*b*^{e}*rēk*^{h}*āh*) in Jerusalem under Hezekiah to the 'Book of the Chronicles of the Kings of Judah' (*Sefer dib*^{h}*rē(y) ha-yāmīm l*^{e}*-malk*^{h}*ē(y) Y*^{e}*hūdāh*). As is well known, the two books of the Kings regularly refer to that work (and also to its counterpart, the 'Book of the Chronicles of the Kings of Israel') for further details concerning certain events which are only summarized or even passed over in silence in the biblical text. The final composition of the 'Book of the Chronicles of the Kings of Judah' is generally assumed not to have taken place before the first decade of the 6th century B.C., since it is quoted in connection with the reign of Jehoia-

[7] According to Diringer, p. 92, »the form of the inscription presents some strange features, one misses something in it«.

kin (609–598); however, less complete editions of it may have been circulating at a much earlier date, and, at any rate, everyone agrees that the book, to a large extent, depended on an annalistic source, which, although it must have been a private rather than an official achievement, nevertheless was obviously based upon the official records of the kingdom[8]. The Shiloaḥ inscription appears to be nothing if not a passage (one feels tempted to say: a pericope, or a *parāshāh*) taken from the 'Book of the Chronicles of the Kings of Judah', or else, if one so prefers, from its annalistic source: someone had the idea of having it carved on the wall of the tunnel as a lasting memorial to an amazing incident in that bold enterprise.

Should the above surmise be correct, the Shiloaḥ inscription would afford an addition to the literary legacy of the ancient Hebrews, the more precious inasmuch as no other extra-biblical literary text has reached us so far, with the only exception, if it is one, of the Lakish letters.

It is obviously impossible to try to identify the »someone« who took the initiative of entrusting stone, a much more durable material than papyrus or hide, with the record of that unusual happening: it cannot have been the king himself, who would not have failed to mention his own name; possibly, it was a high ranking officer of the royal court, since it would have been hardly possible to an outsider to have the wall of the tunnel at his disposal; the great accuracy of the writing makes it likely to have been traced by order of a man well supplied with financial means, and rules out the possibility of the inscription having been set up by the workmen. It would be no less idle to speculate about the reason why only the lower part of the smoothed surface has been inscribed and about the possibility that other inscriptions, now lost, might have existed, where other details of the perforation might have been recorded: the various hypotheses which have been advanced on that subject are mere guesses.

It is no easy task, either, to try to assign a convenient date to the inscription. The assumption, which has been generally admitted without discussion, that it is contemporary with the execution of the tunnel, can by no means be correct, since a certain time must have necessarily elapsed before a report on the work was prepared and had become part and parcel of the royal annals. To be sure, the Recorder, *mazkīr*, who was in charge of writing down the annals, must have kept them up-to-date with the daily events, but we are in no position

[8] See R. H. Pfeiffer, Introduction to the Old Testament, 1941, p. 392–396 and 399–403; Montgomery, op. cit., p. 31–37; O. Eissfeldt, Einleitung in das Alte Testament, 1964[3], p. 382–383 (English translation: *The O. T. An Introduction*, 1965, p. 285–286). I mention some standard works which I happen to have at hand, and do not think that a more copious bibliography would be of any substantial advantage.

to ascertain whether the idea of transferring a section of them on the tunnel wall followed immediately the event or rose only some time later. Any attempt at a satisfactory chronology must be based, therefore, upon the evidence afforded by palaeography. Unfortunately, it is well known how little dependable the palaeographic criterion is when the evidence is scanty or, as in this case, almost completely absent. My personal impression (which I am far from considering as authoritative) is that the writing of our inscription, although this is carved on stone, shows an unmistakable tendency towards the cursive writing as is traced with brush and ink upon sherds (and undoubtedly would be found on papyrus documents, should one of them have escaped destruction): from a comparison with the Samaria and Lakish ostraca the writing of the former appears obviously more archaic (as is well known, they belong to the 8th, if not to the 9th century B.C.) and that of the latter, which are dated with certainty from 599/98 B.C., undoubtedly younger. Therefore, the Shiloaḥ inscription should be assigned to the 7th century, but it remains uncertain to which part of this long span of time it belongs.

If the literary character of our inscription should actually be such as it appears to the present writer, the restoration of the missing initial word would prove easy and would nullify the multifarious suggestions which have been made in the past, such as ... קצת, קץ, פה, עת, ראש, תמם, תם, בים, זאת, זה, הן (see Diringer, p. 85). In the two opening words we ought to recognize the title of the section from the 'Chronicles', or 'Annals', which the inscription reproduces, a title which is repeated, in agreement with a not uncommon stylistic practice, in the first words of the text: »and such was the event of the boring through« (וזה היה דבר הנקבה). Consequently, the beginning should be supplemented as [דבר] הנקבה »The event of the boring through«. *Dābʰār*, as everybody knows, is one of those *voces mediae* which are hard to translate with complete adequacy, since they intimate a variety of meanings: it means an event or an occurrence[9], and, at the same time, it also hints at a report on the same event. I should not be far from surmising that there is some kind of connection between the title of the single section, *dābʰār ha-nĕqābʰāh* (or how else the latter word ought to be vocalized) and the comprehensive title of the book whence it is taken, *dibʰrē(y) ha-yāmīm*. Those who are familiar with the vocabulary of Arabic historiography of the classic age may be reminded of the ambivalence of such terms as *khabar* and *amr* (the latter is typical of the sections of the huge genealogical-historic compilation *Ansāb al-ashrāf* by al-Balādhurī, died c. 892 A.D.) which mean an event as well as the story of it.

[9] Cooke's and Albright's translations (»the manner« and respectively »the way«) fail to do justice to all implications of that word.

The Sources of the Variant Readings to Deuteronomy 1 $_{1}$–29 $_{17}$ of Codex Neofiti 1

By Shirley Lund

(Boston University, Boston, Massachusetts)

In 1956 A. Díez Macho announced the discovery of a complete Palestinian Targum to the Pentateuch–Codex Neofiti 1 of the Vatican Library in Rome[1]. In the fall of 1964 M. Black, very kindly made available to me the microfilm and photostatic copies of this Codex with the suggestion that I make a study of the variant readings found in the margins. Since that time under Black's guidance I have been engaged in examining the variant readings to the book of Deuteronomy. I am happy to present here something of what I have learned about these variant readings.

Number of Sources

It is Macho's opinion that the *marginalia* (hereafter, M) and the interlinear notations of the Neofiti Codex »betray at least three different original sources«[2]. P. Grelot, after a detailed comparative study of Gen 4 3–16 of several manuscripts, decided that »l'origine des gloses marginales de TJN [Neofiti 1] ne se laisse pas aisément discerner .... Ngl [M] serait plutôt fondé sur la collation de plusieurs manuscrits«[3]. Of this conclusion R. LeDéaut writes, »Cette opinion semble confirmée par la lecture de tout le Codex«[4]. However, it can be argued that it is not necessary to postulate more than two sources to account for the M to Dtn 1 1–29 17 inasmuch as at no verse are there more than two M to any one word, or group of words, in the text[5]. Moreover, two M

[1] A. Díez Macho, Una copia de todo el Targum jerosolimitano en la Vatican, Estudios Biblicos, 16 (1956), p. 446–47. For a review of the early literature and correspondence regarding the Codex see Macho's article, Le Targoum Palestinien, Nouvelles Chretiennes d'Israel, 13 (1962), p. 20–25.

[2] Macho, The Recently Discovered Palestinian Targum: Its Antiquity and Relationship with the Other Targums, Suppl VT 7, 1959, p. 237.

[3] P. Grelot, Les Targums du Pentateuque: Étude comparative d'après Genèse, IV, 3–16, Semitica 9 (1959), p. 86, n. 2.

[4] R. LeDéaut, La Nuit Pascale: Essai sur la signification de la Pâque juive à partir du Targum d'Exode XII 42, Analecta Biblica 12 (1963), p. 37.

[5] Beyond 29 17 there is a change in the text and M which warrants a separate study.

to any one textual reading are found in fewer than 5% of the total number of verses (804); for more than 95% of the verses there is only one *marginale* (hereafter, M) to any one word, or group of words, in the text[6]. It would seem in order, therefore, to examine the M in light of a hypothesis of two sources, of which one supplied much the greater number of M. For convenience the latter source may be designated as Source I; the other as Source II.

Source I

A comparison made between the text of Neofiti and the corresponding verses of Deuteronomy extant in the Cairo Geniza fragments yields a total of fifty-seven variants, exclusive of spelling variants unless found in the M of Neofiti[7]. There are M for twelve of these variants. These twelve M include four which substitute the spelling of the Cairo Geniza text for that of the text of Neofiti and three which insert כען after אנה in the clause די אנה מפקד יתכון. The remaining five M effect a change in phraseology or vocabulary. Although the texts of 28 16.17 and 18 of Neofiti differ substantially from those of the Cairo Geniza, there are no M noting the differences. At 28 16 an alternate reading for the verse is given in the margin, but it is a reading different from that of the Cairo Geniza. The evidence is against the Cairo Geniza as a source for the M to Neofiti.

On the other hand, there is abundant evidence that one source for the M is the tradition of the »Fragment Targum« (hereafter, FT)[8]. The M to Neofiti paralleled in the FT includes sixty-one complete and fifty-two partial verses. All the M to thirty-eight complete verses and four partial verses are variant readings to the Neofiti text identical with the readings at these points of the FT. For twenty-eight other partial verses all the M corresponding to the extant portion are identical with the FT readings. For eight complete verses and three partial verses one of the two sources apparent in the M is identical with the FT readings.

In addition, there are many words and phrases in the M to Neofiti which occur repeatedly, either alone or in context. Among these are the following:

[6] The possibility of two sources is indicated by M to the following verses: 1 28 2 15.19.20.21 3 16.17.20 4 26 6 19 8 9 14 1 15 14 17 8 18 14 20 6.8 22 12 23 2.6 24 6.14.15 25 2.9 27 25 29 14.

[7] P. Kahle, Masoreten des Westens, II 1930, p. 26–28. Extant only in MS D.

[8] Published in Rabbinical Bibles beginning with the first Biblia Rabbinica 1515–17) and in »Das Fragmententhargum« (Thargum jeruschalmi zum Pentateuch), M. Ginsburger, 1899). The reader is referred to these volumes for all references to the Fragment Targum.

אליין	1 1 2 4.8.22.29 3 5 4 45 7 20 12 1 18 12 a.e.
הנון	1 1.39 2 11 4 10 5 17.18.20 7 16.26 9 29 a.e.
ההנון	19 17 28 65 29 2.17.
דאית	2 36 3 8.12.25 4 18.47.48 5 8.14.21 a.e.
שיצי	4 26 7 2.20.24 8 19.20 9 3 12 2 17 7.12 a.e.
קורייה	2 34.37 3 4.5.6.10.12 5 14 6 10 12 14 a.e.
שבח (אורייתה הדה)	1 5 4 8 17 18.19 27 3.8.26 28 58 29 8
Gentilic names ending in אי	1 5.7.19.20.27 2 9.10.11.12 a.e.
עוד	3 26 5 25 13 17 17 16 18 16 19 9.
טליתה	22 15.16.19.20.21.25.27.29.
אוף	1 28.37 2 6.15.20 3 20 5 17.20 7 20 9 20 a.e.
זרעיית בני/	1 8.36 4 37 5 29 10 15 11 9 12 25 28 46.
פיקודייה	5 29.31 6 1.2.17 7 9.11 8 1.6.11 a.e.

אליין appears in the margin at 1 1 where it is one of many M identical with the FT reading. It also appears in context at 3 5 in a M which is identical with the FT reading, and at 2 8 it is a one-word M corresponding to the FT text.

A comparison with the extant FT shows the pronoun הנון to be identical to the FT reading at 1 1 14 7 and 15 11, as is ההנון at 29 17.

Twenty-eight times the M דאית replaces די or ...ד of the text. Whenever a FT reading corresponding to the M is extant, that reading is also דאית (4 18.48 7 10 22 4 29 10).

At 7 10 the verb שיצי is found in both the Neofiti M and in the FT reading. At 7 20 it is found in context with אליין. The verb is attested as FT vocabulary also at 7 23 and 33 27, the only other extant verses where a verb of this meaning is required by the context.

At 3 5 and 19 5 קורייה appears as M identical with the FT reading. At 5 14 it appears in context with דאית.

The M (שבח (אורייתה הדה is identical with the FT reading at 27 8 and 29 8. The phrase is found in the FT also at 31 24 and 32 46.

More than forty times there are M which change the spelling of gentilic names to end in אי. The M at 3 11 is identical with the FT reading. At 3 8 4 47 and 12 12 the M are found in context with דאית.

The M עוד is found to be identical with the FT reading at 28 68 and in context with קוריין at 19 9.

טליתה is identical with the FT reading at 22 20 and 22 21.

None of the verses to which אוף appears as M are extant in the FT. It is attested as FT vocabulary, however, at 32 5 and 33 28 and is found in context with הנון in the M at 5 17 and 5 20.

There are no verses extant in the FT with which to compare the M זרעיית בני/, but the phrase appears in the FT at 34 4.

פיקודייה appears in the margins thirty times. It is found in the FT only at 26 18, where, curiously enough, it is not found in the margin of Neofiti even though it is to be expected. It is attested as FT vocabulary at Gen 3 15 and 27 40 Lev 27 34 and Num 12 16 and 15 31.

The simplest hypothesis to hold regarding these recurring M is that every occurrence of each is dependent upon one source; to posit two or more sources for any of them is to multiply sources unnecessarily. There is direct evidence for dependence upon the FT-tradition source for each of the following: עוד, טליתה, אליין, הנון, ההנון, דאית, שיצי, קורייה, (אורייתה הדה), שבח, and gentilic names ending in אי. There is indirect evidence for the dependence upon this source of the M אוף, for it is found in context with הנון. The evidence points to the FT-tradition source as the source for all these M and for every occurrence of them.

The fact that comparison of the M with the extant FT shows that all the M to many verses are from the one source suggests that all the M to other verses for which the FT is only partially extant for comparison may be from one source[9]. When one, or some, of the M to any verse is identifiable by comparison as dependent upon the FT-tradition source, it must be recognized that the others, for which no comparison can be made, may well be from the same source. The M to 3 5 and 5 29 provide examples. At 3 5 one M is attributable by comparison to the FT-tradition source. The other two M include אליין קוריין and קורייתה. At 5 29 one M is attributable by comparison to the FT-tradition source. The other two M include פיקודי and זרעיית בניהון. Since for each verse one M is known to be from the FT-tradition source and the others can be defended as possible FT readings, and since it is known that all the M to other verses are from the FT-tradition source, the more likely explanation for these M is that all are from the one FT-tradition source than that those unidentifiable by comparison are from one or more other sources. It should be noted also that this indirect evidence for the dependence of פיקודי and זרעיית בניהון upon the FT-tradition source is evidence for the dependence of every occurrence of these recurring M upon this source, if what has already been said of the other recurring M is correct.

Finally, let it be said that the postulation of one source for all the M to one verse has the very practical result of making sense of the M. The M to 4 8 provides an example of this. The text reads:

והלא היידה אומה ומלכו דאית לה קיימין וסדרי
דינין זכיין ככל גזירת אוריתה הדה די אנה סדר
קדמיכון יומא הדין:

There are four M: רבה for ומלכו; קשיטין for זכיין; שבח for גזירת; and יהב for סדר. There is no FT extant, but two M can be attributed by indirect evidence to the FT-tradition source. Firstly, the substitution

[9] See above, p. 168.

of רבה for ומלכו is the same reading as that found in 4 7, which is attributable to the FT-tradition source by comparison. Secondly, the third M, שבת, followed in the text by אוריתה הדה, produces a phrase of the FT. The second M, קשיטן, agrees with Targum Onkelos[10]. The fourth M, יהב, cannot be attributed to any extant text. In spite of a word which agrees with Onkelos, another which agrees with no extant text and two which can be attributed to the FT-tradition source only on the basis of other texts, the conclusion which makes the most sense of the M is that they are all from the FT-tradition source.

It can be seen by the foregoing that the amount of FT extant is too limited to give a true picture of the relationship of the Neofiti M to the extant FT when one depends solely upon comparison of extant texts for this picture. In reality, the major source for the M to Dtn 1 1–29 17 of Neofiti–a source with a high degree of continuity–is a manuscript of the FT-tradition.

In order to determine with which of the FT manuscripts the M of Neofiti agree each time the FT disagree among themselves and thus to determine whether the M are more closely related to any one FT manuscript than to the others, the M and the FT readings were collated[11]. The following is a recapitulation of the evidence. BN is shown only when the M agree with it against V or VL, and when the M disagree with all the extant FT. This is done as a matter of economy, for at all other places where there is agreement with BN there is also agreement with either V or L.

Extant	Number of agreements with:			Number of disagreements with:	
FT	V(L)	L(vs. V)	BN(vs. V(L))	VBNL	VBN
VBNL	45	14	8	13	
VBN	25		14		16

Agreement with V(L)	70	Total agreement with VL 84
Agreement with L vs. V	14	

It is evident that the M to Neofiti are more closely related to the readings of the Vaticanus manuscript than to any of the others. The importance of the Leipzig manuscript is also evident in the fourteen

[10] Targum Onkelos, herausgegeben und erläutert von A. Berliner, 1884, p. 199.

[11] In the following presentation V = MS Vaticanus 440: B = fragments first printed in the Bomberg Bible; N = Codex Nuremburg 1; L = Codex Leipzig 1. The MS Paris 110 is disregarded because it proved not to be significant. In collating, I used M. C. Doubles, The Fragment Targum (unpublished Ph.D. thesis, St. Mary's College, University of St. Andrews, 1962), p. 88–104, in which he has set forth the Vaticanus manuscript with a critical apparatus consisting of the significant variants found in the Bomberg edition, Codex Nuremburg and Codex Leipzig. For the readings of MS Paris 110 I used Ginsburger, Das Fragmententhargum, p. 61–65.

agreements with it against V, as well as in the greater number of agreements with BN and disagreements with all extant readings when there is no reading of L extant. The fact that L and BN appear together against V thirteen times and ten of these times the reading of LBN agrees with the M to Neofiti only underlines the significance of L. The manuscript underlying the M to at least 1 1–29 17 of Neofiti would seem to be a manuscript closest to the Vaticanus manuscript but with many of the readings found in the Leipzig codex.

Source II

The question arises whether it is possible to distinguish between Sources I and II. The answer to the question is an affirmative one. An examination of the verses where the FT is also extant shows that the two sources are consistently placed in certain relationships to each other – or, more precisely, in the way in which Source II is placed in relationship to Source I[12]. Source II never appears in the right margin unless in conjunction with Source I. Source II is placed either in the left margin with the corresponding M of Source I in the right margin or, if in the same margin with Source I, below Source I or at the outside margin with Source I next to the text. Furthermore, unless it is obvious that two sources are involved, Source II is given as one reading (in the left margin) while Source I may be rendered by several separate readings, any of which may be in either margin. There is no exception to the positions of the M in those verses which can be compared with the FT. This seems to warrant the conclusion that the relationships exist everywhere. If so, then it is possible to distinguish between the two sources even when there is no extant FT.

At this writing Source II has not yet been identified. It is related to the Pseudo-Jonathan tradition, as can be seen from the marginal reading from this source at 17 8:

(ארום יתכסי מנכון פתגם בדינה בין)דם דכי לדם
מסאב בין דיני נפשא לדיני ממונא בין מכתש סגיר
למכתש תליט מילוי פלוגתא בבית מדרשיך[13]

Although the evidence is limited, there seems to be a greater similarity in the vocabulary and grammar of Source II to Targum Onkelos than to Pseudo-Jonathan. A hint of this similarity to Onkelos in respect of vocabulary is given in the M cited, as a comparison of

[12] The relevant verses are: 8 9 14 1 15 14 17 8 20 6 22 12 24 6.15 25 2 29 14.

[13] Pseudo-Jonathan (Thargum Jonathan ben Usiël zum Pentateuch), herausgegeben von M. Ginsburger, 1903, p. 331. The portion of the verse given in parentheses above is that of the Neofiti text. The Neofiti text concludes as follows: ותקומון ותסקון לאתרה די יתרעי יי/ אלהכון ביה.

texts will show. A relationship to the rabbinic writings is also evident. Source II would seem to have been a late text compounded of many elements. It would seem also to have been fragmentary in nature.

Conclusion

Inasmuch as the complete text behind the FT is not available, the hypothesis here set forth – namely, that there are only two sources for the M to Dtn 1 1–29 17 of Neofiti and that one of these sources is a manuscript of the FT tradition which is not merely a collection of fragments but a manuscript with a high degree of continuity – cannot be proved. Its justification lies, first of all, in the assumption that it is wiser to postulate no more sources than necessary to satisfy the evidence than to multiply sources unnecessarily; secondly, in the fact that the evidence is not only not contradictory but supportive; and thirdly, in the fruitfulness of the hypothesis when tested. So long as the views that the M represent either collations from several sources or from »at least« two sources are entertained, both of which have the effect of setting no limit to the number of possible sources, the M are a confusion of variants, the reason for which is difficult to discover. When the M are examined in the light of an hypothesis of two sources, the seeming confusion gives way to order and valuable information comes to light.

The Horses in Zechariah

By W. D. McHardy

(44 Davenant Road, Oxford)

Zech 1 8 ראיתי הלילה והנה־איש רכב על־סוס אדם .... ואחריו סוסים אדמים־שרקים ולבנים:

ibid. 6 2f. במרכבה הראשנה סוסים אדמים ובמרכבה השנית סוסים שחרים: ובמרכבה השלשית סוסים לבנים ובמרכבה הרבעית סוסים ברדים אמצים:

ibid. 6 6f. אשר־בה הסוסים השחרים יצאים אל־ארץ צפון והלבנים יצאו אל־אחריהם והברדים יצאו אל־ארץ התימן: והאמצים יצאו ויבקשו ללכת להתהלך בארץ ויאמר לכו התהלכו בארץ ותתהלכנה בארץ:

The problems posed by those passages present difficulties which, as in so many places in the Old Testament, may never find a satisfactory solution, but the recognition that this is so does not absolve us from continuing the search or from communicating results, which though admittedly tentative and imperfect may suggest to others a line to pursue. This article, then, seeks only to discover what results from following one line of approach to the difficulties in the above passages, though the problems involved are probably such that a more complex explanation will be required.

The ancient translators were not agreed in their renderings of certain of the colours of the horses. Thus at 1 8[1] while the VSS support the meaning 'red' for אדמים and 'white' for לבנים they are less consistent in rendering שרקים, for which the AV has 'speckled' and the RV 'sorrel'. The RV has the support of 'A and the meaning of the root elsewhere in the Old Testament and in the cognate languages, while the AV agrees with the Vulg. and Pesh. and probably also with the Targ. (קחחין; Jastrow[2]: 'faint-colored, gray[?]'). It agrees also with the LXX, which has a double translation ψαροὶ καὶ ποικίλοι, one a gloss on the other.

Similarly at 6 2f. the VSS support the MT in its descriptions of the first three horses, but there is some diversity in their rendering of the MT's double designation of the fourth group. For ברדים, the adjective used of the sheep and goats at Gen 31 10.12, the LXX has ποικίλοι and the Vulg. *varii*, words used by those VSS at 1 8. The

[1] References without mention of a book are to Zechariah. Standard abbreviations are used, e.g. A(authorized) V(ersion), R(evised) V(ersion), VSS = Versions.

[2] A Dictionary of the Targumim ..... Midrashic Literature.

Targ. has פציחין and ΣΘ πελιδνοί, while the Pesh. has one word ܐܘܟܡܐ for the two in the MT; cf. RV mg., Smith-Goodspeed. For אמצים the LXX (ψαροί cf. RSV) and Targ. (קיטמנים) give colours, but the Vulg. (fortes) and 'A (καρτεροί) with the RV mg. reflect the ordinary meaning of the √אמץ. But clearly only the colour of the horses and not their strength is relevant. To obtain a colour Koehler cites the Arabic اومض 'flash, gleam' (cf. Targ. פציחין 'light-coloured') and translates אָמֹץ as 'piebald'. As suggesting a red colour Perles in JQR[3] compares the Aram. אומצא 'raw meat', though Jastrow[4] gives the definition: 'a thick piece of meat, a piece which can be eaten raw after pressing', connecting the root meaning not with 'red' but with 'press', for he translates אָמַץ 'to press'; but in a later number of JQR[5] Perles accepted the suggestions of Löw, Nöldeke and Ginzberg that אומצא is to be connected with ܚܒܨܢܐ 'bit'.

At 6 6f. again there are four classes, and here ברדים and אמצים are separated. The latter is vouched for by the Vulg'.s *robustissimi*, but 'A (πυρρόι) and the Pesh. (ܣܡܩܐ ܣܘܡܩܐ) support the colour red (אדמים).

This survey of the evidence suggests that originally all the adjectives denoted colours, that there were four of these, and that though white is the only colour occurring in all three groups the others should be red, black and 'dappled', each of which appears in two groups. To produce the required regularity of form in these verses various textual emendations have been suggested. Thus at 1 8 Marti would read שחרים in place of שרקים on the basis of 6 2.6, though it may be objected that the unfamiliar has displaced the familiar. At 6 3 where אמצים is the odd term Houbigant suggested צבעים and Ewald חמצים (cf. Is 63 1). These and other emendations may be found in the commentaries.

But in two articles in Textus[6] G. R. Driver has examined the use of abbreviations in the MT and the part they may play in the recovery of the original text of corrupt passages without emendation. He lays it down that

> »only certain categories of terms are subject to abbreviation, namely: terminations, including pronominal elements; independent pronouns; particles; common nouns of frequent occurrance especially those for numbers and measures; other nouns when they have recently been mentioned; names of persons and places which occur often, especially the divine names; occasional sentences, such as formulae and quotations, and expressions recurring frequently in any given book«.

[3] NS 2, p. 99.

[4] Op. cit.

[5] NS 3, p. 313.

[6] 1, p. 112–131; 4, p. 76–94; cf. Gesenius-Kautzsch, Heb. Gr., § 30 m

He continues:

»At the same time modern readers must never forget that ancient texts were not written down to be read at sight, for amusement or relaxation. Reading was an esoteric art confined to the learned classes (priests, lawyers, and scribes) who generally knew the text by heart, and the written word was merely a *memoria technica* to be consulted to refresh the memory or look up what had been said if or when it failed«.[7]

On the basis of this second quotation we suggest that in addition to the passages which come under Driver's rules we may reasonably expect the use of abbreviation in places where the context or the form of the sentences are such that only an aide-mémoire is required by the skilled and practised reader. Thus in English the context will immediately make clear whether *R* is to be interpreted as Rabbi, Rex or River.

In the verses before us we have what was originally a stereotyped form, horses of four different colours, a tidy pattern which has become disarranged and untidy. The ordinary vicissitudes to which MSS are prone might of course have brought this about, but the very simplicity of the pattern is against this, while at the same time it suggests that a writer might very well have been tempted to use here a form of shorthand writing. The reading שרקים for שחרים at 1 8 is then seen to be a misunderstanding of the abbreviation ש׳, and the objection that שרקים is less familiar than שחרים vanishes if it is recognized that the misunderstanding is due to the presence of the other 'reds', אדם and אדמים.

Turning now to 6 2f. we find red, black and white followed by the duplicate ברדים אמצים. As there were two terms in 1 6 with initial א, so in 6 2f. two begin with א. On our hypothesis ברדים is the outsider, a gloss introduced under the influence of Gen 31 10.12 or an attempt to interpret the unknown אמצים in terms of natural equine appearance, a misguided attempt for ברדים is a pattern, not a colour.

At 6 6f. black and white, in that order each time, though this pair after occupying the last and middle positions now move to the front, are followed by ברדים and אמצים as separate groups. Here the gloss ברדים has displaced the original אמצים in verse 6, while, as the readings of 'A and the Pesh. show, an original אדמים has been replaced by אמצים. This gives, as in the previous passages, two terms with initial א, and, as in them, one of these terms is an adjective from the root אדם, while the second is the name of a colour other than black, white or red. The word, now lost, must have puzzled the ancient copyist who came to extend the abbreviated symbol, the form of which to distinguish it from א׳ = $\sqrt{\text{אדם}}$ may have been אמ׳.

[7] Ibid. 4, p. 94.

There are two pieces of evidence to support the view that our postulated אמ׳ did not represent a pattern-word such as speckled, dappled, spotted or piebald, but a colour-word. The first is versional: ΘΣ represent ברדים by πελιδνοί 'livid' and the Targ. by פציחין 'bright-coloured', while for אמצים the Targ. has קיטמנים 'ashen'. The second comes from the New Testament: the writer of the Apocalypse of St. John, who based his vision in 6 2–8 on Zechariah[8], describes his fourth horse as Χλωρός 'pale, pale yellow, greenish-yellow'[9]. Charles[10], quoting Phavorinus, says pale yellow was the colour of the Nisaean horses, and claims that this is the colour required by Rev 6 7 and probably also by Zech 1 8. If the fourth group of horses in Zechariah were of this shade the symbol אמ׳ might represent the root meaning of אֲמֻנָה for the Greek for this is Χρυσορρόας[11].

If these passages are as stylized as we have suggested then we might look in them for evidence of the further use of abbreviation. Thus at 1 8.10 the divergance of the LXX ὀρέων = ההרים from the MT's ההדסים might point to a confusion due to abbreviation, but a more likely example is to be found at 6 6.7 where there is doubt about the quarters to which the horses go. Just as the points of the compass may be labelled N.S.E.W., so ancient writers used the first letters of words indicating cardinal directions and from them they formed the name ADAM[12].

Clearly the text in 6 6.7 is in some confusion. The words אל־אחריהם make dubious sense and a specific direction is expected to match צפון and התימן. The commentators have put forward various emendations: אל אחרי הים 'to the west of the sea', i.e. the far west; אל אחור (glossed הים); אל־ארץ הקדם. This last suggestion, which comes from Wellhausen, shows that he too regarded the passage as stylized, for he inserts ארץ to conform with the two directions given in full. Further,

[8] The writer borrows the symbolism of the horses and their colours, but in his order (white, red, black, yellow) he is independent, just as he is, for example, in the order of the stones in ch. 21.

[9] That there can be a transition from green-yellow to grey is shown by Delitzsch's note at Ps 68 14 on the root ירק in his Biblical Commentary on the Psalms. ورق is a silver coin, and Charles, Revelation of St. John, I p. 169 translates יֵרָקוֹן as 'lividness'. cf. ΣΘ πελιδνόι.

[10] Ibid.

[11] The colours recall a note in S. R. Driver's Joel (Camb. Bible), p. 88: 'The Arabs say that there are different kinds of locusts, yellow, white, red, black'. Joel remarks on the likeness of locusts to horses (2 4), and the Book of Revelation compares the noise of their flight to the sound of chariots, of many horses rushing to war (9 9).

[12] Secrets of Enoch 30 13; Sibylline Books 30 24–26; cf. Charles, Apoc. and Pseud., II p. 379, 449.

the beginning of 6 7 is defective and LXX ℵ c · b adds ἐπὶ γῆν νότου which Kittel's Bib. Heb.[3] renders אל־ארץ התימן, though as Driver[13] points out νότος represents קדים in nine passages and 'eastwards' may be meant here. It may be added that in several passages where directions are mentioned the text is suspect, e.g. Josh 18 15 I Sam 20 41 Ez 40 2.20.44 42 10.

The Hebrews stuck to no fixed or customary order in indicating the four quarters of the world. Thus while at Gen 13 14 we find N.S.E.W, the order familiar to us and used as early as in the description of the winds as Marduk prepared to do battle with Tiamat, elsewhere there occur the clockwise N.E.S.W. (Ez 47 15ff.), the anti-clockwise N.W.S.E. (I Kings 7 25) and, it seems, every variation. One such is E.N.S.W. which occurs at Rev 21 13 where it has caused commentators some trouble. Charles[14] has an elaborate note, which may very well provide the ultimate explanation of the order, but Rev 21 13 probably took over the order as found at I Chr 26 14–16, which describes the appointment of the gatekeepers, and at Ez 42 16–19, where the angel measures the temple area, for the Apocalyptist speaks both of gates and of an angel with a measuring-rod.

In Zech 6 6.7 only two directions are clearly indicated, the black horses going north, the dappled or yellow going south. Charles[15] writes: 'while the *black* horses rightly go towards the north, the *red* should go to the south and not the spotted, the *white* to the east, and the *yellow* (»spotted« in text) to the west; for the four colours of the horses are said to symbolize the four quarters'. He goes on to give this reconstruction of the text:

הסוסים השחרים יצאים אל ארץ צפון והלבנים יצאים אל ארץ הקדם והברדים יצאים ‹אל ארץ הערב› והאדמים יצאים אל ארץ התימן

It may be noted that in both the suspect terms **אחריהם** and **יצאו** there is an **א**, and this may provide the clue to the restoring of the text. **אל־אחריהם** may be a wrong writing out of **אל־א׳ מ׳**, the abbreviated form of (**מוצא** or) **אל־ארץ מזרח**. The ending of the word **יצאו** may have caused some letters to fall out by haplography, and the original text may have been **יצאו אל־א׳ י׳** i.e. **ארץ ימין**. The reading **התימן**, for which Charles substitutes **הערב** may be explained merely as a mistake for **ים**.

But not all scholars agree with Charles about the directions in which the horses were dispatched. Thus Wellhausen would read after v 6: 'and the red went forth towards the west country', i.e. **אל־א׳ י׳** for **אל־ארץ ים**. The order favoured by G. R. Driver[16] is black northwards,

[13] JTS 39, p. 403; cf. use of λίψ for 'west' as well as 'south'. Deissmann, Bible Studies, p. 141f.

[14] Revelation of St. John, II p. 166ff.

[15] Ibid., I p. 162n.

[16] Op. cit. 39, p. 403.

white westwards, grisled (our 'yellow') southwards, and red eastwards, the scheme accepted also by A. Gelin[17]. Though redness may be associated both with the west and the east (cf. Mt 16 2f.), it is with the east that it has been particularly associated[18]. The text of 6 7 as it stands gives little help, but it is not sure that we have the original text. The subject of ויבקשו cannot be the last-named group, but the horses in general. The next words look like a dittograph of what follows, and there are variant readings which raise doubts about them for LXX^{L} Syr.^{H} omit ללכת, and twelve of Kennicott's MSS read והתהלך for להתהלך. The clause may be taken to be an intrusion. If then יצאו is followed by ויאמר, it is possible to see that אל־א׳ מ׳ may have been dropped by haplography, and the original text read אנ־ארצ מזרח (or מוצא)

The verses may then be rendered:

1 8 I saw last night a man riding a red horse .... and behind him were yellow, black and white horses.

6 2f. In the first chariot were red horses, in the second black horses, in the third white horses, and in the fourth yellow horses.

6 6f. The one in which are the black horses goes out to the north country, while the whites go out to the west country, the yellows go out to the south country, and the reds go out to the east country. He said, 'Go, patrol the earth', and they patrolled the earth.

[17] La Sainte Bible: Zacharie, 1960[3].

[18] See Lewis—Short, A Latin Dictionary, sub Aurora, rubesco, rutilo.

Prolegomena to a Comparative Description of Non-Masoretic Hebrew Dialects and Traditions

By A. Murtonen

(Department of Middle Eastern Studies, University of Melbourne, Parkville, Vic.)

I.

The study of Hebrew language traditions formed a major interest in Paul E. Kahle's many-sided scholarly activity. This concerns particularly those traditions which had been long forgotten, ever since the Tiberian school of grammarians gained the upper hand not only in Palestine, but also in Babylonia, and after having been established in Spain in the beginning of the »Golden Era« determined the standard pronunciation of Hebrew, with some modifications of the original values of some punctuation marks, in the western parts of Europe and therewith in the academic tradition. Most types of the Biblical Hebrew pronunciation in different Jewish communities also appear to be based on the Tiberian tradition; as far as we know only in Yemen has a tradition showing somewhat different derivation been preserved[1]. In Mishnaic Hebrew, divergent traditions seem to enjoy a somewhat wider distribution, but their systematic study has hardly been begun.

It was not until the last decade of the last century that the non-Tiberian traditions of Hebrew began to attract the attention of Hebrew scholars. True enough, a few decades earlier J. L. Barges had published some notes on the Samaritan pronunciation of Hebrew, and J. H. Petermann published the entire book of Genesis in Latin transcription and his »Versuch einer hebräischen Laut- und Formenlehre nach der Aussprache der heutigen Samaritaner« (1868) based on it; but due to his inadequate method, which involved a double transcription process, it failed to provide an adequate basis for future research and was ignored, among others, by Bauer and Leander in their classical grammar.

The supralinear method of punctuation was known in earlier times mainly from those Yemenite manuscripts in which it is used essentially as a transcription for Tiberian pronunciation. Therefore it did not attract any particular attention by Hebrew grammarians; the few exceptions were generally regarded as faulty or aberrant curios and

[1] See S. Morag, The Hebrew Language Tradition of the Yemenite Jews, 1963.

ignored. With the discovery of the old Geniza in Cairo, however, fragments of such texts came to light in so large numbers that this was no longer possible; with them, the earlier known »aberrant Yemenite« manuscripts came again into the focus of attention. Moreover, texts with a totally different supralinear punctuation were also found. The pioneering work on both kinds of punctuation was mainly done, apart from some early, rather dilettante attempts, by Kahle and his pupils, partly in collaboration with I. Rabin. These studies led to the establishment of two traditions of the pronunciation of Hebrew independent of the Tiberian one (abbreviated below: TibH), called Babylonian (= BabH) and Palestinian (= PalH)[2]. Kahle also obtained adequate transcription texts from the Samaritan pronunciation of Hebrew, but mainly because of the limited amount of these his pupil F. Diening tried to use Petermann's publications alongside them in his »Das Hebräische bei den Samaritanern« (1938), and therefore still failed to appreciate the true character of Samaritan Hebrew (= SamH). It is only through the studies of Z. Ben-Ḥayyim and the present writer that the character of SamH as an independent *dialect* of Hebrew has been clearly established; in my opinion, several features of SamH must have been inherited from a stage *before* the Biblical period as different from Jewish Hebrew.

Kahle came also into contact with F. Wutz in his work on the transcriptions of the Septuagint, and one of his early pupils, A. Sperber, went on studying the Greek and Latin transcriptions of Hebrew words in general. His study on »Hebrew according to the Greek and Latin Transliterations« (1937f.) is the best existing summary of the problems in this field, although still rather sketchy and suffering from the misinterpretation of the transcriptions as transliterations. It is a pity that E. A. Speiser never completed his promising study on the subject. E. Brønno's study of the fragment of the Second Column of Hexapla[3] discovered by G. Mercati is very thorough and detailed, but suffers from the author's failure to pay attention to other non-Tiberian traditions and his strong tendency to find an underlying Tiberian pronunciation wherever possible. On the other hand, Schlatter's first-class study of the transcriptions of Josephus[4] has failed to get the attention it deserves. All in all, it seems to me that the tradition of transcribing Hebrew words represented by the Vatican and Sinaitic manuscripts of the Septuagint is too corrupt for a comprehensive and reliable picture of Hebrew,

[2] This may seem overlap with TibH, but the term is so well established that changing it might cause confusion.

[3] Studien über hebräische Morphologie und Vokalismus (Abhandlungen für die Kunde des Morgenlandes), 1943.

[4] A. Schlatter, Die hebräischen Namen bei Josephus, 1913.

while the transcriptions of Jerome are based on sources too diverse to be regarded as an entity. What remains are the transcriptions in the works of Josephus and Origen, and in the younger uncials and related minuscules of the Septuagint; as the Lukianic group seems to play a central role among the latter, we term them JosH, OrH, and LukH, respectively. How far these represent different traditions and/or dialects remains to be determined; in any case, it appears now that OrH represents a later stage than JosH, but hardly as late as Origen's own time. The latter conclusion is based on a study of the main Dead Sea Scrolls[5], which seems to indicate that the vocalization of Hebrew was at its most meagre in the first half of the second century A.D. In the transcription texts, the scarce vocalization is characteristic particularly of OrH. The language of the Dead Sea Scrolls in general or Qumran Hebrew (= QH) appears to represent an intermediary stage between Biblical Hebrew (= BH) and Mishnaic Hebrew (= MH), although some of the youngest Biblical books, e.g., Ecclesiastes, exhibit some organically younger traits than some of the oldest Scrolls. E. Y. Kutscher's otherwise masterly study of the language of the large Isaiah scroll[6] suffers from the failure to pay attention to the systematic differences between the two halves of the manuscript, while R. Meyer's idea of several dialects to be found in the scrolls[7] is based on an erroneous synchronical equation of different stages in diachronical development.

There are still some minor sources for different stages of Hebrew, such as inscriptions found in Palestine[8], a fragment of the Book of Isaiah in Tiberian punctuation, but exhibiting an »aberrant« pronunciation[9], and the so-called Canaanite glosses in the Tell el-'Amarna letters. The latter seem to represent roughly the stage when Hebrew and its sister languages begin to emerge from the common Canaanite language, which may never have been quite uniform, either. NB. the material is strictly limited to the glosses, excluding the »Westernisms« exhibited by the Akkadian of the documents, as such »mixed forms« are very well conceivable in a Canaanite dialect of Akkadian in the light of the theory of languages in contact[10], and at best can be only rough approximations to genuine Canaanite forms.

[5] See A. Murtonen, A Historico-Philological Survey of the Main Dead Sea Scrolls and Related Documents, Abr-Nahrain 4 (1963/64), p. 56ff.

[6] The Language and Linguistic Background of the Isaiah Scroll, 1959.

[7] See, e.g., VT 1 (1951), p. 139ff.

[8] E.g., the Siloah inscription, Samarian and Lachish ostraca; Mesha inscription, however, represents the closely related Moabite language rather than Hebrew.

[9] See A. Murtonen, Spoken Hebrew from the Tenth Century A.D., Abr Nahrain 3 (1961/62), p. 45ff.

[10] See U. Weinreich, Languages in Contact, 1953 (p. 31ff.).

II.

SamH is the best documented dialect of all of these, and therefore it will play the central role in the description of all the non-Masoretic forms of Hebrew. This was already clear to me while writing »A Grammar of the Samaritan Dialect of Hebrew« (Studia Orientalia 29, 1964), and to facilitate the construction work of the final grammar I wrote parts of it as a kind of blueprint for the corresponding sections of the latter. This is implied in the statement that »as always, I have tacitly avoided any statements contrary to facts known from the other Hebrew dialects and related languages« (p. 3), which should have served as a warning to scholars not well versed in the other non-Masoretic Hebrew traditions in reviewing the book, so as not to assume that the volume rests solely on the material presented in it[11]. In addition to the two earlier volumes of my »Materials for a Non-Masoretic Hebrew Grammar«[12], all the other published and unpublished material is presupposed by it. The reason for including it only tacitly and negatively was my desire to avoid, as strictly as possible, getting into a vicious circle, as explained in the Preface to vol. I. For the same reason (cf. ib.) references to other literature were kept at a minimum, except when these directly concerned the tradition or dialect under consideration. Above all, the title of the whole series (»Materials...«) and statements like »The present volume ... is

[11] Admittedly, it could have been stated more explicitly, particularly as in the absence of contrary facts I sometimes bridged gaps in a way which may seem unwarranted on the basis of SamH material only. Moreover, the term *facts* was consciously meant to be understood in opposition to »theories« and »hypotheses«, which was apparently not realized by A. Salonen as he claims (in a privately circulated review) that many a form »is against everything that is known from other Semitic languages« and that primary forms postulated by me are »some kind of *supranatural Platonic ideas* (italics his)«. This conclusion is drawn from n. 2 on p. 123 of »Materials« III, which naturally says only that I am not sure whether the *combination* of the different elements (in this case, *yi'amṣ*) ever existed in the language as such, but the elements themselves (in this case, *yi* and *'amṣ*) certainly did, even if the former probably only as a preformative to *a*-containing verbal stems (dissimilated from *ya*, which also existed independently). Salonen's statement, »The primary forms so frequently cultivated by Murtonen easily give the impression that he believes he is able to reconstruct the Proto-Semitic starting point (sic) of Samaritan Hebrew« (ib.) is simply a malicious insinuation, as he then immediately opposes it to the footnote referred to above, to give the impression that I am not only naive, but blatantly inconsistent at that.

[12] Viz., Liturgical Texts and Psalm Fragments Provided with the So-Called Palestinian Punctuation (Diss. Helsinki 1958), and An Etymological Vocabulary to the Samaritan Pentateuch, Studia Orientalia 24 (1960). The 3rd vol. is the grammar of SamH referred to above.

primarily only material for a future work, nor is it expected to remain a standard work even in its own special field« (II p. 4) should remind reviewers that they are not dealing with completed works, but *materials* which complement each other and still require augmentation from other sources. The construction of the comparative description will follow the principles laid down in another part of the prolegomena, an »Outline of a General Theory of Linguistics«[13]. Samples of continuous texts, however, will not be included, as these have been published, partly in »Materials«, partly by other scholars[14]. Instead, a complete dictionary of non-Masoretic Hebrew, with comparative material from the other Semitic, and occasionally non-Semitic languages to the fullest extent possible will form the first part. The second part, a morpho-syntactical analysis, will be based on a large excerpt from the Samaritan Pentateuch and consist of a preliminary analysis of the continuous text and a subsequent systematic one, which will have a statistical basis, according to the frequency of occurrence of different types of sentences and their different parts in different positions. Results of corresponding analyses of materials from other traditions will be adjoined to this, as far as material is available. The analysis will yield a morphological system as a by-product, complemented by the material included in the dictionary. The morpho-syntactical analysis will furnish material for a phonological analysis, which will follow it on a comparable statistical basis, including full treatment of the length of sounds, consonantal clusters, diphthongs, and incompatibility. The fourth part will consist of a diachronical survey on the lines of § 109 of »Materials« III and of my article on QH[15], except that the whole non-Masoretic Hebrew material will now be adduced and supplemented with material from the other Semitic languages; special samples illustrating the development of phonology from Ugaritic, Middle Babylonian, Babylonian Aramaic, Egyptian Arabic, Zanzibar-Oman Arabic, Moroccan Arabic, Soqotri, Ge'ez, and Harari have been prepared by an electronic counting device, and some others may still be added, if this appears useful. Morpho-syntactical material has been collected also from Biblical Aramaic, Syriac, Old Akkadian, Akkadian in general, Classical Arabic, Maltese Arabic, Tigré, and TibH in addition to the languages mentioned above; even this number may still be increased. The fifth and final part will consist of a panchronistic synthesis, attempting to discover the universally valid rules governing the linguistic change from the particular phonetic rules and effects of morpho-syntactical analogy.

[13] Exists in manuscript which is awaiting publication.

[14] E.g., A. v. Gall, Der hebräische Pentateuch der Samaritaner, 1914/18, apart from the publications of Kahle and his pupils.

[15] See n. 5 above.

III.

Unfortunately I have not seen any detailed discussion of the terminological reform suggested by me in the Introduction to vol. II of the »Materials«. The nearest approximation to it was by W. v. Soden in a privately circulated review, in which he objects to several terms saying: »Seine Umbenennung der 'Tempora' hingegen wird kaum übernommen werden, weil man mit den beiden Bezeichnungen 'afformal' und 'preformal' schon im Hebr. nicht auskommt. Das Akkadische aber hat 3 'preformal'-Tempora! Völlig überflüssig ist die Ersetzung der alteingeführten Bezeichnungen Partizip und Infinitiv durch die äußerst vieldeutigen Ausdrücke nomen agentis — darunter kann man auch die Berufsbezeichnungen nach der Form *fa‘‘āl* verstehen! — und nomen actionis. Partizip und Infini-(tiv[16]) sind ja eben nicht nur Nomina, sondern können auch verbal konstruiert werden... Dr. M. erliegt da öfter der Gefahr, etwas Neues um des Neuen willen ohne eine Rechtfertigung aus der Sache heraus einzuführen«. Has v. Soden ever found a morph of the type *šarrāku* in the Akkadian texts he has read? If such a morph is not a »verbal konstruiert« noun, what is it? Or does he mean that *šarru* and any other noun—adjectives included—inflected in stative in Akkadian is either a »Partizip« or an »Infinitiv«, if these are the only kinds of noun that can be constructed verbally? Or if he means syntactical construction, it is a commonplace that any kind of noun may function as a predicate or in other »verbal« functions in the early Semitic languages. Or finally, if he refers to the fact that it can have an object—first of all, not any »Partizip« or »Infinitiv« can have it, but only those of the transitive verbs; and secondly, those which do have it, have it by virtue of their reference to an action or an agent. As there is otherwise no clear-cut distinction between noun and verb in Semitic languages, this characteristic is amply accounted for by the terms »noun of action«, »noun of agent«, as opposed to plain »noun« or »(noun) substantive/adjective«. The applicability of the term »noun of agent« to the type *fa‘‘al/-āl*, again, is in my opinion a further ground for its introduction rather than against it, as it is nouns based on this type which in most Ethiopic languages stand in a closer relationship to the verbal stems than the type *fa-/fā‘il* more widespread in Asiatic Semitic; both may indeed derive from one and the same basic form, cf. my »Broken Plurals« (1964), p. 35s. It is but another instance of the fluctuation between nominal and verbal categories in early Semitic. As regards the statement that I am introducing »etwas Neues um des Neuen willen« I can only say that I am not

[16] Lacking in the duplicated typescript (at the end of a line).

introducing anything essentially new[17], as the full terms of *preformative/afformative conjugation* as well as *nomen actionis/agentis* have been used by other scholars before me; the former I first met with in R. Meyer's works, cf. Klingenhebens and Rössler's analogous *Präfix-/Suffixkonjugation*, and *nomen agentis/actionis* (or *verbi*) are common in Arabic grammars, deriving as they do from the native terminology, which is based on the actual use of the corresponding forms, whereas *participle* and *infinitive*, far from being »alteingeführte« in Semitic grammar, represent relatively late intruders from the Classical grammar which has quite different structure. It is only the shorter forms *preformal* and *afformal* that I introduced, as I regarded the full forms as too cumbersome for frequent use; v. Soden's objections apply to them no more than to the full forms. And as regards the three preformals of Akkadian, the »present-future« can well be termed Preformal II, with reference to its two stem vowels and etymologically later origin[18], while the »perfect« with its *t*-infix can be termed *t*-Preformal, just as I called the »consecutive imperfect« *w*-Preformal in Hebrew. In general, I expected eventual reviewers to be aware of the several terminological sets being used in Hebrew grammar at present (cf. still Bauer-Leander's *Aorist* and *Nominal*), and therefore did not give specific references. Unfortunately, it seems that even some leading scholars are less well informed than I used to think[19]. Some »Rechtfertigung aus der Sache heraus« he could have found in connection with the proposals (vol. II p. 5sq.) anyway.

It appears to me now that the abbreviation *prf.* for *preformal* may indeed remind readers of the traditional »perfect« too much; therefore I propose to replace it by *pref.* Otherwise the terminology used in the second and third vols. of »Materials« will be used in the final comparative description as such, unless better justified objections to it come to my attention in the meantime. The term, *non-Masoretic* vs. *pre-Masoretic* still remains to be discussed. As is known, Kahle used the latter. This was justified in so far as the two traditions, BabH and PalH, with which he was mainly dealing, essentially represent

[17] Moreover, if I am not introducing anything essentially new, it can hardly be »for the sake of newness«.

[18] Admittedly, this also contradicts a hypothesis of certain Assyriologists; whether it is in contradiction to *facts*, will be discussed in detail in the main work; for the time being, I can only refer to a paper read by me in the Fourth World Congress of Jewish Studies (Jerusalem, July/August 1965) on »The Prehistoric Development of Hebrew Verbal System«.

[19] It is true that assyriology nowadays is so large in scope that one man can hardly hope to have full command of it (according to a favourite saying of A. Salonen); but if this is true of their own special field, Assyriologists should be more careful in their pronouncements about specific West Semitic issues.

earlier stages in the development of Hebrew grammar than the properly Masoretic period, of which TibH is the final product, and SamH also structurally derives from a stage earlier than that period. Nevertheless, as all the source material in SamH are from later periods, and some of it in other traditions also obviously come from the time when TibH already was in existence, and above all, as I do not want to prejudice the issue, I decided in favour of the former alternative.

IV.

As indicated above, this is not the only part of the »Prolegomena«. Another part, dealing with the general linguistic presuppositions[20], will probably also be published separately from the main work. Detailed discussion of sources, as well as of criticisms of the »Materials« and related publications[21], as far as not already published, will be included in the main work by way of introduction. Due to the importance of the comparative material from other languages, and anticipating a result of the investigation, the work will be called »Hebrew in Its West Semitic Setting«.

[20] See above, with n. 13.

[21] These include, apart from Appendix II to Kahle, The Cairo Geniza, 1959², and the articles cited in notes 5 and 9 above, the following as more comprehensive works: »Broken Plurals«, 1964, »Early Semitic«, 1967 E. J. Brill, Leiden), and »Pintupi« (still in manuscript). The last mentioned work, an analysis of a Central Australian language, is a test case for the general linguistic theory referred to above and at the same time a general exercise for »Hebrew in Its West Semitic Setting«.

The Edition of the Kitāb al-Khilaf of Mišael Ben ʿUzziel

by F. Pérez Castro and M. J. Azcárraga

(General Sanjurjo 34, Madrid 3)

I.

Among the studies which Paul E. Kahle devoted to the specification and evaluation of the Hebrew Tiberian Bible text of the masoretic school of Ben Ašer, one of the subjects of which he was fondest was the work of Mišael Ben ʿUzziel, *Kitāb al-Khilaf* (*The Book of the Ḥil·lufim*), Treatise on the Differences between Ben Ašer and Ben Naftali. All those who are familiar with the problems of the Tiberian text of Ben Ašer know the emphasis which Kahle put on the importance of this work of Ben ʿUzziel, mainly contained in the Leningrad manuscripts. He insisted on the usefulness of Ben ʿUzziel's work in the determination of the degree of adherence of a Hebrew Bible manuscript to the punctuation system characteristic of Ben Ašer[1]. His early and continual interest in the subject led him to assign to one of his pupils, L. Lipschütz, the compiling of the critical edition of the *Treatise* based on the manuscripts of Leningrad and Paris, and on those contained in the book *Adat Deborim* which also includes the *Kitāb al-Khilaf*. Lipschütz carried out the assignment entrusted to him, and presented it as his doctoral thesis in Bonn, 1937. Unfortunately, only a small portion of his manuscript could be put into print[2]. For several reasons, the publication of the whole text had to be delayed for more than twenty-five years. During those years, Kahle was unremitting in his constant efforts to increase the interest of those surrounding him in his scientific tasks in this work which he believed to be fundamental to the biblical criticism of the Tiberian text. With his characteristic generosity, he made available to all who wanted it the material which he had at his disposal. This material consisted of the photostats of the Leningrad and Paris manuscripts, the lists of *Ḥil·lufim* Ben Ašer and Ben Naftali based on them, and a transliteration to Arabic letters, from the Hebrew characters in which

[1] Cf. for instance: P. Kahle, Masoreten des Westens, II 1930, p. 60–62; Biblia Hebraica edidit R. Kittel, 1937, Prolegomena p. VIIf.; The Cairo Geniza, 1947, p. 67.

[2] L. Lipschütz, Ben Ascher-Ben Naftali. Der Bibeltext der tiberischen Masoreten. Eine Abhandlung des Mischael ben Uzziel, veröffentlicht und untersucht, 1937.

it was originally written, of Ben ʿUzziel's whole work. This transliteration was made by Kahle himself and it has greatly facilitated the understanding of the work of Ben ʿUzziel.

From the very beginning of my personal acquaintance with Kahle, dating from 1948, he let me have this extremely valuable material which I worked upon with great intensity in connection with the textual-critical research carried out by the »Seminario Filológico Cardenal Cisneros de la Biblia Poliglota (Consejo Superior de Investigaciones Científicas)«. All this provided me with an invaluable tool in several of my papers[3].

Struggling under the lack of the long-awaited complete edition by Lipschütz, the small group of researchers under my direction in the Seminar undertook a systematic investigation based on the material which Kahle had let me have. This investigation led to the setting up of a complete card catalogue of the *Ḥil·lufim*, which consists of the variant readings between Ben Ašer and Ben Naftali, as well as the agreements, between the two according to Mišael Ben ʿUzziel. On my request, Miss C. Muñoz and especially J. L. Lacave, now Secretary of the »Instituto Arias Montano de Estudios Hebraicos«, took upon themselves the task of laying out the ground-work for our further study. Lacave, working directly with the photostats of the manuscripts, had, by 1960, finished the writing up of the whole treatise, which was to have constituted the basis for the new and completed critical edition of the *Kitāb al-Khilaf* in the event that Lipschütz had not been able finally to publish the rest of his study. Fortunately, he broke his long silence during the Third World Congress of Jewish Studies, held in Jerusalem in the summer of 1961, announcing the impending publication of the so long awaited edition of the whole *Kitāb al-Khilaf*. As he had announced, the edition was published in the second volume of »Textus«, Jerusalem 1962[4], later followed by a study of the »*Treatise*« in English in the fourth volume of »Textus«, 1964.

No one will be surprised then at my interest in comparing the new complete edition by Lipschütz with the material we had in the Seminario Cardenal Cisneros, and which was taken directly from the manuscripts of the *Kitāb*. On account of this, I assigned, to my former pupil, now collaborator in the work of the Seminar, Miss M. J.

[3] F. Pérez Castro, Corregido y correcto. El ms. B19a de Leningrado frente al Ms. Or. 4445 (Londres) y al Códice de Profetas de El Cairo, Sefarad 15 (1955), p. 3–30; Idem, Ben Asher-Ben Naftali? Números 13–15 en cinco manuscritos a la luz de Mišael Ben ʿUzziel, »Homenaje a Millás Vallicrosa«, II 1956, p. 141–148.

[4] L. Lipschütz, Mishael ben Uzziel's Treatise on the Differences Between Ben Asher and Ben Naphtali, Textus 2 (1962), p. נ–נח; Idem, Kitāb al Khilaf. The Book of the Hillufim, (with four plates), Textus 4 (1964), p. 1–29.

Azcárraga, the critical comparison of our materials with the Lipschütz edition. For this purpose, she had temporarily to lay aside her work on the collation of the *Ḥil·lufim* Ben Ašer-Ben Naftali with the Biblical text of the Cairo Prophets' Codex and with others attributed to Ben Ašer, which she had been and still is working on, under my direction.

The observations which Miss Azcárraga has made on the Lipschütz edition of the *Kitāb al-Khilaf* seem to me to be of sufficient value as to warrant their publication. The present paper contains only a sample of these observations, which shall soon appear in their entirety in our journal, »Sefarad«. Even so, I believe that in the light of the following sample, our readers will be able to see quite clearly the following:

a) All too often, Lipschütz does not quote the readings of all of the sources which contain the *Ḥil·luf*. Due to this, whoever makes use of this edition cannot have a complete view of the whole textual situation in the manuscripts.

b) At other times, the author's final decision is not documented by any of the manuscript sources, or it is only partly documented by them.

c) Occassionally, his readings do not agree exactly with the text of the manuscript.

d) Sometimes, the manner in which he quotes his sources is erroneous, incomplete, or equivocal.

e) The tendency to come to decisions on the exact contents of a *Ḥil·luf* based more on the testimony of the manuscripts attributed to Ben Ašer than on the sources of the *Kitāb al-Khilaf* is very dangerous. Indeed, this kind of decision can lead to serious errors, and make this type of research a vicious circle, as I pointed out already in another occasion[5].

It is indeed unfortunate, as shown by the above observations, which can be tested out by a careful reading of the following sample, that the Lipschütz edition, in spite of the praiseworthy investigation carried out by its author, has not been able to make unnecessary the direkt consultation of the manuscript sources in order to know their exact testimony in that which concerns the *Ḥil·lufim* Ben Ašer-Ben Naftali. It is to be hoped that the complete work by Miss Azcárraga which, as already said, is to be published in Sefarad, will be successful, not only in pointing out the corrections and additions which are needed in the Lipschütz edition, but also in offering to its readers, in a total and objective manner, the material contained in the *Kitāb al-Khilaf* manuscripts. Only in this way, would it perhaps be possible

[5] F. Pérez Castro, Estudios Masoréticos, Sefarad 25 (1965) p. 313; Idem, En torno a la edición científica del Antiguo Testamento hebreo, Atlántida 4, 20 (1966), p. 140.

to discover if the Hebrew Tiberian Bible manuscripts agree, in each case, with the resultant reading chosen, more or less subjectively, in the Lipschütz edition, or with the reading of one or another of the extant sources.

II.

Observations on the *Ḥil·lufim* of the prophets[6]

Joshua

Josh 3 10. — 151 BA את־הכנעני, BN את הַֽכְנ׳; Ad BA את הכנ׳, BN את הַֽכְנ׳. Lips. follows 151, but does not quote Ad.

Josh 6 18. — 151 BA את־מחנ֤ה, BN אֶֽת מחנ֤ה; Ad BA את־מחנ֤ה, BN אֶֽת־מחנ֤ה; Lips. BA את־מחנ֤ה, BN אֶֽת־מחנה. Lips. creates a *ḥil·luf* in BA insofar as 151 and Ad put the accent both in BA and BN. Regarding the *maqqef*, he follows Ad, but does not quote 151.

Josh 7 24. — 151 BA וְאת אהלו, BN ואת־אהלו; Ad BA וְאת־אהלו, BN ואת אְהלו. Lips. BA וְאֶֽת־אהלו, BN ואֶֽת־אהלו. Lips. does not follow either 151 or Ad. He does not quote the former, and the latter is quoted incorrectly as in its footnote Ad vocalizes BN ואת־אְהלו.

Josh 8 21. — 151 BA וכל־ישר׳, BN וְכֵֽל ישר׳; Ad BA וכל־, BN וְכֵֽל־. Lips. follows Ad, but does not quote 151.

Josh 8 24. — 151 BA כל־, BN כֵֽל; Ad BA כל־, BN כֵֽל־. Lips. follows Ad, but does not quote 151.

Josh 10 20. — 151 BA גדוֹלְה, BN גְדולה־; Ad BA גדוֹלֵֽה, BN גְדלה; Lips. BA גדוֹלְה־, BN גְדולה. Lips. puts *maqqef* in BA disregarding 151 and Ad without saying so.

Josh 10 39. — 151 BA כן־עשׂ֤ה, BN כֵֽן־עשׂ֤ה; Ad BA כן־עשׂ֤ה, BN כְן עשׂ֤ה; Lips. BA כן־עשׂ֤ה, BN כֵֽן־עשה. As in Josh. 6 18 we ask, what led Lips. to believe that the *mehuppakh* is a *ḥil·luf*? Nor does he quote Ad which differs in the *maqqef*.

Josh 13 21. — 151 BA וְכֵֽל, BN וכל־; Ad BA וְכֵֽל־, BN וְכָל־. Lips. follows 151; does not quote Ad.

Josh 17 2. — 151 BA הנוֹתרים, BN הַֽנותרים; Ad BA הנותרים, BN הַֽנתרים.[7] Lips. follows 151, but does not quote Ad.

Josh 22 7. — 151 BA כי־, BN כִּ֣י; Ad BA כְי, BN כִּ֣י. Lips. follows 151; quotes Ad in the following manner: BA כְי־.

[6] Abbreviations used: BA = Ben Ašer, BN = Ben Naftali, Ad = Adat Deborim, Lips. = Lipschütz edition of the *Kitāb al-Khilaf*. Numerals 147–153 indicate the Leningrad manuscripts of the *Kitāb al-Khilaf*, corresponding to the Letters A–G in the Lipschütz edition.

[7] The Cairo Prophet's Codex punctuates הנוֹתרים, that is to say BA, according to the first, but Ms. B 19a of Leningrad, הנותרים would be BA too if we considered Ad.

Josh 22 7. — 151 BA וֽ͏ַיְבָרְכֵם, BN ויברכֵם; Ad BA וַֽיְבָרְכֵם, BN ויברכם. Lips. follows Ad but without indicating that according to 151 the second accent is not a *ḥil·luf*.

Josh 24 19. — 151 BA אֵֽל־, BN אֵֽל־; Ad BA אֵֽל, BN אל־. Lips. follows 151; does not quote Ad.

Judges

Judg 1 4. — 151 BA את־הכנע׳, BN את הַכנעני; Ad BA את הכנ׳, BN את הַכנעני. Lips. follows Ad; does not quote 151.

Judg 11 3. — 151 BA אל־מלאכי, BN אֶֽל מלאכי; Ad BA אל־מל׳, BN אֶֽל־מל׳. Lips. follows Ad; does not quote 151.

Judg 16 2. — 151 BA וַֽיִּתחרשו, BN ויתחרשו; Ad BA ויתחרשו, BN וַֽיִּתחרשו. Lips. follows Ad; but does advise that the *ḥil·luf* in 151 is inverted.

Judg 18 24. — 151 BA וְֽאֶת, BN וְאֶת; Ad BA וְֽאֶת־, BN וְאֶת. Lips. follows 151, but puts *maqqef* in BA and in BN. Does not advise that Ad puts *maqqef* only in BA.

Judg 19 6. — 151 BA וְֽיֵיטַב, BN וְיִטַב; Ad BA וייטב, BN וייטב. The *ḥil·luf* is not discernable; Lips. BA וְֽיֵיטַב, BN וייטב. He puts two ׳ both in BA and in BN. There is no note referring to 151 or to Ad.

Judg 20 13. — 151 BA ונבערה, BN וְנבערה; Ad BA וְֽנבערה, BN ונבערה. Lips. follows 151, but does not point out that in Ad the *meteg* is in BA and not in BN.

Judg 21 18. — 151 BA לתֵת־להם, BN לָֽתֶת להם; Ad BA לתֵת להם, BN לתת־להם; Lips. BA לתֵת־להם, BN לָֽתֶת־להם. He does not follow 151 or Ad, nor does he quote their punctuation.

Judg 21 24. — 151 BA ויתהלכו, BN וַֽיִּתהלכו; Ad BA וַֽיִּתהלכו, BN ויתהלכו. Lips. follows 151, but does not quote Ad.

I Samuel

I Sam 6 3. — 151 BA אַֽל־תשלחו, BN אַֽל תש׳; Ad BA אַל־ת׳, BN אַֽל־תש׳. Lips. follows Ad; does not quote 151.

I Sam 7 14. — Ad BA אשר לָֽקחו, BN לקחו. Lips. indicates the same *ḥil·lufim* which we see in Ad, but in a footnote states the following: Ad (א)אשֶׁר ל׳ (נ) אשר־ל׳. According to this, it seems that Lips. believes that in Ad there is no *ḥil·luf* in לקחו, however, he puts a *ḥil·luf* in אשר, which we do not see, as he includes this word only in BA and not in BN.

I Sam 9 24. — Ad BA שָֽׁמוּר־, BN שמוּר; Lips. BA שָֽׁמוּר־, BN שמוּר־. He does not refer to the *maqqef* of Ad in BA.

I Sam 14 15. — Ad BA במחנה, BN בְּמחנה; Lips. BA במחנה, BN בְּמחנה. He does not indicate that in Ad the accent ˂ is not a *hil·luf*.

I Sam 15 14. — Ad BA קוֹל, BN קול־; Lips. BA קוֹל־, BN קול־. He does not quote Ad which again presents a *ḥil·luf* of *maqqef*, not accepted by Lips.

I Sam 16 1. — Ad BA אשלחך, BN אֲשלחך. Lips. puts the *meteg* in BA, and does not indicate that Ad puts it in BN.

I Sam 20 5. — Ad BA יֵשוב־אשב, BN ישוב אשב; Lips. BA יֵשב אשב, BN ישב אשב. Does not quote Ad.

I Sam 20 36. — Ad BA מְצָא נא, BN מצא־נא. Lips. agrees with Ad in putting *meteg* in BA, and although he puts *maqqef* in BA and BN he does not quote Ad, which only puts it in BN.

I Sam 24 7. — Ad BA אִם־, BN אִם; Lips. BA אִם־, BN אִם־. As above he does not consider the *ḥil·luf maqqef* of Ad.

I Sam 28 10. — Ad BA אִם, BN אִם־; Lips. BA אִם־, BN אִם־. Here Lips. quotes Ad, but not to show that Ad puts *maqqef* only in BN, but only to say that the *ḥil·luf* is inverted (!).

II Samuel

II Sam 4 8. — Ad BA איש־בשת, BN איש בשת־; Lips. BA איש־בשת, BN איש בשת. He does not agree with Ad concerning the *maqqef*, but does not indicate this.

II Sam 7 1. — Ad BA הניח לו, BN הניח לו; Lips. BA הֵנִיחַ־לו, BN הֵנִיחַ־לו. He does not agree with Ad, but quotes it stating that its *ḥil·lufim* are not clear.

II Sam 18 12. — 149 BA כִּי, BN כִּי־; Ad BA כִּי, BN כי־. Lips. follows 149, and quotes the *ḥil·lufim* of the BM Ms. Harl 1528, but omits those of Ad.

II Sam 18 22. — 149 BA לָמה־, BN למה; Ad BA לָמה, BN לָמה; Lips. BA לָמה־, BN למה־. He quotes Ad, but not 149.

II Sam 19 44. — 149 BA לי במ׳, BN לי במ׳; Ad BA ידות, BN ידות לי. Lips. follows 149, but does not explain that the *ḥil·luf* according to Ad is in ידות and not in לי.

II Sam 20 1. — 149 BA נחלָה, BN נַחלה; Ad BA נחלָה, BN נחלה(?). Lips. follows 149, but does not quote Ad.

II Sam 22 32. — 149 BA מִבלעדי, BN מבלעדי; Ad BA וּמִי צור מבלעדי, BN ומי־צור. Lips. follows 149. In a footnote referring to the BM Ms. Harl 1528 he says: BA וּמִי, BN וּמִי, but does not state that this *ḥil·luf* is included in Ad, too.

II Sam 24 17. — 149 BA אֶת, BN אֶת־; this *ḥil·luf* does not appear in Ad. Lips. BA אֶת־, BN אֶת־. He does not quote the *ḥil·luf maqqef* of 149.

I Kings

I Reg 3 9. — Ad BA אֶת־, BN אֶת; Lips. BA אֶת־, BN אֶת־. He does not quote Ad.

I Reg 8 33. - Ad BA והתפללו, BN וְהִתפללו; Lips. BA והתפַּללו, BN same reading as in Ad, but does not point out that in Ad there is no *meteg* in BA.

I Reg 8 37. — Ad BA כָּל־, BN כל; Lips. BA כָּל־, BN כָּל־. He does not quote the *ḥil·luf maqqef* of Ad.

I Reg 10 16. — Ad BA שֵׁשׁ, BN שש־; Lips. BA שֵׁשׁ־, BN שֵׁשׁ־. He does not quote Ad.

I Reg 11 31. — Ad BA לירבעֹם, BN לְירבעם. Lips. BA לירבעֹם, BN לְירבעם. What led him to believe that the *zaqef* is a *ḥil·luf*? In Ad it is not a *ḥil·luf*, but Lips. does not state this.

I Reg. 11 36. — Ad BA לְדָוִד, BN לדוִד; Lips. BA the same as Ad, BN לדוִד־. He does not quote Ad.

I Reg. 16 7. — Ad BA כל־, BN כָּל; Lips. BA כָּל־, BN כָּל־. No quotation.

I Reg 17 1. — Ad BA אִם־, BN אִם; Lips. BA אִם־, BN אִם־. He does not quote the variant reading *maqqef* of Ad.

I Reg 18 26. — Ad BA בשם, BN בְשֵׁם־; Lips. BA בשֵׁם־, BN בְשֵׁם־. He does not quote Ad.

I Reg 18 26. — Ad BA ועד הַצהרים, BN ועד־הצה׳. Lips. does not agree with Ad on the *maqqef*, but does not point this out.

I Reg 22 34. — Ad BA הַפֵּוך, BN הפוך; Lips. BA הַפֵּךְ, BN הַפֵּךְ. He does not point out that the accent of BN is not discernable in Ad.

II Kings

II Reg 1 2. — Ad BA אִם־, BN אִם. Lips. disagrees with Ad on the *maqqef*, but does not point this out.

II Reg 2 15. — Ad BA וישתחוו־לו, BN וישתחוו־לו; Lips. BA וישתחוו־לו, BN וישתחוו לו. He does not quote Ad.

II Reg 4 29. — Ad BA משענתי, BN משענתי־. Lips. BA agreeing with Ad, BN משענתי. Does not quote Ad.

II Reg 4 39. — Ad BA אחד אל־ה׳, BN אחד אֶל־ה׳. Lips. BA אל־, BN אֶל־. He does not make any reference to the *ḥil·luf* in אחד of Ad.

II Reg 10 33. — 148 BA אשר־על, BN אשר על, Ad BA אשר על, BN אשר על. Lips. follows 148, but does not quote Ad.

II Reg 12 19. — 148 BA את כָּל־, BN את כֶּל־; Ad BA את כל־, BN את כֶּל. Lips. follows 148, but does not quote Ad.

II Reg 13 17. — 148 BA חֵץ־, BN חֵ֫ץ־; Ad BA חֵץ־, BN חֵץ. Lips. follows 148, but does not quote Ad.

II Reg 14 6. — 148 BA בְּסֵפֶר־תורת, BN בְּסֵפר תור׳; Ad BA בְּסֵפר תור׳, BN בספר ת׳. Lips. follows 148, but does not quote Ad.

II Reg 17 40. — 148 BA אִם־, BN אִם־; Ad BA אִם, BN אם־. Lips. follows 148, but does not quote Ad.

II Reg 18 28. — 148 and 149 BA דְבַר־, BN דְּבַר־; Ad BA דבר־, BN דבַר. Lips. follows 148 and 149, but does not quote Ad. Refers to fact that BM Ms. Harl 1528 puts BN דבַר. We believe that Ad puts the accent in the same place as above Mss. Why does Lips. overlook it? He does not mention the *maqqef* that Ad attributes to BA either.

II Reg 18 37. — 148 BA אשר־על־הב׳, BN אֲשֶׁר על־ה׳; 149 BA אשר־על־ה׳, BN אֲשֶׁר־על־ה׳; Ad BA אֲשֶׁר על הב׳, BN אשר עַל־הב׳. Lips. follows 149, but does not quote 148. Points out the *ḥil·luf* in אשר of Ad, but not the one which refers to על (BN).

II Reg 19 18. — 148 BA אִם־מע׳ ידי א׳, BN אִם־מע׳ ידי־א׳; 149 BA אִם־מע׳ ידי־א׳, BN אִם־מע׳ ידי־א׳; Ad BA אם־מע׳ ידי א׳, BN אִם מע׳ ידי א׳. Lips. follows 149, but does not quote 148, his base Ms. nor Ad.

II Reg 23 3. — 148 and 149 BA עַל־, BN עַל־; Ad BA עַל, BN על־. Lips. follows 148 and 149, but does not quote Ad.

II Reg 23 11. — 148 and 149 BA וְאֶת־, BN וְאֶת־; Ad BA וְאֶת־, BN וְאֶת. Lips. follows 148 and 149, but does not quote Ad.

II Reg 23 12. — 148 and 149 BA וְאֶת־, BN וְאֶת־; Ad BA וְאֶת, BN וְאֶת־. Lips. follows 148 and 149, but does not quote Ad.

II Reg 25 8. — 148 and 149 BA תְשַׁע־, BN תשַׁע; Ad BA תְשַׁע־, BN תשע. Lips. follows 148 and 149, but does not point out that in Ad there is no accent in BN.

II Reg 25 19. — 148, 149, and Ad BA אֲשֶׁר, BN אשר. Lips. ignoring the punctuation of first three sources, writes BA אשר, BN אֲשֶׁר.

Isaiah

Is 1 18. — 148 BA (deteriorated), BN לְכוּ נָא וְנִוָּכְחָה, 149 BA לכו־נא ונִוָּכְחָה, BN לכו־נָא ונִוָּכחה; Ad BA לכו־נָא ונוכחה, BN לְכוּ נָא ונוכחה; Lips. BA לכו־נָא ונוכ׳, BN לְכוּ נָא ונוכחה. He agrees partly with 148 and partly with Ad. Quotes 149, but does not point out that in Ad נָא does not have a *ḥil·luf*.

Is 10 12. — 148 BA אֶת כָּל־, BN אֶת־כָּֽל־; 149 BA אֶת־כָּל־, BN אֶת־כָּֽל־; Ad BA אֶת כָּל־, BN אֶת כָּֽל־. Lips. follows 149 and Ad (although in the latter there is is no *maqqef* joining אֶת כָּל, either in BA or in BN), but does not quote 148.

Is 16 1. — 148 and 149 BA מוֹשֵׁל, BN מֽוֹשֵׁל־; Ad BA מוֹשֵׁל, BN מושל־. Lips. BA מוֹשֵׁל־, BN מֽוֹשֵׁל. Lips. disagrees with the three sources on the *maqqef*, but does not state it, nor does he point out that the *ḥil·luf meteg* of BN is not discernable in Ad.

Is 29 24. — 148 BA ילמדו[8], BN יִֽלְמְדוּ; 149 BA ילמדו־, BN יִֽלְמְדוּ; Ad BA ילמדו, BN יִֽלְמְדוּ־. Lips. follows 149, but does not quote Ad nor 148. The fact that one cannot discern clearly whether the Ms. 148 puts *maqqef* in BA does not change anything, as it can be seen in BN, which is where 149 and Lips. do not put it in.

Is 33 23. — 148 BA בַּל־, BN בַּֽל־; 149 and Ad BA בַּל־, BN בַּֽל.
Lips. follows 148, but does not quote 149 or Ad.

Is 34 11. — 148 and 149 BA קָו תֹהוּ, BN קַו־תֹהוּ. Ad BA קַו תֹהוּ, BN קַו־תֹהוּ. Lips. agrees with all in BA, but in BN (קַו־תֹהוּ) disagrees with all, although he does not point this out.

Is 34 12. — 148 and 149 BA וְאֵין־, BN וְאֵין־; Ad BA וְאֵין, BN וְאֵין־.
Lips. follows 148 and 149, but does not quote Ad.

Is 36 22. — 149 BA אֲשֶׁר־, BN אֲשֶׁר־; Ad BA אשר־, BN אֲשֶׁר. Lips. follows 149, but does not quote Ad.

Is 37 19. — 149 and Ad BA כִּי אִם־, BN כִּי אִם; Lips. BA כִּי אִם־, BN כִּי־אִם. From where does he take the *ḥil·luf maqqef* of BN? He does not quote 149 and Ad.

Is 40 31. — 149 BA יַעֲלוּ אֵבֶר, BN יַעֲלוּ־אֵבֶר; Ad BA יַעֲלוּ אֵבֶר, BN יַֽעֲלוּ אבר[9]. Lips. follows 149, but does not quote Ad.

Is 43 2. — 149 BA אִתְּךָ־, BN אִתְּךָ; Ad illegible; Lips. BA אִתְּךָ־, BN אִתְּךָ־. He does not quote the *ḥil·luf maqqef* of 149.

Is 44 20. — 149 BA הֲלֹא שֶׁקֶר, BN הֲלֹא־שֶׁקֶר; Ad BA הלא שֶׁקֶר, BN הלא־שֶׁקֶר; Lips. BA הֲלוֹא שֶׁקֶר, BN הֲלוֹא־שֶׁקֶר. Only quotes Ad not concerning these *ḥil·lufim* but concerning the adition in Ad: BA יִתְקַבְּצוּ, BN יתקבצו.

Is 45 2[10]. — 149 BA כִּי־אֲנִי יְיָ, BN כִּי אֲנִי יְיָ; Ad BA כִּי־אֲנִי יְיָ, BN כִּי אֲנִי יְיָ. Lips. follows Ad, but does not point out the *ḥil·luf* in יי of 149.

Is 45 20. — 149 BA וּמִתְפַּלְלִים, BN וּמִתְפַּלְלִים; Ad BA וּמִתְפַּלְלִים, BN וּמִתְפַּלְלִים. Lips. follows 149, but does not quote Ad.

[8] It is blurred and cannot be seen if there is a *maqqef*.

[9] Ad is very blurred.

[10] Lips. Is 45 3.

Is 50 5. — 149 BA פָּתַח, BN פְּתַח; Ad BA פִּתַח, BN פְּתח. Lips. follows Ad, but does not quote 149.

Is 63 7. — 149 BA אֲשֶׁר־, BN אֲשֶׁר־; Ad BA אשר־, BN אֲשֶׁר. Lips. follows 149, and even though he quotes Ad in order to point out that according to it, the *meteg* belongs to BN he does not consider the *ḥil·luf maqqef*.

Jeremiah

Jer 1 7. — 149 BA אֶשְׁלָחֲךָ, BN אשלָחֲךָ; Ad BA אֶשְׁלחך, BN אשלחך.
Lips. follows 149, but does not quote Ad.

Jer 2 6. — 149 BA המעלה, BN הַמַּעֲלֶה; Ad BA המעלה, BN הַמַּעלה.
Lips. BA המעלה, BN הַמַּעלה. Does not quote the *ḥil·lufim* of 149 and Ad.

Jer 2 22. — 149 and Ad BA אִם־, BN אִם־. Lips. disagreeing with 149 and Ad writes: BA אם־, BN אִם.

Jer 3 9. — 149 BA ותחנף, BN וַתֶּחֱנַף; Ad BA ותחנף, BN וַתחנף. Lips. follows 149, and does not quote Ad.

Jer 10 24. — 149 BA אל־, BN אַל; Ad BA אל־, BN אַל־. Lips. follows Ad, but does not quote 149.

Jer 11 7. — 149 BA ועד־, BN עד־; Ad BA ועד, BN עד. Lips. BA ועד, BN עד־. Neither 149 nor Ad consider that the *maqqef* is a *ḥil·luf*. Why does Lips.?

Jer 14 18. — 149 BA כי־, BN כִּי; Ad BA כי־, BN כִּי. Lips. follows 149, but does not quote Ad.

Jer 18 11. — 149 BA אל־איש, BN אל־אִישׁ; Ad BA אל־אִיש, BN אל־אִיש. Lips. follows 149, and quotes Ad thus: BA אל־אִיש, BN אל־אִיש.

Jer 21 9. — 149 BA על־הכש׳, BN עַל הכש׳; Ad BA הכשדים, BN עַל־הכשדים. Lips. BA על־הכשד׳, BN עַל־הכשדים. Makes no reference to 149 or Ad.

Jer 22 28. — 149 BA אִם־כלי, BN אִם כלי; Ad BA אם כלי, BN אִם כלי. Lips. follows 149, but not quoting Ad.

Jer 23 25. — 149 and Ad BA אשר־אמרו, BN אֲשֶׁר אמרו. Lips. ignoring the punctuation of these Mss. writes BA אֲשֶׁר־, BN אֲשֶׁר־.

Jer 25 29. — 149 BA אֲשֶׁר־נקרא, BN אֲשֶׁר נקרא; Ad BA אשר נקרא, BN אשר־נקרא; Lips. BA אֲשֶׁר־נקרא, BN אֲשֶׁר־נקרא. Quotes the *ḥil·lufim* of Ad, but not those of 149.

Jer 34 1. — 149 BA וכל חילו וכָל־, BN וְכל חילו וכָל־; Ad BA וכל־חילו וכל. BN וְכל חילו וכל, Lips. BA וכל־חילו וכל, BN וְכל־חילו ובכל (!).

Jer 35 15. — 149 BA שובו־, BN שׁוּבוּ־; Ad BA שֻׁבו, BN שׁוּבו; Lips. BA שובו־. BN שׁוּבו. Lips. does not take into account 149 and Ad, nor does he quote them.

Jer 37 13. — 149 BA אֶת־, BN אֶת־; Ad BA אֶת, BN את־. Lips. follows Ad, but does not quote 149.

Jer 37 19. — 149 BA אֲשֶׁר־, BN אֲשֶׁר; Ad BA אֲשֶׁר־, BN אֲשֶׁר־; Lips. BA אשר, BN אֲשֶׁר־. Does not quote 149 and Ad.

Jer 38 11. — 149 BA וישלחם אֶל־, BN וְישלחם אֶל־; Ad blurred; Lips. BA אֶל־, BN אֶל־. Does not follow 149 concerning the word וישלחם, but neither does he quote it.

Jer 42 1. — 149 and Ad BA בן־הוֹשַׁעְיה, BN בן־הוֹשעיה; Lips. BA בן־הוֹשַׁעְיה, BN בן הוֹשעיה. Does not quote 149 and Ad.

Jer 43 2. — 149 BA בן הושעיה, BN בן־הוֹשעיה; Ad omits this *hil·luf*. Lips. BA בן־הוֹשַׁעְיה, BN בן־הוֹשעיה. Does not quote 149.

Jer 44 14. — 149 BA לגוּר־, BN לגוּר־; Ad BA לָגוּר, BN לָגוּר. Lips. follows 149 and quotes BM Ms. Harl 1528: BN לָגוּר. Why does he not quote the same reading of Ad?

Jer 48 13. — 149 BA מִבֵּית אל, BN מבית־אל; Ad BA מִבֵּית אֵל, BN מבית אל; Lips. BA מִבֵּית אֵל, BN מִבֵּית־אֵל. Does not agree with 149 or with Ad, but does not quote them.

Jer 48 19. — 149 BA מה־נֶּהיתה, BN מַה־נהיתה; Ad BA מה־נהיתה, BN מַה־נהיתה. Lips. follows 149, but does not point out that for Ad the only *hil·luf* is מַה (BN).

Jer 51 10. — 149 BA ונספרה, BN וְנספרה; Ad BA ונספרה בציון את־מ׳, BN ונספרה בציון אֶת מעשה. Lips. follows 149, but does not quote the *hil·lufim* of Ad, which does not affect the word ונספרה.

Ezekiel

Ez 1 11. — 149 BA שְׁתַּים, BN שְׁתַּים; Ad BA שְׁתַּים, BN שתים. Lips. follows 149 and does not quote Ad.

Ez 3 15[11]. — 149 BA אֶל, BN אל; Ad BA אֶל, BN אֶל־. Lips. BA עַל־, BN עַל־.

Ez 12 19. — 149 and Ad BA כָּל־, BN כָל־[12]. Lips. BA כָּל, BN כָל־. He does not quote 149 and Ad.

Ez 16 33. — 149 and Ad BA לְכָל־, BN לְכָל; Lips. BA לְכָל־, BN לְכָל־. Does not consider the *maqqef* as a *hil·luf*, but neither does he quote 149 and Ad.

Ez 18 4. — 149 BA לִי, BN לִי; Ad BA לי־, BN לִי. Lips. BA לִי־, BN agrees with 149 and Ad. In BA he does not follow any source, at least not in its entirety, but does not point it out.

[11] Lips. Ez 1 3. Because of this writes על instead of אל. In 1 3 there is a similar case, but it seems more probable that it concerns 3 15.

[12] Ad does not put *maqqef* either in BA or in BN.

Ez 20 28. — 149 BA ויזבחו־, BN וַיִּזְבחו; Ad BA ויזבחו־, BN וַיִּזְבחו. Lips. follows Ad (although he does not write *maqqef* either in BA or BN) but does not quote 149.

Ez 21 28. — 149 BA כקסם, BN כִּקְסם; Ad BA כקסם־, BN כִּקְסם. Lips. follows 149, but does not quote Ad.

Ez 23 5. — 149 BA עַל־, BN עַל־; Ad BA עַֽל, BN על־. Lips. follows 149 and does not quote Ad.

Ez 23 44. — 149 BA ואל אָהליבה, BN ואל־אהליבה. Lips. follows only the *ḥil·luf* ⌟ of 149. Does not refer to the *maqqef*.

Ez 29 7. — 149 BA ובהִשָּׁעֲנָם, BN ובהִשָּׁעֲנָם; Ad BA ובהִשָּׁעֲנָם[13], BN ובהִשָּׁעֲנָם. Lips. follows Ad, does not quote 149.

Ez 31 12. — 149 and Ad BA אֶל־ההרים, BN אֶל־הֶהָרִים; Lips. BA אֶל־ההרים, BN אֱֽל־ההרים. Lips. does not quote 149 and Ad although they present a completely different *ḥil·luf* and do not include the one he presents in his edition.

Ez 37 14. — 149 and Ad BA כי־, BN כִּי. Lips. BA כי־, BN כִּי־. Does not quote 149 and Ad.

Ez 45 17. — 149 and Ad BA בְּכָל, BN בכל־; Lips. BA בְּכָל־, BN בְּכָל־. Lips. puts a *maqqef* in BA, ignoring the reading of 149 and Ad and does not quote them.

Ez 48 8. — 149 and Ad BA אֲשֶׁר־, BN אשר־ (Ad does not put *maqqef* in BA or BN). Lips. BA אֲשֶׁר, BN אֲשֶׁר־. Does not quote 149 and Ad.

Minor Prophets

Hos 2 1. — 149 BA אשֶׁר־, BN אֲשֶׁר־; Ad BA אשר־, BN אשֶׁר. Lips. follows 149 and does not quote Ad.

Hos 4 1. — 149 BA ואין־דַּעַת, BN ואין דעת־; Ad BA ואין דעת, BN ואין־דעַת; Lips. BA ואין־דעת, BN וְאֵין דעת. Does not quote 149 and Ad.

Hos 9 12. — 149 BA אם־, BN אִם; Ad BA אם־, BN אִם־. Lips. follows Ad, but does not quote 149.

Obad 20. — 148 BA אֲשֶׁר־, BN אשר־; Ad BA אשֶׁר, BN אשר־. Lips. follows 148, and does not quote Ad.

Zech 6 14. — 148 BA ולידעיה, BN וְלִידעיה; Ad BA ולידַעיה, BN וְלִידַעיה. Ad presents the same *ḥil·luf* as 148. Lips. follows 148, but quotes Ad in an erroneous, equivocal manner. He says: «according to Ad BA reads ולידַעיה». He seems to want to indicate that Ad considers this *meteg* a *ḥil·luf*, but we are not in agreement, as in BN we find

[13] Because it is very blurred, one cannot see if there is an accent on the נ.

that same *meteg*, as well as the *meteg* in לֽ, which is, in our opinion, the only *ḥil·luf*.

Zech 8 17. — 148 BA אֲֽל־, BN אל־; Ad BA אְֽל, BN אל־. Lips. follows 148 and does not quote Ad.

Zech 11 7. — 148 and Ad BA ואקֽח־, BN וָֽאקח־; Lips. BA ואקֽח BN וָֽאקח־. Does not quote either of the two Ms.

Zech 12 10. — 148 and 149 BA כהמר עַֽל־, BN כהמר על־; Ad BA כהמר־עַֽל, BN כהמר עַל. Lips. follows 148 and 149, but does not quote Ad.

Zech 14 7. — 148 and 149 BA לְעֵֽת־, BN לעת־; Ad BA לְעֵֽת, BN לעת־. Lips. follows 148 and 149 and does not quote Ad.

Zech 14 14. — 148 and Ad BA כָֽל־, BN כָֽל־; 149 BA כל־, BN כָֽל. Lips. follows 148 and Ad, but does not quote 149.

Mal 2 5.— 148 and 149 BA ואתנֽם־, BN ואתנם־; Ad BA ואתנֽם, BN ואתנם־. Lips. follows 148 and 149, but does not quote Ad.

Mal 2 7. — 148 and Ad BA יִֽשמרו־, BN יִֽשמרו־; (Ad does not put *maqqef* in either BA or BN); 149 BA ישמרו־, BN יִֽשמרו. Lips. follows 148 and Ad, but does not quote 149.

Mal 3 16. — 148 BA ולחשבֵי, BN וְֽלחשבֵי; 149 BA לְֽיראה ... ולחשבֵי, BN לְֽיראה ... וְֽלחשבֵי; Ad the *ḥil·luf* is not discernable. Lips. follows 148, but does not refer to the *ḥil·lufim* which are included in 149.

The Cultic Role of the Pig in Ancient Times

By Alfred von Rohr Sauer

(Concordia Seminary, 801 DeMun Avenue, St. Louis, Missouri)

During the past two generations a number of studies have been made on the role which the pig has taken in the cultic rites of the Ancient Near East. Most recently R. de Vaux devoted his attention to the sacrificial use of pigs in the Holy Land and its immediate environs[1]. A generation earlier P. E. Newberry had investigated the relationship of the pig to the worship of the Egyptian god Seth[2]. The fact that additional evidence has come to light on this subject from such important sites as Megiddo, Shechem, Hazor, and Taanach justifies the preparation of a brief study on the cultic role of the pig for the Paul Kahle memorial volume. The following article will therefore review briefly what has been published in this area and make such additions as the new evidence warrants.

That serious objections are raised against the pig in the Bible is evident in the dietary proscriptions of the Old Testament. The use of pork for food is forbidden in the Levitical laws on the basis of the fact that, even though the swine is cloven-footed, yet it does not chew the cud, and therefore is unclean[3]. A number of prophetic texts speak against the use of pigs, but these will be taken up in a later paragraph. The pig appears in the New Testament as the symbol of shame and degradation. The low point in the life of the prodigal son is reached when he associates himself with the work of a swine-herd[4]. Jesus warned his followers not to cast their pearls before the swine[5] and Peter compared false prophets to sows who are washed only that they may wallow in the mire[6]. The wisdom writer fitly summarizes the anti-pig stance of the Bible in the words, »Like a gold ring in a swine's snout is a beautiful woman without discretion«[7].

1 R. de Vaux, Les Sacrifices de Porcs en Palestine et dans l'Ancien Orient, in: O. Eissfeldt-Festschrift, BZAW 77, 1958, p. 250–265.

2 P. E. Newberry, The Pig and the Cult-Animal of Set, JEA 14 (1928), p. 211–225.

3 Lev 11 7 and Dtn 14 8.

4 Lk 15 20.

5 Mt 7 6.

6 II Pet 2 22.

7 Prov 11 22.

Are similar attitudes of abhorrence and disdain over against the pig to be found among other peoples than the Hebrews? A brief survey of Eastern Mediterranean cultures will help to supply an answer. Newberry has pointed out that the pig does not fit into a pastoral way of life[8]. While the domestication of the wild boar (sus scrofa) is known in pre-historic times, it is associated only with the settled land. For the bedouin the pig provides no wool like the sheep and no milk like the goat and that makes the only useful pig a dead pig. How then did the pastoral Semitic tribes learn to know the domesticated pig? They must have come into contact with worship rites involving the pig in such settled lands as Babylon, Canaan and Egypt. It is apparent that not all of the Semites reacted in the same way toward the domesticated swine. Some associated themselves with the worship of the pig and therefore prohibited the eating of its sacred flesh. Others refused any contact with the pig because that would be condoning the sacrifice to other gods.

In the agrarian land of Egypt there is a reference to the domestic pig as far back as the Third Dynasty (2900 B.C.)[9]. An agricultural overseer under Sesostris I was called the Keeper of the Swine ca. 1950 B.C. Mayor Renni of El-Kab in the New Kingdom is said to have owned as many as 1500 pigs. The sacredness of the swine in Egypt is connected with the worship of the god Seth. According to the myth of »The Pig in the Sun's Eye« Horus was half-blinded by a black pig (Seth) which got into one of his eyes[10]. As the story goes, Re asked Horus to let him see what was in his eye and Re discovered that it was a black pig that caused the hurt. Horus reacted by blaming Seth for hurting his eye and Re agreed that Seth had transformed himself into a black pig. It is therefore quite natural that the ancient Egyptians occasionally thought of the souls of the wicked as being brought to the place of condemnation in the disgraceful form of swine. It should also be noted that the cult animal of Seth has been identified by Newberry with the pig[11]. Over against earlier scholars who regarded this animal as an imaginary creature like a Sphinx or a Griffin Newberry persisted in his contention that because of the erectness of the tail, the prominence of the ears, the dark and light striations and the striking resemblance to a greyhound, the animal must indeed be a pig. While the breeding of swine was extensive in Graeco-Roman Egypt, pigsties in Egypt today are found almost solely in Coptic villages.

[8] Newberry, op. cit., p. 214.

[9] Newberry, op. cit., p. 211.

[10] The Mythology of All Races, ed. L. H. Gray and G. F. Moore, 1916–1932, v. 12, p. 124.

[11] Newberry, op. cit., p. 217–219.

The earlier view of Bertholet that the pig was the dominant sacrificial animal in Babylon has been challenged by de Vaux[12]. Swine were raised and eaten and portrayed in art in Mesopotamia, but only rarely were they used for any kind of worship. On the other hand, they were used in the two river country to exorcise demons. The blood and members of a young pig were used to conjure away illness. Lamashtu, the demon feared by pregnant women, could be despatched to the underworld by an application of a pig's heart and boar's grease.

It has long been recognized that the pig was the foremost sacrificial animal in both Greece and Rome[13]. The origin of such use of the pig has been associated with the story of Demeter and Triptolemus. It was said that Demeter, the goddess of the soil, taught Triptolemus all kinds of agricultural arts. When Triptolemus discovered that his first sowing had been uprooted by a pig, he brought the animal to Demeter's altar and sacrificed it to her. Ever since the worship of Demeter has been characterized by the offering of a pig[14]. This may well be the reason why in Etruria, Latium and Greece the bride and groom were wont to sacrifice a swine together and why the posts of the entrance to the bridal chamber were painted with swine's blood. It should not be surprizing that Schliemann found thirty teeth of a wild boar in a tomb at Mycenae and that Graeco-Roman warriors adorned their shields and helmets with the figure of a wild boar. The pig was not only the object of worship, it was also regarded as a formidable opponent[15]. De Vaux notes that as part of the feast of Demeter and Persephone little pigs were thrown into ditches alive and afterwards their spoiled remains were taken out and sacrificed on Demeter's altar[16].

The question arises quite naturally at this point, why practically all of the Semites abstain from pork and thus distinguish themselves so radically from the Graeco-Roman peoples and from the rest of the Western world. Some rather down-to-earth reasons have been recorded, e.g., the pig lives in dirt, it communicates leprosy, its eyes are so earth-bound that it cannot see the upper regions, it ruins the fields, it conceives when the moon is waning, it devours its own offspring[17]. For the Hebrews however the answer was very likely a theological one, namely, the sharp thrust of their monotheist faith. As Elijah once called a halt to religious syncretism with his searching question,

[12] De Vaux, op. cit., p. 253 ff.

[13] Pauly's Realencyclopädie der Classischen Altertumswissenschaft. Zweite Reihe, dritter Halbband, 1921, col. 811 ff.

[14] The Mythology of All Races, v. 1, p. 230.

[15] Pauly's Realencyclopädie der Classischen Altertumswissenschaft, col. 804.

[16] De Vaux, op. cit., p. 259.

[17] De Vaux, op. cit., p. 262.

»How long halt ye between two opinions?« (1 Kings 18 21), so the Biblical prohibition against the eating of pork probably had a strongly polemic accent, it probably constituted a summons to the people of God to have no part in the cultic practices of their neighbors and contemporaries.

De Vaux raises the question of the date of such an anti-pork polemic. His starting point is not the Levitical legislation referred to above, but rather a number of late prophetic texts. Is 65 4 and Is 66 17 condemn the people of God, because they provoked their Lord to anger by eating the flesh of swine. Volz had assigned these texts to the Hellenistic period, but de Vaux finds this untenable. His argument is based on the fact that there were ancient animal rites involving the pig not only in the Aegean world, but also throughout the Near East. Moreover there is a recognizable anti-swine attitude in Ez 8 7–13. If this text reflexts conditions in Jerusalem between the first and second deportations and if Is 65–66 are assigned to the period after the return, but before the rebuilding of the temple, then Israel's succumbing to the eating of pork may be assigned to the exilic or immediate post-exilic period. This may of course represent the re-introduction in a time of national laxity of pig rites which had been practiced in Israel much earlier[18]. Arguing along another line, Ehrlich has taken the view already referred to above that the prohibition to eat pork originated in pre-Israelite times. It was then adopted by the Hebrews and given a new motivation as a polemic against contemporary pagan practices[19].

There is one more question which needs to be taken up briefly before the archaeological evidence is presented. Is the anti-pork attitude discussed thus far based on the view that the pig is unclean or that it is holy? R. Smith called attention to the fact that the ideas of holiness and uncleanness are closely related[20]. Among the Semites the boundary between rules of holiness and rules of uncleanness is often quite vague. It is difficult to determine, e.g., whether the Syrian taboo on swine's flesh is traceable to the animal's holiness or to its uncleanness. There is also considerable ambiguity in the Jewish attitude toward the pig. Did the people of God really abhor swine, especially in later times, or were they led to venerate swine in imitation of their pagan contemporaries? Surely they could have been forbidden to kill pigs because of their sacredness; but they could also have been forbidden to eat them because of their uncleanness[21].

[18] De Vaux, op. cit., p. 265.

[19] E. L. Ehrlich, Die Kultsymbolik im Alten Testament und im nachbiblischen Judentum, in: Symbolik der Religionen, III 1959, p. 126.

[20] W. R. Smith, Lectures on the Religion of the Semites, First series, 1889, p. 427ff.

[21] J. G. Frazer, The Golden Bough, Part V, vol. II, 1919, p. 16–22.

May one infer that originally the pig was worshipped rather than disdained? Some of the practices in Egypt and Cyprus seem to point in that direction. Once a year the pig was eaten and sacrificed in Egypt. The Greek scientist Eudoxus maintained that the Egyptians venerated the pig because it helped their agriculture. Pigs trampled the seed into the wet earth after the Nile waters receded. Historically, however, it would appear that the pig was more a source of terror than of worship, because it was the embodiment of Seth, the enemy of Osiris, as was noted earlier. The annual sacrificial feast involving the pig is also noted among the pagan Harranians by Al Nadim and the Cyprians allegedly sacrificed a wild boar to Aphrodite on every second day of April[22].

What evidence does archaeology provide to help recognize the cultic role of the pig in the Bible and in the ancient Near East? De Vaux has dealt with the material up to 1957–1958 which has thrown valuable light on the problem[23]. In 1955 at Tell el-Farah (the presumed site of ancient Tirzah) de Vaux came upon an underground room which he dates ca. 1800 B.C. and which he is convinced has a cultic context. In its later phases the room is closely parallel to the 16th century subterranean sanctuary which Woolley found at Alalakh. In this underground sanctuary two sets of small animal bones, one embryonic group preserved in a jar, have been identified as those of pigs which could only have been used for some sort of sacrificial rite.

Similar findings at other sites would seem to confirm the above interpretation of the Tirzah material. From the second millennium B.C. there is an alabaster statuette which was discovered at Gezer and which has some very striking features. A naked man is holding the hind quarters of a young pig against his breast with his right hand grasping the animal's genitals. Both figures are hollow and it is proposed that the piece was a receptacle of some kind used for libations. In the Palestine Archaeological Museum in Jerusalem there is a restored alabaster piece from Early Bronze Ai which de Vaux regards as the hind quarter of a pig. Its feet are tucked under its belly with a cord attached, apparently implying that the animal was being prepared as a sacrifice. A bronze figurine from 16th century Megiddo is tentatively associated by de Vaux with the figure of a wild boar, but he grants that it was not discovered in a cultic context[24].

Discussion of evidence that has accrued since the publication of the de Vaux article may begin with the Hazor Pig Skeleton[25]. South

[22] Frazer, op. cit., p. 23; Smith, op. cit., p. 392.

[23] De Vaux, op. cit., p. 250–265.

[24] De Vaux, op. cit., p. 251f.

[25] S. Angress, The Pig Skeleton from Area B, Hazor 2, An Account of the Second Season of Excavations 1956, 1960, p. 166.

of the Citadel (Area B) a pig skeleton was found which is dated in the last half of the 8th century. When the skull was almost completely restored, Angress concluded that it must represent a domestic breed of pig. Its importance was increased by the fact that none of the seven domestic pig skulls described in Lachish III as suffering from pachyostosis were accompanied by photographs or measurements. Even though its length (110–115 cm), is considerably shorter than that of the average wild boar (130–170 cm), Angress sees the Hazor skull as resembling that of a young wild boar more than that of an adult domestic pig. But if it resembled its wild ancestors, there is evidence that it did not have complete freedom of movement. Some of its bones were afflicted with pachyostosis which probably was caused by a continuous series of hard blows as well as insufficient fodder. Having had such a hard life, it may well have been a very early example of interbreeding of domestic and wild pigs. Perhaps the Hazor pig was derived from the wild boar in the neighboring swamps of Lake Huleh. Its cranial features present a strange combination of rigorous domestication and the typical characteristics of the wild pig[26].

The first campaign of the Joint Concordia-ASOR Excavation at Ta'annek contributed to our knowledge of the cultic role of the pig in the Near East in a rather unique way[27]. Three groups of astragali (ankle bones) of pigs were found in the context of an ash layer directly next to a well cut block of flint, a destruction which has been tentatively dated as coming from the time of Shishak's campaign in Palestine in 918 B.C.[28]. It is a striking phenomenon that 140 such bones should be found in the proximity of a stone that may well have functioned as a gaming board or in some distinctive cultic capacity. No other pig remnants were found next to the ankle bones. One fragment of an astragalus from Ta'annek was pierced, another had been affixed to a piece of iron. The latter features are quite analogous to an earlier find of astragali in a cultic situation at Megiddo[29]. This group consisted of 640 pig and 3 sheep astragali heaped together in a crater which is listed as Mus. No. 36–1943 in the Palestine Archaeological Museum in Jerusalem. Lapp examined the Megiddo collection and noted that eleven of the pig astragali are perforated with little holes and two of them had been affixed to a bar of bronze. The holes and metal rods point to the fact that these bone objects had been put to some kind of use by the people of Ta'annek and Megiddo.

[26] Angress, op. cit., p. 166f.

[27] P. W. Lapp, The 1963 Excavation at Ta'annek, BASOR 173 (1964), p. 35.

[28] Lapp, op. cit., p. 8.

[29] Lapp, op. cit., p. 35.

Additional material on the pig is provided in the Preliminary Report of the Fifth Campaign at Balatah (Shechem). In Area 3 an Iron Age sanctuary was enclosed within a massive wall. The sanctuary was destroyed late in the 10th century B.C. and an unfinished stela or massebah was lying on the floor. Beneath a brick platform which could have functioned as an altar there was a jar that contained among other things four astragali. These bones too must have been put to use, for several of them had become smooth from wear. If the jar is connected with the establishment of this cult building, as the excavator proposes, the astragali too will have had some connection with religious rites[30].

What function these great numbers of astragali served in the lives of ancient Near Eastern peoples is a question that additional study and perhaps more archaeological finds will help answer. Whether they were used for oracular purposes like the ancient Urim and Thummim, or whether they were amulets that served as good luck charms, or whether they were used in games like our modern chess or checkers cannot be determined at the present. The fact that some were worn smooth and others had perforations and were attached to metal rods may be a clue that will help to lead to a plausible solution. The evidence of the astragali is there in abundance; what it means should be a challenge to future scholars.

30 J. A. Callaway, The Fifth Campaign at Balatah (Shechem), BASOR 180 (1965), p. 11.

Von den Gebetbüchern der Proselyten

Von A. Scheiber

(Kún-u. 12, Budapest)

Die Christen, die in Europa zum Judentum übergetreten waren, mußten in ihrer Furcht vor der Kirche und ihrer Familie von ihrem Aufenthaltsort fliehen. Es kam vor, daß sie ihren Weg nach anderen Ländern Europas nahmen. So mochte wegen der Judenmassaker der ersten Kreuzfahrer nach dem damals sicheren Ungarn jene Proselytenfamilie flüchten, die hier ihren Namen in die Geschichte der jüdischen Wissenschaft eingeschrieben hat[1]. Der Vater hieß Abraham, die zwei Söhne hießen Isaak und Josef-Jehosafia. Den ersten nennen die verschiedenen Quellen entweder קצין, oder ויסקונטי. Es scheint wahrscheinlich, daß in diesem Falle קצין die hebräische Übersetzung von Viscount ist. Selbst noch anfangs des 16. Jh. besuchen bettelnde Proselyten in Ungarn die Gemeinden von Tyrnau Nagyszombat, Preßburg Pozsony, Ofen Buda, Gran Esztergom, Stuhlweißenburg Székesfehérvár und Totis Tata, wo sie von den wohlhabenderen Juden unterstützt werden[2].

In größerer Zahl hingegen gehen sie nach dem Orient[3]. In Fostat erreichen sie eine große Zahl. Es gibt unter ihnen auch enttäuschte Kreuzfahrer. Diese erhalten zumeist eine Unterstützung von der Gemeinde und leben dort unter ihren Mitgliedern. Über einen ist klar zu lesen, daß er in der den babylonischen Ritus befolgenden Synagoge zu finden ist (T.-S.K. 15^{45})[4]. Es gibt einen, der acht Denare Steuer zahlt (T.-S. Misc. Box 26^{37}).

Es ist natürlich, daß, wenn sie am jüdischen Leben teilnahmen und die Synagoge besuchten, der eine oder der andere Lust bekam, sich — dem Brauche des Zeitalters gemäß — ein Gebetbuch abzuschreiben. Auf meiner Studienreise in England 1965, die mir ein Stipendium der Memorial Foundation for Jewish Culture ermöglichte, habe ich von den Gebetbüchern zweier Proselyten je ein Fragment gefunden.

[1] E. E. Urbach, REJ 100 (1935), S. 173–174; בעלי התוספות, Jerusalem, 1955. S. 193–194; B.-Z. Wacholder, JQR 51 (1960/61), S. 313 Anm. 109; A. Scheiber in: The World History of the Jewish People. The Dark Ages. 1966, S. 317.

[2] Monumenta Hungariae Judaica, ed. A. Scheiber, VIII 1965, S. 170, No. 190.

[3] J. W. Hirschberg, A History of the Jews in North Africa (Hebräisch), II 1965, S. 140, 360 Anm. 122.

[4] E. Ashtor, Zion, 30 (1965), S. 69–70.

I. Aus dem Gebetbuch des Proselyten Obadja

Die Melodieaufzeichnungen in Obadjas Gebetbuch, dessen Autorschaft der Schreiber dieser Zeilen und N. Golb — voneinander unabhängig — erkannten[5], lenkten die Aufmerksamkeit der Forscher auf die Frage und eröffneten eine reiche Literatur[6]. Ich habe schon früher festgestellt, daß sein Gebetbuch den palästinischen Ritus befolgt[7]. Nun bin ich in Cambridge unter den noch nicht geordneten Genisastücken auf ein interessantes Fragment gestoßen, das ich in den von mir sortierten Karton (T.-S. N.S. 325[50]) legte.

Ein Blatt, Papier, 12×17,5 cm. Nicht punktiert. Auf der Seite 1a ist das Ende eines gereimten, alphabetischen Pijjuts zu lesen. Es kommt heraus das Akrostichon der Buchstaben ר-ש-ת und des Wortes תמים. Im Pijjut klagt der Verfasser über seine Feinde. Auch orthographische Fehler sind vorhanden. Das Akrostichon des zweiten liturgischen Gedichtes ist עבדיה הגר. Dann folgt die arabische Bemerkung מא הי תאמה, dies bedeutet: »unvollendet« (nämlich der Text). Daraus können wir vielleicht mit Recht folgern, daß die weggebliebenen Strophen noch das Akrostichon enthielten: הנורמנדי, der Normanne. Es ist in einem einigermaßen kindlichen Hebräisch geschrieben. Am Ende bittet es Gott um Hilfe gegen seine Feinde. Die aus der Bibel gelernte hebräische Sprache ist in beiden vorherrschend.

Aus dem Ton und dem Rhythmus des Gedichtes von Obadja glaube ich die der mittelalterlichen lateinischen Hymnen herauszuhören. Seine Reimart (a, a, a, b) ist in der Hymnologie ganz gewöhnlich.

Ein Beispiel aus dem 11. Jh.[7a]:

Sripturae sacrae mystica
Mire solvis aenigmata,
Theorica mysteria
Te docet ipsa veritas.

Die Schrift ist nicht die des normannischen Proselyten Obadja. Auch den Namen Gottes schreibt er anders als er: ׳׳י׳. Andererseits sind nur von dem normannischen Obadja Schriften auf uns gekommen.

Wir können derzeit nicht befriedigend entscheiden, ob auch dieses Fragment von ihm stammt oder nicht. Vielleicht hat es sich nur in einer Abschrift erhalten — dafür spricht die arabische Bemerkung —,

[5] N. Golb, JR 45 (1965), S. 153–156; A. Scheiber, Tarbiz 34 (1965), S. 366–371; Studia Musicologica 8 (1966), S. 173–187; I. Adler, Revue de Musicologie 51 (1965), S. 19–51; H. Avenary, JJS 16 (1965), S. 87–104; L. Levi in: Scritti sull' Ebraismo in memoria di Guido Bedarida, 1966, S. 105–136.

[6] N. Allony, Sinai 57 (1965), S. 43–55; Haaretz, 11. VI 1965; L. Levi, a.a.O. 2. VII 1965; J. Schweitzer, Isr. Wochenblatt 65 (1965), XI, 19.

[7] A. Scheiber, Sinai 46 (1959/60), S. 268–270.

[7a] J. Szövérffy, Die Annalen der lateinischen Hymnendichtung, I 1964, S. 382.

jedoch ist er der Verfasser. Wir wollen hoffen, daß weitere zum Vorschein kommende Stücke dies aufklären werden.

Hier folgt der Text selbst (Abb. 1–2):

T.-S. N. S. 325[50]

[1a] [רְעָתָם] // תָּבוֹא לְפָנֶיךָ[1] וּמַעֲלָם
וְאַל יַצְלְחוּ לָנוּ בְמַעֲשֵׂיהֶם וְלֹא בְמִלּוּלָם
וּמְאֵירָה תְשַׁלַּח בָּם[2] עַד שֶׁיֹּאבְדוּ כּוּלָּם
וְיִהְיוּ לַחֲרָפוֹת לְדִרְאוֹן עוֹלָם[3]:

שַׁבֵּר מַחֲשַׁבְתָּם[4] וְהָשֵׁב גְּמוּלָם בְּרֹאשָׁם[5]
וְתוֹלַעְתָּם לֹא תָמוּת[6] וְלֹא תִכְבֶּה אִשָּׁם
וְיִרְאוּ רַבִּים צָרָתָם וְחֶרְפָּתָם וּבָאְשָׁם
וְיָשׁוּבוּ בְּפַחֵי נֶפֶשׁ[7] בְּחָקְרָם וְדָרְשָׁם:

תָּשִׁיב לָהֶם גְּמוּל[8] וְתִמְחֶה אֶת זִכְרָם[9]
וְיִהְיוּ לְמָשָׁל וְלִשְׁנִינָה[10] וְתַחְשִׁיךְ אוֹרָם
וְאַל יְהִי לָהֶם מוֹשֵׁךְ חֶסֶד[11] וַעֲלֵיהֶם אַל יָחוּס צוּרָם
יִרְאוּ וְיִתְיַסְּרוּ בָּם כָּל אַנְשֵׁי עִירָם:

תַּעַן לְשׁוֹנִי אִמְרָתֶךָ[12]
וּלְבָבִי יַאֲמִין בְּצִדְקָתֶךָ
וְנַפְשִׁי תָגִיל[13] בִּישׁוּעָתֶךָ
וּלְשׁוֹנִי תָמִיד תְּסַפֵּר תְּהִלָּתֶךָ:[14]

מִמְּכוֹן שִׁבְתְּךָ[15] בְּחַסְדְּךָ עֲנֵנִי
וּבְנֵה בְרַחֲמֶיךָ הֵיכָלִי וְאַרְמוֹנִי

1 איכה א, כב.
2 דב׳ כח, כ.
3 דנ׳ יב, ב.
4 כמו קלקל מחשבתם.
5 עובדיה א, טו.
6 יש׳ סו, כד.
7 פסיק׳ דר״כ כרך א׳ ,הוצ׳ מנדלבוים, ניו־יורק, תשכ״ב, עמ׳ 261: ,,והיה יוצא משם בפחי נפש״.
8 איכה ג, סד.
9 דב׳ כה, יט.
10 דב׳ כח, לז.
11 תה׳ קט, יב.
12 שם, קיט, קעב.
13 שם, לה, ט.
14 שם, כח.
15 מל׳ א, ח, ל.

וּזְבוּלְךָ תְּיַסֵּד וּלְבֵיתְךָ תַּעֲלֵנִי
חָנֵּנִי יְיָ כִּי אֻמְלַל אָנִי[16]:

יֵבוֹשׁוּ רוֹדְפַי וְאַל אֵבוֹשָׁה אָנִי
יֵחַתּוּ מְרִיבַי[17] וְאַל אֵחָתֶה[18] אָנִי
הָבֵיא עֲלֵיהֶם זַעַמְךָ וְאַל תַּכְלִימֵנִי
וּרְצֵנִי וְזַכֵּנִי וּמִלְּפָנֶיךָ אַל תַּשְׁלִיכֵנִי[19]:

מִשָּׁמַיִם תִּשְׁלַח[20] וְתַשְׁקִיף וְתוֹשִׁיעֵנִי
וּמֵחַטְאוֹתַי[21] וּפְשָׁעַי וְאַשְׁמוֹתַי טַהֲרֵנִי[22]
[1 b] וּמִשְּׁגִיאוֹת וּמִנִּסְתָּרוֹת תְּחַטְּאֵנִי וּתְכַבְּסֵנִי[23]
וְעַל[24] אַף אוֹיְבַי[25] וְשׂוֹנְאַי וְצָרַי תַּעַזְרֵנִי:

עֶלְיוֹן לְךָ מוֹדֶה
שׁוֹמֵר וְגַם פּוֹדֶה
אוֹתִי וְעַם עוֹשֶׂה
צֶדֶק וּמֵישָׁרִים:

בָּרוּךְ אֱלֹהֵינוּ
בּוֹחֵר אֲדוֹנֵנוּ
מֹשֶׁה לְהוֹרֵינוּ
תּוֹרָה לְדוֹר דּוֹרִים:

דִּבֵּר לְכָל אַחַי
הָאֵל אֲשֶׁר הוּא חַי[1]
עֵדוּת עֲלֵי סִינַי
חֻקִּים לְכָל עוֹבְרִים[2]:

יָהּ רָם שְׁמוֹ נִקְרָא[3]
גָּדוֹל מִכֹּל אֲשֶׁר בָּרָא[4]
בָּרוּךְ בְּכָל־שִׁירִים[5]:

16 תה׳ ו, ג.
17 שמ׳ א, ב, י.
18 כאלו נגזר מן שרש תתה בנפעל.
19 תה׳ נא, יג.
20 ז.א. ידיך כמו בתה׳ קמד, ז.
21 בכ״י ,,ומחטותי״.
22 תה׳ נא, ד.
23 שם, ט.
24 בראשונה ,,ואל״ ותוקן.
25 תה׳ קלח, ז.
1 תה׳ מב, ג.
2 כמו לכל באי עולם.
3 עפ״י יש׳ נז, טו.
4 השווה יש׳ מ, כה.
5 כמו ,,מלך מהולל בתשבחות״.

הָיְתָה שְׁבוּעַת אֵל
לָתֵת לְיִשְׂרָאֵל
עַל יַד יְקוּתִיאֵל[6]
מֹשֶׁה וְגַם הוֹרִים[7]:

הַגֵּר[8] הֲלֹא גָר שָׁם
מַקְרִיב עֲלֵי רֹאשָׁם[9]
רֹאשׁ הוּא לַמַּזְהִירִים[10]:

גֵּאִים וְחַיָּבִים
שָׂרִים[11] וְכָל אוֹיְבִים
אֶל אֵל בְּמִסְתָּרִים:

רְאֵה אֱלוֹהַּ חַי:
מא הי תאמה[12]

II. Aus dem Gebetbuch des Proselyten Jehuda

Ebenso fand ich in einem der nicht geordneten Kartons ein aus zwei Blättern bestehendes, auf Papier geschriebenes Fragment, das gleichfalls im erwähnten Karton (T.-S. N.S. 325[64]) plaziert worden ist. 13,5 × 20 cm. Es ist nicht punktiert. Es enthält die mit **אתה הנחלת** beginnenden Azharot, und zwar das Ende des 7. Teils (vom zweiten Wort des Buchstaben **פ**)[8] und den ganzen 8. Teil[9]. Die Schrift ist ziemlich ungeübt, die Buchstaben sind ungleichmäßig und nicht schön. Im Text gibt es Fehler, da es den Kopisten nicht leicht ankam, den schweren Pijjut zu verstehen.

Zum Schluß ist der Kolophon zu lesen (Abb. 3): **כמלת בעזרה̈ האל אמן נצח וכתב יהודה גר טהור ס״ט סלה** »Vollendet mit Gottes Hilfe. Amen auf ewig. Geschrieben von Jehuda, dem reinen Proselyten, es sei im guten Zeichen, Sela«.

Offenbar ist auch dies ein Teil eines Gebetbuches. Über seinen Kopisten wissen wir — bedauerlicherweise — nichts Näheres, jedoch

[6] זה משה.
[7] אלו האבות. ה„וו״ מעל לשורה.
[8] זה אברהם.
[9] מרמז על העקדה.
[10] ז.א. ראש המאמינים.
[11] תה׳ קיט, קסא.
[12] בעברית: אין היא נגמרה.

[8] I. Davidson, Thesaurus of Mediaeval Hebrew Poetry, I 1924, S. 78.

[9] I. Davidson, a.a.O., III 1930, S. 543.

darüber, daß die Proselyten sich ein Gebetbuch abzuschreiben pflegten, liegt uns darin eine in jeder Hinsicht interessante Angabe vor[10].

Mit Pietät widme ich diese, zwei Genisa-Texte behandelnde Arbeit dem Andenken Prof. Paul E. Kahles, des Historikers der Genisa, dessen Briefe — Symbole unserer langen Beziehung — ich stolz bewahre. Auch sie zeugen von seiner wissenschaftlichen und menschlichen Größe.

[10] S. W. Baron schreibt neulich: »Much yet remains to be done before the story of medieval Jewish proselytism will be more fully clarified«. A Social and Religious History of the Jews, IX 1965, S. 251 Anm. 24.

»A Drop of a Bucket«? Some Observations on the Hebrew Text of Isaiah 40 15

By D. Winton Thomas

(4 Grantchester Road, Cambridge)

V. 12–31 of Is 40 have as their theme the omnipotence of Yahweh, and in v. 12–16 his might is seen manifested in the creation of the sea, the heavens, and the earth, and his wisdom knows no bounds. The divine majesty transcends all creation, the nations are of no account before Yahweh, and not even the wood of Lebanon and its denizens would suffice to make a worthy sacrifice to him. V. 15, a triple line[1], runs in Hebrew as follows:

הֵן גּוֹיִם כְּמַר מִדְּלִי
וּכְשַׁחַק מֹאזְנַיִם נֶחְשָׁבוּ
הֵן אִיִּים כַּדַּק יִטּוֹל:

which is translated in the English Versions[2]:

»Behold, the nations are as a drop of a bucket, and are counted as the small dust of the balance; behold, he taketh up the isles as a very little thing«.

The meaning »a drop of a bucket« for כמר מדלי is found in all the chief ancient versions. Thus the LXX translates the phrase by ὡς σταγὼν ἀπὸ κάδου, the Vulg. by *quasi stilla situlae*, the Pesh. by ܐܝܟ ܢܘܛܦܬܐ ܡܢ ܕܘܠܐ, and the Targ. by כטיפא מדול[3]. This same meaning is found in the commentaries of Rashi and Kimchi. The former's comment on the two Hebrew words is כטיפה מרה המטפטפת משולי הדלי ומשקע טנופת המים ורוקבין העץ לימנויד״א בלע״ז »Like a bitter drop that drips from the rim of a bucket and deposits at the bottom the impurity of

[1] For the verse of three members in Second Isaiah, see C. C. Torrey, The Second Isaiah, p. 154ff.

[2] R. S. V. »a drop from a bucket«; so B. Duhm, Das Buch Jesaia, p. 263, cf. E. König, Das Buch Jesaja, p. 356; Torrey, op. cit., p. 226; C. R. North, The Second Isaiah, p. 33; P. Volz, Jesaia II, übersetzt u. erklärt, p. 7.

[3] Similarly the Arabic version (B. Walton, Polyglot, ad loc.), and the Ethiopic version (J. Bachmann, Der Prophet Jesaia nach d. aethiop. Bibelübersetzung, p. 69). The Wisdom of Solomon 11 22 may be compared — ὅτι ὡς ῥοπὴ ἐκ πλαστίγγων ὅλος ὁ κόσμος ἐναντίον σου.

the water and it rots the wood—*l'immonde* in the gentiles' language«[4]. Kimchi's comment is כמו הטיפה מדלי שהוא דבר מועט כנגד מי הדלי »Like a drop from a bucket which is a small thing compared with the water in the bucket«. This traditional meaning »a drop of a bucket« is found generally in commentaries[5] and lexicons[6]. The aim of this article is to raise the question whether this meaning, despite the long tradition behind it, is in fact correct. Before we proceed to suggest another possible translation, it is necessary first to consider the precise meaning of two other phrases in this verse, namely, כשחק מאזנים and כדק יטול. We shall consider them in turn.

The basic meaning of the Hebrew root שחק, which occurs only four times in the Hebrew Bible, is »rubbed away, beat fine, pulverized«. In Job 14 9 waters »rub away« stones; in Ex 30 36 Moses is commanded to »beat fine« the incense; and in II Sam 22 43 (= Ps 18 43) the verb is used of »beating small as dust, crushing« enemies (here שחק is parallel to דקק »crushed«). The same verb is found in Sir 6 36[7] ראה מי יבין ושחריהו ותשחוק בסיפו רגלך »If thou seest one who is understanding, be sure to seek him out, and let thy foot wear out (rub away, LXX ἐκτριβέτω) his door-step«, that is, make thy visits to him frequent (cf. Lat. iter terere)[8]. This basic meaning «rubbed away, pulverized«, is that which is borne by the cognate verbs in other Semitic languages. Thus in Arabic سَحَقَ (a synonym of دَقَّ = Hebrew דקק) means »bruised, pounded, pulverized«, also »wore out« (of a garment)[9], and in Aramaic[10] שְׁחַק and in Syriac[11] ܫܚܩ bear similar meanings.

The Hebrew substantive שַׁחַק thus basically means »that which is rubbed, crushed, made fine« like dust, and is used in the Hebrew

[4] The French *l'immonde* renders only the Hebrew word טנופת. J. L. Teicher has kindly discussed this passage from Rashi, which is not without its difficulties, with me.

[5] Cf. n. 2 above, and E. J. Kissane, The Book of Isaiah, II p. 11.

[6] See the lexicons of Brown-Driver-Briggs, Gesenius-Buhl, Zorell, and Koehler-Baumgartner.

[7] See R. Smend, Die Weisheit des Jesus Sirach, Hebr. u. Deutsch, p. 6 (of Hebrew text); Die Weisheit des Jesus Sirach erklärt, p. 61.

[8] Cf. H. L. Strack, Die Sprüche Jesus', des Sohnes Sirach, p. 6.

[9] Lane, Arab.-Eng. Lex., 1318.

[10] G. Dalman, Aram.-Neuhebr. Wörterb., etc., p. 400.

[11] P. Smith, Thes. Syr., 4122f. The Akkadian *šaḫāqu* »sneeze« is compared by Koehler-Baumgartner, p. 96, but this meaning is regarded as doubtful by C. Bezold, Bab.-Assyr. Glossar, p. 268. The form *i-ši-ḫi-iq* in a Babylonian medical text is compared with Hebrew שחק »rubbed away« by C. Frank, OLZ 12 (1909), 482; cf. Ges.-Buhl, Hebr. u. Aram. Handwörterb. über das A.T., 16th. ed., p. 819.

Bible twenty times of »(thin) clouds«, usually in the plural שְׁחָקִים. It frequently stands in parallelism with שָׁמַיִם (e.g., Dtn 33 26 Is 45 8 Jer 51 9 Ps 36 6 Job 35 5[12]); twice it is opposed to תְּהוֹם (Prov 3 20 8 28); in II Sam 22 12 (= Ps 18 12) the phrase עָבֵי שְׁחָקִים »thick clouds» occurs; and in Job 37 18 (plural) and Ps 89 7.38 (singular) it means »sky«[13]. In Arabic سَحْقٌ means »thick clouds«, which are likened to an old and worn out garment[14] (as rubbed away; cf. Aramaic שְׁחִקְתָא »worn out, thin, clothes«)[15]. The one example of the singular שַׁחַק in the Hebrew Bible is in the passage at present under discussion. Most commentators and lexicographers, as well as the English Versions and the Revised Standard Version, give the meaning here »fine dust«, the phrase »fine dust of the scales« being a simile of insignificance; fine dust in the scales is too small a thing to be reckoned of any account in weighing. This meaning »fine dust«, literally »what has been rubbed away, crushed, pulverized«, may be accepted as correct for Is 40 15[16], even though elsewhere in the Hebrew Bible the meaning (in the plural) »clouds« predominates. The two meanings »fine dust« and »(thin) cloud« are, however, not so dissimilar that they cannot be brought into association (cf. the English phrase »a cloud of dust«)[17].

The substantive שַׁחַק occurs again with the meaning »dust« in Sir 42 4. The Hebrew text runs — על שחק מאזנים ופלס ועל תמהות איפה ואבן »(Do not be ashamed) concerning the dust on the scales and the tongue of the balances nor of testing the ephah measure and weights«, that is, do not hesitate to take account even of the fine dust on the scales in watching the merchant's balances for exactness (for על שחק מאזנים the LXX has περὶ ἀκριβείας ζυγοῦ). R. Smend sees in שחק an in-

[12] Possibly also in Ps 68 35, where השמים may have to be read in place of ישראל; cf. BH[3] ad loc.

[13] For the meanings in these passages, see Brown-Driver-Briggs, p. 1007; P. Joüon argues that שחקים never means »clouds«, but always »heaven«. It is a poetic synonym of שמים, with the nuance »the high part of heaven« (שחק II »was high«); it means »the heights«, just as שמים (Arabic *samā* »sky« is from *sāmi* »high«), ZKTh 27 (1903), p. 592f. For a similar view, see M. Lambert, REJ 68 (1914), p. 113f. The LXX renders שחק here by ῥοπή, the Vulg. by *momentum*, the Pesh. by ܢܛܠܐ, and the Targ. by עיול; similarly the Arab. and Eth. versions. Ibn Janāḥ (ed. A. Neubauer) explains by سحالة »filings, particles« (p. 714).

[14] Lane, op. cit., 1319.

[15] Dalman, op. cit., loc. cit. Cf. כתן[ש]חיק »an old coat« (A. Cowley, Aramaic Papyri of the Fifth Century B.C., 42 10, p. 142, 144).

[16] North, op. cit., p. 33, translates »moisture on scales«, which »in a market place would not need to be taken into reckoning« (p. 84). Dust on scales, however, seems a more likely phrase when an oriental market is in mind.

[17] According to Midr. Till. to Ps 18, the clouds are called שחקים »because they rub against one another« (M. Jastrow, A Dict. of the Targumim, etc., p. 1550).

finitive[18], but since, as he himself remarks, there is a clear connection between this verse in Sir and Is 40 15, it is preferable to regard it as a substantive[19], and to give it the same meaning which, as we believe, it has in the Isaiah passage, namely, »dust«.

Since in our view כשחק מאזנים means »like the fine dust of the scales« in Is 40 15, we find unacceptable H. Torczyner's suggestion that it means »like the rags of the clouds«. This suggestion has a twofold basis. In the first place it is argued that שחקים in the sense »rags« is used metaphorically for שחקים »clouds« — »For do we not see also the clouds of the rainy season ragged and torn by wind and weather, as black shreds of garments!«[20] And secondly, it is argued that מאזנים here does not mean »scales«, but »clouds«. Comparing the Arabic مُزْن »cloud«, Torczyner reads מְזָנִים in place of מֹאזְנַיִם, and he finds support for this reading in the Isaiah scroll, which has מזנים in v. 15, whereas in v. 12, where it is agreed that it means »scales«, it is spelt מוזנים[21]. It must, however, be considered hazardous to attach much significance to this difference in spelling, for not infrequently the Isaiah scroll exhibits similar differences in the spelling of a word, *ḥôlem* sometimes being written with an accompanying *wāw* and sometimes not. In illustration it will suffice to refer to משלה (40 10), but מושלים (49 7, both participles); to the participle אומר (42 22), but אמר (45 8); to עוונה (40 2), but ועונכה (43 24); and to חטאתיכה (plural, 43 25), but חטאותיכה (44 22)[22]. There would appear, therefore, to be no compelling reason for differentiating, on the basis of spelling, between מזנים and מוזנים in the scroll, for the former could have been pronounced exactly the same as the latter. It is worth remarking in this connection that in the scroll v. 15 is written by a different hand from that of v. 12. Where different scribes are concerned, it is surely unsafe to argue from the spelling of the one to that of the other. It does not appear to the present writer that Torczyner has made out his case, and his view

[18] Die Weisheit des Jesus Sirach, Hebr. u. Deutsch, p. 74 (»Wage und Setzwage zu prüfen«); and of the verb he says »Eigentl. abreiben, dann ins Gleichgewicht bringen«. He suggests that the word תמהות should be read המחות or תמחות (noun; N. H. מחה Hiph.« tested weights«; the basic meaning of מחה also is »rubbed away«; Die Weisheit des Jesus Sirach erklärt, p. 389).

[19] So I. Lévi, L'Ecclésiastique ou la sagesse de Jésus, fils de Sira, Première Partie, p. 46f.; N. Peters, Hebr. Text d. Buches Ecclesiasticus, p. 397.

[20] St Th 1 (1948), p. 190. He continues—»out of this very conception we have to understand the English word *cloud* (unsatisfactorily explained till now), simply as another pronunciation and spelling of *clout*, a ragged piece of cloth«.

[21] Ibid. 2 (1949/50), p. 98; cf. Ben Iehuda, Thes. totius Hebraitatis, 7032f.

[22] See M. Burrows, The Dead Sea Scrolls of St. Mark's Monastery I, The Isaiah Manuscript and the Habakkuk Commentary, ad loc.

seems all the more unlikely since Is 40 15 is concerned throughout, as will be suggested later, with the idea of weighing, so that the meaning »scales« for מאזנים is entirely consonant with the context, as too is שחק in the meaning »dust«. The meaning »scales« has been rightly handed down by the chief ancient versions (LXX ζυγοῦ, Vulg. staterae, Pesh. ܡܣܐܬ̈ܐ, Targ. מאזניא), as also by Kimchi העפר הדק ההוא אשר במאזנים »that thin dust which is on the scales«.

We pass now to a consideration of the phrase כדק יטול, translated in the English Versions »he taketh up (the isles) as a very little thing«[23], the subject being Yahweh. The verb יטול has been connected with the root טול »cast, threw«[24], but is more generally connected with נטל. This latter root, as used in the Hebrew Bible, normally means »lifted up, bore«, and this is the meaning commonly given to it by commentators and lexicographers in Is 40 15, the sense being that as given by the English Versions. Much more likely, however, נטל here has the sense it bears in Syriac (ܢܛܠ) »turned the scale, weighed heavy, was weighty«[25]. Several derivatives meaning »weight«, »weighty«, »heaviness«, are known in Syriac[26], and Hebrew knows the substantive נֵטֶל »burden, weight« (Prov 27 3 ‖ כֹּבֶד) and the adjective נָטִיל (in נְטִילֵי כָסֶף »laden, weighed down, with silver«, Zeph 1 11). If, with some commentators[27], the plural יטולו be read in place of יטול (cf. the plural verbs in the LXX and Pesh.) — the final *wāw* may have been assimilated to the following לבנון[28] — the whole phrase איים כדק יטולו may then be translated »the isles weigh only as fine dust«. The root דקק runs throughout the Semitic languages[29] in

[23] LXX ὡς σίελος λογισθήσονται (כדק read as כָּרֹק, an ocular error on the part of the Greek translator; see J. Fischer, In welcher Schrift lag das Buch Isaias den LXX vor?, p. 54). Hieron, »*quasi saliva reputantur* ... Aiunt autem Hebraei hoc verbo significari *tenuissimum pulverem*« (F. Field, Orig. Hexapl., II p. 511); Pesh. ܐܝܟ ܕܩܝܩܐ ܢܬܚܫܒܘܢ; Vulg. *quasi pulvis exiguus*; Targ. כדוקא דפרח »like fine dust that flies about«. See further J. Ziegler, Isaias (Septuaginta Vet. Test. Graec., Göttingen), p. 269.

[24] So Kimchi מבנין נפעל משרש טיל. In more recent times the connection with טול has been held by P. A. H. de Boer, though he regards נטל as possible (Second-Isaiah's Message, OTS 11 (1956), p. 4, 41).

[25] See Volz and North, ad loc.; F. Feldmann's objection to נטל = ܢܛܠ can hardly be sustained (see his Das Buch Isaias, II p. 35).

[26] P. Smith, op. cit., 2349f.

[27] E.g., Marti, Volz, North, op. cit.

[28] Cf. North, op. cit., p. 81.

[29] Akkad. *daqāqu* (Bezold, op. cit., p. 109), Arab. دقّ (Lane, op. cit., 895), Aram. דְּקַק (Dalman, op. cit., p. 98), Syr. ܕܩܰܩ (P. Smith, op. cit., 936f.), Eth. *daqaqa* (Dillmann, Lex. Ling. Aeth., 1009 f.). The adjective דק is found in Phoenician (»thin,

the sense »crushed, pulverized, broke in pieces«, the sense which, as we have seen, is the basic meaning of the verb שחק, and as שַׁחַק literally means »what is crushed, pulverized«, and so »fine dust«, so too דַּק here similarly means »what is crushed, pulverized«, and so again »fine dust« (as the Revised Standard Version). While דַּק is normally an adjective, it is here used substantivally[30]. To give to דַּק here the meaning »thin foil«[31] — as if דַּק here has the same meaning as דֹּק in v. 22 — is to miss the point of the parallelism between שַׁחַק and דַּק.

Since then the second and third members of the verse under consideration should, as we believe, be translated »and like fine dust of the scales are they (the nations) reckoned«, and »behold, the isles weigh only as fine dust«, respectively, it may well be asked whether the first member also contains a reference to dust and scales. Certainly, in view of the translation of the other two members favoured here, the first member in its traditional translation — »behold, the nations are like a drop of a bucket« — seems out of context. Is there any basis for the belief that in the first member of the verse there is some reference to weight? We may suggest that there may be. Before we advance a suggestion, we may take a brief look at the etymologies which are commonly given for the words מַר and דְּלִי, both of which occur in this passage only.

According to Brown-Driver-Briggs[32], מַר in the sense »drop« is derived from a root מרר, unused in Hebrew, but known in Arabic (مَرَّ »passed by, ran, flowed« [of water], مَرْمَرَ »made [water] to pass, go, upon the surface of the ground«[33]). If »drop« is in fact the meaning of מַר, then this etymology may be thought to be reasonably, but only reasonably, satisfactory. Torczyner, however, goes so far as to say that there is no linguistic justification for the sense »drop«[34].

---

fine«, Z. S. Harris, A Grammar of the Phoenician Language, p. 96), and in Ugaritic *dq* means »fine, small« (G. R. Driver, Canaanite Myths and Legends, p. 153; J. Aistleitner, Wörterb. d. ugar. Sprache, ed. O. Eissfeldt, p. 81).

30 So Brown-Driver-Briggs, op. cit., p. 201; Ben Iehuda, op. cit. 981; cf. Kimchi כמו הדבר הדק. As an adjective דַּק is used with אָבָק »dust« in Is 29 5. For the verb דקק used with עָפָר (»crushed to dust«), cf. Dtn 9 21; further, Ex 30 36, 32 20 II Kings 23 6.15 II Chr 15 16 34 4. In Is 40 22 דֹּק »veil«, »curtain« (as thin) is distinguished from דַּק, a distinction which is not recognized by the Targ. (זעור) or by Aq. Symm. and Theod. (λεπτόν).

31 So Koehler-Baumgartner, op. cit., cf. E. König, op. cit., p. 357 (»wie ein dünnes Blättchen«).

32 P. 601.

33 Lane, op. cit., 2699f.

34 StTh 1 (1948), p. 196.

This meaning perhaps owes its origin, at least in part, to the interpretation of דְּלִי as »bucket«, an interpretation which is quite uncertain[35]. It was said above that דְּלִי, like מַר, occurs only in this passage. This statement needs justification, since דָּלְיָו in Num 26 7 is generally connected with דְּלִי »bucket«. It must suffice here to say that the Hebrew text in Num 26 7 is very dubious. W. F. Albright, for example, abandons all attempt to translate it[36], while others drastically emend the text so that דָּלְיָו disappears from it[37]. In these circumstances a connection between דְּלִי in Is 40 15 and דָּלְיָו in Num 26 7 must remain problematical.

How then may we explain כמר מדלי in a sense consistent with the meaning of the rest of the verse as we have interpreted it? L. G. Rignell has, we believe, pointed the way to an answer. While allowing that the traditional interpretation of the phrase may be correct, he thinks that it »may also be possible that מדלי as well as the following מאזנים refers to a type of balance«, and he remarks that Ethiopic has a verb *dalawa* »weighed«[38]. To this it may be added that from this verb a noun *madlôt* (plural *madâlewe*) »weight, scales« is formed[39], and that in South Arabic *mdlw* is found with the meaning »weight«[40]. Nouns with prefixed *mem* from ל״ה roots are generally formed, as is well known, on the pattern מִשְׁתֶּה, מַרְאֶה, and so on, and so from a root דלה (= Eth. *dalawa*) a noun מַדְלֶה or מִדְלֶה »scales« would be expected, whereas מדלי is the form found in the Massoretic text. Is מִדְלֵי, מַדְלֵי, a possible vocalization? In the Isaiah scroll there are several examples of the representation of an *e*-sound at the end of a word by *yôdh* instead of *hē*. Thus, for example, in 21 9 the scroll has ויעני for ויענה (MT ויען); in 37 19 60 21 מעשי (MT מעשה); and in 65 10 לנוי (MT לנוה). Others scrolls too provide examples of similar spelling[41]. Perhaps then

[35] Ibid., loc. cit. In Akkadian *madlu* means »draw-well«, and Ugaritic *mdl* and Arabic *dalwu* both mean »bucket« (cf. G. R. Driver, op. cit., p. 161).

[36] JBL 63 (1944), p. 218.

[37] See BH³ ad loc.; cf. S. Mowinckel, ZAW 48 (1930), p. 245f.; A. v. Gall, B. Stade-Festschrift, ed. W. Diehl et al., p. 34f.; E. Burrows, The Oracles of Jacob and Balaam, ed. E. F. Sutcliffe, p. 72 (דליו »his testicles«, comparing the LXX's paraphrase τοῦ σπέρματος αὐτοῦ). Rignell, op. cit., p. 16, »perhaps a special irrigation arrangement, not necessarily a bucket«. Torczyner, op. cit., 1 (1948), p. 196, »his boughs«, with Jewish commentators, like דליותיו, Jer 11 16 Ez 17 6 f.

[38] Op. cit., loc. cit.

[39] Dillmann, op. cit., 1082f.

[40] K. C. Rossini, Chrest. Arab. Meridionalis Epigraphica, p. 126; cf. W. W. Müller, ZAW 75 (1963), p. 308.

[41] See M. H. Goshen-Gottstein, JJS 4 (1953), p. 43f. (reprinted in: Text and Language in Bible and Qumran, p. 86f.).

in our passage there is a case of like orthography (cf. מַדְוֵי Dtn 7 5, for which forty-eight manuscripts have מדוה).

It remains to find a suitable meaning for מַר. Can it mean »dust«, like שַׁחַק and דַּק? Perhaps we may think of Arabic مَارَ »moved from side to side, to and fro« (مَارَ الغُبَارُ means »the dust moved to and fro«, or »became raised by the wind«). From this verb there is a derivative مُور »dust moving to and fro in the air«, »dust raised by the wind«, or »carried to and fro by the wind«[42]. Was there in Hebrew a word מוּר (מַר) meaning something similar? (For the form, cf. רוּחַ = Arabic رُوح). If such a word with this meaning is postulated[43], the whole verse is then seen to consist of three well balanced members, a similar thought being expressed in each. We may accordingly translate it, with the sole change of יטול to יטולו[44] —

»Behold, nations are like the dust of the balances,
And like the fine dust of the scales are reckoned,
Behold, the isles weigh only as fine dust«.

Philological advance in the study of Hebrew must proceed by trial and error, and if the present writer has not succeeded in answering completely the question posed in this article, he may perhaps at least hope that he may have given a fresh turn to the discussion of the text and meaning of Is 40 15.

This small contribution is offered in gratitude to the memory of a great orientalist, to whose outstanding work all students of the text of the Hebrew Bible stand indebted.

[42] Lane, op. cit., 2743f.

[43] It may be pointed out that from a biliteral root מר a number of triliteral roots are formed in the Semitic languages with the meaning „rubbed, made smooth" (e. g. Akkad. *marāsu*, Syr. ܡܪܣ, Heb. מרח; in Ethiopic *marēt* means „dust"). Is some derivative from such a root concealed beneath the Hebrew מַר? If it were, the parallelism between מַר, שַׁחַק, and דַּק would be complete.

[44] The emendations of Torczyner (כַּמְּרֹם דִּלִּי „he lifts up (the isles) as the heights", דִּלִּי standing for דִּלָּה, op. cit. 1, 1948, p. 196), and of Kissane, op. cit., p. 13, who substitutes מַיִם „water" for גוים „nations" and reads וּשְׁחָקִים כְּמוֹ־נֹאדִים „and the sky like water-skins", comparing Job 26 8 38 37 are thus unnecessary.

Du prologue de Qirqisānī à son commentaire sur la Genèse

Par Georges Vajda

(Institut de Recherche et d'Histoire des Textes, 40 Avenue d'Iéna, Paris)

Les travaux préparatoires, à vrai dire très peu avancés, car souvent interrompus, que nous poursuivons depuis bien des années en vue d'une édition et d'une traduction commentée du *Kitāb al-Muḥtawī* du théologien karaïte Yūsuf al-Baṣīr, nous ont ramené une fois de plus à un autre grand représentant de sa secte, Ya'qūb al-Qirqisānī[1]. Cette fois-ci nous voudrions soumettre au lecteur quelques pages provenant d'un autre ouvrage élaboré simultanément à son *Kitāb al-anwār* où il est cité d'ailleurs à maintes reprises[2]: le commentaire sur la Genèse. Nous n'ignorons pas que M. Zucker, l'un des meilleurs spécialistes en la matière, prépare une édition critique de tout ce qui subsiste de cet écrit volumineux. Cette édition ne se profile pas encore sur l'horizon et nous le regrettons. Dans l'incertitude du lendemain, nous avons jugé expédient de ne pas attendre davantage et de nous contenter bon gré, mal gré, de la publication, très moyenne, de H. Hirschfeld[3], quitta à en corriger, chemin faisant, quelques unes des fautes les plus flagrantes. Telle quelle, la pièce que nous versons au dossier de l'histoire intellectuelle du judaïsme arabophone du Xe siècle de l'ère usuelle, ne manquera pas, nous osons l'espérer, de rendre service aux arabisants et aux historiens qui ne font pas leur occupation quotidienne de l'étude du karaïsme, secte religieuse animée d'idéologies assez diverses et jouissant à l'époque d'une importance qu'elle aura tôt fait de perdre, un siècle à peine après Qirqisānī.

»... Louange de Dieu, l'un, l'unique, qui a existé dans la prééternité, alors que nulle chose n'existait hormis Lui. Il n'a pas d'attribut qui puisse être appréhendé, ni de définition qui permette de formuler des similitudes à son sujet; il n'a pas de qualité[4] existante[5];

[1] Il suffit de rappeler ici l'édition si méritoire de son *Kitāb al-Anwār* procurée par le labeur de M. L. Nemoy, et la série d'études de valeur très inégale, auxquelles cette publication nous a permis de procéder: voir en dernier lieu REJ 120 (1963), p. 7–74.

[2] La liste de ces citations a été dressée dans l'édition de Nemoy, vol. V p. 43, s.v. *Tafsīr Berēshīth*.

[3] Qirqisānī Studies (Jews' College, Publication no. 6), 1918, p. 39–43 (analyse sommaire, p. 14–19); le texte est emprunté au ms. Or. 2557 du British Museum.

[4] *na't* »caractère, trait descriptif«.

[5] Autrement dit, »distincte de son essence simple«.

on ne saurait fixer un terme (à son existence); Il n'a ni commencement, ni fin; Il a imposé une limite aux choses en les créant; elles sont les indices de son existence, de son unité et de ce qu' Il les a produites du néant[6]. Los à Lui, sa Gloire est exaltée.

[Dans le présent ouvrage], nous voulons assumer la tâche de commenter[7] le livre de notre Seigneur qu' Il a révélé par l'intermédiaire de Moïse, la paix sur lui, je veux dire la Tora, et d'en expliquer les thèmes (*ma'ānī*) autres que les commandements et les préceptes; à ceux-ci, en effet, nous avons consacré une monographie[8]. Nous y exposerons les questions qui se posent à propos des expressions ambigües (*al-kalām al-mutašābih*), des énoncés qui insinuent (faussement) quelque contradiction donnant prise (aux objections) des adversaires et des hérétiques (*al-muḫālifūn wal-mulḥidūn*) comme les Manichéens et d'autres. J'ai dessein de ne laisser sans réponse aucune des questions générales ou particulières[9] que les gens posent habituellement. J'ai constaté, en effet, qu'un certain nombre de nos coreligionnaires, adeptes de la spéculation rationnelle et de la science[10], dédaignent les questions et thèmes de peu de conséquence pour réserver tout leur effort à la discussion des problèmes subtils.

Agissant ainsi ils manquent à leur devoir à deux égards: premièrement [en méconnaissant] qu'il convient de commencer par les questions générales de la science et du *Kalām*, en remontant de là à ce qui est subtil et difficile;

deuxièmement, il arrive plus d'une fois qu'un savant, *mutakallim* sagace, s'entende poser par un homme inculte du vulgaire une question qui, en raison de son insignifiance dans son esprit, lui paraît méprisable; et pour cela même, il reste court, si bien que faute de pouvoir répondre, il se couvre de honte. C'est pour cela qu'il ne convient pas de négliger ces sortes de problèmes; au contraire, il faut commencer par les traiter avant les autres.

Abordons donc notre étude en exposant les thèmes de la péricope *Berēšīt* puisque ce texte constitue le début de la Tora et qu'il renferme des thèmes obscurs et des questions difficiles qui ont besoin d'être

[6] *abda'ahā lā min šay'*; Hirschfeld a imprimé *'ḪBR 'M'* ce qui n'a aucun sens ici.

[7] Dans ce contexte, *tafsīr* a le sens de »commentaire« comme en arabe musulman, et non de »traduction«, comme souvent en judéo-arabe.

[8] Ou plus simplement »un livre à part«, *Kitāb mujarrad*, allusion probable au *Kitāb al-anwār*, encore que celui-ci, d'ailleurs plus tardif quant à sa rédaction définitive, ne soit pas exclusivement un code juridico-rituel.

[9] *bimā daqqa wajalla min al-masā'il*; l'auteur imite ici les termes musulmans *al-jalīl* et *ad-daqīq min al-kalām*, dont l'emploi n'est peut-être pas absolument homogène non plus; voir à ce sujet nos observations REJ 108 (1948), p. 69 n. 14, précisées dans nos »Brèves notes sur la *Risāla fi l- 'ulūm* d'Abū Ḥayyān al-Tawḥīdī«, *Arabica* 12 (1965), p. 196.

[10] *ahl an-nazar wal-'ilm*, autrement dit, qui acceptent de pratiquer les procédés de raisonner et de discuter admis par les *Mutakallimūn*. Qirqisānī les étudiera dans la quatrième partie du *Kitāb al-Anwār*, ch. 58–68, que nous avons essayé de traduire dans REJ 122, p. 13–50.

discutés et examinés avec une méthode efficace[11], Ce devoir s'impose particulièrement à qui veut faire oeuvre d'exégète rationnel et philosophique[12].

En effet, des gens qui voulurent faire oeuvre d'exégète sans posséder conjointement l'habileté [requise] dans les deux domaines s'imaginèrent faussement (*tawahhamū*) que la création et son ordonnance telles que les rapporte l'Ecriture sont en contradiction avec les lois[13] philosophiques et physiques.

La réalité dément cette allégation. Tout au contraire, celui qui possède une connaissance correcte des deux domaines sait que chacun des deux confirme l'autre, voire que l'Ecriture est une des sources[14] de la philosophie. C'est le résultat auquel parviendra le chercheur lorsqu'il aura rejeté loin de lui la passion et la partialité. Nous expliquerons cela selon notre capacité. L'assistance vient de Dieu.

David b. Marwān ar-Raqqī, connu sous le nom d'al-Miqmāṣ, a composé sur la Genèse un bon ouvrage qu'il avait tiré de l'exégèse des Syriens[15]. Néanmoins, en plusieurs endroits, son commentaire n'a pas l'ampleur nécessaire en la matière alors qu'à d'autres endroits il multiplie les discours vains et se laisse aller à des longueurs dont la nécessité ne s'imposait pas. Un autre auteur, contemporain[16], a également rédigé sur ce sujet un bon ouvrage dans lequel il suit une méthode semblable à celle de David. Nous leur emprunterons le meilleur de leur exposé, tout en suppléant[17] ce que, à notre avis, ils ont omis ou traité de façon insuffisante[18].

Avant de commencer cet exposé, nous avons à élucider la question des éléments rationnels et des doctrines philosophiques contenus dans l'Ecriture[19], en rappelant quelques énoncés scripturaires qui se laissent interpréter en ce sens et fournissent des indices à cet égard.

Nous procéderons[20] ainsi parce que nombre de nos coreligionnaires manifestent de la répugnance lorsqu'ils entendent une interprétation

[11] Lire *šāfin*; *šāff* »transparent« de l'édition n'est pas en contexte.

[12] L'original est plus vague: *man yataʿāṭā iḫrāj ḏālika ʿala l-maʿānī l-ʿaqliyya al-falsafiyya*, litt: »qui s'occupe à faire ressortir cela selon les significations rationnelles, philosophiques«.

[13] Lire *LLQW'NYN* (*lil-qawānīn*) au lieu de *LLTW'BYN* qui n'a aucun sens ici.

[14] *aṣl*, »racine, principe«; *al-kitāb aṣl min uṣūl al-falsafa*.

[15] *naqalahu min tafsīr as-suryāniyyīn*, c'est-à-dire, le commentaire dont il s'agit n'était qu'une adaptation d'un commentaire syriaque chrétien sur la Genèse, plus exactement peut-être d'un *Hexaemeron*; sur les relations entre les chrétiens et Ibn al-Muqammiṣ (pour le désigner de son nom le plus usuel), voir provisoirement les références dans la première note à notre article, La finalité de la création de l'homme selon un théologien juif du IXe siècle, Oriens 15 (1962), p. 61.

[16] *min ahl hāḏā l-ʿaṣr*, donc contemporain de celui qui écrit, non de David b. Marwān. Je m'abstiens de formuler des hypothèses concernant son identité.

[17] Lire *NḌYF* (*nuḍīf*) à la place de *NṢF*.

[18] Pour *WQṢD'*, lire *WQṢR'* (*waqaṣ*[*ṣ*]*arā*.

[19] *'amr al-maʿqūl wal-awḍāʿ al-falsafiyya min al-kitāb*.

[20] Lire *NFʿL* (*nafʿal*), non *NʿQL*.

scripturaire à laquelle se mêle quelque discours rationnel inspiré par la philosophie; ils la considèrent comme superflue et quelques uns même comme répréhensible et illicite.

Si les yeux de leur intelligence étaient ouverts, ils sauraient que ces choses-là sont des instruments du Livre [révélé], des échelles et des voies de passage conduisant à la connaissance des vérités puisqu'aussi bien l'authenticité du Livre et de la religion n'est connue que grâce à la raison[21]. Or, comme les thèses philosophiques sont, elles aussi, construites uniquement sur les déductions rationnelles (*maqāyis ʿaqliyya*) fondées sur les données des sens et des notions premières *ʿulūm al-ḥawāss waḍ-ḍarūrāt,* quiconque nie les propositions (*aqāwīl*) rationnelles et philosophiques, nie [de ce fait] tout savoir abstrait et sensible (*kull maʿlūm wakull maḥsūs*).

Nous avons dit quelques mots de cette question au livre (!) septième du deuxième traité (*maqāla*) de notre ouvrage consacré aux préceptes[22], Nous y reviendrons brièvement ici, car nous en avons besoin pour commenter (l'Ecriture) et particulièrement (la péricope) *Bērēšīt.* Nous nous sommes bornés à rappeler ici ce qui confirme [la nécessité de] la spéculation rationnelle et des sciences philosophiques.

En effet, les savants de notre nation n'hésitaient pas à user de ces méthodes, à preuve que Salomon a été qualifié par l'Écriture[23] du plus docte des mortels pour avoir disserté sur toutes les espèces de plantes, de la plus grande, qui est le cèdre, jusqu'à la plus petite, qui est l'hysope[24], et toutes les espèces d'animaux, bétail, oiseaux, poissons et insectes. Comment en aurait-il disserté si ce n'est en en exposant la nature, les causes, les espèces utiles et les espèces nuisibles, enseignement que les philosophes grecs et autres ont reçu de lui[25] et qui se trouvent actuellement dans leurs livres[26].

[21] Thèse cardinale de la théologie muʿtazilite fortement affirmée au premier chapitre de *Kitāb al-Muḥtawī*; nous l'étudierons en détail en commentant ce texte dans l'ouvrage annoncé au début du présent article.

[22] Voir, en effet, *Anwār* II 7, éd. Nemoy, op. cit., p. 73–77, traduction abrégée REJ 107 (1946/47), p. 64 sq.

[23] Voir I Rois 5 11–13.

[24] Qirqisānī a rendu ce mot par *azāb*, transcription plutôt que traduction par un mot authentiquement arabe. Saadia fait de même en Ps 51 9, au moins d'après certains manuscrits (voir Dozy, Supplément, I 19) alors que dans sa version de Pentateuque (Ex 12 22), il l'a rendu par *ṣaʿtar* (cf. Ibn ʿEzra *in loc.* et Y. Qāfiḥ, *Pērūšey Rabbēnū Saʿdyah Gāʾon ʿal ha-Tōrāh*, 1963, p. 58 n. 11; David b. Abraham al-Fāsī retient également *ṣaʿtar* (*Jāmiʿ al-alfāẓ*, éd. S. Skoss, I 53), non sans protester contre l'interprétation historico-allégorique donnée par le Targum au verset du livre des Rois.

[25] Lire *TQBLH* (*taqabbalahu*) au lieu de *YQLBH*.

[26] A propos de la tendance qui se manifeste dans la littérature arabe et juive du moyen âge de faire dériver la science grecque de l'enseignement de Salomon et des prophètes d'Israël, on peut voir les indications que j'ai rassemblées dans mon article »Galien-Gamaliel«, dans Annuaire de l'Institut de Philologie et d'Histoire Orientales et Slaves 13 (Mélanges I. Lévy, 1955), p. 643–644. Les textes de

Des spéculations de ce genre sont également portées par l'Ecriture au crédit de Daniel, Ḥanania, Miša'el et ʿAzaria, lorsqu'il est dit[27]: *Et sur quelque point de sagesse ou de prudence qu'il les interrogeât, le roi les trouvait dix fois supérieurs à tous les magiciens et devins de son royaume tout entier.* Ceci prouve on ne peut mieux qu'ils furent des savants pénétrants en toutes les disciplines philosophiques, puisque leur science dépassait dix fois celle des magiciens. Si nous ne possédions pas d'autre indice de l'existence de la philosophie au sein de la nation d'Israël que ce que nous venons de rappeler, cela serait déjà d'une parfaite valeur probante. De fait, maints autres passages de l'Écriture contiennent des indications similaires. Nous en avons rappelé une partie ici-même[28] et nous en rapporterons un certain nombre d'autres par la suite, lorsque l'occasion s'en présentera au cours du commentaire.

Voici encore d'autres passages bibliques qui confirment [la valeur du] donné rationnel et [recommandent] son utilisation: *Pour qu'ils voient et qu'ils sachent, qu'ils observent et comprennent tous que la main du Seigneur a fait cela, que le Saint d'Israël l'a créé* (Is 42 20), [exemple de] démonstration rationnelle qui conclut de l'oeuvre à l'auteur (*aṣ-ṣanʿa tadull ʿala ṣ-ṣāniʿ*).

Pour qu'on sache du levant au couchant que tout est néant sauf moi; je suis le Seigneur, sans égal (Is 45 6), également preuve rationnelle de l'unicité.

Des textes comme *tu as entendu et vu tout cela* (Is 48 6) et [*choses*] *qui viennent d'être créées à l'instant* (v. 7) constituent des preuves de l'adventicité (*ḥidaṯ*) du corps, preuve déduite de la constatation que jamais le corps n'est sans (*yaḫlū*) des choses adventices (*muḥdaṯāt*), qui sont les accidents (*aʿrāḍ*).

Souvenez-vous des choses passées depuis longtemps [litt. »premières«] *je suis Dieu sans égal, Dieu qui n'a pas de pareil* (Is 46 9), formule la preuve de l'impossibilité de remonter indéfiniment d'un conséquent à son antécédent[29].

Qirqisānī dont j'ai eu tort de ne pas avoir tenu compte, me font revenir sur le jugement trop timide que j'ai émis alors »... les attestations de cette volonté de revendiquer la science grecque comme un bien légitime de la postérité d'Abraham ne semblent apparaître nettement dans la littérature juive qu'à partir du XIIe siècle... « Non, les deux textes de Qirqisānī sont formels et ils nous ramènent au milieu du Xe siècle:

Qirqisānī Studies, p. 41, lig. 5–6: *waḏālika huwa mā taqabbalahu l-falāsifa ʿanhu min al-yūnāniyyīn wagayrihim wahuwa l-āna mawjūd fī kutubihim* et *Anwār* II, 7, Nemoy, op. cit., p. 75, lig. 3–5: *waḏālika ʿalā sabīl mā takallamat bihi l-ḥukamāʾ wal-falāsifa wahuwa mudawwan fī kutubihim bal huwa l- aṣl fī ḏālika aʿnī Sulaymān waʿanhuʾ ʾuḫiḏa*; »c'est Salomon qui est à l'origine de la science aujourd'hui consignée dans les livres des philosophes«.

27 Dan 1 20 d'abord inexactement cité puis paraphrasé.

28 Phrase maladroite qui se rapporte sans doute aux exemples de Salomon et de Daniel et ses compagnons qui viennent d'être allégués.

29 Littéralement »il n'est pas admissible qu'une chose soit avant une chose, sans terme«.

En proclamant: *sachez que lui, YHWH, est Dieu, lui nous a faits et non pas nous*[30]; le Psalmiste (100 3) énonce [l'axiome): il n'est pas admissible que les choses se soient faites elles-mêmes.

Les paroles de l'Ecclésiaste (7 27): *voici ce que j'ai trouvé, dit Qohélet, en les additionnant l'un à l'autre pour trouver le compte*, reviennent à dire: j'ai constaté que toutes les choses avaient besoin les unes des autres afin que tu découvres cette pensée[31], à savoir la preuve de la cause et de l'effet et de l'interdépendance de tous les êtres[32].

Un texte comme: *l'oreille apprécie le discours, comme le palais goûte les mets; la sagesse est l'affaire des vieillards, le discernement, le fait du grand âge* (Job 12 11f.) recommande le recours au raisonnement[33] de même que: *et maintenant ils ne voient pas la lumière qui resplendit* [pourtant] *dans les nuages* (37 21) revient à dire: celui qui nie Dieu est comme s'il niait la lumière, car la raison aperçoit clairement Dieu par la démonstration comme la lumière est directement perçue par l'organe sensoriel.

Il y a des textes[34] qui expriment la preuve tirée par les *Mutakallimūn* de la coopération de la sphère et des qualités élémentaires à la production de l'univers, sous la direction d'un Auteur sage: Alors que *les fabricants des idoles sont des hommes qui, rassemblés, seront couverts de honte* (Is 44 11), il est dit plus loin (45 8): *cieux, déversez la rosée d'en haut*, allusion au mouvement venant de l'éther, je veux dire la sphère du feu qui disperse les vapeurs, au sujet desquelles l'Écriture dit

[30] D'après le *Ketib* : *l'*. Le texte imprimé par Hirschfeld ne reproduit pas les mots *welo' 'anaḥnu*, qui sont le nerf de la »preuve«; *ilā* qui suit la citation hébraïque est altéré, mais le sens de la phrase ne fait pas de doute.

[31] Galimatias, trop fréquent dans le style de cet auteur, mais le sens est clair: ayant observé les choses en particulier, j'ai découvert un principe général: elles sont liées par des rapports de cause à effet et de dépendance mutuelle.

[32] A la place de *NF'QH* que l'éditeur a marqué d'un point d'interrogation, il faut lire *WF'QH*, *wa-fāqa*, »et le besoin«. — A la page 16 n. 1 de son mémoire, Hirschfeld reproduit, d'après un autre manuscrit du British Museum (Or. 2492 fol. 3), un passage du commentaire sur Gen 1 1 où le même verset est allégué dans un contexte un peu différent, l'accent y étant mis sur la preuve de l'existence de Dieu que nous offre le spectacle de la réunion et de la conciliation des éléments aux qualités opposées; voir, au sujet de cette démonstration, le commentaire contemporain, de Dūnaš b. Tāmīm sur le *S.Y.* III 1–2, dans REJ 112 (1953), p. 6–11 (l'original arabe, ibid., 113 (1954), p. 47, lig. 22 sqq.) et nos observations, p. 20 sq. – Sur les preuves de l'existence de Dieu dont Qirqisānī prétend découvrir ici les homologues scripturaires, l'on trouvera une vue d'ensemble dans l'ouvrage de M. A. Nader, Le système philosophique des Muʿtazila, 1956, p. 119–124; la documentation dont nous disposons actuellement, surtout grâce à l'édition de plusieurs volumes du *Muġnī* du cadi ʿAbd al-Jabbār, invite à reprendre toutes ces questions.

[33] Traduction *ad sensum*; le texte édité est corrompu.

[34] Pour plus de clarté, nous intervertissons l'ordre de la phrase arabe que nous nous sommes permis également de délayer un peu; la rédaction de l'original, trop concise, par maladresse stylistique plutôt que par densité de pensée, exige ce traitement.

ailleurs (Gen 2 6): *une vapeur monte de la terre*; (la suite du verset d'Isaïe) *que les nuées fassent pleuvoir selon l'ordre établi*[35], indique le mouvement descendant, en direction de la terre, imposé à la partie [de l'exhalaison] transformée en élément aqueux, et l'ondée que [cette chute] produit; *que la terre s'ouvre pour qu'abonde le salut*, signifie la réception de cet effluve par la terre et les forces que celle-ci prend à cause de cela[36], l'ensemble du processus étant la cause de la végétation, *qu'elle fasse germer la délivrance*. Nous reprendrons cet argument, lors de la démonstration de l'existence de Dieu, à propos du troisième mot [de Gen 1 1], *Elōhīm*[37].

La fin du même verset d'Isaïe: *moi, YHWH, je l'ai créé* revient à dire que Dieu a fait ces choses telles qu'elles démontrent son existence. Ce sont là les preuves rationnelles fondées sur les connaissances sensibles.

C'est pourquoi, faisant le portrait de la Tora, David dit (Ps 19 8–10) qu'elle concerne à la fois la raison et l'expérience sensible[38].

La loi de YHWH est parfaite: elle est appréhendée par les intelligences saines[39].

Les préceptes de YHWH mettent la joie dans le coeur: le coeur y acquiesce en vertu de prémisses et de conclusions correctes[40].

Le commandement de YHWH est clair; il illumine les yeux: il s'agit de la clarté et de la limpidité[41] du discours[42], dès que les incertitudes[43] en sont éliminées et écartées.

La crainte de YHWH subsiste à jamais: la doctrine tient ferme et ne s'écroule pas devant les objections et les difficultés[44] soulevées

[35] Le sens »philologiquement« exact de *ṣedeq* n'importe aucunement dans ce contexte où le verset entier est interprété dans un sens cosmologique et physique et non comme un appel à la manifestation de la puissance divine dans l'histoire.

[36] Traduction incertaine; *talaqqi l-arḍ waquwā-hā liḏālika*; si *talaqqī* doit se construire avec *liḏālika*, le sens serait plutôt »la réception de cet effluve par la terre et ses forces«.

[37] Hirschfeld, op. cit., p. 17 n. 2, cite à ce propos un texte qui dit seulement que la démonstration du caractère créé des choses apporte du même coup la preuve de l'existence d'un Auteur (*ṣāni'*), puisque l'oeuvre postule l'artisan; l'ouvrage ne nous étant provisoirement connu que par les citations de Hirschfeld, il est difficile de dire si celui-ci a reproduit le passage le plus topique en l'occurrence.

[38] *W'LḤSN* dans l'imprimé est une faute pour W'LḤS (= *wal-ḥiss*).

[39] Littéralement »exemptes de vices« (*as-salīma min al-āfāt*) le mot arabe *salīm*, »intact, sain et sauf« équivaut exactement à *tāmīm* que nous avons ici dans le texte hébreu.

[40] Le verbe *sakana ilā* que l'auteur emploie ici évoquait pour ses lecteurs avertis *sukūn an-nafs*, »assentiment *sine formidine alterius partis*«, thème capital dans la théorie de la connaissance du *Kalām* mu'tazilite; nous y reviendrons dans une étude ultérieure.

[41] Mot à mot: »l'éclat (*ḍiyā'*) et la lumière (*nūr*)«.

[42] *Kalām*, »raisonnement dialectique«.

[43] *šubah*, »dubitationes«, dans la langue de l'Ecole.

[44] Le terme employé par l'original (*mu'āraḍāt*) a un sens technique dans la dialectique du *Kalām*, et Qirqisānī disserte très longuement là-dessus (voir *Anwār* IV,

contre elle. La vérité éclate alors grâce à la coopération de ces cinq facteurs[45]: *les statuts de YHWH sont vérité; ils sont tous ensemble avérés.*

Salomon dit (Prov 18 4): *des eaux profondes, (voilà) les paroles de l'homme, un torrent debordant, source de sagesse:* il enseigne par là que Dieu a confére aux sages le pouvoir de dégager les concepts (*ma'ānī*) et de les rendre accessibles à la compréhension des gens par la synthèse et l'analyse, la mise en ordre et l'agencement, tout comme il a mis dans leur entendement l'esprit d'invention (*ḥīla*) qui les rend capables de faire monter l'eau des profondeurs du sol.

Celui qui nierait, dans ces conditions, le donné rationnel et la valeur probante des démonstrations et des syllogismes qu'il nous fournit, ferait-il preuve[46] d'autre chose que d'une extrême insolence jointe à une ignorance excessive?

Existe-t-il parmi les hommes une autre échelle de valeurs que la raison et ce qu'impose le donné rationnel? N'étaient ces moyens de déduire à partir du visible ce qui est inconnu et échappe aux sens, quelle supériorité l'homme posséderait-il sur les animaux[47]. C'est [en pensant à cela] que l'Écriture dit (Job 35 11): *Il nous rend plus avisés que les bêtes sauvages, plus sages que les oiseaux du ciel*[48]. Il est vrai, tel est le sens de ce texte, que les bêtes et les oiseaux possèdent une certaine sagesse, comme les abeilles qui confectionnent leurs ruches, les fourmis qui préparent dès l'été leur nourriture d'hiver, ainsi que

ch. 61 sq. traduits et expliqués REJ 122, p. 20 sq.), mais je ne crois pas qu'il soit nécessaire de le prendre ici stricto sensu.

[45] Littéralement: »composition et réunion de ces cinq principes« (*bita'līf hāḏihi l-ḫams uṣūl wajtimā'hā*); en fait, l'auteur n'a interprété que quatre qualifications de la Loi révélée qu'il a appliquées au sujet pensant et à la pensée: intégrité de l'intelligence, correction du raisonnement, élimination des incertitudes et *irréfragabilité* devant les objections; le cinquième »principe« serait alors la synthèse marquée par les mots »tous ensemble avérés« ou bien l'expérience sensible évoquée dans la phrase introductive du développement.

[46] Traduction d'après le contexte; le verbe *ta'āfā* imprimé par Hirschfeld signifie »recouvrer la santé«. Contre les adversaires de l'examen rationnel, Qirqisānī prend position dans *Anwār* I 1, éd. Nemoy, op. cit., p. 3–5, texte malheureusement mal conservé.

[47] J'ai simplifié, sans rien sacrifier du sens, la phrase embrouillée et mal construite de l'original; au surplus l'imprimé porte derechef *'LḤSN* pour *'LḤS(al-ḥiss)*.

[48] Voir sur ce thème nos observations dans: La Théologie ascétique de Bahya Ibn Paquda, p. 25–27. Il n'est pas sans intêret de noter que si Baḥya cite le verset de Job à deux reprises (II 2, éd. Yahuda, p. 99 = version de Juda Ibn Tibbon, éd. Zifroni, 1928, p. 61, trad. française d'A. Chouraqui, p. 121, et VIII 3, éd. Yahuda, p. 309 = version d'Ibn Tibbon, p. 212, trad. Chouraqui, p. 463), dans un contexte semblable à celui qui nous occupe ici, Saadia ne l'allègue point dans *Amānāt* et ne s'y arrête pas dans ses notes sur sa traduction de Job. Ce n'est pas la seule congruence entre Qirqisānī et Baḥya, et elle suggère peut-être une source commune qui pourrait être, al-Muqammiṣ. Nous espérons revenir un jour sur cette question.

l'Écriture le rappelle (Prov 6 6–8), l'araignée qui confectionne et tisse sa toile[49] pour y prendre les mouches dont il se nourrit, et l'on pourrait multiplier ces exemples. Cette sagesse n'est cependant qu'instinctive[50], tandis que l'homme a été gratifié par dessus tous les animaux de la sagesse élective qui opère par[51] déduction et élaboration [progressive de la vérité], opération comparable, nous l'avons dit, à la mise en oeuvre d'un mécanisme ingénieux pour faire monter l'eau des profondeurs du sol.

Les mêmes idées sont exprimées par David dans le Psaume 8 v. 2 *Tu as placé ta majesté sur le ciel*: tu fais servir le ciel et sa structure à la démonstration[52] de ta majesté et de ta puissance; idée répétée au début du Ps 19: *les cieux racontent la gloire de Dieu*; nous donnerons des explications plus détaillées à ce sujet en parlant du ciel[53].

v. 3 *De la bouche des tout petits, des nourrissons tu as fondé* (la) *force*: après avoir placé (la preuve de ta majesté) dans le ciel, tu as introduit la connaissance de ta force et de ta justice dans la raison naturelle d'un chacun[54] si bien que même les petits enfants en sont conscients. En effet, si un homme impose à un jeune enfant de faire une chose dont celui-ci est incapable, l'enfant lui dira: je ne le puis; et si, non content de lui avoir imposé (une telle tâche), l'homme s'irrite contre lui et le punit, l'enfant estimera certainement que l'individu en question est injuste à son égard[55]. La connaissance de la justice de Dieu et de sa force est donc fermement établie chez tous, jusqu'aux petits enfants.

Puis le Psalmiste revient au thème de la démonstration que le ciel offre de (son) Auteur:

v. 4 *Lorsque je vois le ciel* ...

Ensuite, il parle de l'homme et des qualités qui font de ce dernier un être plus éminent que toutes les créatures, développement qu'il achève

49 »Un filet«, dit l'original.

50 »Nature et greffe« (*ṭibāʿ wa-tarkīb*), dans la langue de l'auteur.

51 Mot à mot: »la sagesse du choix lequel est«.

52 Littéralement: »tu as placé dans ... une démonstration«.

53 A l'occasion du mot *ha-šāmayim* dans Gen 11? La phrase citée par Hirschfeld, op. cit., p. 18 n. 2 nous laisse, une fois de plus, sur notre faim.

54 *fiṭar* pluriel, au sens distributif, de *fiṭra*; à propos de cette notion, l'on peut se reporter à l'article, aujourd'hui périmé, de D. B. Macdonald, dans l'Encyclopédie de l'Islam, repris tel quel dans la seconde édition, II 953 sq. et à A. J. Wensinck, The Muslim Creed, 1932, passages marqués à l'index (p. 293), s.v.

55 Lire *jā'ir*^an^, non *jā'iz*^an^; la paraphrase de l'éditeur, fondée sur cette mauvaise leçon, montre qu'il s'est mépris sur le sens du passage (p. 18: »If a person set a boy a task which he is unable to discharge, this boy may confess his inability to do so, but if the man wax angry and punish him for it, he may, no doubt, accomplish it«.). Pour le fond, il s'agit du problème du *taklīf mā lā yuṭāq*: »Dieu peut-il exiger de l'homme ce que ce dernier est hors d'état d'accomplir?« (formulation de M. R. Brunschvig, dans son étude récente sur la question: Devoir et Pouvoir, Histoire d'un Problème de Théologie Musulmane, dans Studia Islamica 20, 1964, p. 5–46).

par les mots (v. 9) *il passe par les sentiers des mers*; autrement dit, non seulement tu lui as conféré la domination sur tous les animaux, mais encore tu lui as donné la capacité et le savoir nécessaires pour traverser les mers et cheminer au milieu de leurs flots, grâce à son art et à son industrie (*bit-tadbīr wal-ḥīla*). Tous ces textes et d'autres semblables que l'on pourrait citer de la Bible confirment l'importance du rationnel, de l'inférence et de la déduction (*al-ma'qūl wal-istinbāṭ* (*wal-istiḫrāj*)... «[56].

[56] Encore une phrase à la syntaxe confuse et au texte peut-être mal établi, dont seul le sens général se laisse établir.

The Decalogue and the Minim

By Geza Vermes

(University of Oxford)

»It used to be lawful to recite the Ten Commandments every day. Why then do they not recite them now? Because of the claim of the Minim: so that they may not say, Only these were given to Moses on Sinai«. (Y. Ber. i, 3c).

This famous and much debated passage from the Palestinian Talmud records and explains a major change in the Jewish liturgy. From having been an integral part of Temple worship, at about the end of the first century of the Christian era the Decalogue was abruptly dropped from daily public prayer and at the same time excluded from the phylacteries »because of the claim of the Minim«[1]. To understand the magnitude of the decision it is necessary to realize the importance accorded to the Ten Commandments until then within Judaism.

The Mishnah fortunately preserves in one of its tractates a Temple rubric enjoining the daily recitation of four Scriptural texts: the Decalogue (Ex 20 1ff. Dtn 5 6ff.), the Shemaʿ, the supreme confession of Jewish faith (Dtn 6 4ff.), and two further excerpts relating to the symbolical reminders of the Law, the *tephillin*, the *mezuzah* and the *ṣiṣith* (Dtn 11 13ff. Num 15 37ff.)[2]. From the order of their arrangement it would seem that the most important of these pericopes was the Decalogue, and in fact this conjecture is substantiated by a variety of literary sources.

In the Nash Papyrus[3], which is possibly the oldest of our documents, the following formula is inserted between the Ten Commandments and the Shemaʿ:

»These are the statutes and judgements that Moses commanded the children of Israel in the wilderness when they came forth out of the land of Egypt«.

The same wording (except for »the Lord« in place of »Moses«) appears also in the Septuagint on Dtn 6 4. The most reasonable interpretation of this gloss is that the »statutes and judgements« of the Decalogue were thought to represent the sum total of the entire Sinaitic legislation.

[1] Cf. Sanh. 11 3; Men. 3 7; Kel. 18 8; Siphre—Deut. § 34–35; Ber. 12a.

[2] Tam. 5 1.

[3] Cf. S. A. Cook, A Pre-Massoretic Biblical Papyrus, PSBA 25 (1903), p. 34–56; W. F. Albright, A Biblical Fragment from the Maccabaean Age: the Nash Papyrus, JBL 56 (1937), p. 145–176.

Philo of Alexandria recognizes the δέκα λόγοι as the quintessence of the Torah, as the kernel of divine revelation in which all other laws are contained. In his treatise »De Decalogo« he writes:

»We must not forget that the Ten Commandments are κεφάλαια (summaries) of the special laws which are recorded in the Sacred Books and run through the whole of the legislation«[4].

He discovers two distinctive features lifting them high above other biblical laws given by God. Firstly, they are expressed »in the form of simple commands and prohibitions without laying down any penalty, as is the way of legislators, against future transgressors«[5]. In this way, the Decalogue is a true reflection of the nature of God himself. He, »the cause of good only, and of nothing ill«, is not concerned with the punishment of sinners but, as »Great King« and »Prince of Peace«, delegates it to one of his »subalterns«, Justice[6]. Secondly, he submits that the Ten Commandments were proclaimed by God using a miraculously created voice[7].

»For it was in accordance with his nature that the pronouncements in which the special laws were summarized should be given by him in his own person, but the particular laws by the mouth of the most perfect of the prophets«[8].

In brief, Philo holds that the Decalogue's uniqueness lies in its all-inclusiveness, pure goodness, and immediate divine origin.

Josephus's thought, as is clear from his account of the Sinai events, ran on similar lines. The paramount holiness of the Ten Commandments demanded that they should be uttered by a heavenly voice, »that the excellence of the spoken words might not be impaired by human tongue«[9]. The historian even insinuates that the Decalogue shares the sanctity of the ineffable Tetragrammaton: »These words it is not permitted us to state explicitly, to the letter«[10]. He does not, of course, deny that the Law as a whole comes from God, but seems to suggest that all but the Ten Words were phrased by Moses.

»Such were the provisions concerning sacrifices and the purification relating thereto that Moses made for his countrymen; and here are the further laws which he drew up for them«[11].

The Gospel tradition of the New Testament does not argue the preeminence of the Decalogue explicitly, as do Philo and Josephus,

[4] Decal. 154.
[5] Ibid. 176.
[6] Ibid. 176–178.
[7] Ibid. 32–35.
[8] Ibid. 175.
[9] Ant. iii, 89.
[10] Ibid. iii, 90.
[11] Ibid. iii, 273.

but there is no doubt that Jesus also conceived it as the sum of all religious duties.

»What must I do to inherit eternal life?« ...
»You know the commandments. Do not kill. Do not commit adultery. Do not steal. Do not bear false witness. Do not defraud. Honour your father and mother«[12].

Archaeological findings in the form of fragmentary phylacteries from Qumran Caves 1 and 4 bring further support to this literary evidence. They are remarkable for the inclusion of Dtn 5 with the Decalogue. The *tephillin* of Murabbaʿat, by contrast, which is identical with that of the Rabbis, contains only the four customary texts[13].

*

The purpose of the present paper is to explore the mystery of the Minim responsible for the removal of the Decalogue from its privileged place in Jewish worship. To this end, we propose to *a*) trace the genesis of their »false doctrine« as seen by the Rabbis; *b*) attempt to reconstruct the exegetical justification of the »claim of the Minim«; *c*) answer the vital question: who were they?

a) The Rabbis accused the Minim (heretics or sectaries)[14] of faith in two creative Powers[15], of disbelief in resurrection, of setting a wicked example, and above all of denial of the Torah[16]. All these charges, except the first, were found to originate in the biblical past and were attached to biblical personalities, the implication being that *minuth* was based on an immemorial tradition held and transmitted by the wicked in Israel and that the heterodox of their own age were the imitators of the heresiarchs of Scripture, Cain, Balaam and

[12] Mk 10 17–19. Cf. Mt 19 16–19 Lk 18 18–20.

[13] Cf. G. Vermes, Pre-Mishnaic Jewish Worship and the Phylacteries from the Dead Sea, VT 9 (1959), p. 65–72; H. Schneider, Der Dekalog in den Phylakterien von Qumran, BZ 3 (1959), p. 18–31. See also A. M. Habermann, *ʿAl ha-tephillîn bîmê ḳedem, ʾEreṣ Yisrael* 3 (1954), p. 174–177.

[14] Cf. I. Broydé, Min, JE 8, p. 594–595; K. G. Kuhn, Giljonim und sifre minim, in: Judentum, Urchristentum, Kirche (Jeremias-Festschrift), BZNW 26 (1960), p. 24–61; M. Simon, Verus Israel, 1964², p. 215ff., 500ff. Originally a min had to be a Jew: Ḥul. 13b; Shab. 116a.

[15] Cf. Sanh. 4 5; Hag. 15a. That they did not teach full dualism but rather a doctrine in which the Creator is helped by an assistant is attested quite clearly by the sources. For example, the creation of Adam on the sixth day is explained as follows: »So that the Minim might not say, God had a partner in his work« (T. Sanh. 8 7).

[16] T. Sanh. 13 5.

Korah[17]. Of these three, it is Korah's fault that is most enlightening. The Bible describes him as a rebel (Num 16 1ff.), but for post-biblical Judaism Korah was a heretic who opposed the teaching of Moses on the subject of the *ṣiṣith* (Num 15 37ff.), the law set out in the paragraph immediately preceding[18]. In the (contemporary) words of Pseudo-Philo:

»In illo tempore precepit illis de fimbriis et tunc restitit Chore, et ducenti viri cum eo, et locuti sunt dicentes: Quid si ponitur nobis lex intolerabilis«[19].

Targum Pseudo-Jonathan tells the story more fully.

»They (Korah and his band) rose impertinently and in the presence of Moses decreed a halakhah in the matter of the blue colour. Moses said, I have heard from the mouth of the Holy One ... that the tassels are to be white with only one blue filament in them. But Korah and his fellows made both their garments and the tassels all of blue, which the Lord had not commanded«[20].

A trivial matter of priestly fashion? No. A rebellion against God's authority, the creation of a »division«, a sect[21]. A haggadah inserted into the Palestinian Talmud recounts that Korah accused Moses of error in regard to other laws also, and that when Moses retorted by quoting the relevant verses from the Bible, Korah exclaimed: אין תורה מן השמים, The Torah is not from Heaven[22]. Another later midrash on Numbers places almost literally the »claim of the Minim« in the mouth of Korah and his followers, besides alleging that some of the Scriptural statutes were invented by Moses for his own and Aaron's benefit.

»God has given us only the Ten Commandments. Of dough-offering, heave-offering, tithes and fringes we have not heard except from yourself. You have spoken in order to establish rulership for yourself and glory for Aaron your brother«[23].

From these texts it emerges that to the Rabbis the Minim were sinful disciples of Korah, who not only wilfully refused to obey the

17 They are named together as chief sinners in T. Sot. 4 19 and as models of heterodoxy in Jude 11. I have discussed Cain in: The Targumic Versions of Genesis 4 3–16, The Annual of Leeds University Oriental Society 3, 1961/62 (1963), p. 101–103, and Balaam in: Scripture and Tradition in Judaism, Haggadic Studies, 1961, p. 134, 172. For Korah, see A. Marmorstein, Religionsgeschichtliche Studien, I. Heft: Die Bezeichnungen für Christen und Gnostiker im Talmud und Midraš (1910), p. 79; H. Schneider, op. cit., BZ (1959), p. 28.

18 The interpreters consider the two passages as forming a continuous narrative: *samûkh* (post hoc, ergo propter hoc).

19 Pseudo-Philo's Liber Antiquitatum Biblicarum, ed. G. Kisch, 1949, xvi. 1, p. 155.

20 1JT on Num 16 2.

21 See 2JT, Onk. and Pesh. on Num. 16 1.

22 Y. Sanh. X, 27d–28a. Cf. also Tanḥ. (ed. Buber), IV, p. 97.

23 Sefer ha-Likkutim. Sammlung älterer Midraschim und wissenschaftlicher Abhandlungen. IV. Teil enthält Collectaneen aus dem alten Midrasch Jelamdenu zum 4.en Buch Moses, 1900, p. 41a.

sacred code of statutes and ordinances granted by God to Israel, but jealous of the authority of the heirs of Moses dared also to misuse Judaism's age-old veneration of the Ten Commandments by employing it to devalue the Torah[23a].

b) Needless to say, no scholar would accept as objective or authentic a judgement of this kind. He knows that the Minim were religious non-conformists and that however shocking their teaching may have seemed to the Pharisees it must have been erected on a Scriptural, or rather exegetical, foundation. Indeed, the reaction of the Rabbis proves that this was so and that it caused them much embarrassment. But in the absence of direct sources can it be discovered? As so often happens, the Palestinian Targum, in its treatment of Dtn 5 22(19), provides the clue. The biblical verse following the Decalogue records Moses's comment on the manner of its revelation:

»These words the Lord spoke to all your assembly at the mountain ... with a loud voice; and he added no more«.

The final clause, ולא יסף, which is peculiar to the Deuteronomic account, states plainly that God limited himself to the Ten Commandments in his direct communication with the whole congregation of Israel on Sinai. The Septuagint finds no difficulty in accepting this and renders it literally: καὶ οὐ προσέθηκεν. But not so the Targums. Apart from a minor variant, the Geniza fragment published by Paul Kahle[24], Codex Neofiti 1, Pseudo-Jonathan, and Onkelos, all agree on a paraphrase which departs conspicuously from the original:

»These words the Lord spoke to all your assembly at the mountain ... with a loud voice which/and he ceased not«[25].

In a deliberate effort to avoid having to suggest that God proclaimed no laws beyond the Decalogue, all the Aramaic translators derive the verb, not from the root יסף, but from סוף or אסף (to end, to cease, to be taken away)[26]. Having thus confused the issue artificially, the school of thought represented by the Targums sets off at a tangent and alleges that »he ceased not« means that God did not interrupt his peroration but »spoke the Decalogue with a single utterance«[27].

23a According to Pseudo-Philo (LAB xxv 13), the unfaithful of the tribe of Benjamin were guilty of *min* tendencies: »Nos voluimus in hoc tempore librum legis perscrutantes cognoscere utrum manifeste Deus scripsisset qua erant in eo aut Moyses docuisset ea per se«.

24 Masoreten des Westens, II 1930, p. 26.

25 דלא פסיק (Geniza, 1JT; cf. Pesh.) or ולא פסיק (Neof., Onk.).

26 See also the Targums on Num 11 25.

27 Mekh. on Ex 20 1 (ed. Lauterbach, II p. 228). Cf. Rashi's comment on Dtn 5 22 combining this interpretation with the original meaning of the sentence: »God did not cease and, since he did not cease, he added nothing«.

These exegetical acrobatics on the part of the Pharisees incline us to believe that they must have been prompted by the insistence of the Minim on the literal significance of Dtn 5 22. Such an interpretation leads to the conclusion that the Torah (as distinct from the Ten Commandments) was either not revealed at all but was invented by Moses, or (which is more likely) that it was not revealed by God himself or intended as a binding rule for all the generations of Israel[28]. It may be noted in parenthesis that, as a response to the threat of heresy, the arguments of the Rabbis and the practical measures which they took in the liturgical field were negative and show signs of panic. Later, the Tannaim recovered their balance and directed their efforts towards a positive demonstration that the whole Torah comes from God[29], both the written and the oral Law[30].

c) One crucial problem remains: who were the Minim? Can we associate them with any of the known branches of ancient Judaism outside the Pharisaic fold? Were they Sadducees, Essenes or Judeo-Christians?

The first two may be eliminated straight away. The Sadducees cannot have failed to acknowledge the heavenly origin of laws relating to the Temple and priestly matters, and the Essenes were the staunchest protagonists of all things Mosaic. The case of the Judeo-Christians is different. In fact, in the late nineteenth and early twentieth century most experts tended to regard »Minim« as the rabbinic name for that community, on the grounds that the Minim rejection of the Torah is mirrored in the 'antinomianism' of the Church, and that the parallel of Minim and Noṣerim in the Palestinian recension of the ʿAmidah suggests that they were one and the same[31]. But although

[28] The latter opinion may have been held by Pseudo Philo if »precepta eterna *qua non transient*« refers, as it seems to do, only to the Decalogue; cf. LAB 11 5.

[29] R. Ishmael expounds the opening words of the Code of the Covenant thus: »These are added to the former ones (the Decalogue). Just as the former were given on Sinai, so were the latter«. (Mekh. on Ex 21 1, ed. Lauterbach, III p. 1). An anonymous exegete discussing Dtn 1 3, »Moses spoke to the children of Israel«, asks the question: »Did Moses prophesy only the Ten Commandments? «—»Whence do we know that he prophesied all the words of the Torah? Scripture says, (Moses spoke to the children of Israel) *according to all that the Lord had given him in commandment to them*«. (Siphre—Dtn 1 3, § 2).

[30] Moses received on Sinai the Decalogue, the Torah, the Prophets and Writings, the Mishnah and the Talmud, according to Simeon b. Laḳish commenting on Ex 24 12 in Ber. 5a.

[31] Cf. M. Bloch, Les 613 lois, REJ 1 (1880), p. 205; W. Bacher, Le mot »minim« désigne-t-il quelquefois des chrétiens? REJ 38 (1899), p. 38–45; I. Lévi, Le mot »Minim« désigne-t-il jamais une secte juive de gnostiques antinomistes ayant exercé son action en Judée avant la destruction du Temple? Ibid. p. 204–210; Un papyrus biblique, REJ 44 (1903), p. 214; F. C. Burkitt, The Hebrew Papyrus of

M. Simon has recently shown that Christians were referred to as Minim in the fourth century[32], the title scarcely fits the Judeo-Christians of the apostolic and sub-apostolic age. For one thing, it seems a priori unlikely that they made a strong enough impact on Judaism so soon after the death of Jesus. More important still, none of the parties within the early Church taught an 'antinomianism' as radical as the complete denial of the divine origin of the Torah. The Jerusalem Church would certainly not have done so, and neither would the disciples of Paul, who merely preached that the Mosaic Law was not universally obligatory. The most extreme views expressed in the Syriac Didascalia and the Pseudo-Clementine writings are still mild compared with the doctrine attributed to the Minim. The author of the Didascalia insists only too vehemently that the sacrificial and dietary laws were inflicted by God upon the Jews in punishment of their apostasy in worshipping the Golden Calf[33]. The Pseudo-Clementine assertion that after the death of Moses false pericopes were interpolated into the Torah is perhaps the nearest Christian approach to the heresy of the Minim, but even this fails to measure up to the rabbinic accusation[34].

We thus come by way of elimination to the thesis advanced by M. Friedländer[35], A. Marmorstein[36] and others[37], identifying the Minim as Jewish Gnostics. Although the word »Gnostic« is, as I

the Ten Commandments, JQR 15 (1903), p. 398–399; R. T. Herford, Christianity in Talmud and Midrash, 1903; S. Schechter, Genizah Specimens, JQR 10 (1898), p. 654–659. E. G. Hirsch, Shemoneh Esreh, JE 11, p. 281; L. Finkelstein, The Development of the Amidah, JQR 16 (1925), p. 19, 157; I. Elbogen, Der jüdische Gottesdienst in seiner geschichtlichen Entwicklung, 1931, p. 36–38.

32 Verus Israel, p. 218.

33 »The Law is in the first place that which the Lord God spake, before the people made the calf ... which is the Ten Commandments and statutes; and after they had worshipped idols He justly put on them chains as they deserved«. (M. D. Gibson, The Didascalia Apostolorum in English, 1903, p. 5).

34 According to Pseudo-Peter's words to Pseudo-Clement, the falsified passages detract from God's transcendental greatness. Our author no doubt refuses to accept as genuine texts implying that God desires a temple or sacrifices, but nowhere does he restrict the Sinai revelation solely to the Decalogue. Cf. Hom. II, 38–44. See also H. J. Schoeps, Urgemeinde, Judenchristentum, Gnosis, 1956, p. 27.

35 Der vorchristliche jüdische Gnosticismus, 1898; Encore un mot sur Minim, Minout et Guilionim dans le Talmud, REJ 38 (1898), p. 194–203; Die religiöse Bewegungen innerhalb des Judentums, 1905, p. 171 ff.

36 The Background of the Haggadah, HUCA 6 (1929), p. 141–204 (Reprinted in: Studies in Jewish Theology, 1950, p. 25 ff.).

37 E.g. J. Mann, The Jews in Egypt under the Fāṭimid Caliphs, I 1920, p. 223; Genizah Fragments of the Palestinian Order of Service, HUCA 2 (1925), p. 283–284; S. Krauss, Die Mischna, Sanhedrin-Makkōṯ, 1933, p. 165.

believe, misleading, all the available evidence tends to show that these scholars were on the right track, and that the first century antinomian Minim came from the ranks of Hellenistic Judaism. After all, Dtn 5 22 in the Septuagint version is absolutely clear and, unlike the Hebrew original, difficult to misconstrue. The Greek reader of the Bible learns that God added nothing to the proclamation of the Decalogue. For example, Pseudo-Philo (who was not a Min) concludes his account of the Ten Commandments, the only section of the Torah which he gives in extenso, with the words: »Et ... quievit Dominus loqui«[38]. Furthermore, we know from the excerpts from Philo and Josephus quoted earlier that their Hellenistic contemporaries were accustomed to the idea of the Decalogue's superiority since many of them found it physically or morally impossible to do more than observe the ethical demands of Judaism.

Additional support for the argument that the Minim had their origins in a Greek environment is found in the New Testament. When Stephen asserts that the Torah was delivered to Israel, not by God, but by the angels[39] which, according to the Septuagint, accompanied him to Sinai[40], he is voicing with some difference of emphasis the »claim of the Minim«. He is also, it should be noted, speaking as the acknowledged leader of the »Hellenists«[41], as a Jew of the Dispersion and not as a pre-Pauline Christian. Again, it is a Minim exegetical argument that the Hellenistic author of the Epistle to the Hebrews advances when he contends that, since Jesus is greater than the angels who transmitted the Torah, his teaching must surpass the Jewish Law[42].

The relation between the Minim and Hellenistic Jewry seems therefore sure. But can we be more precise? From the alarm they caused among the Palestinian Rabbis, from their distinction between permanent moral values and customs linked to a certain social structure, and from their acquaintance with Greek philosophical thought[43], I believe we may safely deduce that they came from among

[38] LAB xi 14. As has been seen, in xxv 13 doubt concerning the divine origin of the whole Torah constitutes a capital offense.

[39] Act 7 53; cf. Act 7 38; Gal 3 19.

[40] Cf. LXX on Dtn 33 2, »His angels were with him on his right hand«. By contrast, 2JT renders the verse as, »He stretched out his right hand from the midst of the flames of fire and gave the Torah to his people«. See also 1JT which combines both traditions but maintains the Palestinian bias.

[41] Cf. M. Simon, St. Stephen and the Hellenists, 1958.

[42] Cf. Heb 2 1–2.

[43] The Alexandrine doctrine of a creative Logos is no doubt the basis of the accusation that the Minim believed in two Powers, and the Hellenistic emphasis on the immortality of the soul can be understood as a denial of bodily resurrection.

the progressive, enlightened and intellectual *élite* of the Mediterranean, and especially Egyptian, Diaspora; that they were the ancient forebears of what is known today as »Liberal« Judaism.

This study, dedicated to the memory of Paul Kahle, is intended not only as a public tribute to the father of modern targumic research, but also as a personal testimony of deep gratitude for his help and kindness to me.

Nouveau fragment de la Massorah Magna du Targum de Babylone

Ms. heb. d 62 Fol. 45
Bodleian Library — Oxford

Pr. Gérard E. Weil

(Faculté des Lettres, 23 boulevard Albert Ier, Nancy)

Je dédie l'édition de ce fragment à la mémoire de mon défunt maître Paul Kahle qui après Berliner et Landauer, mais avec plus d'acuité que ses deux prédécesseurs, a appelé l'attention du public lettré sur l'importance de ces fragments manuscrits. Nous nous sommes souvent, au cours de la dernière décade de son existence, entretenus de l'urgence qu'il y avait à dresser le catalogue des fragments inédits de ce type de Massorah. J'ai entrepris à sa demande le récolement de ces documents afin d'éditer le moment venu l'ensemble le plus complet représentant la *Massorah Magna du Targum de Babylone* à défaut de disposer d'ouvrage exhaustif comme la *Okhlah* pour la Massorah Magna de la BH. La Massorah du Targum a certainement été réunie sous une forme ou sous une autre, mais ne nous a été transmise qu'à travers les fragments épars et retrouvés dans les Genizōt ou encore par des gloses marginales au long des pages de certains manuscrits.

Les fragments que j'ai édités jusqu'à présent n'offraient pas l'intérêt exceptionnel de celui que j'édite aujourd'hui. Nous disposons pour la première fois d'un fragment qui nous révèle le commentaire massorétique du Targum à partir du début d'un des livres de la Bible[1].

Ce fragment unique devait appartenir à coup sûr à un commentaire de la Massorah du Targum du Lévitique. Nous ne disposons cependant pas d'assez de données pour affirmer qu'il ait appartenu à un commentaire de toute la Torah. Cependant, l'état de conservation dans lequel il nous est parvenu après son passage dans la Genizah du Caire, pourrait permettre de supposer qu'il ait appartenu à un ensemble plus vaste. Le recto du fragment ayant très peu souffert, on peut supposer qu'il n'a pas été longtemps le premier feuillet d'un volume.

Folio de parchemin de 243 × 160 mm réglé, sur ce qui est aujourd'hui le verso, à 24 lignes de justification, entre deux réglures ver-

[1] Lev 1 1–3 4.

ticales tracées à 130 mm de distance l'une de l'autre. Le parchemin semble avoir été réglé pour servir à la copie d'un livre de la Bible et le feuillet a fini comme substrat à notre commentaire. Celui-ci est rédigé sur 25 lignes au recto et 26 au verso d'une écriture carrée de type babylonien assez régulière[2]. Le scribe n'a pas graphié les potences et autres parties horizontales hautes de ses lettres directement sous la réglure comme l'on pourrait s'y attendre. Certaines lignes sont même manifestement écrites entre deux réglures. L'écriture est du même type carré que j'ai déjà reconnu dans un article précédemment publié[3].

Les signes vocaliques supralinéaires appartiennent au système babylonien simple décrit par P. Kahle dans ses différentes oeuvres[4]. Il faut noter que le scribe, auteur du fragment, n'a utilisé aucun signe séparateur entre les versets ou entre les divers enseignements qu'il a colligés dans son manuscrit et que l'on rencontre d'ordinaire dans les manuscrits de type babylonien.

L'auteur a rassemblé dans son manuscrit trois sortes d'enseignement:

1⁰ Les équivalences araméennes des diverses expressions de la Bible hébraïque telles que la tradition qu'il pratique les a fixées.

2⁰ Quelques rudiments de listes qui signalent le nombre de fois ou certaines expressions ont telle ou telle acception dans la paraphrase, prémices de la Concordance de la paraphrase araméenne et de la BH que les sémitisants attendent aujourd'hui encore. Nous connaissons par ailleurs des listes de ce type qui ont déjà été éditées.

3⁰ Enfin, il profite pour signaler les graphies particulières de certains mots hébreux et surtout leur énonciation selon la tradition babylonienne en notant la vocalisation dans le système qu'il utilise.

Avant de passer à l'étude détaillée de ce fragment, je crois qu'il est important de signaler une fois encore une des hypothèses qui conduisent les recherches que je poursuis. J'ai conclu dans un précédent article que l'étude de la *Massorah du Targum araméen* laissait entrevoir l'origine des commentaires de la *Massorah Magna de la Bible hébraïque*. La recherche par les écoles babyloniennes d'une paraphrase canonique a tendu à fixer les formes des paraphrases, à réunir ces formes fixées en catalogue et à fixer de même le texte biblique, base de ces travaux.

[2] S. A. Birnbaum, The Hebrew Scripts II. 1954–1957, pl. 188 datée de 835, babylonien carré.

[3] Quatre fragments de la Massorah Magna babylonienne, Textus 3 (1963), p. 74–120.

[4] Der masoretische Text des Alten Testaments nach der Überlieferung der babylonischen Juden, I 1902; Masoreten des Ostens. Die ältesten punktierten Handschriften des Alten Testaments und der Targume, 1913; § 6–9 de H. Bauer — P. Leander, Historische Grammatik der hebräischen Sprache des Alten Testaments. 1962.

Dans le commentaire de ce fragment, je ne relèverai que les versets ou les mots dont l'existence, l'orthographe ou la paraphrase soulèvent un problème.

II

Recto

ע א ויקרא	Lev 1 1
דיל אדם	Lev 1 2
ניג מכם	
ו א קרבן כול	
עלה כול	Lev 1 3
אא זכר כול	
ע ע יקריבנו כול	
: ע א לרצנו לרעוא ליה תרג	
אכ - : וסמך כול ויסמוך תרג	Lev 1 4
ריש עלתא [תרג]	
ע ונרצה ?	
אע ושחט כו[ל]	Lev 1 5
עע אשר פתח כול דביתרע תרג	
ע ונתח אתה יתה תרג כו[ל]	Lev 1 6
לאיברהא איברהא כול אלף והשור ? והכרתי ?	
וערכו ויזדרון תרג אית דאמר ויסדרון ויסדר	Lev 1 7.8
ע אעיא על אישתא	
ע ע ירחץ תר דק	Lev 1 9
וקרבו Lev 1 9	
עע ע והקרב יחליל תרג Lev 1 13	
ואם מן הצאן ואם מן ענא תרג	Lev 1 10
מן הכשבים מן אימריא תרג	
או מן בני עיזיא [תרג]	

Lev 1 2

אדם La note abrégée דיל qui surplombe ce mot ne semble pas avoir été encore rencontrée et reste pour moi totalement obscure. Cette note ne semble pas avoir été rédigée par la même main que le reste du manuscrit, ni par celle qui a rajouté certains mots entre les lignes.

מכם Le scribe a noté ניג abréviation de ניגרא -paroxyton- ce mot du texte hébreu dont il tient à fixer la position tonique.

ו א
קרבן כול L'auteur signale que le mot du texte hébreu est toujours écrit et vocalisé ainsi. On notera la vocalisation *shureq* qui correspond en babylonien à la vocalisation du *qamaṣ bref* tibérien.

Lev 1 3

עלה כול Le scribe note l'habituelle graphie défective dans la Torah de ce mot du texte hébreu. La seule divergence à cette graphie dans la Torah figure sous Num 28 27 noté dans L: ל מל בתור

אא
זכר כול Vocalisation courante de ce mot dans le texte biblique.

ע ע
יקריבנו כול Vocalisation courante de ce mot dans le texte de la BH. L'absence de signe pour le *sègol* dans le système babylonien le fait noter par le signe du *pataḥ* .Les grammairiens hébreux du Moyen Age avaient nommé cette voyelle: *pataḥ bref*.

: ע א
לרצנו לרעוא ליה Le mot hébreu est amené avec l'expression araméenne composée de deux mots qui le paraphrase. Le scribe en vocalisant le mot hébreu par le *ḥolam* signale la graphie défective de cette expression qui par ailleurs est hapaxe.

Lev 1 4

אכ - :
וסמך כול ויסמוך תרג: l'expression וסמך de l'hébreu est toujours paraphrasée ainsi en araméen[5].

..
ריש עלתא: J'ai ajouté תרג à l'édition; le scribe n'a pas trouvé nécessaire de faire précéder l'araméen de l'expression hébraïque ראש העלה.

ע
ונרצה Le texte du manuscrit peut être lu ונרצנה ce qui ne correspond pas au texte original. Il est possible que ce soit une double graphie de la même lettre ע, correction de cette lettre mal rédigée une première fois. La vocalisation *pataḥ* est en opposition avec le sens du mot dans le verset hébreu. Il justifierait seulement le Ketib תִּרְצֶנָה de תִּרְצֹנָה de Prov 23 26.

Lev 1 5

עע
אשר פתח כול דביתרע תרג, TS. propose la leçon défective דבתרע. Le *yod* assurant la lecture dans notre fragment me paraît simplement superfé-

[5] Ex 29 10.19 Lev 1 4 3 2.8.13 4 4.24.29.33 16 1 et aussi Am 5 19.

tatoire. L'araméen **דבתרע** paraphrase toujours et seulement l'hébreu **אשר פתח**[6].

Lev 1 6

ונתח אתה יתה תרג כו[ל] Le scribe signale que l'araméen rend l'hébreu **אתה** par **יתה**. Cette même expression rend cependant deux fois l'hébreu **לָהּ** sous Gen 17 16 et Num 12 13. A l'inverse, sous Lev 1 16 et 17 10 **אתה** est rendu par **יָתֵיהּ** signalé par notre scribe dans ce fragment.

Lev 1 11 ירך שידא דמדבחא ציפונא

וזרקו תר זרק

Lev 1 11 דאם מן הצאן

Lev 3 2 דואם זבח

ויזרקון תרג כול פרש בני אהרן הכהנים בחד.

Lev 1 12 וערך כול ויסדר תרג

Lev 1 14 התרים

היונה יונא תרג

Lev 1 15 ומלק כול ויקרביניה כהנא למדבחא

וימלוק תרג

ית רישיה

ונמצה [תרג] ויתמצי דמיה על כותל מדבחא

Lev 1 16 והסיר מראתו בנצתה

ויעדי ית זפקיה באוכליה וײרמי יתיה [תרג]

ביסטר מדבחא קידומא באתר דמקרין

אית דאמר: באתר בית קיטמא

הדשן כול קיטמא תרג

Lev 6 2 (3.4) אית דאמר דצו את אהרן דישנא תר[ג]

אתה דמי[תרג] יתיה תר[וי] בא[ורייתא].

Lev 1 16 והשליך

Lev 17 10 והכרתי

אל מקום דמ[יתרג] באתר

[6] Gen 19 11 Lev 1 5 4 7 et 18.

?? אל המקום דמי[תרג] באתרא תר[וי] בא[ורייתא].

Lev 1 16 והסיר

Deut 16 6(9) כי אם אל המקום דעילוי שבעה שבעות

Lev 1 17 ושסע ויפריק יתיה

בכנפיו בא[ורייתא] בכנפוהי לא יפריש

כל אשה ריח ניחה קורבן דמי[ת]קבל ברעוא תרג

לאיברהא איברהא Le scribe note que les deux expressions araméennes citées ont le *aleph* de la forme déterminée. לאיבראה[7] paraphrase l'hébreu לְנְתָחֶיהָ. Le second terme présente une forme aberrante qui a dû venir par entraînement pour איבריא[8] qui paraphrase l'hébreu הַנְּתָחִים.

Le premier mot de notre note a assimilé par haplographie le ל de l'expression [כו[ל dans la note qui précède. Le mot איברהא qui commence la ligne — 4 — a été ajouté après que le scribe avait déjà écrit le כול de fin de titre, qu'il a effacé pour y substituer ce mot qui en fait n'existe pas tel que dans le texte et doit donc être considéré comme superfétatoire.

והשור והכרתי Ces mots qui semblent désigner les références aux versets 9 et 13 du même chapitre où se retrouve l'expression לאיברהא semblent sans rapport avec les versets intéressés.

Lev 1 7.8

ויזדרון תרג TBS. a la seconde leçon proposée et ne semble jamais avoir rencontré la première leçon proposée par notre manuscrit, ce qui confirme la leçon de Lev 1 12.

אעיא על אישתא TBS. propose דעל pour le verset 8 et suit notre leçon pour le verset 7.

Lev 1 9

ירחץ תר דק Le scribe babylonien vocalise l'hébreu ירחץ que le tibérien lit ירחץ. La vocalisation babylonienne du *yod* semble proposer une lecture *sègol* à cause de la proximité de la gutturale. L'araméen יחליל paraphrase deux fois l'hébreu ירחץ.

Lev 1 11

ירך Le Targum ne paraphrase pas ce mot strictement, mais le glose en une métaphrase qui tient compte du *Midrash* qui décrit l'autel.

ציפונא a dans notre manuscrit une leçon pleine que TBS. ne connaît pas.

וזרקו תר זרק Le scribe écrit זוק pour זרק, Les deux références désignent

[7] Lev 1 6 9 13.

[8] Lev 1 8 8 20.

les versets où l'hébreu וזרקו n'est pas suivi de l'expression בני אהרן הכהנים. L'araméen ויזרקון paraphrase encore l'hébreu וזרקו sous Lev 1 5 3 8.13, mais est alors suivi de l'expression בני אהרן הכהנים. Dans le manuscrit le *ḥireq* supralinéaire a été noté par erreur sur le *resh*.

Lev 1 14

עא

היונה Pour notre scribe cette expression hébraïque est paraphrasée par l'araméen יונא avec graphie emphatique *aleph*. TBS. ne semble pas connaître cette leçon et propose la leçon יונה. La leçon יונא semble être une leçon tibérienne.

Lev 1 15

אכ

ומלק L'auteur n'a pas indiqué que cette même expression est encore paraphrasée וימלוק sous Lev 5 8.

א

ונמצה est paraphrasé par l'araméen ויתמצי pour lequel TBS. propose la graphie וייתמצי.

Lev 1 16

אכה: :או ..

והסיר מראתו בנצתה La leçon usuelle de l'hébreu est את מראתו. Le manque de la particule ne semble pas être une leçon particulière aux Orientaux. BG. ne signale rien à ce sujet.

כ עע

באתר דמקרין TBS. a la leçon באתר דמקרין קטמא alors que notre auteur semble terminer sur דמקרין קטמא proposant comme leçon divergente: באתר בית קיטמא.

הדשן כול קיטמא תרג On retrouve sous Lev 4 12 cette même paraphrase, alors que sous Lev 6 3 et 4 l'hébreu הדשן est paraphrasé דישנא.

אתה דמי[תרג] יתיה Selon notre scribe, l'hébreu אֹתָהּ est deux fois paraphrasé יתיה sous Lev 1 16 et 17. En fait trois fois, mais le scribe n'a pas tenu compte de la répétition de cette expression dans le second verset. Berliner[9] et Landauer[10] citent cette même leçon.

אל מקום דמ[יתרג] באתר L'hébreu אל מקום est paraphrasé une seule fois באתר, alors qu'il est paraphrasé de nombreuses fois לאתר, לאתרי.

Pour l'hébreu אל המקום paraphrasé באתרא, l'auteur nous propose une liste de deux références: Lev 1 16 et Dtn 16 6. Cette liste semble être erronée et rappelle une autre liste: המקום דמתרג אתר ב באור Gen 20 13, Ex 20 24[11] donnée par la Massorah du Targum. Dans la liste proposée par notre scribe

a) la première référence est en contradiction avec la note qui précède;

[9] A. Berliner, Die Massorah zum Targum Onkelos enthaltend Massorah Magna und Massorah Parva, 1877, p. 45.

[10] S. Landauer, Die Mâsôrâh zum Onkelos auf Grund neuer Quellen lexikalisch und kritisch beleuchtet. 1896, p. 17.

[11] Berliner, op. cit., p. 20, et Landauer, op. cit., p. 122.

b) la seconde référence ne se retrouve pas dans le texte de TBS. qui propose la leçon לאתרא signalant en apparat que certains manuscrits de tradition tibérienne lisent באתרא.

Lev 2 1

כל תו[רה] דגבי נפש יוד תרג כגון Si l'expression יוד dans le titre de cette liste signifie 10, les 12 références données dans la liste infirment déjà sa signification. L'auteur a réuni en catalogue les expressions נפש, ונפש, הנפש paraphrasées אנש non déterminé, avec un sens pronominal indéfini. En réalité les exemples sont bien plus nombreux et l'on comprend mal les raisons qui ont fait réunir ces 12 exemples en un catalogue. Réf. Lev 23 29 תעננה pour תענה? Réf. תגעל incompréhensible pour הנגעת? Il faut noter cependant que lorsque notre auteur donne des références, il n'en donne pratiquement aucune hors du livre du Lévitique. ce qui fait que l'on peut s'étonner de trouver des références aux *Nombres*.

ג ו .. א ..ע ..
ואינש ארי יקריב קרבן La leçon de ואינש avec *yod* n'est pas connue de TBS. et semble être de tradition tibérienne, de même que קרבן à graphie défective alors que TBS. et le reste de notre manuscrit écrivent קורבן.

Lev 2 1 — כל תו[רה] דגבי נפש יוד תרג̇ כגון:

	תקריב	Lev 2 1 (ע)
	תטמא	Num 12 22
	תחטא	Lev 4 2 *passim.*
	תשבע	Lev 5 4
	תמעל	Lev 5 15
	תאכל	Lev 7 20 *passim.*
	תשא	Lev 7 18
	תפנה	Lev 20 6
	תגע	Lev 5 2 *passim.*
? [תענה]	תעננה	Lev 23 29
? [הנגעת]	תגעל נפשי	Num 19 22
	תעשה	Lev 23 30 *passim.*

ג ו .. א ..ע ..
Lev 2 1 ואינש ארי יקריב קרבן
סולתא

.אע
ויצק ויריק תרג̇

א
Lev 2 6 ויצקת ותריק תרג̇

ע   ע כה
Lev 2 2 והביאה וייתינה תרג̇

קדמ̇ לות

י ו אה   ——   ו כה
מסלתה בירתא מסולתה

[Début du verso]	עה וממישחה כה : לבונתה א עה תרג̇ אידכרתה	ו עצה ומשמנה אה : לבנתב א אה אזכרתה

[Fin du recto]

Lev 2 2

L'auteur de notre Massorah donne en ligne les mots hébreux du verset et leurs équivalents dans la paraphrase araméenne. Pour rendre l'exposé plus didactique, j'ai édité ces mots face à face. On notera l'usage du ה supralinéaire pour marquer le *mapiq* tibérien. Après le mot hébreu **מסלתא** et au-dessus de la ligne, on lit בירתא dont je ne comprends pas le sens ici.

II

Verso

Lev 2 3 והנותרת והנותר ודיישתאר תרג̇

Lev 2 4 תקרב (ע) קרבן וארי תקריב (א)

מאפה תנור (ע.. ו) ק ו ת [קרי ותרג̇]

סלת ק ו ת תלת בפרש

Lev 2 4 וכי

Lev 2 5 ושלא̇

Lev 2 7 ושלא̇

כל קרבן (ו ג) קורבנא? (ו א) תרג̇

Lev 2 1 בריש כי תקריב

Lev 2 4 וכי תקרב (ע)

Lev 2 12 קרבן ראשית

Lev 2 13 קרבן מנחתך (ו ע)

Lev 9 7 ועשה את קרבן

Lev 9 15 ויקרב את קרבן

Lev 2 4 בלולת כול דפילן תרג̇

כל בלול דפיל תרג̇

כל [ויקרא] בלולה דפילא תרג̇

Lev 2 4 כל ורקיקי ואיספוגין תרג̇

א
מצא   Lev 2 5

א
כל ורקיק ורקיק ואיספוג   תרג֗
ע
מסריתא
∴
סלת   קות

ע   ו   _ ע
[פתות] בצע יתה ביצועין ותריק עלה   Lev 2 6
אע
שמן
·
הפי סוף פסוקי מן היא אר[חון ?] בפרש֗.

                    פתות   Lev 2 6
                    ונתת   Lev 2 15
          [ו]אם [לא] תשיג   Lev 5 11
        ע   אה
                  והביאה   Lev 5 12

      · דיח אע   ∴   י ע   · ע
סלת בשמן תעשה   סלת במשח תיתעביד [תרג֗]   Lev 2 7

                לקדם שבע בפרש֗.   Lev 2 8

                  והבאת   Lev 2 8
        ע
              והביא את הפר   Lev 4 4
                  ונודעה   Lev 4 14
              והביא את אשמו   Lev 5 6
              ואם לא תגיע   Lev 5 7
              נפש כי תמעל   Lev 5 15
              ואת אשמו   Lev 5 25
        ע
          ..
ותיתי בא[ורייתא]
ע   ..
  ..ע   _ א עה   מיש   ע   עה
דתיתעביד מיאילין לקדם ייי וייקרבינה לות כהנא ויקרבינה למדבחא

          ·   ..
והרים   כול ויפריש תרג֗   Lev 2 9

      אע ..
תעשה   Lev 2 11
      ..ע
    א   ו   י
כל מנחתא דיתק[ר]בן קדם ייי לא תיתעביד
      ע ו
תסקון   [תרג֗]
        ע
ממנו   מיניה [תרג֗]
              ע
כול אשה כול קורבנא תרג֗ בר מן:

        ע
      לחם אשה   Num 28 24
      אך בכור שור   Num 18 17

Lev 2 12	קורבן ראשית קורבן קדמי תרג באורייתא
	יעלו יתסקון תרג
	בין ריח ניחח ובין לריח ניחח
	כול לאיתקבלא ברעוא תרג
Lev 2 13	קורבן
	במלח תמלח במילחא תימלח תרג
Lev 2 13(1)	תבטיל מלח קדמ ניג קרא ותרג מלח
Lev 2 13(2)	מילחא בתר מתרג

Lev 2 4

מאפה תנור noté ק״ות, sigle de קרי ותרגום. La tradition tibérienne donne la graphie מאפה à l'expression paraphrasée, alors que la tradition babylonienne l'écrit מאפי.

כל קרבן קורבנא תרג La leçon קורבנא donnée par notre auteur est fausse selon toutes les traditions. קורבן reste indéterminé aussi en araméen. Pour le reste le catalogue est juste; il s'agit bien de tous les cas où קרבן est ainsi paraphrasé dans le Lévitique, à l'exception de Lev 7 14 qui est déterminé à la paraphrase: קורבנא et des formes très nombreuses dans ce même livre paraphrasées . . . קורבנא ד.

בלולת כול דפילן Les formes hébraïques בלולת sont rendues par דפילן en araméen dans ce livre (Lev 2 4 7 12.12), alors que בלול sous Lev 14 21 est rendu par דפיל. Ces leçons se vérifient pour d'autres livres de la Bible.

Lev 2 6

הפי סוף פסוקי מן היא Liste des versets dans la péricope dont le dernier mot הִוא est rendu en araméen par הִיא.

Lev 2 7

סלת בשמן On lit au-dessus de la ligne דיח note de cantilation babylonienne que P. Kahle avait déjà signalée[12] et que l'on retrouve sous Lev 3 2 dans notre commentaire.

Lev 2 8

לקדם שבע בפרש Liste donnant les 7 cas où ליי est paraphrasé לקדם יי dans notre péricope. Berliner[13] et Landauer[13] citent ce même enseignement.

[12] Der masoretische Text des Alten Testaments nach der Überlieferung der babylonischen Juden, I 1902, p. 16–17.

[13] Berliner, op. cit., p. 45; Landauer, op. cit., p. 40.

דתיתעביד...לות כהנא L'expression **לות כהנא** est surmontée du sigle massorétique **מיש** abréviation de **מישתמשים** — divergences —, qui signale le risque d'un choix contraire à la tradition du scribe tel que **לכהנא** cité par TBS. qui semble être de tradition tibérienne.

Lev 2 11

כול אשה כול קורבנא תרג בר מן Sous Num. 18 17 **אשה** est paraphrasé **קורבן לאתקבלא**, sous Num 28 24 **לחם אשה** est paraphrasé **לחים קורבן** alors que partout ailleurs **אשה** est paraphrasé **קורבנא**.

Lev 2 13

תבטיל מלח noté **קדמ ניג קרא**. Le premier est lu *mil'eyl* et paraphrasé **מלח**. Le second est paraphrasé **מילחא** et lu *milra'*.

Lev 3 1

מלח קר ותר Liste des deux cas où la forme hébraïque **מֶלַח** est conservée en araméen. Cette liste semble extrapolée à cette place. Cf. Berliner[13] et Landauer[14].

תרבא Début d'un catalogue non ordonné des différentes flexions de **תרב** équivalent araméen de **חלב** hébreu, à l'exception de **תרבהון** Num 18 17 qui n'a pas été colligé par le scribe. Ce catalogue qui devrait figurer sous Lev 3 3 est donné entre deux enseignements concernant Lev 3 1. L'expression **תרבהין** est notée **קיפ תר** équivalant à la note **רפי** des tibériens, mais dont le sens m'échappe ici.

Lev 2 14	בכורים	ביכורין תרג
	אביב	אביב תרג
	גרש כרמל	קלי בנור פירוכן
Lev 2 15	ותיתין [תרג]	
	ותשוי [תרג]	
Lev 2 16	אזכרתה	אידכרתה
	מגרשה	מיגירשה
	ומשמנה	ומימשחה
	לבנתה	לבונתה תרג
Lev 3 1	מקריב [דמ.....	

[14] Landauer, op. cit., p. 81.

מלח קר׳ ותר׳ [ ]

[מלח] ברית Lev 2 13 (1)
ברית מלח Num 18 19

Lev 3 3 *passim* תרבא
תרביה
תרבה
דתרבי [תרבי]
תרביא
תרבהין קיפ תר׳
[תרבהון]

Lev 3 1 בׄ מקריב תר[ג] בא[ורייתא].
ואם זבח Lev 3 1
וקדשתו Lev 21 8

Lev 3 4 *passim* יעדינה כתׄ במידר פיס

אם מן תורי הוא מקריב Lev 3 1

Lev 3 2 ושחטו
וזרקו בני אהרן הכהנים

Lev 3 4 כול וית תרתין .... [Fin du verso]

מקריב תר[ג] L'auteur de notre catalogue signale que l'expression [מקריב] est deux fois paraphrasée מקריב. A-t-il oublié de citer un troisième Lev 3 7 ou l'a-t-il exclu de sa liste parce qu'il est construit avec la particule ית? Il est difficile de trancher cette question, d'autant que dans Berliner p. 45 et Landauer p. 127 on rencontre le même enseignement avec la même exclusive.

Lev 3 4
אהרן הכהנים Cette expression est surmontée du sigle דיח déjà cité[15].

Conclusion

La place nous a manqué pour étudier le système vocalique babylonien assez particulier utilisé dans ce manuscrit ainsi que les variantes pleines et défectives, dont l'étude devrait enrichir nos connaissances en matière d'établissement du texte de la paraphrase canonique babylonienne. Nous consacrerons à ces problèmes une étude particulière.

[15] Cf. note 12.

Tafeln

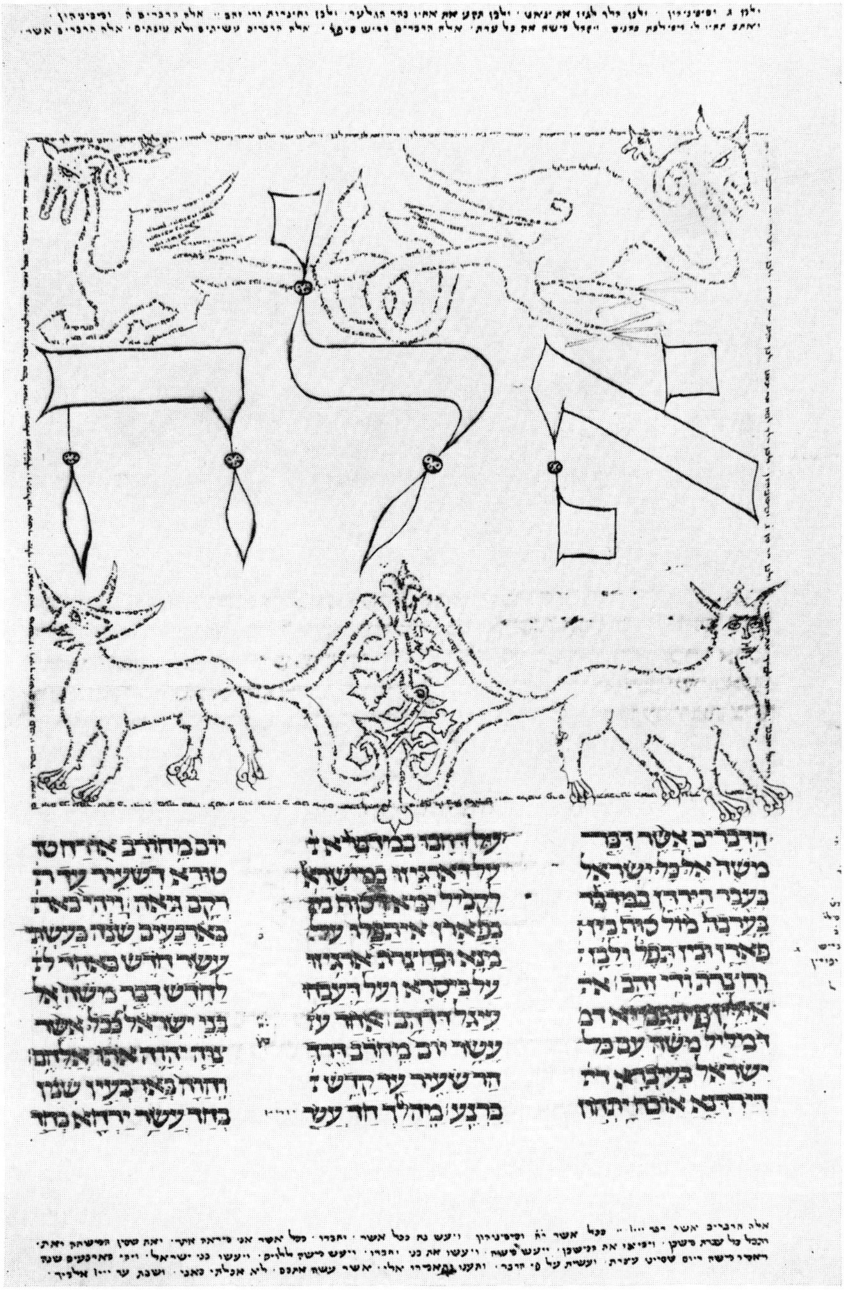

de Boer. Plate I. No. 1. Deventer, Athenaeum-Bibliotheek, cod. or. 1, fol. 165b.

de Boer. Plate II. No. 2. Deventer, Athenaeum-Bibliotheek, cod. or. 2, fol. 42b.

de Boer. Plate III. No. 4. Leiden, University Library. Leaf in cover Scal. 4, (recto).

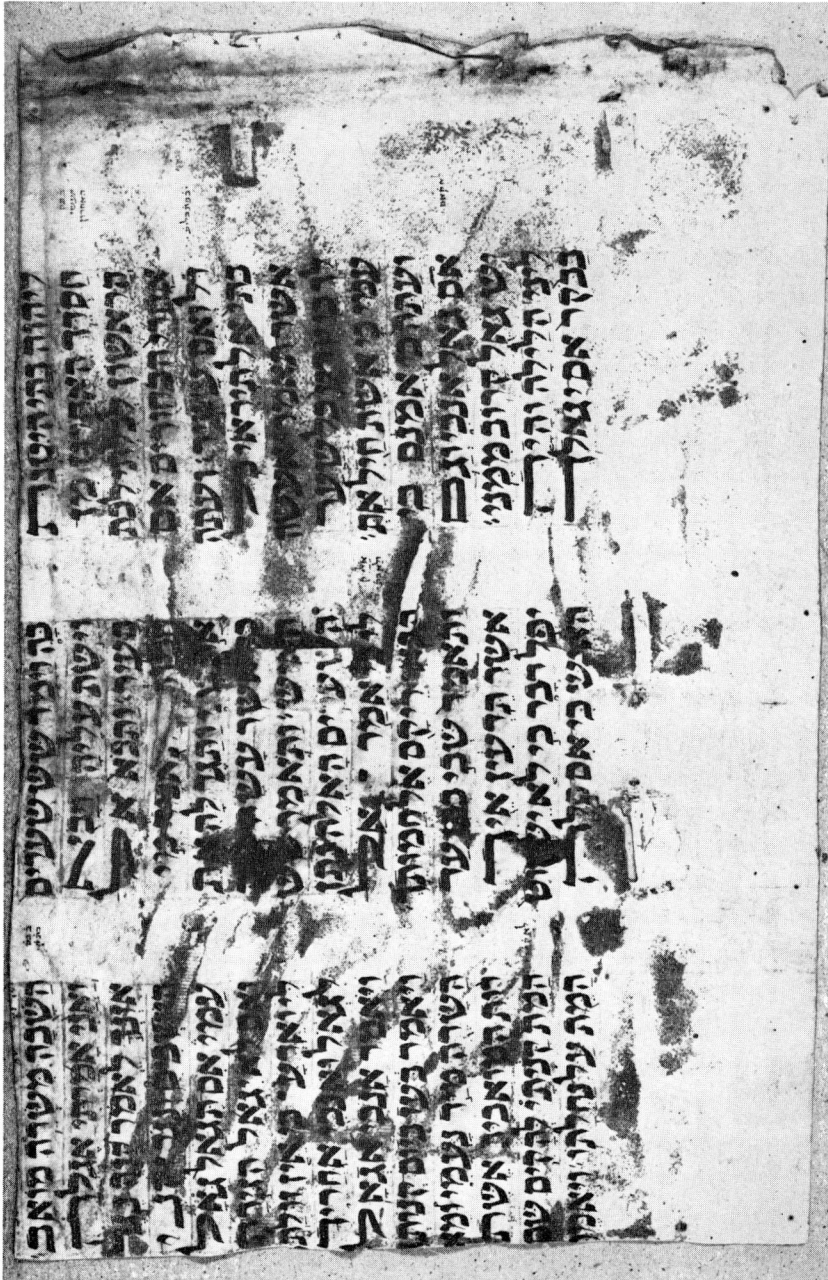

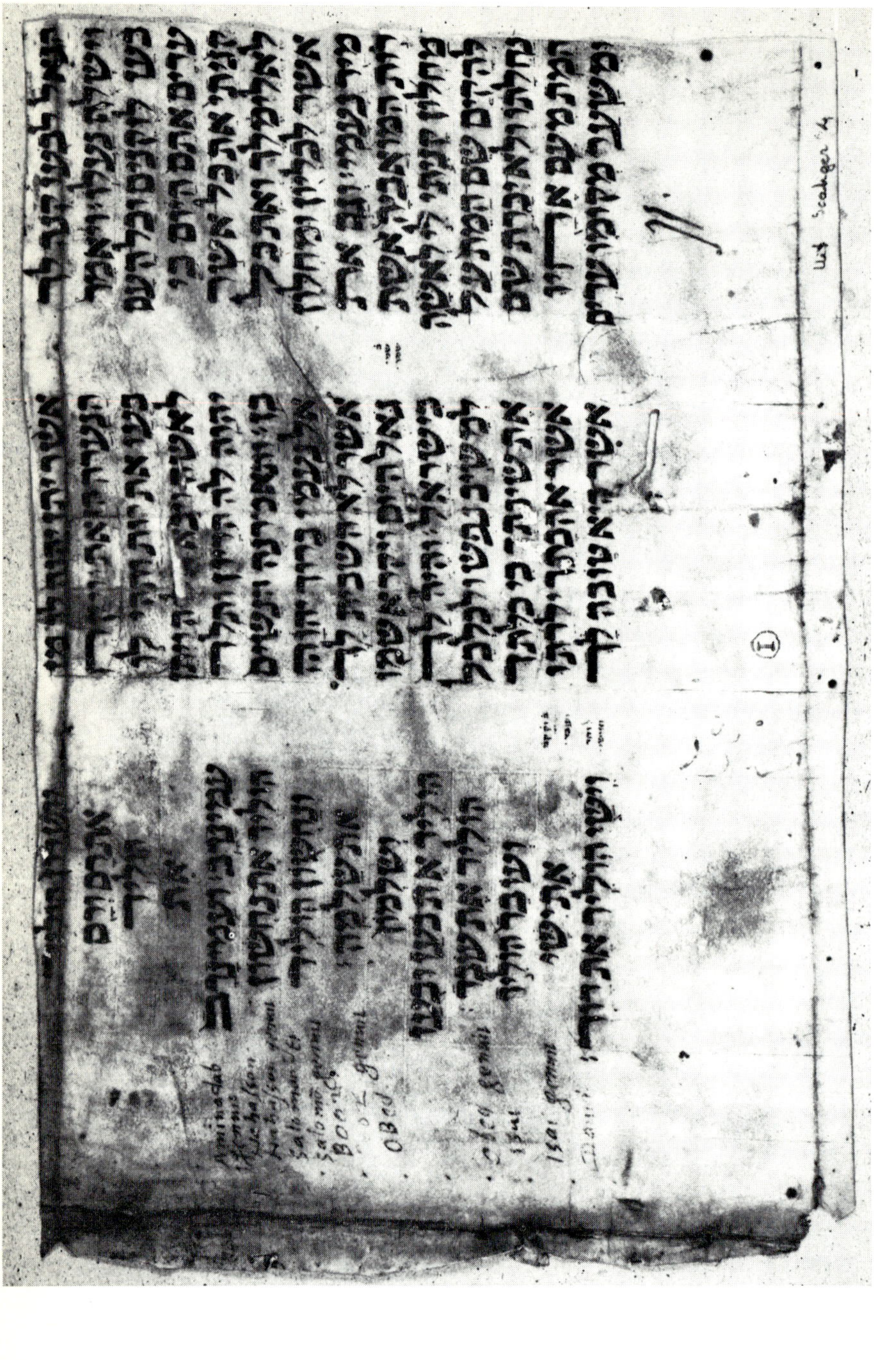

de Boer. Plate IV. No. 4. Leiden, University Library. Leaf in cover Scal. 4, (verso).

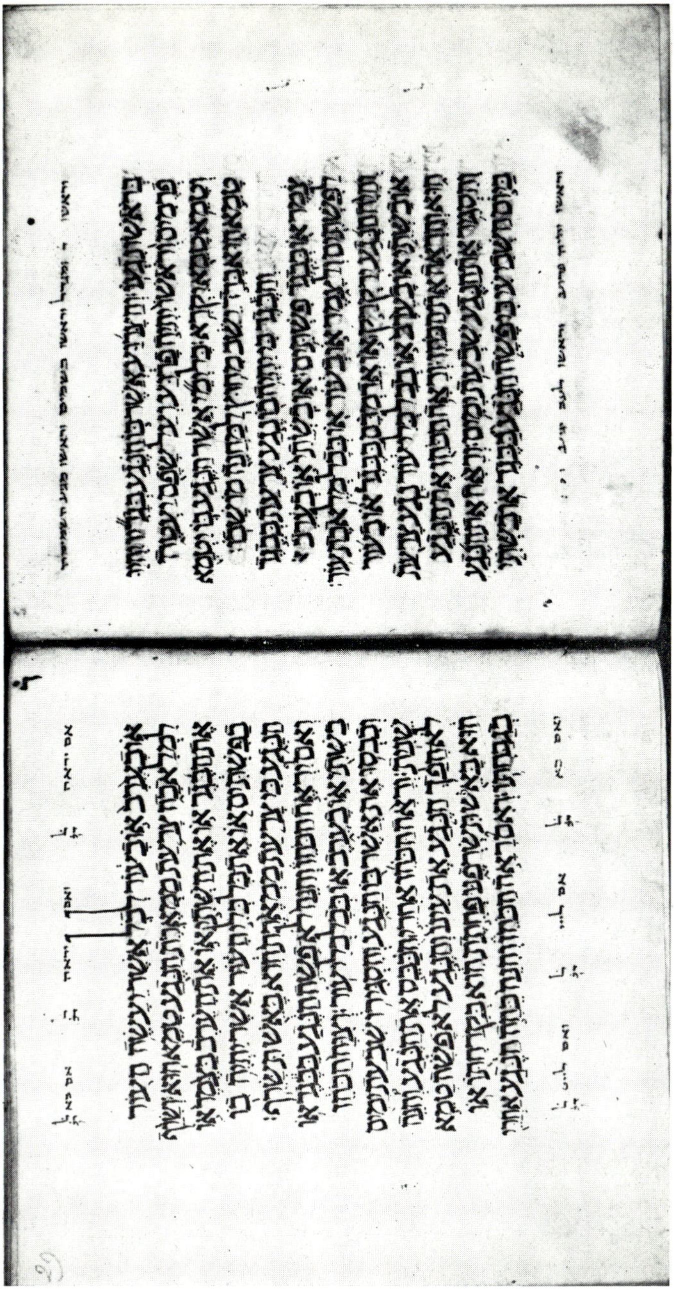

de Boer. Plate V. No. 6. Leiden, University Library, Scal. 20. folio's 28b + 29a.

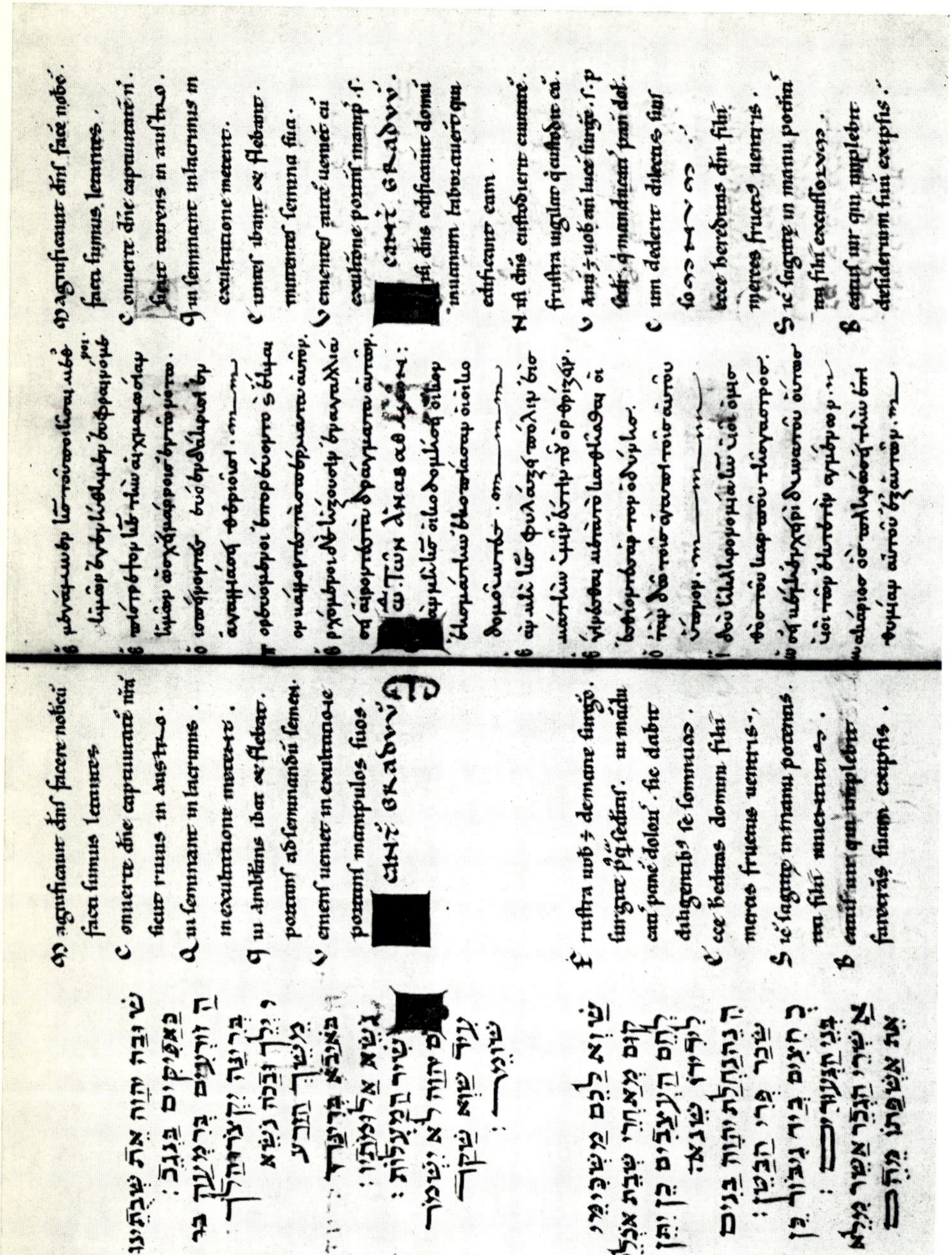

de Boer. Plate VI. No. 7. Leiden, Univ. Libr. Bibl. pub. graeca 49 A, folio's 267b + 268a

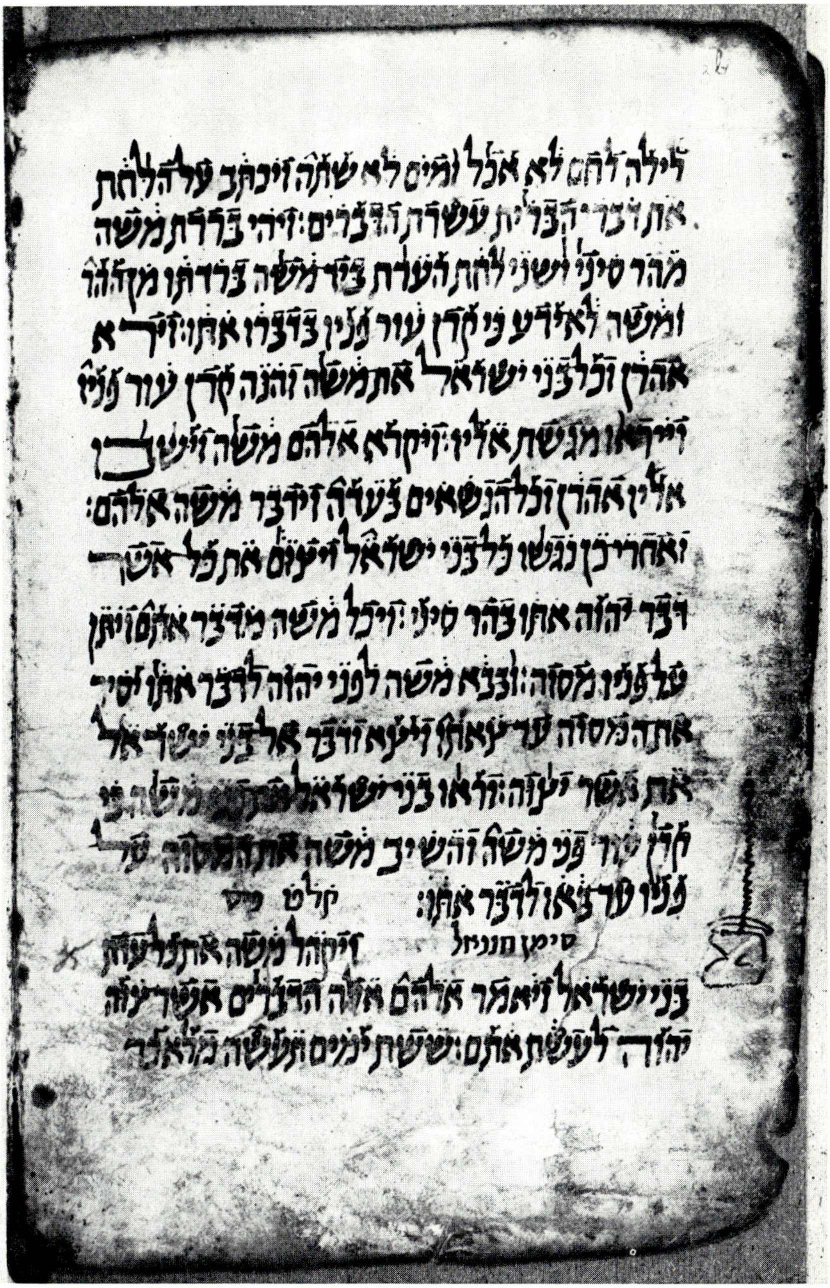
לילה לחם לא אכל ומים לא שתה ויכתב על הלחת
את דברי הברית עשרת הדברים: ויהי ברדת משה
מהר סיני ושני לחת העדת ביד משה ברדתו מן ההר
ומשה לא ידע כי קרן עור פניו בדברו אתו: וירא
אהרן וכל בני ישראל את משה והנה קרן עור פניו
וייראו מגשת אליו: ויקרא אלהם משה וישבו
אליו אהרן וכל הנשאים בעדה וידבר משה אלהם:
ואחרי כן נגשו כל בני ישראל ויצום את כל אשר
דבר יהוה אתו בהר סיני: ויכל משה מדבר אתם ויתן
על פניו מסוה: ובבא משה לפני יהוה לדבר אתו יסיר
את המסוה עד צאתו ויצא ודבר אל בני ישראל
את אשר יצוה: וראו בני ישראל את פני משה כי
קרן עור פני משה והשיב משה את המסוה על
פניו עד באו לדבר אתו: קלט פס
סימן חנניאל ויקהל משה את כל עדת
בני ישראל ויאמר אלהם אלה הדברים אשר צוה
יהוה לעשת אתם: ששת ימים תעשה מלאכה

de Boer. Plate VII. No. 11. Leiden, University Library. Hebr. 248, fol. 3b.

Eißfeldt. Abb. 1

Eißfeldt. Abb. 2

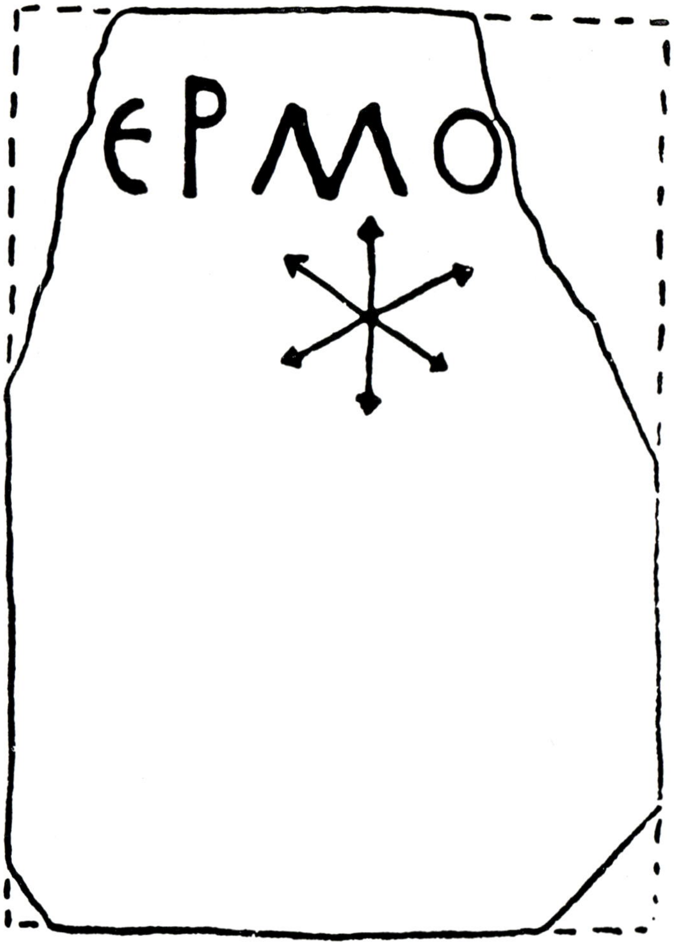

Eißfeldt. Abb. 3

Eißfeldt. Abb. 4

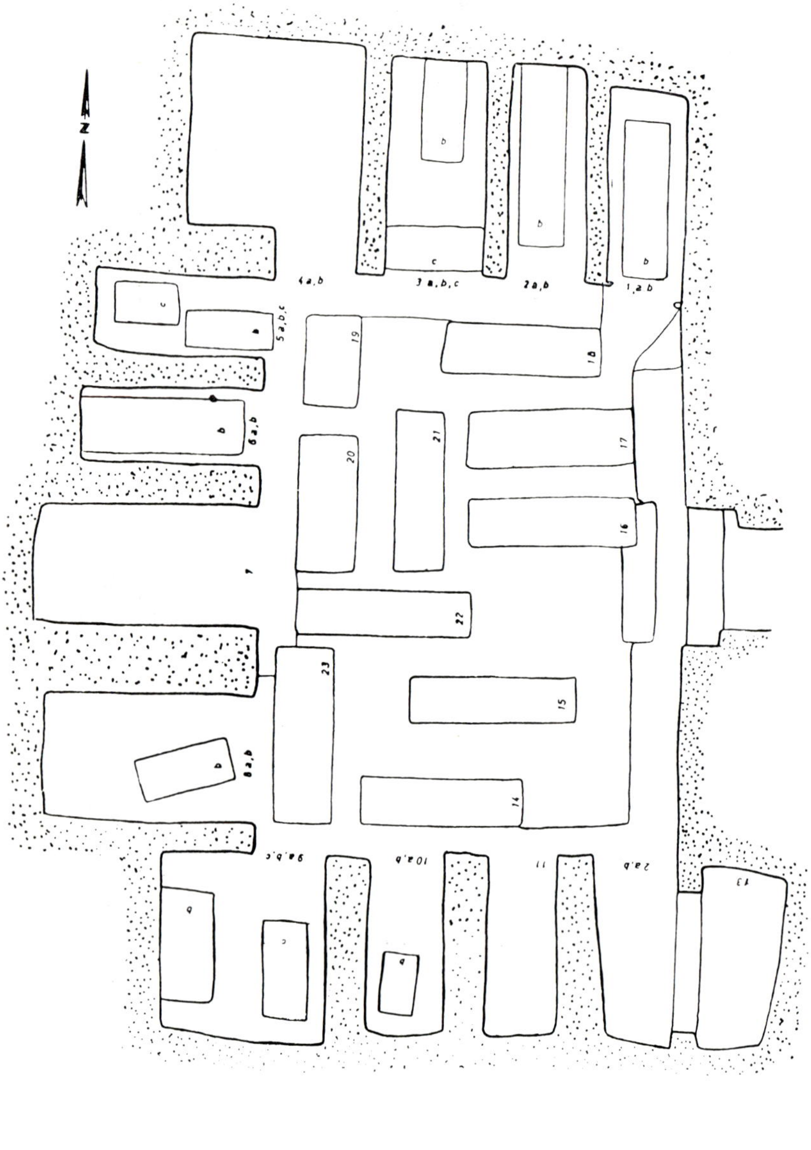

Eißfeldt. Abb. 5

Eißfeldt. Abb. 6

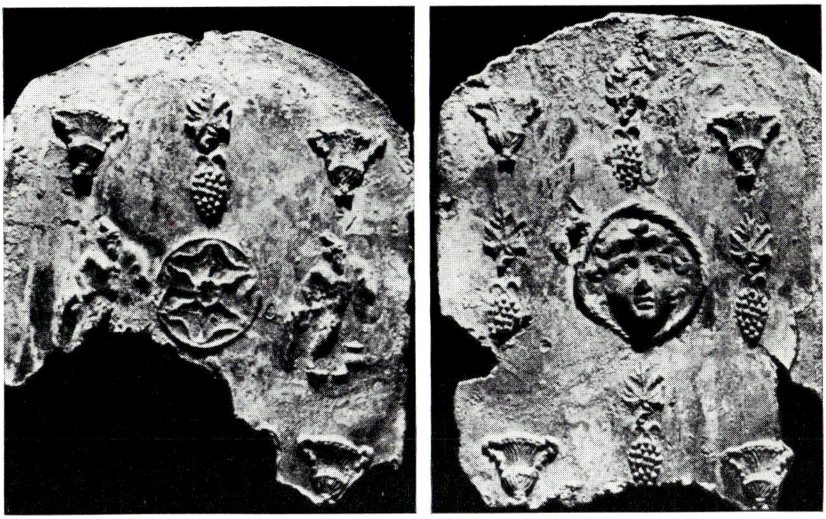

Eißfeldt. Abb. 7

Eißfeldt. Abb. 8

Eißfeldt. Abb. 9

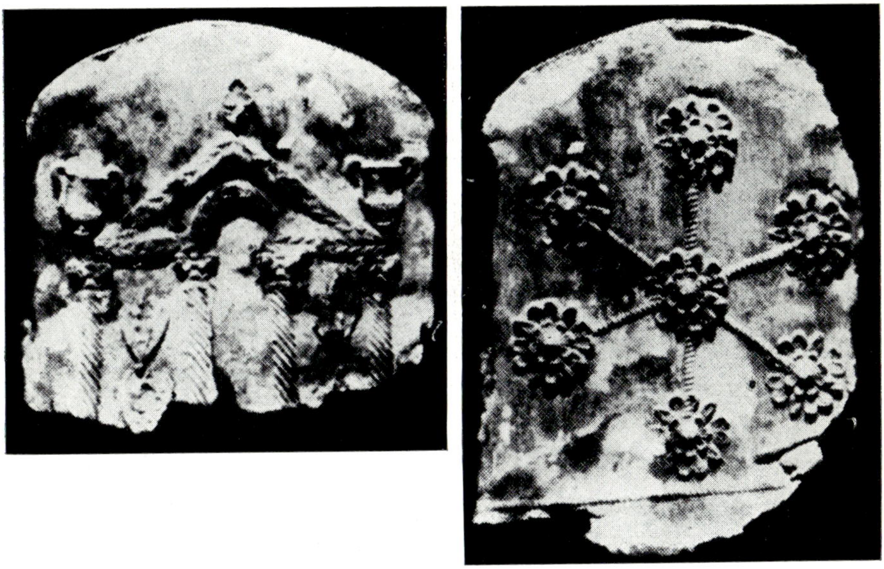

Eißfeldt. Abb. 10

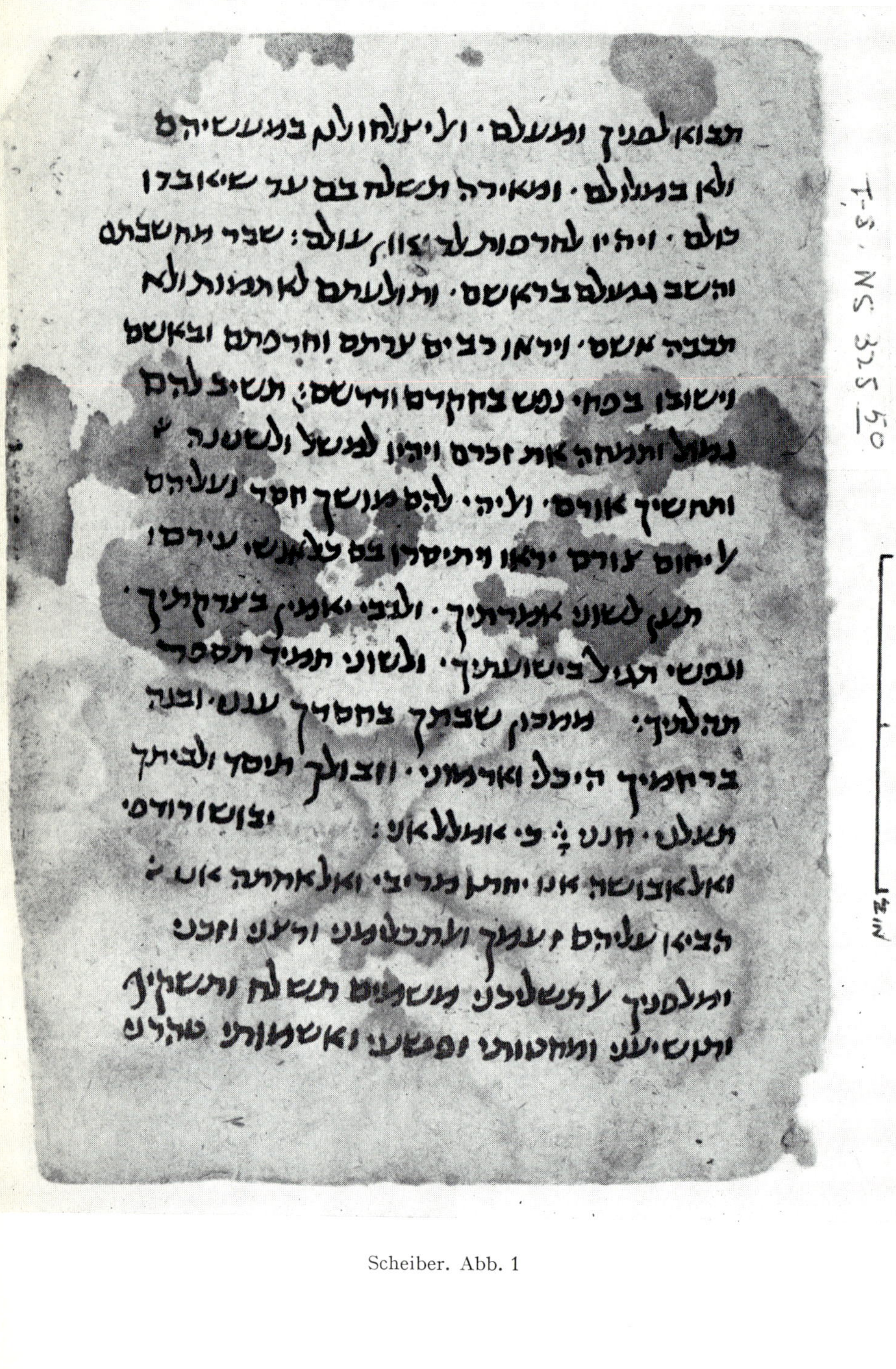
תבוא לפניך ומעלם · ולא יצלחו ולא במעשיהם
ולא במעלם · ומאירה תשלח בם עד שיאובדו
כולם · ויהיו לחרפות עד יצוו עולם : שבר מחשבתם
והשב גמולם בראשם · ותולעתם לא תמות ולא
תכבה אשם · ויראו רבים ערותם וחרפתם ובאשם
וישובו בפחי נפש בחקרם ודרשם : תשיב להם
גמול ותמחה את זכרם ויהיו למשל ולשנינה
ותחשיך אורם · ולא יהי להם מושך חסד עליהם
לאיום עורם יראו ויתיסרו בם כל אנשי עירם ·
תען לשוני אמרתיך · ולבבי יאמין בצדקיך ·
ונפשי תגיל בישועתיך · ולשוני תמיד תספר
תהלתך : ממכון שבתך בחסדך עננו · ובנה
ברחמיך היכלך וארמוני · ובזולך תוסד ולביתך
יבואו ורודם ·
תשלון · חננו יי כי אומללאנו :
ואל אבושה אנו יהוה כי דיבי ואל אחרה אף
הביאו עליהם ... ועתה ... ורענו וזכנו
ולפניך להשליך משמים תשלח ותשקיף
ותושיענו ומחטאותי ופשעי ואשמותי טהרני

Scheiber. Abb. 1

ומשגעאות ונסתרות תחתאני ותכבסני ואלאף
אויבי ושוטי ועלי תעזרני : 𐄂

ע עליון לך אודה שומר ועם פורה · אויב ועם
עושה צדקה ומישרים :

ב ברוך אלהינו בוחר אהרון משה להורים תורה
לדור דורים :

א רצה למלאתי האל אשר הולכי שדי מעל
טיע חקים לכל עפרים :

ל יה רם שמו נקרא גדול מכל אשר ברא ס
ברוך בכל שיריס :

ה היתה שבועתך לאב לישראל עליך
יקראו משה עם לויים :

ה הגד הלא גד שם מקריב על ראשם ראש
הוא לעשרים :

ג נאים וחייבים שרים ולאויבים אלון
במסתר סס :

ל ראוה עוה חיים   מאורי מותר

𐄂

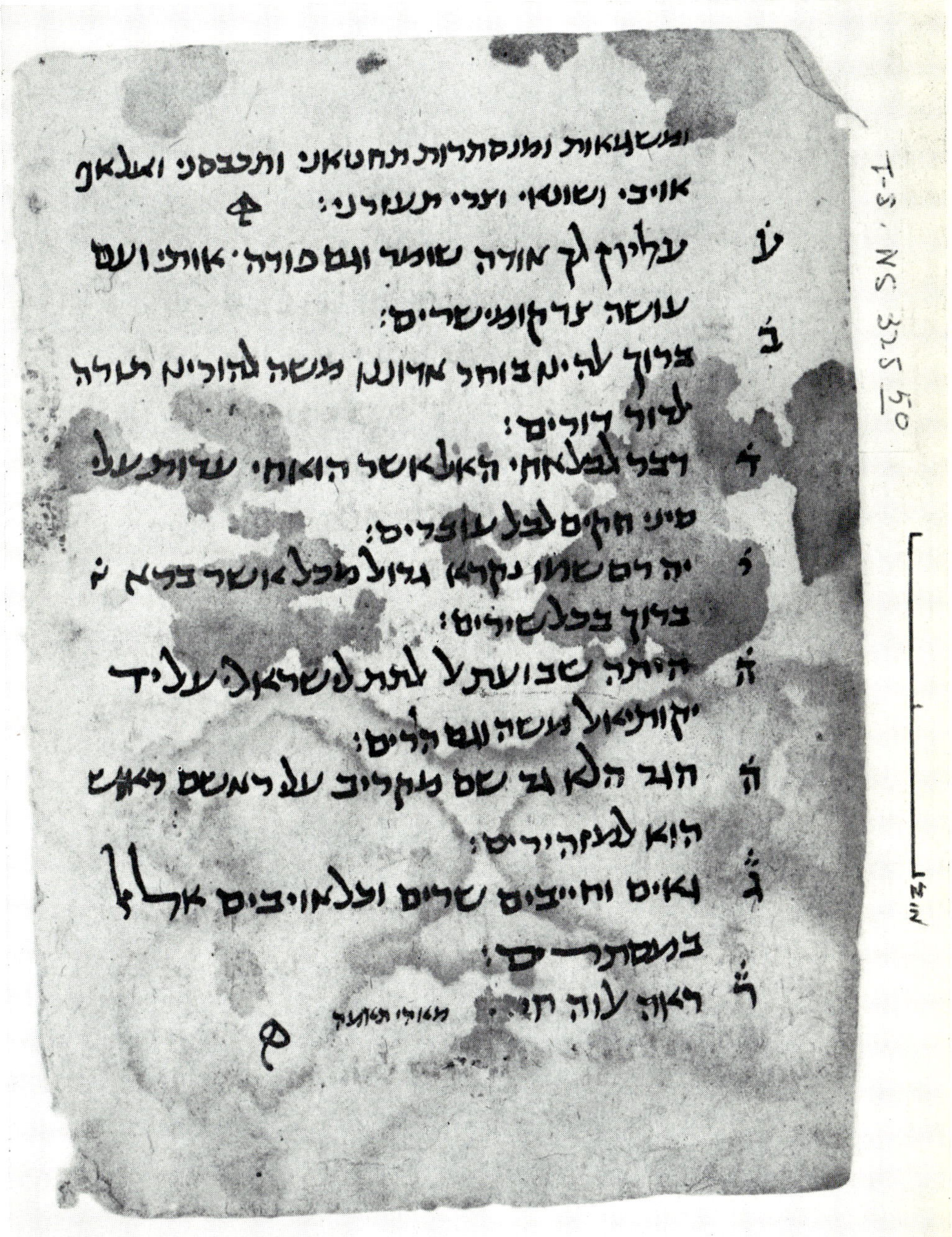

Scheiber. Abb. 2

Scheiber. Abb. 3

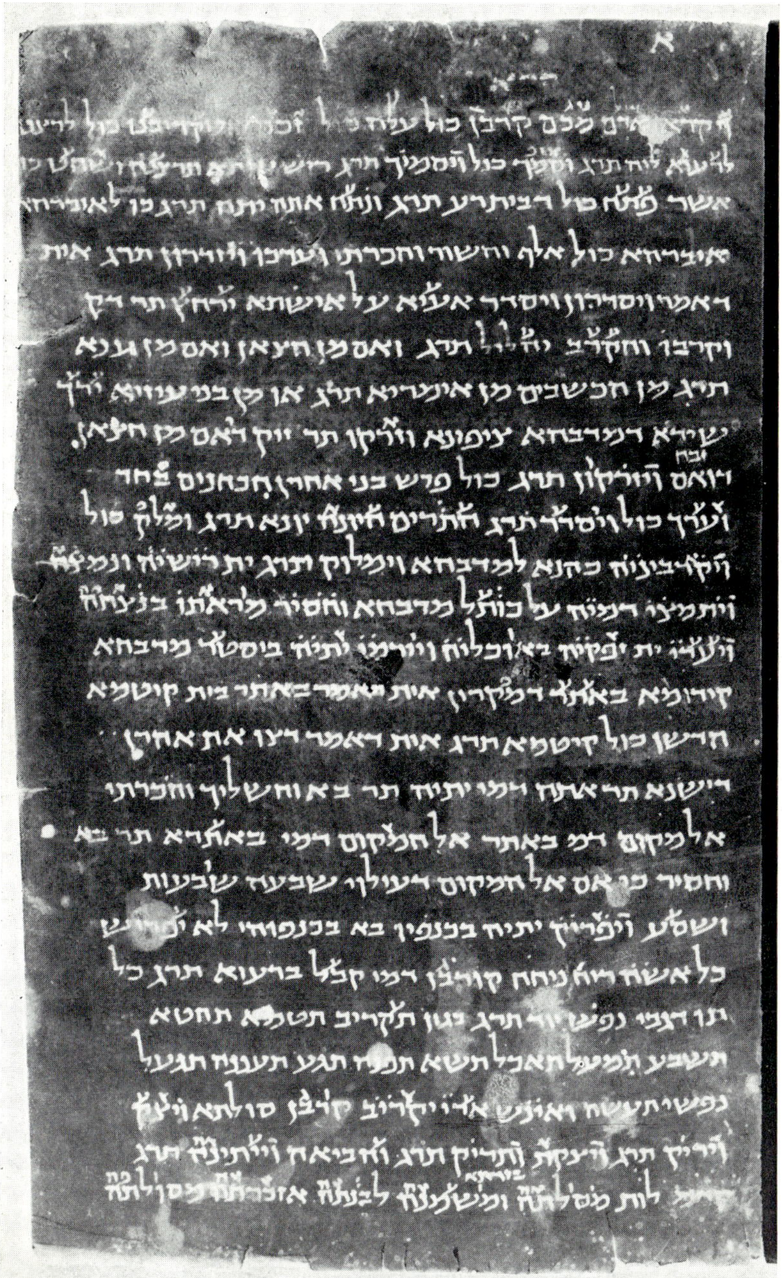

Weil. Abb. 1

Ms. heb. d. 62 fol. 45a Bodleian Library - Oxford

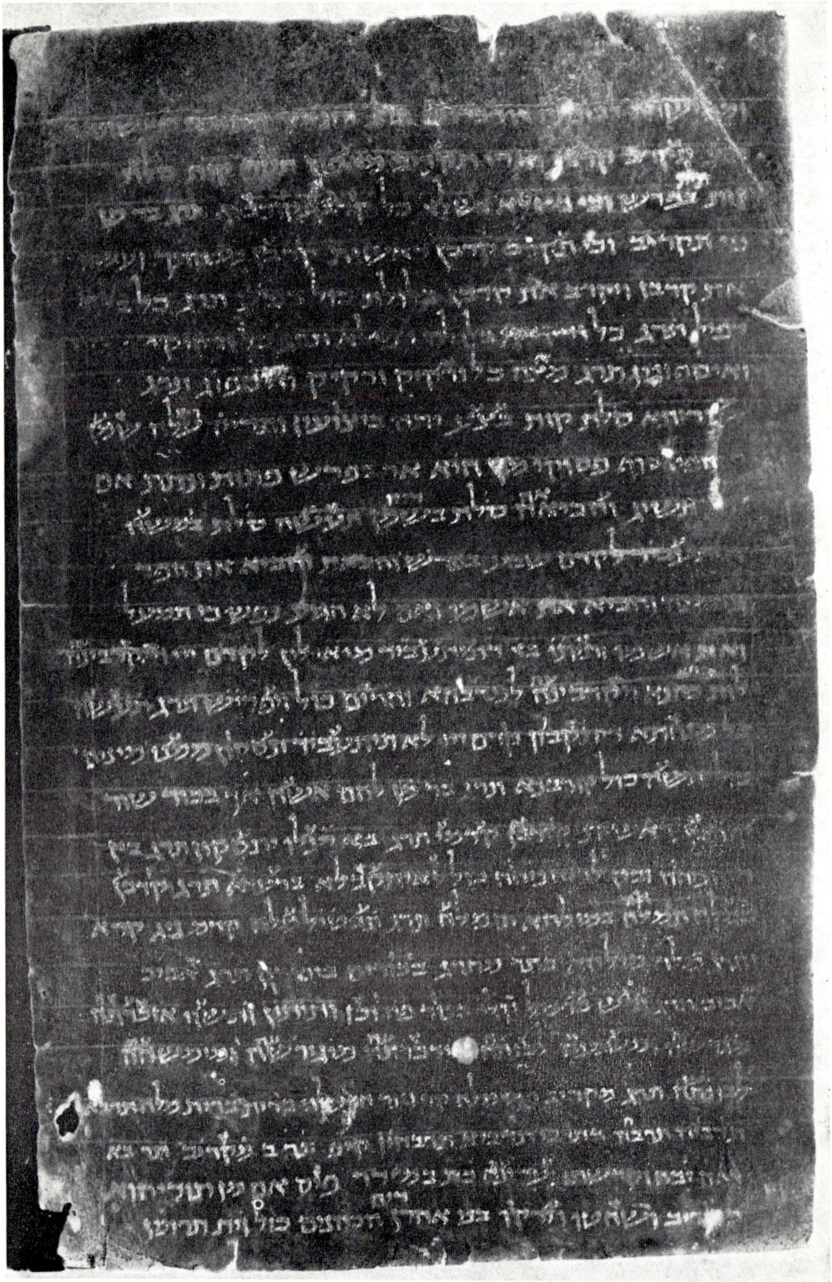

Weil. Abb. 2

Ms. heb. d. 62 fol. 45b Bodleian Library - Oxford